THE MURDER OF JOE WHITE

AMERICAN INDIAN STUDIES SERIES

Gordon Henry, SERIES EDITOR

Shedding Skins: Four Sioux Poets
Edited by Adrian C. Louis | 978-0-87013-823-2

Writing Home: Indigenous Narratives of Resistance
Michael D. Wilson | 978-0-87013-818-8

National Monuments
Heid E. Erdrich | 978-0-87013-848-5

The Indian Who Bombed Berlin and Other Stories
Ralph Salisbury | 978-0-87013-847-8

Facing the Future: The Indian Child Welfare Act at 30
Edited by Matthew L. M. Fletcher, Wenona T. Singel, and Kathryn E. Fort | 978-0-87013-860-7

Dragonfly Dance
Denise K. Lajimodiere | 978-0-87013-982-6

Ogimawkwe Mitigwaki (Queen of the Woods)
Simon Pokagon | 978-0-87013-987-1

Plain of Jars and Other Stories
Geary Hobson | 978-0-87013-998-7

Document of Expectations
Devon Abbott Mihesuah | 978-1-61186-011-5

Centering Anishinaabeg Studies: Understanding the World through Stories
Edited by Jill Doerfler, Niigaanwewidam James Sinclair, and Heidi Kiiwetinepinesiik Stark | 978-1-61186-067-2

Follow the Blackbirds
Gwen Nell Westerman | 978-1-61186-092-4

Bawaajimo: A Dialect of Dreams in Anishinaabe Language and Literature
Margaret Noodin | 978-1-61186-105-1

Sacred Wilderness
Susan Power | 978-1-61186-111-2

Ottawa Stories from the Springs: anishinaabe dibaadjimowinan wodi gaa binjibaamigak wodi mookodjiwong e zhinikaadek
Translated and Edited by Howard Webkamigad | 978-1-61186-138-9

The Murder of Joe White: Ojibwe Leadership and Colonialism in Wisconsin
Erik M. Redix | 978-1-61186-145-7

∞ The paper used in this publication meets the minimum requirements of ANSI/NISO Z39.48-1992 (R 1997) (Permanence of Paper).

Michigan State University Press
East Lansing, Michigan 48823-5245

Printed and bound in the United States of America.

20 19 18 17 16 15 14 1 2 3 4 5 6 7 8 9 10

Library of Congress Control Number: 2014936051

ISBN: 978-1-61186-145-7 (pbk.)
ISBN: 978-1-60917-432-3 (ebook: PDF)
ISBN: 978-1-62895-032-8 (ebook: ePub)
ISBN: 978-1-62896-031-0 (ebook: Mobi/prc)

Book design by Scribe Inc. (www.scribenet.com)
Cover design by Shaun Allshouse, www.shaunallshouse.com

green press INITIATIVE Michigan State University Press is a member of the Green Press Initiative and is committed to developing and encouraging ecologically responsible publishing practices. For more information about the Green Press Initiative and the use of recycled paper in book publishing, please visit www.greenpressinitiative.org.

Visit Michigan State University Press at
www.msupress.org

THE MURDER OF JOE WHITE

Ojibwe Leadership and Colonialism in Wisconsin

Erik M. Redix

Michigan State University Press
East Lansing, Michigan

For Ogie Martin
and Aanakwad Redix

Contents

Acknowledgments

This book is the direct result of the generous support of many individuals who have shared their expertise with me over the years. This project has its roots from when I first picked up William Warren's *History of the Ojibway People* as a teenager. A love of Ojibwe history was a part of my family: my great-aunt Caroline Martin Benson did exhaustive genealogical research for our family; my cousin Larry Martin, former chair of American Indian studies at the University of Wisconsin–Eau Claire, showed me the possibilities of engaging in academia and has always been very warm and gracious in his support of my career. Entering college at the University of Wisconsin–Madison, I was anxious to learn more about Native people in North America and Latin America. I would like to give thanks to Florencia Mallon for her generous support and mentorship of my senior thesis and throughout my time at Madison; she was always there to answer the many questions of a curious undergrad. I am also indebted to Ned Blackhawk, Patty Loew, and Rand Valentine for taking the time to support my intellectual growth and making a big university seem much smaller.

After graduation, I returned home to work at Lac Courte Oreilles Ojibwe Community College (LCOOCC) and eventually served as chair of the Division of Native American Studies. My five years at LCOOCC shaped my professional and personal life immeasurably. I learned so much from my colleagues at LCOOCC including Tom Antell, Melissa Crow, Lisa La Ronge, Keller Paap, and Karissa White. I am forever grateful for the late Sky Houser and his support during my time at LCOOCC. I am appreciative of the patience and support of LCOOCC librarian Carol Pfaff; the extensive microfilm collections of the LCOOCC were crucial as I developed my courses and this project. Library staff Mel Hall and Cynthia Tudjen were incredibly patient and helpful during my many hours of research. I also learned much from my students at LCOOCC. In particular, Austin Bartold, Richard Denomie Jr., Bezhig Hunter, Nicole Matrious, Nicole Nalewaja, and Michael Sullivan Sr. were among the engaged students who have remained lifelong friends.

The University of Minnesota is a great place for graduate work in American Indian studies. Thanks to the many fellow graduate students in American Indian studies at Minnesota who provided so much support and fellowship through the years. Heidi Kiiwetinepinesiik Stark was especially helpful as I developed this project. Karissa White and I made the transition from tribal college to graduate school at the same time, and her fellowship was crucial during my time in graduate school. Special thanks to Mark Lindberg and Michael Foster at Minnesota's cartography lab for their work on the maps and their patience with me as I sought to include many remote locations on the maps. Thanks to my incredible committee, whose continued support has been essential for this project. John Borrows has supplied insightful criticism and was always positive and encouraging. The expertise of John Nichols has been invaluable to my project. From the time I began coursework through this project's completion, David Chang consistently provided helpful critiques and creative ideas.

My coadvisor Jean O'Brien brought so much into this project by supplying challenging, yet prompt, critiques and ideas. I am truly indebted to Jeani for teaching me the art of how to make precision critiques rather than blunt statements. My coadvisor Brenda Child took a special interest in my work, even prior to my entrance into graduate studies, when we were both participants in the Lannan Summer Institute at the Newberry Library. I feel privileged that Brenda found potential in me and nurtured it into a passion and skill for scholarship. Brenda has been unwavering in her enthusiasm for this project, and its completion is a direct result of her continued support.

The D'Arcy McNickle Center at the Newberry Library has been extremely generous in their support of my work over the years. The earliest research for this project occurred when I participated in the Lannan Summer Institute for the summers of 2003 and 2004. I returned to the Newberry in 2008 for the Committee on Institutional Cooperation Fellowship and again the following year when I was awarded the Susan Kelly Power and Helen Hornback Tanner Fellowship. As dozens of scholars who study Native people know, the Newberry is an amazing environment in which to work. I give a special thanks to Brian Hosmer, Fred Hoxie, and Scott Stevens for their support during my time at the Newberry. While at the Newberry, I made numerous trips to the National Archives Great Lakes Branch. I extend a special thanks to Scott Forsythe at the National Archives for helping me navigate their vast collections.

A Summer Fellowship in North American History by the Indian Treaty Signers Project, a Phillips Fund for Native American Research Grant from the American Philosophical Society, and the A. Beebe White Fellowship from the University of Minnesota also supported my research for this project. While writing my dissertation, I was extremely fortunate to receive a Consortium for Faculty Diversity Fellowship at Macalester College in American studies. My two years at Macalester were incredibly productive, and the students, faculty, and staff of the Macalester community provided an extremely supportive intellectual environment. Macalester is well known for its excellent students but I found people at Macalester to be equally as friendly. John Bennett and Ajuawak Kapashesit were among the exceptional students who made me feel welcome during my time at Macalester. My colleagues in American studies were extremely generous with their time and always expressed interest in this project. My thanks go to Karin Aguilar San-Juan, Duchess Harris, Jane Rhodes, and Kathie Scott.

My colleagues in American Indian studies at the University of Minnesota–Duluth (UMD) were helpful and supportive as I began the process of turning my dissertation into a book. UMD is a great place to teach, due in large part to the strength of American Indian studies, and I am fortunate that my colleagues are always available for me to stop in and bounce an idea off of. My thanks go to Joseph Bauerkemper, Jill Doerfler, Linda Grover, Tadd Johnson, Gordon Jordain, Tami Lawlor, Elyse Lawrey, Brian McInnis, Ed Minnema, and Larry "Amik" Smallwood. Thanks also to Steve Graham in UMD's cartography lab for taking the time to teach me how to create maps and being incredibly patient with me as I struggled to learn the software. UMD's students were eager to learn and provide insights as I explored different ideas in lectures. Chad Auginash, Gabrielle Benjamin, Ge-Waden Dunkley, Alexa LaMontagne, Jesslynn Poitra, and Morgan Rose were among the excellent UMD students who showed interest in my work.

Many people outside academia shaped this book. Tribal Historic Preservation Officer and Lac Courte Oreilles spiritual leader Jerry Smith added so much to my teaching skills and abilities and to this project throughout the years. Despite his incredibly busy schedule Jerry has always been there to answer questions. A special thanks to Sylvia Bracklin, who was extremely generous in sharing her family stories and letters and provided critical input to the book. Frank Zufall of the *Spooner Advocate* shared photographs and research that he completed for his newspaper article about the murder of Joe White.

I need to extend a special thanks to my lifelong mentor, David Scott Bisonette. Without David this book would not exist. I met David while still in college and a few years later was fortunate enough to be his colleague in Native American studies at LCOOCC. I knew very little about the history of Lac Courte Oreilles prior to meeting David. David has always been there to share his vast expertise about Ojibwe culture and history, much of it based on his own exhaustive research. David has been a continued mentor to me beginning when I was developing courses at LCOOCC and continuing as I developed this project.

The love and support of my family was crucial to me completing this book. My great-aunt Rose Martin would have enjoyed this book immensely and was always positive and supportive of my studies. I have always relied on my cousins Jeff, Paul, Andrew, and Amy Suralski as my support system, including through the years of working on this book. I am forever indebted to the support of my parents, Joan and Mike Redix. This book would not have been completed without their patience and support during the writing process. My parents have always been supportive of my goals, both academic and personal. I come from a background where college degrees were uncommon and advanced degrees nearly unheard of. My parents did not have the opportunity to pursue a higher education, and I understand the privilege I have been afforded by being able to pursue a career in something I am passionate about.

This book is dedicated to two Ojibwe people born one hundred years apart. My grandfather Jerome Leo Martin Sr. was born in 1907. He was known to everyone as "Ogie," as his father jokingly called him *ogimaa*, meaning chief. He worked at the Winter Co-op for sixty-two years, starting in his teens and retiring in his seventies. He was the father of ten children. He died in 1992 and toward the end of his life was very interested in his heritage. As a young teen I accompanied him and my mom around the reservation on trips so he could find out more about things that he had been too busy working all of his life to do. I looked up to my grandfather, and after he passed I wanted to continue to learn more about the things that interested him. In 2007 my son, Aanakwad Quaderer Redix, was born. The poverty that my grandfather experienced during his childhood is a far cry from my son's comfortable life of video games and watching YouTube clips on his iPad. My son's life is a direct result of the hard work of his great-grandfather and all of his forbearers whose lives were shaped in large part by the events described in this book. As we go forward we must be mindful of the privileges we enjoy that were denied to those who came before us who lived through the difficult times that are the subject of this book.

Introduction

On December 13, 1894 Lac Courte Oreilles Ojibwe *ogimaa* (or chief) Giishkitawag was shot to death by game warden Josiah Hicks on the orders of his superior, Horace Martin. The game wardens were serving Giishkitawag with an arrest warrant for hunting deer out of season. Giishkitawag, or Joe White, as local whites knew him, was the leader of an Ojibwe community at Rice Lake, Wisconsin. The shooting occurred north of Rice Lake at Long Lake, an important site for Ojibwe fishing and wild rice gathering. Giishkitawag was traveling from Long Lake to the Lac Courte Oreilles Reservation when the Rice Lake game wardens caught up with him. According to witnesses including family members present that day, Giishkitawag took a single step back as Martin and Hicks attempted to place him in handcuffs. This seemingly small action nonetheless provoked Martin and Hicks, and they began to beat Giishkitawag with the handcuffs and the end of a shotgun. As Giishkitawag began to fear for his life and attempted to flee, Hicks shot Giishkitawag, killing him almost instantly. At the time of his murder, Giishkitawag, like all Lake Superior Ojibwe, was guaranteed the right to hunt off-reservation in treaty rights, reserved rights never extinguished. While this shocking act of violence might today appear a quick or random event in an era when racial violence was common, it was in fact an event decades in the making, an action that was the direct result of the history of American colonialism operating against Native people in Wisconsin.[1]

Rice Lake, Wisconsin, is a town of about eight thousand in the northwest part of Wisconsin. It is so named because of a shallow, 859-acre lake that borders the town. Wild rice, the food source for which the lake is named, is not rice at all but a highly nutritious grain, which once grew in dense stands over the entirety of the lake. Vital to the survival of the Ojibwe and other Native people of the region for centuries, wild rice can be stored for long periods of time without spoiling. Though small by many standards, Rice Lake is still the largest city in this part of northwest Wisconsin and draws people of surrounding smaller towns from a radius of over sixty miles.

One of these communities is Hayward, Wisconsin, fifty miles northeast of Rice Lake. Ten miles south of Hayward is the Lac Courte Oreilles Ojibwe Indian Reservation. The Lac Courte Oreilles (or LCO) Reservation includes 69,072 acres, of which the tribe or individual tribal citizens own just over fifty thousand acres; 2,252 of the 6,154 enrolled tribal citizens live on the reservation.[2]

At the beginning of the nineteenth century the Lac Courte Oreilles Band consisted of seven communities spread out in a vast area along the Chippewa River watershed. The band originated and took its name from the community at Lac Courte Oreilles, but by the nineteenth century the largest and most influential Ojibwe community was at Rice Lake. The community was influential because the Ojibwe at Rice Lake had access to the rich prairie hunting grounds to the south and the vast wild rice beds of Rice Lake and nearby Prairie Rice Lake. Their influence was sustained by the military success of the leader of the community, Nena'aangabi, in campaigns against Dakota people to the southwest.

The rise of Nena'aangabi coincided with American expansion in the western Great Lakes. In the Treaty of Prairie du Chien in 1825, the Native nations of the western Great Lakes agreed to boundaries among one another that paved the way for future land cessions. In 1837, Ojibwe leaders sold their lands in northwest Wisconsin in exchange for yearly payments of cash and goods over a twenty-year period. However, the majority of the signers of the treaty were leaders who represented communities outside of the territory ceded. Although Nena'aangabi attended the council, he refused to sign the treaty. Despite selling their lands, under the treaty, the Ojibwe retained their essential rights to hunt and fish throughout the ceded territory, and the federal government made no effort to remove them.

When removal pressures came, it was not from the federal government but from local officials, in the person of Minnesota Territorial Governor Alexander Ramsey. In 1850, Ramsey plotted to remove the Wisconsin Ojibwe to Sandy Lake in northern Minnesota in order to benefit his fur-trading cronies in Minnesota who stood to profit from the payment of Ojibwe treaty annuities. Ramsey schemed to trap the Wisconsin Ojibwe in Minnesota by having the annual treaty payment at Sandy Lake but withholding the payment until after the waterways had frozen, making travel back to Wisconsin more difficult, in the hope that the Ojibwe would locate there for the winter. With no provisions, more than four hundred Ojibwe, or 12 percent of the total Wisconsin Ojibwe population, died as a direct result of Ramsey's plans. After the deaths at Sandy Lake, Ojibwe leaders were anxious to retain reservations. In 1854, the Lac Courte Oreilles and other Lake Superior Ojibwe bands retained reservations. In this treaty, as in prior land cession treaties, the Lake Superior Ojibwe also retained their rights to hunt, fish, and gather throughout the territory ceded. Tragically, the following year, at the height of his influence, Nena'aangabi was killed in battle with the Dakota.

His son Waabizheshi succeeded Nena'aangabi. During the following twenty-two years of his leadership, Waabizheshi would face unprecedented challenges from American expansion. The old-growth forests of northern Wisconsin were razed, providing the building materials for homes in the treeless prairies of the west. Timber companies built dams to store logs temporarily during the winter, then in the spring logs were released downstream to sawmills for processing. Logging dams devastated wild rice crops, resulting in the complete destruction of wild rice beds at Rice Lake and Prairie Rice Lake. In the midst of these changes, white settlers poured into Rice Lake and the surrounding area. Unlike the traders who previously lived in the territory, these new settlers adamantly separated themselves from Ojibwe people, insisting that the Ojibwe remove north to a reservation at Lac Courte Oreilles. In the midst of these mounting pressures, a member of the Ojibwe community killed Waabizheshi in 1877.

In this turbulent environment, Giishkitawag inherited the mantle of leadership from the Ojibwe community at Rice Lake. The ensuing decade brought even more direct challenges to Ojibwe sovereignty. Allotment policies threatened to break up the reservation, and federal officials sought to alienate Ojibwe children from traditional culture through education in off-reservation boarding schools. Even more disruptive to the Lac Courte Oreilles, the state of Wisconsin aggressively pursued its own agenda to curb the sovereignty of the Ojibwe. Despite the reserved rights of the Ojibwe to hunt, fish, and gather off-reservation, which had been guaranteed in federal treaties, the state of Wisconsin vigorously enforced its own game laws, depriving Ojibwe people of their economic means of survival. In the early winter of 1894 a Rice Lake judge, Franklin Angel, issued a warrant for the arrest of Giishkitawag for hunting deer out of season. On December 13, 1894, Game Warden Horace Martin and his assistant Josiah Hicks left Rice Lake headed for a logging camp where the leader was employed, intending to serve him with a warrant and place the leader under arrest.

Following Giishkitawag's murder, conducted in full daylight in front of his distraught wife and terrified children, both Martin and Hicks were charged with manslaughter with a trial date set for the spring. During the trial, the defense never denied beating or shooting Joe White. Furthermore, examination of the scene clearly demonstrated that Joe White did not posses weapons prior to or throughout his violent encounter with Martin and Hicks. In late nineteenth-century Wisconsin, justice for Native people in local courts was rare. Not only was the jury all white, but it was composed of recent immigrants, and many held negative views of Native people. The murder of Joe White illustrates the atmosphere of violence in northern Wisconsin, and the trial of his killers shows how courts upheld the interests of white citizens and an encroaching state and local government, contributing to a complex colonialism for the indigenous Ojibwe living in their own homeland.

AMERICAN COLONIALISM

The murder of Joe White occurred four years after the massacre of four hundred Lakotas at Wounded Knee. While very different events, both incidents were part of the process of American colonialism. Historians have only recently begun to see American expansion in the nineteenth century and its impact on Native communities as examples of settler colonialism. In *The Plains Sioux and U.S. Colonialism* historian Jeffrey Ostler explains the interaction between the Lakota and the US government as colonialism: "the term colonialism makes explicit the fact that expansion almost always involves conquest, displacement, and rule over foreign groups."[3] American military campaigns against the Lakota make it relatively easy to understand American actions against the Lakota as colonialism. However, Americans did not mount a military campaign against the Ojibwe. Instead the Ojibwe experienced American colonialism as a complicated, sometimes contradictory, broad spectrum of violence and displacement, and through the extension of a brutal and unjust governmental authority.

It is important to distinguish colonial expansion in places like the Americas, Australia, and New Zealand from colonialism elsewhere in the nineteenth century. Scholars have termed colonialism in these areas settler colonialism, meaning nonindigenous settlers came to stay and in most areas formed the majority of the population and in all areas were the power holders in national governments. For scholar Patrick Wolfe, settlers themselves drove colonialism: "Rather than something separate from or running counter to the colonial state, the murderous activities of the frontier rabble constitute its principal means of expansion."[4] Wolfe's ideas about the role of the "frontier rabble" are useful for understanding settler colonialism, but also obscure the different structures of the colonial apparatus and how they often contradicted each other. The Ojibwe experienced colonialism not just on the federal policy level, but also from the state of Wisconsin, in addition to local governments run by recent immigrants from northern Europe and even corporations, such as timber and power companies. These conditions made it much more difficult to resist, as the Ojibwe faced not just a centralized federal government or settlers. How could the Ojibwe resist? Even if the Ojibwe were so inclined to offer armed resistance, who or what would they fight? Who would be their allies?

Colonialism is a foundational aspect of American nationhood. Despite the tendency in most historical literature about Native peoples in the United States to deny colonialism, it is an important and useful way to conceptualize the unprecedented challenges faced by the Lac Courte Oreilles Ojibwe from the nineteenth century to the present day. For Wolfe "invasion is a structure rather than an event."[5] While the American colonialism against the Ojibwe never included acts of war, it was a relentless process that effectively undermined their communities and ways of life. Most Native people understand their history as being impacted by American colonialism, even if the term "colonialism" does not yet have everyday currency among many Native people. On the other hand, most non-Natives refuse to acknowledge America's colonial past and how the legacy of colonialism continues to shape current socioeconomic realities. As Ostler says: "Although Americans have often been reluctant to acknowledge imperialism and colonialism in their history, the expansion of the United States clearly involved both, insofar as it entailed the conquest of and eventual rule over Native people."[6]

Many studies of Native American history place a heavy emphasis on the federal government as the principal force driving American colonialism. Indeed, the narrative of Native history is often tied to changes in federal Indian policy. A common way to conceptualize changes in federal Indian policy is through the idea of pendulum swings. However, as historian Donald Fixico argues, "the 'pendulum's' wide sweep obscures as much as it reveals."[7] For Fixico and others, the idea of the pendulum is problematic due to its exclusive focus on the federal government's impact on Native people and their land and institutions. Instead, I argue that colonialism at the state, municipal, and corporate levels deeply affected Lac Courte Oreilles economic conditions and sovereignty as much as if not more than federal policies of the time including the allotment of reservation lands to individual ownership or enrollment of Native children in boarding schools. Timber companies flooded rice beds, and the state of Wisconsin prosecuted Ojibwe fishers and hunters, undermining an entire economy. The result of these acts of colonialism was that by the end the nineteenth century most Ojibwe struggled on a day-to-day basis to feed their families.

Constructing a narrative of Native history using the pendulum model is also problematic because it rests on the assumption that federal policies only impacted Native peoples for a limited amount of time. For example, in many historical studies scholars treat the removal of Native people from ancestral homelands to reservations as limited to one or two decades following passage of the Indian Removal Act of 1830.[8] I seek to challenge this narrative by arguing that, for the Lac Courte Oreilles Ojibwe, the immediate impact of removal was not limited to the mid-nineteenth century, but carried on for decades. For decades after the 1854 treaty, which created the reservation, Ojibwe people remained in traditional areas. Furthermore, as Joe White's activities prior to his murder illustrate, Ojibwe people continued to assert their sovereignty by practicing traditional labor in areas off-reservation into the late nineteenth century, even at the expense of their lives and safety. This book seeks to expand the common narratives of Native American history by arguing that removal and the struggle for sovereignty was a complex, decades-long contestation between Native people and federal, state, municipal, and corporate interests.

AMERICAN COLONIALISM AND THE LAW

The murder of Joe White occurred during an era when law shaped American colonialism. While federal policy initiatives were influential on the lives on Native people, it took laws to drive these policies. Legal scholar Sidney Harring effectively articulated the relationship between law and federal policy:

> The image of U.S. law replacing the gun as the agent of civilization reveals the coercive core of the application of criminal law to Indians. Even if the law could not accomplish this end, it was inextricably intertwined with other assimilationist institutions. BIA schools could not function without compulsory attendance laws and BIA police to arrest or threaten parents for not sending children to school. BIA farmers could not teach the Indians to farm without laws and police to prevent Indians from killing their stock for food. Christian churches could not convert without laws to ban traditional ceremonial activities. Land could not be allotted without laws to punish Indians who resisted.[9]

For Harring, assimilation policy of the era could not have existed without the backing of individual laws that attacked tribal sovereignty. However, the impact of the law on Native people was not just laws passed to assimilate

Native people. Equally as damaging to tribal sovereignty was the failure to enforce those laws that protected tribal sovereignty, such as treaty provisions.

New laws also shaped American colonialism against Native people. For example, in 1885 Congress passed the Major Crimes Act, making seven offenses committed on Native lands by and against Native peoples a federal offense. The Major Crimes Act came about as a response to the Supreme Court ruling in *Ex Parte Crow Dog* in 1883. There the court ruled that American courts had no authority in the murder of one Lakota by another Lakota on the reservation due to the sovereignty of Native nations.[10] As legal scholar Robert Clinton argues, passage of the Major Crimes Act represented the first time in the nearly four hundred years since contact that a colonial power sought to assert governing authority over Native people in North America. Furthermore, Clinton points out that the Major Crimes Act established governing authority over noncitizens. Clinton further notes that this extension of governing authority had no basis in constitutional law, treaties, or consent of Native peoples, but merely in the racism justifying colonialism.[11]

Another example of the law as an effective and lasting tool of American colonialism during the era when Joe White was murdered was the establishment of the Plenary Power Doctrine in the Supreme Court's decision in *United States v. Kagama* in 1886. With *Kagama*, and later in 1903 in *Lone Wolf v. Hitchcock*, the court ruled that the federal government holds absolute power over Native nations.[12] In his analysis of *Kagama*, Robert Clinton argues that the Supreme Court found no constitutional basis or treaty justifying plenary power.[13] Nevertheless, the doctrine of plenary power has been utilized since the late nineteenth century to attempt to diminish tribal sovereignty.[14] As Clinton argues, *Kagama* enshrined racism and colonialism in US law. Clinton sees the continued use of the case for precedent highly problematic in a democracy:

> The closest analogy might be the Court unabashedly citing *Dred Scott v. Sanford* or *Plessy v. Ferguson* to make a controlling point in a modern affirmative action case. If such an event occurred, the uproar from the public and the legal and academic community undoubtedly would be deafening.[15]

For Clinton, the continued citation of plenary power by the courts means that American colonialism is not confined to the nineteenth and early twentieth centuries. Instead, the lasting legal legacy of nineteenth-century colonialism remains to the present day. Change is a difficult task, as in its over two-hundred-year history the Supreme Court has in only one instance invalidated a congressional law dealing with Native peoples.

On top of all this, Native people were not US citizens before allotment, some not until 1924. Not only were Native people subject to laws and policies that attacked their sovereignty, but also at the same time, they were not afforded the same basic legal protections of American citizens. This left Native people with no constitutional protections and increasingly fewer protections from their own political institutions. Just one example of the vulnerability of Native people during this time was Bureau of Indian Affairs efforts to suppress Native religion coupled with the lack of citizenship status that would have allowed Native people to seek protection under the Bill of Rights.[16] Federal policies and their lasting effect, federal and state law and the selective enforcement thereof, local governments, and corporations were all part of the complicated way that American colonialism operated against the Ojibwe. While lacking the centrality and clarity of a military campaign, this colonialism was equally as effective at creating poverty and other social problems that made it more difficult for Ojibwe people to assert their sovereignty.

TRIBAL SOVEREIGNTY

Native nations in the United States possess inherent sovereignty. Native nations were autonomous, sovereign entities prior to contact with European nations. Although colonialism reshaped Native nations, they retained their sovereignty. For the Lac Courte Oreilles Ojibwe and other Native nations in the Great Lakes, sovereignty was maintained for nearly three hundred years of contact with the French and British. The United States recognized the sovereignty of Native nations in hundreds of ratified treaties, federal legislation, court decisions, and the commerce clause of the Constitution. The commerce clause of the Constitution delegates the Senate to make treaties with foreign nations and "Indian Tribes," essentially recognizing the sovereignty of Native nations as equal to other sovereigns.[17]

Treaties form the basis of subsequent relationships between the US government and the over five hundred recognized tribal nations in the United States. By the act of making treaties, the United States recognized the sovereignty of Native nations. Article 6 of the US Constitution declares that treaties are the "supreme Law of the Land." The first treaty between the United States and Native nations was with the Delaware in 1778, and treaties continued to be made until 1871, when Congress passed a rider to cease treaty making, although the US government continued to make "agreements" with Native nations that were de facto treaties after that date. Over five hundred treaties were made between the federal government and Native nations. It cannot be overemphasized that no other groups of peoples or states engaged in treaty making with the federal government.[18]

The sovereignty of Native nations was further reflected in early federal law with the Northwest Ordinance, which stipulated that Native lands could not be taken without consent, and the Trade and Intercourse Act of 1790, which stipulated that only the federal government, not states or private individuals, could acquire Native lands.[19] Many Supreme Court decisions attempted to define the relationship between Indian nations and the government. Most notably, Chief Justice John Marshall in *Cherokee Nation v. Georgia* defined Native nations as "domestic dependent nations." In this case and others, the court has often produced decisions that have lasting effects on Indian law that often were based more on political realities of the day rather than the historical evolution of Native peoples' inherent sovereignty.[20]

What many non-Natives (and perhaps some Native people themselves) fail to understand is that sovereignty is a dynamic, fluid process.[21] While tribal sovereignty is inherent and thus in many ways independent of historical chronology, tribal sovereignty is also an ever-changing historical process. Even the terminology employed to describe tribal sovereignty has differed vastly at particular historical moments. The Lac Courte Oreilles asserted their sovereignty in very different ways in contexts ranging from the late nineteenth-century response to American colonialism, to the 1930s debate over the Indian Reorganization Act, to the grassroots and legal activism of the 1960s and 1970s, to the advent of gaming in the 1990s. Despite the numerous challenges to tribal sovereignty leveled by American colonialism, Native nations remain sovereign. Tribal sovereignty can only be diminished by Native people themselves. For the Lac Courte Oreilles and other Native nations, tribal sovereignty is practiced in a variety of ways including their organization of a government under the Lac Courte Oreilles Constitution, running a gaming operation, regulating citizenship, and exercising off-reservation treaty rights to hunt, fish, and gather.

Understanding tribal sovereignty is an essential task of writing a history such as this. While it is important that the work of historians working in Native history speak to other historians, equally important is how their work is rooted in Native American studies and Native communities. The central task of Native American studies should be to empower Native people and non-Natives with a better understanding of tribal sovereignty. While many studies exist that explore the historical development of how the federal government viewed tribal sovereignty, few historical studies discuss how Native people themselves viewed, understood, and asserted their sovereignty as their own institutions evolved. This approach is vital to scholarship on Native people as it emphasizes that tribal sovereignty is not merely a concept resulting from the benevolence of the federal government, but is and always has been an inherent aspect of Native political life with its own historical development. The stakes are high. Scholars have the power to not only influence future policy makers, but also shape how Native people themselves understand their sovereignty.

METHODOLOGY AND SOURCES

Most accounts of Ojibwe history are topic centered and specific to a time period. This study attempts to understand changes in Ojibwe history over a longer period of time. It is important to be comprehensive whenever possible and to include the social, cultural, economic, political, gender, and legal histories of a single community. Furthermore, we must situate Ojibwe history within the framework of American and Canadian colonialism. This work seeks to accomplish both tasks by providing a comprehensive historical account of an Ojibwe community while at the same time enriching our understanding of American colonialism as a driving force throughout American history.

Even though this book is about Ojibwe communities in the nineteenth century, Michael Witgen's recent *An Infinity of Nations* is influential on this study. Witgen demonstrates how the western Great Lakes were Native territory prior to the nineteenth century. Through his exhaustive and meticulous research, Witgen skillfully interrogates how French and British claims of empire in the region were mere rhetoric.[22] In many ways, this study is an extension of Witgen's work. The eventual dispossession of Ojibwe lands was by no means inevitable even decades after the land cession treaties were signed. There were moments in the second half of the nineteenth century when white settlers made broad claims and threats to remove Ojibwe people when in fact they possessed no such ability. Throughout the nineteenth century, Ojibwe leaders proposed viable alternative visions of their relationship to Americans that did not diminish Ojibwe sovereignty. Reading sources mindful of the actual realities of the time they were produced and not what eventually happened is important for any study of Native history.

Records of annuity payments due under treaties have been essential to my understanding of Joe White's family and other Ojibwe families moving onto the reservation. These records are rarely cited in works of American Indian history. As historian Frederick Hoxie argues, these records are of great value to historians studying Native peoples: "The major method or approach that Indian historians have ignored is the quantitative analysis of manuscript census data. . . . Together they provide a rich resource for the study of population composition, family life, and cultural change."[23] Hoxie made this argument over twenty years ago. Since then, these types of records have become even less fashionable in academic histories. As a result, historians of Native people are even less likely to utilize these sources than when Hoxie argued for their wider use. However, methodological approaches to studying Native peoples should utilize all available evidence, regardless of the latest trend in academia.

Annuity records are also underutilized because many scholars do not possess Ojibwe language ability. As a result, scholars often confuse the names of Ojibwe leaders. In the nineteenth century, there was no standardized orthography of Ojibwe. Furthermore, government officials and other writers of archival sources rarely had Ojibwe language ability and spelled Ojibwe names phonetically. This makes having Ojibwe language ability imperative, as names of the same Ojibwe leaders do not appear similar. Furthermore, scholars face the challenge of deciphering the identity of Ojibwe leaders with common names such as Waabizheshi, Noodin, and Bizhiki.[24] As a result, Ojibwe leaders are often peripheral to many studies. In this study, I have standardized all Ojibwe names in the Fiero orthography or double vowel system that is most commonly utilized by Ojibwe speakers in the United States. By utilizing historical evidence such as annuity records and census data, this study places Ojibwe leaders at the center of the story.

DESIGN

The chapters of this book are organized chronologically and analyze a line of Ojibwe hereditary leaders from the early nineteenth century through the first decades of the twentieth century. Chapter 1, "The Rise of Nena'aangabi and American Expansion in the Western Great Lakes, 1825–1837," traces the historical development of the Ojibwe community at Rice Lake and how this community soon became the largest and most important among the Lac Courte Oreilles Band. Much of this had to do with the ability of the community's leader, Nena'aangabi, to defend the region, which was rich in wild rice, from the Dakota. This expansion coincided with increased American presence in the region, resulting in the Treaty of Prairie du Chien in 1825, where Native leaders from throughout the Great Lakes agreed to boundaries among them. Chapter 2, "Nena'aangabi and the Language of Treaties, 1837–1855," chronicles Nena'aangabi's role in treaties, including the 1837 treaty that Nena'aangabi refused to sign that ceded the territory of the Lac Courte Oreilles Band and the 1854 treaty where the Lac Courte Oreilles Band retained a three-township reservation. This chapter concludes with Nena'aangabi's death on the battlefield against the Dakota in 1855.

Chapter 3, "Waabizheshi's Vision of an Intercultural Community at Rice Lake, 1855–1877," discusses the twenty-two-year struggle of Nena'aangabi's son and successor, Waabizheshi, to establish a new community at Rice Lake, one that accommodated the increasing presence of white settlers but included continued Ojibwe occupation. Timber companies made this more difficult with the destruction of wild rice beds throughout the region, including the complete destruction of the extensive wild rice bed on Rice Lake in 1864. At the same time, white settlers poured into northwestern Wisconsin and the city of Rice Lake grew. The chapter concludes with Waabizheshi's murder by Bidad, a member of the Ojibwe community in 1877. Chapter 4, "Aazhaweyaa and Ojibwe Women in Transition," chronicles the life of Aazhaweyaa, Waabizheshi's sister. As a young woman, Aazhaweyaa experienced a series of visions where she fought alongside her father in battle against the Dakota. When these visions came to fruition, she became famous throughout Ojibwe country. However, like other Ojibwe women of her generation, Aazhaweyaa's life changed dramatically in her early adulthood as a result of American expansion in the region. Aazhaweyaa felt these changes dramatically as in a few short years she went from being a famous warrior to being married to James Bracklin, an American lumber baron and the first mayor of the city of Rice Lake.

Chapter 5, "Giishkitawag Confronts Removal, 1879–1894," discusses the leadership of Waabizheshi's brother and successor, Giishkitawag, who adopted a more aggressive style to resistance to removal. In 1878, the Barron County Board petitioned the federal government for the removal of the community village to the reservation. Giishkitawag was able to resist this effort, but the allotment of the reservation increasingly brought the community into the reservation near Whitefish Lake, when timber sales from allotment provided the Ojibwe income. However, the Ojibwe continued to work off-reservation in traditional labor and in lumber camps as timber harvest on allotments was plagued by fraud and federal mismanagement of Ojibwe timber resources, prompting a Senate investigation in 1888.

The heart of my study is chapter 6, "The Murder of Joe White and the Culmination of Removal," which chronicles the murder of Giishkitawag, the trial of his killers, and how the state of Wisconsin sought to suppress the treaty rights and sovereignty of Ojibwe people by any means, including violence. This chapter interrogates how white settlement impacted the Ojibwe and their ability to remain off-reservation by examining the various whites involved with the trial of Giishkitawag's killers, including timber workers, defense attorneys, jurors, and the killers themselves. Each of these people had a vastly different relationship to the Ojibwe. However, all of them benefitted from Ojibwe dispossession even though these individuals were not directly involved with removing the Ojibwe from their lands. The trial of Joe White's killers illustrated the breadth of American colonialism: white settlement, the role of the timber industry, the state of Wisconsin's enforcement of its game laws on Ojibwe people, and the failure of American courts to provide Native people effective legal protections.

The final chapter, "Maggie Quaderer, Steve Grover, and the Creation of Community at Whitefish, 1894–1920," examines Joe White's community following removal and the new community they built at Whitefish Lake on the reservation. At Whitefish, Nena'aangabi's grandson Steve Grover emerged as a spiritual leader in *Chi-dewe'igan*, or Big Drum ceremonies. Big Drum came to Ojibwe communities in the late nineteenth century from the Dakota. Grover built on his family's rich legacy of leadership and made Whitefish a center for Big Drum, drawing hundreds of followers from as far away as Oklahoma. However, Grover's leadership was extremely controversial, and tensions emerged that were the result of challenges to Ojibwe sovereignty.

AAZHOGAN (BRIDGE)

This book is my attempt to answer the many questions I had about my northern Wisconsin home growing up in the 1980s at the height of controversy over spearfishing and the practice of Ojibwe treaty rights. Why do we have treaty rights? Who were our leaders? Why does our reservation have such an odd shape? Why is there no rice in Rice Lake? I have since learned all of these questions are connected to the murder of Joe White. The murder of Joe White is a telling event in American history, one that addresses how

Native people sought to assert their sovereignty despite the unprecedented challenges they faced. Joe White's story is not widely known outside of Lac Courte Oreilles. The murder of Joe White is not mentioned in Wisconsin history and has never been discussed in any published work. My hope is that this book will help my own community better understand our history and the problem of American colonialism, remember important figures in the struggle, and appreciate that our sovereignty has never been extinguished.

Pronunciation Guide

In this study, I have standardized all Ojibwe personal and place names in the Fiero orthography or double vowel system that is most commonly utilized by Ojibwe speakers in the United States. Consonants in the double vowel system sound roughly like their English equivalents. Vowels, however, have the following pronunciations:

Vowel	*Phonemic*	*A Similar Sound in English*
a (short)	uh	*a*bout
aa (long)	aah	f*a*ther
e (long)	ay	caf*é*
i (short)	ih	p*i*n
ii (long)	ee	s*ee*n
o (short)	oh	*o*pen
oo (long)	oo	b*oo*t

Note: Much of this guide was adapted from Anton Treuer, *The Assassination of Hole-in-the-Day* (St. Paul: Minnesota Historical Society Press, 2011), 220–221.

CHAPTER 1

The Rise of Nena'aangabi and American Expansion in the Western Great Lakes, 1825–1837

At the 1855 annuity payment at Madeline Island, thousands of Lake Superior Ojibwe from Minnesota, Wisconsin, and Michigan gathered. Also present was Richard Morse, a Detroit physician. Dozens of Ojibwe leaders were there, yet the one that most captivated Morse was Nena'aangabi:

> He is rather less than the medium height and size, an intelligent face and mild expression, a very keen eye, and when animated in speaking, a sort of fiery look or twinkle. Like most of the warriors, his face is highly colered with vermillion. At the head of his warriors and in council, he wears an elaborate turban of turkey feathers over his head and shoulders—giving him a fuller appearance in person than he really has, an *unique* look even for an Indian.
>
> It was not long after this chief arrived, before he became the favorite orator and chief.[1]

Nena'aangabi was the ogimaa of the Ojibwe community at Manoominikaan, or Rice Lake, the southernmost village of the Lac Courte Oreilles Band in northwest Wisconsin. Nena'aangabi was not born "the favorite orator and chief": he was not a hereditary leader but ascended to his position through military success. Writing in 1831, Henry Schoolcraft noted that Nena'aangabi was a leader "whose influence is entirely of his own creation."[2] Nena'aangabi's leadership in warfare made Ojibwe presence at Manoominikaan possible.

Nena'aangabi's father was not an ogimaa. Prior to his assumption of leadership, there was not an Ojibwe community at Manoominikaan. The area was rich in wild rice, the mainstay of the Ojibwe diet, due to the massive rice bed on Rice Lake and an even richer rice bed on Prairie Rice Lake, fifteen miles to the south. The area was also rich in game, as the mixed forest and prairie lands around Rice Lake and areas to the south provided more food sources for deer than the heavily forested areas of Lac Courte Oreilles, fifty miles to the northeast. By the 1830s, these vast resources made the community the most vital of the Lac Courte Oreilles Band, larger and more important to Ojibwe survival than the original community at Lac Courte Oreilles.

The rise of Nena'aangabi coincided with American expansion in the western Great Lakes. After centuries of trading relationships with the French and British marked by mutual cooperation, the Ojibwe were confronted by Americans who pushed west in the nineteenth century with the intent of fully incorporating Ojibwe territory into the United States. Despite the claims of the French and the British prior to the nineteenth century, the Ojibwe fully controlled their own territory. As treaties proceeded, fur traders demanded payment from the government for Ojibwe debts, claiming Ojibwe dependence on the fur trade. In reality, the fur trade was a declining industry due to declining demand for fur products in Europe. Prominent fur traders saw Ojibwe treaties as an opportunity to subsidize the industry. While American settlers were uninterested in Ojibwe lands during the time of Nena'aangabi, federal officials were bent on securing the timber and mineral resources. The first treaty that the Ojibwe made with the American government created borders among Native nations in the western Great Lakes that set the stage for future land cession treaties. However, Nena'aangabi and other Native leaders attempted to use these borders to their benefit as well. Nena'aangabi's vision of Ojibwe sovereignty brought complaints from American officials who hoped to get him to bend to their will, and yet his vast charisma also inspired respect from American officials. Treaties gave Ojibwe leaders like Nena'aangabi new opportunities for asserting influence that were not present in the eighteenth century. Nena'aangabi proved adept at utilizing these conditions on his way to becoming the "favorite orator and chief" of the Lake Superior Ojibwe.

OJIBWE MIGRATION TO MANOOMINIKAAN

Although Ojibwe oral traditions vary on the exact details of Ojibwe migration, all share certain commonalities: a westward movement along the Great

Lakes from a starting point on the east coast. Ojibwe migration took several centuries, and Ojibwe people had common origins with Odawa and Potawatomi people. A common thread to Ojibwe migration stories is the role of Mooningwanekaan, or Madeline Island in Lake Superior.[3] Madeline Island is a central place for Ojibwe people. In 1831, Henry Schoolcraft described it this way: "It appears to be the focus from which, as radii from a centre, the ancient population emigrated; and the interior bands consequently look back to it with something of the feelings of parental relations."[4]

Ojibwe society was organized in small geographically based bands. While autonomous from one another, bands were linked through common language, history, kinship, and clan ties. By the mid-nineteenth century, there were four bands of Ojibwe in Wisconsin: La Pointe, St. Croix, Lac du Flambeau, and Lac Courte Oreilles.[5] Bands were usually identified by the waterways that linked the villages in a band together. For example, the Lac du Flambeau Band is named for Waaswaagan Zaaga'igan, the lake from which the band originated. Lac du Flambeau is the literal French translation of the Ojibwe name, which means Torch Lake, named after the Ojibwe practice of spearing fish at night using torchlight. The St. Croix Band is named for the St. Croix River, which links the villages in that band. The Ojibwe name is Manoominikeshinh Ziibi, after the small birds that inhabit wild rice, as the St. Croix River valley contains massive amounts of wild rice, perhaps the most on Earth. The villages of the La Pointe Band were all linked through Chequomegon Bay, including villages at Madeline Island (which the French termed La Pointe or the Point), across the bay at Red Cliff, and at the mouth of the Bad River.

The Ojibwe name for Lac Courte Oreilles is Odaawaa Zaaga'igan, or Ottawa Lake, so named because early in the eighteenth century an Ojibwe hunting party found a dead Odawa on the lake's shores.[6] Both oral tradition and archeological evidence suggest that Lac Courte Oreilles was at one time home to a substantial Odawa community. In the late nineteenth century, future Bad River Ojibwe Tribal Chairman John Condecon was laboring as a surveyor at Lac Courte Oreilles. In the 1930s Condecon was interviewed for the Bad River Works Progress Administration historical project: "When the mounds are dug, there are found skeletons in various positions of Ottawas who died suddenly and without warning. It is said they died suddenly of some epidemic."[7] Lac Courte Oreilles in French literally means "lake of the short ears." Bizarre explanations as to why Lac Courte Oreilles is identified this way abound including the unique shape of the ears of Ojibwe people of the area or that bays in Lac Courte Oreilles resemble short ears. However, the French name for the Lac Courte Oreilles is simply a translation of the Ojibwe name, much like Lac du Flambeau is a direct translation of Waaswaagan Zaaga'igan. Historical sources indicate that French fur traders identified Odawa people as *courte oreilles*. Thus, in the French vernacular of the time, Lac Courte Oreilles meant Odawa Lake, the same as its Ojibwe meaning.[8]

Band cohesiveness was strong and rooted in recognition of common origin, kinship, and geographical proximity. Villages within the same band were typically linked geographically by a common waterway, travel along lakes and rivers by birchbark canoe being the primary means of transport.[9] Ojibwe bands contained anywhere from four to seven villages, each led by an ogimaa, identified in federal records from the nineteenth century as chiefs.[10] Each ogimaa was autonomous. However, leaders could assert influence within the band or in larger Ojibwe politics based on their success in war, the importance of their community, and the number of persons living in the community.

Central to nineteenth-century Ojibwe life was the clan, or *doodem*. English speakers sometimes called clans totems in the nineteenth century. The importance of clans is reflected in the meaning of the word. *Ode'* means heart, and the word part *doo-* refers to the breast area. Nineteenth-century ethnographers found that Ojibwe people were guarded about not speaking their name aloud out of humility. At the same time, Ojibwe people stated their clan affiliation with pride.[11] Inherited from one's father, historically clans were central to Ojibwe society. According to Ojibwe oral tradition, each of the original clans had specific duties. For example, the *ajijaak*, or crane clan, was associated with leadership. By the nineteenth century these traditional roles had faded, so not all *ogimaag* (the plural of *ogimaa*) belonged to the crane clan. However, clans remained an integral part of the fabric of Ojibwe society, most significantly in kinship. One was responsible to a member of their clan the same way as to a blood relative, even if this person was in no way related biologically.[12] This tied Ojibwe communities together, as one could travel a vast area, from Lower Michigan to Manitoba, and have kinship ties in different Ojibwe communities.

The Lac Courte Oreilles Band had its origin in 1745, when Ojibwe who lived on Lake Superior and frequented the area on hunting trips made Lac Courte Oreilles their year-round base. According to mixed-descent historian William Warren, Ojibwe people utilized the area around Lac Courte Oreilles increasingly in the early eighteenth century for seasonal activities as Dakota peoples slowly moved out of the area. According to Warren, this was risky: "For a number of years, however, these hunters made no permanent stay on any spot throughout this country, because danger lurked behind every bush and every tree from the prowling war parties of the Dakotas and Odugamees [Fox]." In 1745, things changed when three brothers of the bear clan were hunting in the area. One of the brothers lost a child while hunting in the winter on the shores of Lac Courte Oreilles. When they buried the child, the devoted parents would not leave: "There was a silent charm about that silent little grave, which caused the mourning parents to brave all dangers, and isolated from their fellows, they passed the spring and summer in its vicinity, and eventually made the spot where it stood the site of a permanent village." Soon, more families with kinship ties to the original family began moving to Lac Courte Oreilles.[13]

The natural beauty of the Lac Courte Oreilles area cannot be overstated. Even today the crystal-clear waters and sandy shores of Lac Courte Oreilles and other lakes in the area beckon visitors from Minneapolis-St. Paul, Milwaukee, Chicago, and other metropolitan areas in the western Great Lakes. Pristine, bubbling rivers and creeks linked to the Chippewa River connected areas to the south where the Ojibwe hunted, fished, made maple sugar, and harvested wild rice. In addition, a pipestone quarry was nearby, an important cultural resource to Native peoples in the Great Lakes. From the first community at Lac Courte Oreilles, Ojibwe families then established other villages in the area including Bakweyawaa (later called Post) east of Lac Courte Oreilles on the Chippewa River, and at Lake Chetac, south of Lac Courte Oreilles.[14] By 1860, government officials paid treaty annuities to communities at Lac Courte Oreilles, Lake Chetac, Pacwawong Lake on the Namekagon River north of Lac Courte Oreilles, Rice Lake, and three on the Chippewa River.[15] These communities, although autonomous, were all part of the Lac Courte Oreilles Band.

Although nineteenth-century Ojibwe villages were important geographic posts, we should not think of them as being the same as towns today since they were rarely continuously occupied. Instead, village sites were the base of operations for seasonal labor, including making maple sugar, gathering wild rice, hunting, trapping, and fishing.[16] Indian Agent Henry Schoolcraft noted: "They are not fixed in their habitations at any point, during the whole of the year, being compelled to go in search of game, fish, and other spontaneous productions, on which they depend."[17] Village sites were most populated in the warmer months following splitting off into smaller family groups in order to more effectively harvest resources. However, even during the summer months, village sites could be devoid of people due to labor activities such as gathering berries or social events in other communities. For example, in July 1831 Schoolcraft passed through the village at Pacwawong Lake on the Namekagon River and gave this description: "We found it completely

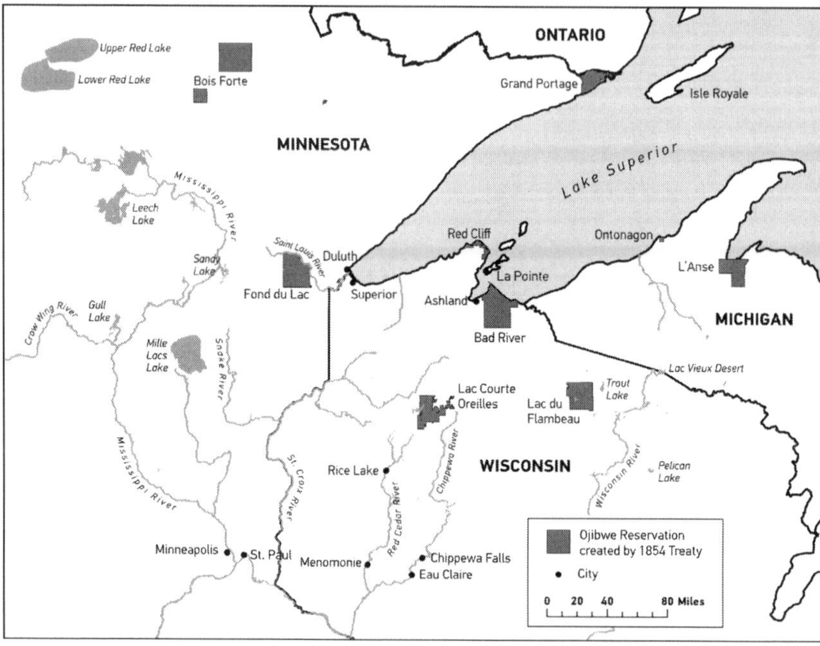

Reservations created by the treaty of 1854.

deserted, according to the custom of the Indians, who after planting their gardens, leave them to go on summer hunts, gather berries, etc."[18]

Furthermore, the sites of Ojibwe villages in the nineteenth century were not fixed in one location as the community eventually exhausted the firewood supply adjacent to the village. For example, the site of the village at Lake Chetac moved to different locations on the lake throughout the nineteenth century. In 1831, Henry Schoolcraft found the village site on an island, while in the late nineteenth century, according to early settler Paul Kirkendall, the village site was located on the eastern side of the lake.[19]

In the case of the Ojibwe at Manoominikaan, the community split their time between Manoominikaan and Long Lake, a large irregularly shaped lake about fifteen miles north of Manoominikaan. Long Lake is extremely narrow, and most of its body more resembles a river. By land, it is thirteen miles from the northernmost point of Long Lake to its southernmost point. Historically, Long Lake had an excellent walleye fishery, and its shallow bays supported excellent stands of wild rice. *Rice Lake Chronotype* editor August Ender wrote: "The headquarters of Chief Nay-Na-Ong-Gay-Bee were on the site of the present city of Rice Lake, and also on a point off the northeast shore of Long Lake."[20] A different location on Long Lake was given by

Ira Isham (who was married to one of Nena'aangabi's granddaughters) in 1925: "Na-Non-Gabe, like most of his predecessors, made his headquarters a great deal of the time at Rice Lake and also on the point below the island on Long Lake."[21] It is likely the community occupied two different sites on Long Lake over the course of the nineteenth century due to exhausting fire wood. Regardless, late in the nineteenth century, when faced with threats of removal to the reservation at Lac Courte Oreilles, the Ojibwe retreated completely from Manoominikaan and spent most of their time at Long Lake. In the closing years of the nineteenth century, when many Native children were educated in distant federal boarding schools, the children of the Ojibwe community at Manoominikaan instead attended a public school on Long Lake alongside the children of white settlers.

Ojibwe people established a permanent community at Manoominikaan in the late eighteenth century. William Warren claimed that Nena'aangabi's father, Gekek, founded the community.[22] Gekek was a direct descendent of the hunter who lost his child on Lac Courte Oreilles and established the permanent Ojibwe community there in 1745. Much like how the Ojibwe settled at Lac Courte Oreilles, the abundant wild rice supply at Manoominikaan rapidly drew more and more Ojibwe families to Gekek's community.[23] In July 1831, Henry Schoolcraft noted: "On coming into Rice Lake we found the whole area of it, except a channel, covered with rice not yet ripe."[24] Furthermore, Schoolcraft noted the abundance of rice along the Red Cedar River (which flows into and out of Rice Lake) north of Rice Lake.[25]

However, there was no better ricing area in northwest Wisconsin (and perhaps anywhere on Earth) than Prairie Rice Lake, about twenty miles south of the Ojibwe village on Rice Lake. In the nineteenth century, the skinny lake was eight miles long and about a quarter mile wide at its widest with a four-acre island in the middle. Prairie Rice Lake is located on a stream just off of the Red Cedar River. It was named Mashkode-Manoominikaan, or Prairie Rice Lake, because the area surrounding the lake was ravaged by fire, making it an open expanse with few trees. William Warren claimed that it could feed two thousand people per season. In 1850, Warren visited Prairie Rice Lake during the height of ricing season and found five hundred people gathering rice there.[26] At the annuity payment that fall, there were 203 people in Nena'aangabi's community.[27] This means that there were hundreds of other Ojibwe people from other communities that utilized Prairie Rice Lake.

All Ojibwe village sites were located on ricing lakes or rivers, and most battles Ojibwe people fought in Wisconsin were over access to ricing areas. Wild rice was the resource that enabled human survival in northern Wisconsin, northern Minnesota, and Upper Michigan prior to the advent of refrigeration and large-scale importation of food into the area. It is a highly nutritious and delicious grain that could be easily stored in caches throughout the year without spoiling so long as it does not get wet. An annual, wild rice grows in shallow bodies of water with murky bottoms. Wild rice yield varies considerably from year to year depending on weather conditions.[28]

Given the importance of rice to surviving the harsh climate of northern Wisconsin, the Dakota attempted numerous times to dislodge the Ojibwe from Prairie Rice Lake in the late eighteenth century. In 1798, the Dakota launched a surprise attack on an Ojibwe ricing camp on Prairie Rice Lake. William Warren claimed that, although the Ojibwe were outnumbered ten to one, only four Ojibwe were killed, while many more Dakota were killed. A few years later, two hundred Dakota attacked a single Ojibwe family camped at Prairie Rice Lake while the head of the household was gone spearing fish. After finding his dead family, the man pursued the Dakota party and killed five Dakota warriors before making his skillful escape. The Dakota attacked another Ojibwe family at Prairie Rice Lake a short time later. Warren asserted, "Almost every bend on the Chippeway and Menominee rivers has been the scene of a fight, surprise, or bloody massacre, and one of their chiefs remarked with truth when asked to sell his lands that 'the country was strewn with the bones of their fathers and enriched with their blood.' "[29]

As valuable as the area's rice beds were, there were other valuable resources in the region important to Ojibwe survival. In the nineteenth century, vast, old-growth forests dominated the landscape around Lac Courte Oreilles. While the massive white pines, hemlocks, and sugar maples were awe-inspiringly beautiful, old-growth forests are not the best landscapes for sustaining an abundant deer population. The forest canopy of old-growth trees chokes out sunlight to the ground, resulting in very little vegetation for deer to eat. In 1919, Mrs. Gustave Robert remembered her childhood at a fur trade post on the Chippewa River south of Lac Courte Oreilles near modern Cornell, Wisconsin: "The whole country around was almost an unbroken pine forest and one could walk for hours without seeing the sun."[30] Describing Ojibwe seasonal labor, Lac Courte Oreilles Ojibwe Prosper Guibord told anthropologist Robert Ritzenthaler, "January—Indians would be in hunting grounds—go to hunt deer, sometimes way down to Eau Claire—there were no deer around here."[31] Moving south from Lac Courte Oreilles toward Rice Lake, there were more open areas (as there are today) with more food sources for deer at ground level. In addition, the soil quality was much better. The sandy soils around Lac Courte Oreilles give way to much richer soils to the south, something evident today in the amount of agriculture around

Rice Lake. Schoolcraft wrote: "the whole country puts on a sylvan character, as beautiful to the eye as it is fertile in soil."[32]

South of Rice Lake were even better hunting grounds, as the woodlands totally gave way to open prairie. While traveling south of Rice Lake on the Red Cedar River in 1831 Henry Schoolcraft wrote: "We now entered a prairie country, of a pleasing and picturesque aspect. We observed a red deer during the morning; we passed many hunting encampments of the Indians and the horns and bones of slaughtered deers, and other evidences of our being in a valuable game country."[33] Accordingly, this area was fought over by Ojibwe and Dakota living to the south throughout the nineteenth century right up until the United States forcibly removed the Dakota from Minnesota following the Dakota War in 1862. The area in between the Ojibwe village at Rice Lake and the Mdewakanton Dakota village near the confluence of the Mississippi and Minnesota Rivers was a buffer zone between the two nations where neither had any permanent villages but instead made brief travels for labor activities. Despite the soil quality mentioned by Schoolcraft, no one (including non-Indians) dared stay long enough to plant, maintain, and harvest crops.

The vast resources of Rice Lake had drawn Native people for centuries, as evidenced by the numerous mounds around Rice Lake, some of which survive today as part of Indian Mounds City Park in Rice Lake.[34] While Wisconsin was the site of thousands of effigy and burial mounds, the highest concentration was in the southern part of the state, most notably around Madison. There were only scattered mounds in northern Wisconsin. Rice Lake is the one exception, which by far had the highest concentration of mounds in northern Wisconsin. The mounds at Rice Lake are believed to be several-centuries-old burial mounds of Dakota or Mesquakie peoples.[35] In addition, there were valuable cultural resources, such as a nearby pipestone quarry. Despite the fact that the quarry is surrounded by swamp and inaccessible in the summer months, it served as an important site for acquiring pipestone. Archeological evidence suggests that Native peoples utilized the site for hundreds of years prior to the Ojibwe establishing a village at Rice Lake.[36]

A LEADER WHOSE INFLUENCE IS ENTIRELY OF HIS OWN CREATION

Nena'aangabi was a self-made man: Schoolcraft wrote that Nena'aangabi's "influence is entirely of his own creation." Estimates of Nena'aangabi's age vary. He was born sometime in the late eighteenth century, when Ojibwe struggled against Dakota attacks at Prairie Rice Lake. One account says he was seventy-six when he died in 1855, while another says he was "past sixty" at his death.[37] As Schoolcraft pointed out, he was "not in the line of the ancient chiefs." Indeed, Nena'aangabi's father, Gekek, was not a chief, despite his role in establishing the Ojibwe community at Manoominikaan.[38] The fact that Nena'aangabi wielded so much influence is all the more remarkable given that Moozojiid, leader of the community on Lac Courte Oreilles, was a hereditary leader and leader of the original community of the band.[39] However, by 1831, Nena'aangabi's charisma and success in war made him the most influential leader of the Lac Courte Oreilles Ojibwe and one of the most influential among all Wisconsin Ojibwe leaders.

Ojibwe clans are patrilineal, and Nena'aangabi was a direct descendent of the original settlers of Lac Courte Oreilles, who were members of the bear clan. Despite the fact that specific clan duties had faded, clans still exhibited common characteristics in the nineteenth century. William Warren claimed:

> It is a general saying, and an observable fact, amongst their fellows, that the Bear clan resemble the animal that forms their Totem in disposition. They are ill-tempered and fond of fighting, and consequently they are noted as ever having kept the tribe in difficulty and war with other tribes, in which, however, they have generally been the principal and foremost actors.

Warren backed his claim by noting that influential war chiefs such as Nena'aangabi, famed Gull Lake ogimaa Bagone-giizhig, and Bizhiki of Leech Lake were members of the bear clan. Warren even claimed that members of the bear clan exhibited physical characteristics related to bears: "the writer has observed the fact, that they are possessed of a long, thick, course head of the blackest hair, which seldom becomes thin or white in old age."[40]

Writing in 1831, Henry Schoolcraft found a robust, growing Ojibwe community at Manoominikaan: "The population is enterprising and warlike. They have means in *comparative* abundance. They are increasing in numbers."[41] An 1843 federal census showed 153 people at Manoominikaan, making it the most populated community of the Lac Courte Oreilles Band. More people lived at Manoominikaan than the flagship community at Lac Courte Oreilles.[42] In 1850, just seven years later, the community grew to 203 people.[43] The growth of the community was directly related to Nena'aangabi's ability to provide security and resources to Ojibwe families. Nena'aangabi's leadership made harvesting rice at Prairie Rice Lake safe for

Ojibwe families, in marked contrast to the violent episodes of the late eighteenth century.

This security and access to important resources made Nena'aangabi a popular leader. When Henry Schoolcraft visited Manoominikaan in 1831, he marveled at the presence of many young warriors "who appeared to be ardently attached to him." Schoolcraft then pressured Nena'aangabi to stop fighting the Dakota: "After a pause, Neenaba got up, and spoke to the question, connecting it with obvious considerations, of which mutual rights, personal safety, and the obligation to protect women and children, formed the basis. The latter duty was not a slight one."[44]

However, it was not just his military accomplishments that sustained Nena'aangabi's influence. Schoolcraft noted that Nena'aangabi's personal qualities were equally a factor in his popularity: "His manner was frank and bold equally free from servility and repulsiveness." These were important characteristics for Ojibwe leaders. Schoolcraft claimed Nena'aangabi was a leader "whose endowments, personal and mental had not been misrepresented by the Indians on my route, who uniformly spoke of him in favorable terms." It was due to all of these factors that Nena'aangabi became the most influential leader in the Lac Courte Oreilles Band. Schoolcraft noted that "upon him rests essentially the conduct of affairs in this quarter."[45]

What was also remarkable about Nena'aangabi was that Americans respected him despite the fact that he made absolutely no effort to compromise Ojibwe sovereignty or assimilate to American culture. While over in Minnesota famed Gull Lake Ojibwe leader Bagone-giizhig built a house and began farming in 1855 to show his commitment to American officials, Nena'aangabi made no such concessions.[46] He remained, utterly and completely, what the government would later refer to as a "blanket Indian" right to his death. Despite this, Americans loved him. In 1831, Schoolcraft referred to Nena'aangabi as a "distinguished young man" and had nothing bad to say about him despite the fact that Nena'aangabi spurned Schoolcraft's plea to stop fighting the Dakota.[47] Beyond his considerable military success, intelligence, and political skill, Nena'aangabi's popularity rested on the fact that he was a straightforward, honorable, and moral person.

Nena'aangabi was not only the most influential leader within the Lac Courte Oreilles Band, but as the nineteenth century wore on, his influence grew among the Wisconsin Ojibwe. Ogimaag were leaders of a particular community or village and exercised autonomy from each other. Authority was never vested in one central figure. However, leaders of large villages were able to assert influence outside their own village. The size of one's village was directly related to the quality of one's leadership as Ojibwe families could leave the village at any time to join relatives in another village if they felt the leader was not effective. Other factors shaped how much a leader could exercise influence outside of their own community such as how long they had been a leader, oratorical abilities, and the historical importance of the leader's community. For example, until his death in 1854, Bizhiki of La Pointe was the most influential Ojibwe leader in Wisconsin based on his own individual qualities as a leader, his advanced age, and the historical importance of the Ojibwe community at La Pointe. All of these factors in turn reflected the large size of his community.[48] At the time of Bizhiki's death, however, Nena'aangabi's influence among Ojibwe in Wisconsin and even American officials rivaled the old chief. After Bizhiki's death there was no question Nena'aangabi was the most influential Ojibwe leader in Wisconsin.

In the first decades of the early nineteenth century, Nena'aangabi ascended to leadership as a war chief due to his bravery in battle with the Dakota. There was a distinction between war chiefs and civil chiefs. William Warren explained:

> The war-chiefs, though second in rank to the civil chiefs, have often attained a paramount influence over the villages or sections of the tribe with whom they resided; but this influence (before they learned to follow some of the evil ways of the whites) they always used towards sustaining and strengthening the hereditary civil chiefs. The war chieftainship was usually obtained by courage and exploits in war, and success in leading a war party, through spiritual vision, against an enemy. It sometimes descended from father to son, in fact always, where the son approved himself in a manner to secure the confidence of the warriors.[49]

By the time Warren wrote *History of the Ojibway People*, the main distinction between war chiefs and civil chiefs was merely how each attained their position: Nena'aangabi was more influential than Moozojiid, the leader at Lac Courte Oreilles who was a civil chief. As historian Theresa Schenck notes, while civil chiefs inherited their position from their father, it was not always the eldest son who ascended to leadership, but the son with the most merit.[50] However, the sons of war chiefs also inherited their father's position, as Nena'aangabi's son Waabizheshi did in 1855, following Nena'aangabi's death.

Many of the duties of the ogimaa occurred at the community level where each ogimaa made autonomous decisions that had little impact outside the village or even in the larger structure of the band. These included decisions about the allocating of resources and territory. It was an ogimaa's responsibility to provide for his community, and their influence depended on it. It was difficult for a successful ogimaa to accumulate wealth. In the 1850s German ethnographer Johann Kohl wrote: "Frequently, when a chief receives very handsome goods, either in exchange for his peltry, or as a recognition of his high position, he will throw them all in a heap, call his followers, and divide all among them."[51]

However, in other areas ogimaag worked together outside of the community. This was where certain ogimaa exercised greater influence. Prior to the nineteenth century, this was mostly in warfare. Leaders gained prominence outside their community by their ability to raise military groups and the subsequent success of those groups. However, in the mid-nineteenth century, treaties opened up new opportunities for Ojibwe leaders to distinguish themselves. Despite the claims of Warren about how the "evil ways of the whites" corrupted Ojibwe political structures, in many ways the advent of treaty making and the execution of provisions contained in treaties, such as annuity payments, gave ogimaag new avenues for asserting influence outside their own communities that had not been there in the eighteenth century.

In reality, it made little difference how an ogimaa obtained their position since the authority of the ogimaa was based solely on their ability to provide effective leadership and access to resources. Members of the community could leave at any time to join family in other villages if they felt the leadership of the ogimaa was not effective. William Warren noted the presence of "made" chiefs, who were appointed by traders. For Warren, the presence of made chiefs illustrated how traditional Ojibwe political institutions were corrupted by outsiders. A made chief enjoyed advantages that civil chiefs and war chiefs did not. Since traders appointed them, a made chief had greater access to goods. However, despite Warren's lamenting, if the leader was not a good provider to his community or was of low moral character, members of his community would leave, circumventing the impact of the traders.[52]

In the Lac Courte Oreilles Band, one leader who was a made chief was Misko-manidoons, leader of a community on the Chippewa River. The case of Misko-manidoons illustrates how the way a leader ascended to leadership was irrelevant to how much influence they could assert. Warren noted that Misko-manidoons sustained his popularity with his "courage in war, and especially his success in the chase."[53] In the early nineteenth century, Misko-manidoons built on this to become an influential leader within the Lac Courte Oreilles Band. After Misko-manidoons's death in the late 1820s, his son Gichi-Waabizheshi (not to be confused with Nena'aangabi's son and successor Waabizheshi) assumed leadership and, early on at least, inherited his father's influence. For example, in 1831, Gichi-Waabizheshi was influential enough to represent the Lac Courte Oreilles Band along with Nena'aangabi during Henry Schoolcraft's first visit as Indian agent to northwest Wisconsin from his headquarters at Sault Ste. Marie.[54] Schoolcraft noted that Gichi-Waabizheshi's influence within the band had slipped and was being surpassed by Moozojiid, leader of the community at Lac Courte Oreilles.[55] However, Gichi-Waabizheshi was still influential enough in 1843 to speak for the Lac Courte Oreilles Band in protest of the treaty of 1842.[56] Within a few years of that, Gichi-Waabizheshi's influence eroded quickly. This receding influence is reflected in the number of people in Gichi-Waabizheshi's community, which declined drastically from 161 in 1847 to 75 in 1850. During the same time period, the community at Bakweyawaa on the Chippewa River under Gwiiwizenzish in 1847 and then his son Ozhaawashko-giizhig in 1850 increased from 107 to 177.[57] Thus, the ability to maintain influence really had little to do with how a leader ascended to leadership, but was more about providing for the needs of his community.

OJIBWE-DAKOTA WARFARE

Success in war was a major factor in the growth and maintenance of Nena'aangabi's influence. Warfare with the Dakota was a constant aspect of Ojibwe life in Wisconsin and Minnesota in the nineteenth century right up until the Dakota War in 1862, after which the Dakota were forcibly removed from Minnesota. Historical sources in the nineteenth century tended to portray Ojibwe-Dakota warfare in terms that had more to do with stereotypes of Native savagery. For example, Thomas Randall wrote in his *History of the Chippewa Valley*: "Nothing can be more dastardly, or better calculated to induce a mean, cowardly disposition, than their mode of conducting war—assassination or murder, better defines their treacherous, stealthy, fiendish butcheries than any other terms."[58] While Randall's characterization is rooted more in white stereotypes of Indian savagery than actual knowledge of Ojibwe warfare, Ojibwe-Dakota warfare (like all warfare) was in fact marked by intense violence. Fear of this violence shaped Ojibwe communities in the nineteenth century, especially communities like Manoominikaan that bordered Dakota Territory. While there are no recorded accounts from Ojibwe people from Manoominikaan, non-Indian accounts reveal the genuine terror of Ojibwe-Dakota warfare. At the Bakweyawaa community on the Chippewa River in 1803, teenaged fur trader George Nelson described a tense night: "We were in a most unenviable plight—we knew not what to do, where to fly—sometimes erect or half standing, sometimes lying flat on the ground as possible to avoid the balls of our enemies we were every moment expecting to hear whizzing again amongst us."[59]

While out on a hunting expedition with his family and far from his main Plains Ojibwe village, John Tanner spotted Dakota peoples:

> The night before my departure was one, at my lodge, of terror and alarm, greater even than is commonly felt among the Indians. I had mentioned the tracks that I had seen, and I did not doubt that a party of Sioux were in my immediate neighbourhood, and would fall upon me before morning. More than half the night had passed, and not one of us had slept, when we heard a sudden rushing without, and our dogs came running in evident alarm. I told my children that the time was come for us to all die together. I placed myself in the front part of my lodge, and raising the door a little, put the muzzle of my gun, and sat in momentary expectation of the approach of the enemy. Footsteps were distinctly audible, but the night being dark, I could as yet see nothing. At last a little black object, not larger in appearance than a man's head, came slowly and directly to my lodge. Here again I experienced how much fear influences the power of sight for this little object, as it came near, seemed at instant to shoot up to the height of a man, and at the next to be no larger than it really was. When I was entirely convinced that it was nothing but a small animal, I stepped out, and finding it to be a porcupine, killed it with my tomahawk. The remainder of the night was spent in the same manner as the beginning. Early in the morning, I fled to the fortified camp.[60]

Having to tell one's children that "the time was come for us to all die together" vividly illustrates the harsh realities of Ojibwe-Dakota warfare on Ojibwe families. While Tanner and his family were able to escape to safety, it is important to remember that dozens of Ojibwe and Dakota families in nineteenth-century Wisconsin and Minnesota were not so lucky.

American officials and early white settlers saw these raids as an endless cycle of savage revenge, but in fact they served important cultural and spiritual purposes. When a person was killed in an Ojibwe community, it was the responsibility of their relatives to receive either material compensation or some form of retribution in order for the spirit of the murdered person to go on to the spirit world. Warfare operated very similarly. The main difference was that, instead of a ceremony within the community, there was a scalp dance. Scalps served an important spiritual purpose, as they contained the spirit of the person. Because of this, it was not just enough to kill a Dakota, but it was imperative to take the scalp and have the scalp dance so that the killed person could go on to the spirit world.[61] Likewise, for Nena'aangabi and other war leaders, it was required to do things in a proper way spiritually before initiating a military campaign. In the 1850s Johann Kohl wrote: "When a chief is meditating a war expedition, or preparing for it, either a dream he has had was the incitement to it, or in case the determination preceded the dream, he now seats himself for the express purpose, concentrates his every thought on the subject, and seeks to gain good dream for it before he proceeds to carry it into execution."[62]

In the eighteenth century, the Ojibwe fought the Dakota for territorial gain. Historian Anton Treuer argues that, by the beginning of the nineteenth century, most Ojibwe-Dakota military conflict was no longer large campaigns to gain (or in the case of the Dakota, regain) territory, but instead involved small raids to avenge dead relatives. Many times these small raids involved noncombatant civilians.

According to Treuer, because most Ojibwe-Dakota warfare in the nineteenth century was just smaller raids to avenge relatives, casualties in both Ojibwe and Dakota communities were much lower than in the eighteenth century. Even though the immediate purpose of these raids was to avenge prior deaths, they served a secondary purpose in defining and maintaining Ojibwe territorial gains made in the eighteenth century.

At the same time, Ojibwe and Dakota people practiced truces in order to exchange hunting territory. However, these truces were not just about economic exchange: they often entailed social exchange including friendships and intermarriage.[63] The Lac Courte Oreilles Band practiced truces with the Dakota in 1841 and 1846. The 1841 peace came about after a Dakota party was killed on the Red Cedar River in 1840 and six Ojibwe were killed in retribution. A peace council was held in Eau Claire. Another peace council was held in 1846 at Chippewa Falls. Dakota leaders Wabasha, Red Wing, and Big Thunder attended the council accompanied by 150 mounted warriors. According to sources, the "head chief," most likely Nena'aangabi, approached the Dakota with a large pipe in one hand and a hatchet in the other. Upon reaching the Dakota, he threw the hatchet in the ground "with considerable force as to bury it in the earth."[64] While the surviving account of this council does not identify whether it was in fact Nena'aangabi, this dramatic gesture was in keeping with his dramatic diplomatic style. Furthermore, by the 1840s, Nena'aangabi was unquestionably the "head chief" in the region.

TRADERS, TREATIES, AND THE MYTH OF OJIBWE DEPENDENCE

In 1828, Leech Lake Band Ojibwe leader Eshkibagikoonzh or Flat Mouth told Henry Schoolcraft, "The Americans are not our masters; the English are not our masters; the country is ours."[65] Eshkibagikoonzh's words reveal how, despite the claims of the British and later Americans, Ojibwe communities remained autonomous well into the mid-nineteenth century. Similarly, traders pushed for payments of Ojibwe debt at the treaties, arguing that the Ojibwe were poor and dependent on the fur trade. However, recent scholarship reveals that these claims of Ojibwe dependency were exaggerated, and that neither the British, Americans, nor traders were the "masters" of the Ojibwe.

In *An Infinity of Nations*, historian Michael Witgen demonstrates that the Great Lakes remained Native territory during the seventeenth and eighteenth centuries, despite the cultural, political, and economic shocks sustained by Native peoples.[66] As Witgen argues: "European claims of discovery and possession in this region represented the rhetoric of empire rather than a genuine expansion of political sovereignty."[67] Other scholarship suggests that actual French and British influence on Ojibwe life was minimal. Historian Theresa Schenck argues that the Ojibwe were slow to enter the fur trade in the seventeenth century and characterizes Ojibwe participation in the trade as sporadic, rather than of steadily increasing dependence.[68] Bruce White's excellent study of the fur trade, "A Skilled Game of Exchange," emphasizes the precarious position occupied by traders doing business with Ojibwe people. White discusses how traders had to give gifts to Ojibwe people to get them to participate in the trade and points out how important it was for traders to have kinship ties to Ojibwe people in order to have an advantage over competing companies.[69] As German ethnographer Johann Georg Kohl observed in 1855: "It may be conjectured that a trader can only be successful through caution and exercise of tact."[70] Women in particular exercised a central role, with traders often negotiating directly with Ojibwe women over food supplies, given the role of Ojibwe women in producing these supplies.[71] In his 1894 autobiography, Benjamin Armstrong noted that intermarriage was a tactic that Ojibwe leaders used in the nineteenth century when the monopoly of the American Fur Company resulted in high prices. Having a kinship relationship to an individual trader tempered the ability of the company to impose high prices, as the trader was obligated to be fair through his kinship relationship to Ojibwe leaders.[72]

In fact, much of the time, traders were dependent on the Ojibwe, not the other way around. One example was fur trader George Nelson at his fur trade post at Bakweyawaa on the Chippewa River. The teenage Nelson was utterly dependent on Ojibwe ogimaa Babaamikawe, or as Nelson termed in him French, "La Piste" (the Track). On February 29, 1803, Nelson wrote, "LaPiste today gives me two small Pike & about 6 quarts of rise—Charity!" A week later Nelson wrote, "La Piste gives me a bag (small) of wild rise, & another mixed with Corn & rise half full." By March 17, things we even more dire: "We subsist upon indian Charity."[73] At the Treaty of St. Peter's in 1837, Eshkibagikoonzh told the treaty commissioners regarding the demands of traders seeking a payment from the Ojibwe: "Where have they got the Fish they have eaten, and the wood they have burned? They were caught from our Lakes, & Rivers, and taken from our Land—And they talk to us about paying them our debts!"[74]

Taken together, this literature suggests that accounts of Ojibwe dependence on the fur trade in the nineteenth century were highly exaggerated. Recent scholarship has more directly challenged the notion of Ojibwe dependence on the fur trade. In their excellent study on Ojibwe traditional labor in northwestern Ontario, scholars Tim E. Holzkamm, Leo G. Waisberg, and Joan A. Lovisek point out that the diversity of Ojibwe food sources and participation in cultural activities, suggesting that Ojibwe people had free time for leisure pursuits even in winter, indicate that descriptions of Ojibwe poverty and dependence during the mid-nineteenth century were exaggerated.[75] Instead, it wasn't until the late nineteenth century when the ecological changes brought about by clear-cutting of timber resources, enforcement of provincial game laws off-reservation, and dispossession of Native reserve lands threatened traditional Ojibwe labor, resulting in poverty.

Likewise, in *The Ojibwa of Western Canada*, historian Laura Peers argues against increasing dependence on the fur trade among the Plains Ojibwe. Peers argues that the relative abundance of historical evidence from those involved in the fur trade has tended to overemphasize dependence on the fur trade:

> these sources must be used carefully, for they were generated by non-Native people for particular purposes. The cultural biases of the authors, and the topical gaps created in our understanding by what they did not record, mean that the window they open on western Ojibwa life and history is narrow, and the view through it is limited and at times distorted. Traders' and missionaries' accounts tell us largely what happened around the trading posts and mission stations, and reliance on them tends to produce historical interpretations that over-emphasize the role of these institutions in Native society.[76]

Peers goes on to make a convincing argument that Plains Ojibwe culture and labor went through several ups and downs in this time period and was not characterized by a linear increasing dependence. Peers notes that Plains Ojibwe dependence on traders peaked in the early nineteenth century, and traders increasingly were frustrated as Western Ojibwa turned to bison hunts and away from trapping in the nineteenth century. Another example Peers cites is how increasingly in the nineteenth century Plains Ojibwe used skins of animals instead of blankets obtained by traders. Peers also offers compelling evidence that changes in the top of the trade, most notably the 1805 demise of the XY Company and the 1821 merger of the North West Company and Hudson's Bay Company did not devastate Plains Ojibwe communities or even lessen the role of the Plains Ojibwe in the trade. Rather, Peers demonstrates that the Plains Ojibwe turned to alternative furs by hunting different animals. Even when beaver epidemics coincided with changes at the top of the trade, Peers argues that the Plains Ojibwe were able to survive and even thrive in these conditions.

The work of Holzkamm, Waisberg, and Lovisek in northwest Ontario and Peers with the Plains Ojibwe suggests that American officials in Wisconsin and Minnesota also exaggerated dependence on the fur trade. Instead, it may be more useful to think of how the decline of fur trade revenues impacted the top levels of the industry rather than Ojibwe producers of furs. Henry Schoolcraft noted this in 1832, when he argued that the supply of both furs and goods going into Ojibwe communities had declined over the past forty years.[77] However, throughout the nineteenth century traders remained present in Ojibwe communities, giving the Ojibwe access to goods they could not produce themselves such as guns and powder. Furthermore, Ojibwe people were resourceful and knew how to produce alternatives to goods not available through the fur trade.

The excellent work of these scholars also informs the role of traders in Wisconsin Ojibwe treaties. Many of the early politicians in local governments in Wisconsin, Michigan, and Minnesota were either former traders or still held major interests in trading enterprises. Nearly all of the treaty commissioners for Ojibwe land cession treaties had ties to trading interests. Therefore, it may be helpful to think about the large amounts of money paid to traders in the treaties not so much as illustrating Ojibwe dependence on the fur trade, but instead as the federal government subsidizing an industry that saw profits eroding at the very top levels.

In Ojibwe land cession treaties, traders secured direct payments from the US government. Despite the payments made directly to traders at the time of the treaties, traders continued to siphon off Ojibwe yearly annuities after treaties, sometimes in collusion with government officials. Benjamin Armstrong noted that the agent would "allow the traders places by the pay table, especially the American Fur Company, with an open sack in which to take the money claimed to be due them from the Indians and as soon as an Indian had touched the pen the bill against this Indian was handed to the agent and the money poured into the traders' sack, and the bill was generally enough to cover the Indians' dues."[78] Rather than seeing Ojibwe dependency on the fur trade, a better way to think about the fur trade in the nineteenth century was that well-connected individuals involved in the fur trade saw an opportunity to make more money off of Indians. This occurred because the traders had a voice in the US government, and the Ojibwe did not.

On the ground, Lac Courte Oreilles leaders felt the effects of declining profits at the top of the fur industry. In 1828, Henry Schoolcraft described a visit to his agency at Sault Ste. Marie by Lac Courte Oreilles ogimaa Misko-manidoons, who complained to Schoolcraft that traders were charging exorbitant prices for goods and that non-Ojibwe hunters were trespassing on Ojibwe hunting grounds.[79] These sentiments were echoed the same year by Gidagaa-bizhiw, the ogimaa of the village on Lake Chetac. In particular, Gidagaa-bizhiw complained that the traders were charging high prices for ammunition.[80] Perhaps local traders were trying to recoup losses at the top levels of the industry by overcharging Ojibwe people at the local level.

AMERICAN EXPANSION AND THE TREATIES OF 1825 AND 1826

In 1825, the American government made its first real attempt to assert its authority over Native nations in the western Great Lakes with the Treaty of Prairie du Chien. Despite American claims to the region dating back to the Treaty of Paris in 1783, on the ground Americans exercised little to no influence in Ojibwe communities. The relationship Americans sought with the Ojibwe differed dramatically from the relationships established between the Ojibwe and the French beginning in the seventeenth century and continuing later with the British. Both the French and the British maintained economic relationships with the Ojibwe founded on cooperation, as the Ojibwe traded beaver and other furs for technology useful in seasonal labor activities.[81] Americans had little interest in economic relationships rooted in respect for Native sovereignty and sought to incorporate Native territory and remove Native peoples from the land. In the course of a few decades American colonialism disrupted a pattern of two centuries of interaction between Ojibwe people and French and later British traders. While American officials claimed the treaty of 1825 was meant to solely promote peace by setting up boundaries between Native nations, in reality the government used the boundaries to procure land cessions in the immediate years following the treaty in northern Illinois and southern Wisconsin, areas rich in lead.[82]

Another distinction between the Americans and the French and British who preceded them was the role of bureaucrats. While the president of the United States theoretically represented the American government, on the ground Native nations mostly dealt with a changing cast of bureaucrats. The Office of Indian Affairs, later known as the Bureau of Indian Affairs, was initially a division of the War Department. In 1849, the Office of Indian Affairs moved to the Interior Department. The commissioner of Indian affairs who headed the Office of Indian Affairs reported to the secretary of war (after 1849, the secretary of the interior). Within the Office of Indian Affairs were Indian agencies, federal outposts staffed by an Indian agent, an individual charged with managing the day-to-day basics of the federal government's relationship with Native communities. In the early nineteenth century, the Indian agent for the Lac Courte Oreilles Ojibwe was located at Sault Ste. Marie, at the far eastern tip of Michigan's Upper Peninsula, over four hundred miles from Manoominikaan. The president authorized a treaty commissioner to represent the interests of the federal government and negotiate treaties. Treaty commissioners were typically an Indian agent or territorial official, as treaties were conducted prior to statehood.

Ojibwe treaty councils were highly ritualized diplomatic exchanges, marked by protocols of Ojibwe diplomacy, such as gift giving. Missionary Leonard Wheeler's description of the 1842 treaty council was typical of all Ojibwe treaties:

> The making of a treaty with the Indians is one of the most important occasions for which they ever assemble together. It is an occasion which calls out a greater number of people than ordinarily meet for the transaction of other business. It is a time when the wise men of the nation are called for, and when the talents and oratory of the people are brought into requisition. It is a time also for paint and ornaments and all that display, which exhibits national character. The number of Indians present, was between three and four thousand.[83]

While many attended treaties, only individuals of influence signed them. In some of the Lake Superior Ojibwe treaties, only ogimaag signed. In other treaties, individuals known as headmen and warriors signed. "Headmen" led small family groups when the larger village split up for labor activities, while "warriors" were typically younger individuals of military renown in the community.[84]

Despite popular notions about treaty making, Lake Superior Ojibwe leaders were not plied with alcohol in order to coerce them to sign the treaties. In his work on Plains Indian treaties anthropologist Raymond DeMallie notes: "American Indian leaders were not mere pawns of the U.S. government. They did use political strategies to combat whites on their own ground and sometimes they were able to gain important concessions."[85] This was even truer for the Lake Superior Ojibwe. No settlers clamored for Ojibwe lands in the mid-nineteenth century, and the Ojibwe still exercised complete autonomy. Lake Superior Ojibwe leaders signed the treaties because they hoped to establish a relationship with the United States that would benefit their communities by bringing money and goods into the communities they led. Based on the minimal American presence in the western Great Lakes and what American officials told the Ojibwe, ogimaag had little reason to believe that the treaties would be the basis of dispossession of their lands.

In the treaty of 1825, the federal government claimed to be only interested in promoting peace among Native nations by drawing borders between tribes in the western Great Lakes including the Ojibwe, Dakota, Ho-Chunk, Menominee, Potawatomi, Odawa, Sauk, Fox, and Iowa. The treaty commissioners were Michigan Territorial Governor Lewis Cass (the states of Michigan, Wisconsin, and Minnesota were all part of the Michigan Territory at this time) and St. Louis Indian Agent William Clark of the Lewis and Clark expedition fame. Cass later served as the secretary of war during the Jackson administration when removal of the Cherokee and other southern tribes was underway. Cass told the tribes, "We tell you again your Great Father does not want your land. He wants to establish boundaries and peace among you." Despite American imperial designs in the region, Native nations were still powerful, and the discourse of diplomacy was still very much rooted in Native protocols. For example, Clark told the tribes, "My Children, this belt of Wampum now in our hands is considered to be a religious contract between all the Tribes which are represented on it and is intended by your Great Father to draw you as a part of his Children still nearer under his protective wing."[86] Furthermore, gifts were a central part of the diplomacy between Native nations and the Americans, all revealing how much Native nations themselves dictated the process of diplomacy.

After the treaty, Clark and Cass wrote Secretary of War James Barbour,

"This Treaty will form an era in our Indian relations." However, Native leaders had mixed reactions to American goals. Many tribal leaders voiced uncertainty about the idea of boundaries. Noodin, an ogimaa of the Snake River Band, told the commissioners, "I wish to leave here in peace. But in running marks around our country or in giving into our enemies it may make new disturbances or breed new wars."[87] One of the issues that would impact the Lac Courte Oreilles Band was the widely diverging claims made by Ojibwe and Dakota leaders about the southern border of Ojibwe territory south of Manoominikaan. Dakota leader Little Crow claimed lands all the way up to Chippewa Falls, while Snake River Band ogimaa Bayezhig told federal officials that Ojibwe territory went all the way down to the mouth of the Chippewa River.[88] American officials located the boundary where the Eau Claire River empties into the Chippewa River (modern-day Eau Claire, Wisconsin), about ten miles south of Chippewa Falls and about fifty miles north of the mouth of the Chippewa River. On the Red Cedar River, the boundary was drawn just north of modern-day Menomonie, Wisconsin, some fifteen miles north of the mouth of the Red Cedar.[89]

While these areas were contested in the eighteenth century, by 1825 Ojibwe people held the upper hand in the region. Furthermore, as Nena'aangabi grew in influence as a leader in the 1830s, Ojibwe at Manoominikaan exercised even more control of the area south of the boundary. Ojibwe leaders were supposed to be represented by Henry Schoolcraft, the agent in far-off Sault Ste. Marie. However, Schoolcraft was marginal to the proceedings at Prairie du Chien. At the same time, Dakota leaders such as Little Crow and Wabasha had day-to-day interaction with agents at Prairie du Chien and Fort Snelling who were much more influential at the treaty. How could Schoolcraft assert anything for the Ojibwe? After all, Sault Ste. Marie was over six hundred miles from Prairie du Chien: he had no pull among leaders in the developing lead-mining region of southwest Wisconsin. The boundary was no small matter. While Ojibwe at the time exercised control on the ground south of the boundary, the federal government allowed the Dakota to later lease a mill and ultimately cede the land in 1837. This meant that money and goods flowed into Dakota communities for lease and sale of what was in reality Ojibwe land.

Following the treaty, Schoolcraft argued that the Wisconsin and Minnesota Ojibwe were well represented at the treaty.[90] Schoolcraft's claim is borne out by the number of leaders who signed the treaty. Of the Lac Courte Oreilles Band, Gidagaa-bizhiw of Lake Chetac and Chippewa River leaders Misko-manidoons and Babaamikawe signed the treaty. In addition, it is possible that Nena'aangabi's father, Gekek, signed the treaty as "Ka ka ka, The

Sparrow, Lac Courte Orielle."[91] Despite his influence during the Schoolcraft visit in 1831, there is no evidence to suggest that Nena'aangabi had achieved influence by 1825. It is unknown why Moozojiid, leader of the community of Lac Courte Oreilles, did not sign the treaty, since Henry Schoolcraft claimed he was present.[92] Despite the fair turnout from Lac Courte Oreilles Ojibwe leaders, treaty commissioners recognized the vastness of Ojibwe territory and that many leaders could not attend since Prairie du Chien was a long journey for most Ojibwe. Accordingly, Article 12 called for another treaty in 1826 on Lake Superior for just the Ojibwe, so "that the objects and advantages of this treaty may be fully explained to them."[93]

In 1826, American presence among the Wisconsin Ojibwe increased when a subagency was established at La Pointe, a branch of the agency headquarters at Sault Ste. Marie.[94] Later in the year, the treaty with the Ojibwe mandated in the 1825 treaty was held at Fond du Lac, on Lake Superior's far western shore. Lewis Cass again served as treaty commissioner. This time, however, the commissioner of Indian affairs, Thomas McKenney, joined Cass. McKenney chronicled his massive journey from Washington to the far end of Lake Superior, which was published the following year as *Sketches of a Tour to the Lakes.*[95] A major task of the treaty was to get Ojibwe leaders to develop an exclusive diplomatic relationship with the United States and to end British influence in the region. Article 8 read: "The Chippeway tribe of Indians fully acknowledge the authority and jurisdiction of the United States, and disclaim all connection with any foreign power."[96] The kinship ties Ojibwe leaders cultivated with the British after 1763 were viewed by Ojibwe leaders as binding and not easily broken. Furthermore, Ojibwe leaders no doubt had a sense of how Americans were handling other Native nations to the south and east and felt that the British had more of an interest in maintaining a trading relationship with Ojibwe people and not settling in the area or exploiting Ojibwe resources aside from furs. American officials were keenly aware of this and actively sought to stem the role of the British in the years after the Treaty of Prairie du Chien. For example, in 1828 Henry Schoolcraft refused to give any gifts to Misko-manidoons after the Lac Courte Oreilles ogimaa visited British officials.[97]

The primary reason for the treaty, however, and the reason for the presence of the commissioner of Indian affairs, was American interest in the mineral resources of the western part of the Upper Peninsula of Michigan. Americans were captivated by stories of aboveground boulders of pure copper in the Ontonagon River valley. Most famous of these was the Ontonagon Boulder, three thousand pounds of pure copper. McKenney tried and failed to bring the Ontonagon Boulder back to Washington with him.

Accordingly, Article 3 of the treaty read: "The Chippewa tribe grant to the government the right to search for, and carry away, any metals or minerals from any part of their country. But this grant is not to affect the title of the land, nor the existing jurisdiction over it." Despite the fact that the treaty explicitly said the right of exploration did not relinquish Ojibwe land title, subsequent treaty commissioners twisted the meaning of the article to pressure Ojibwe leaders to sign. Other provisions of the treaty included land for persons of mixed descent. A section of land was granted near Sault Ste. Marie for over sixty persons of mixed descent or wives of persons of mixed descent, including such recognizable names as Michel Cadotte, William Warren, and the children of John Tanner. Another provision gave the Ojibwe an annuity of $2,000. However, the Senate struck these last two articles out of the treaty.[98]

According to Thomas McKenney, there were over seven hundred Ojibwe at the treaty. Fond du Lac is an island on the St. Louis River. McKenney wrote: "Bark canoes are constantly passing to and from the island, which gives animation to the scene."[99] While other Ojibwe bands were well represented at the treaty, Lac Courte Oreilles leaders were not. According to influential La Pointe Band ogimaa Bizhiki: "The people who live at the Tawa Lakes have not come. But their ears are not shut. They are as open as ours. But they heard bad birds singing at the Prairie."[100] It is clear that "the Prairie" referred to is Prairie du Chien. There is no historical evidence that explains what specifically Lac Courte Oreilles leaders objected to at Prairie du Chien. Only Babaamikawe, ogimaa of a community on the Chippewa River, signed the treaty.[101]

THE LEGACY OF 1825 AND THE IMPACT OF INDIAN-INDIAN BOUNDARIES

While the treaties of 1825 and 1826 were an attempt to extend American influence in the region, in reality life changed little for the Ojibwe at Manoominikaan. American attempts to assert power near the community in the immediate years after the treaties were sometimes laughable. For example, in the late fall of 1829, a party of seventy soldiers left Prairie du Chien to build a small fort on the Red Cedar River near its mouth, about sixty miles south of Manoominikaan. Their journey up the Mississippi and Chippewa Rivers to the mouth of the Red Cedar was an utter debacle: half the boats got stuck in quicksand on the Chippewa River and in ice fifteen miles from the mouth of the Red Cedar. The commanding officer remained on the Red Cedar to guard the supplies while the remainder of the group went back to rescue the marooned boats. In the meantime, the commanding officer spotted a group of Ojibwe and fled in terror, dropping his goods, which the Ojibwe group rescued. According to pilot John Fonda, "The warriors had no idea of disturbing anything" and later, "the oldest chief" returned the goods. Although unidentified in Fonda's account, it is likely the "oldest chief" was Nena'aangabi. The commanding officer was missing for three days. When finally discovered, his feet and legs were completely frozen to his knees. The fort was completed, although the commanding officer was immediately returned to Prairie du Chien to face his superior: future president Zachary Taylor.[102] That Taylor chose to dispatch the group so late in the year, when ice was forming, shows how completely unfamiliar Americans were with an area they claimed to be theirs.

Just as the federal government sought to utilize these boundaries set at Prairie du Chien in 1825 for subsequent land cessions, Native leaders too attempted to utilize the boundaries for their benefit. As early as 1822, Mdewakanton Dakota leader Wabasha negotiated an agreement with Prairie du Chien fur traders James Lockwood and Joseph Rolette to cut timber and build a sawmill on the Red Cedar River on what would become the city of Menomonie, only sixty miles downstream from Rice Lake. Wabasha had close ties with the traders who, like others in the declining fur industry, saw timber as the next way to make money in Wisconsin. Wabasha located the sawmill on the far northern extent of what he thought of as Dakota Territory. Wabasha's own community was located at modern-day Winona, Minnesota, hundreds of miles by river from the sawmill site. For the Dakota, it mattered little to them if Americans established themselves on the Red Cedar so long as they could utilize western Wisconsin for hunting. However, approval for the contract stalled, and in the meantime the 1825 Treaty of Prairie du Chien defined the Ojibwe border just above the sawmill site, something Wabasha likely pushed for. After languishing for a few more years, Lockwood personally lobbied Michigan Territory's congressional representative, and in 1830 the agreement was approved. That summer work began on the mill.[103]

Nena'aangabi was not happy about the mill. However, evidence suggests that Nena'aangabi was less bothered by the actual presence of Americans close to his community. After all, he was not bothered by the fort construction on the Red Cedar, even returning the commanding officer's goods. What bothered Nena'aangabi was Dakota claim to territory that by 1830 the Ojibwe exercised clear control of. Indian Agent Henry Schoolcraft visited Manoominikaan in 1831 to sort out the issue of the boundary and the mill. Nena'aangabi stated unequivocally that the mill was on Ojibwe land and made a map for Schoolcraft detailing the boundary. Nena'aangabi was upset that the Ojibwe received no payment for the presence of the mill within Ojibwe territory. Nena'aangabi told Schoolcraft that the mill "had been built, as it were, by stealth." After Schoolcraft left Manoominikaan, he traveled downriver to the mill where he found eleven men working. Schoolcraft noted that even the man in charge "believed that land in this vicinity belonged to the Chippewas. He said it was seven years since any Sioux had visited the mill."[104]

The purpose of the treaty at Fond du Lac in 1826 was to clarify the terms of the 1825 treaty for Ojibwe leaders and sort out any disputes over the boundaries. Had Nena'aangabi and Moozojiid been involved, they could have asserted their right to the territory of western Wisconsin. Instead, Wabasha was able to exploit these boundaries for the benefit of his own community. This matter is not just a historical one. Today, this boundary defines ceded territory where Lac Courte Oreilles and other Lake Superior Ojibwe can practice off-reservation treaty rights. As a result, Ojibwe cannot practice off-reservation hunting and fishing in western Wisconsin where Nena'aangabi and other Ojibwe routinely engaged in traditional labor activities because Wabasha and other nineteenth-century Dakota leaders claimed the lands were within their territory. In reality, Dakota presence in these lands was minimal, and it was only Wabasha's close ties to influential traders at Prairie du Chien that enabled him to assert this bogus claim at the 1825 treaty. Dakota leaders further exploited this claim when they ceded the land to the United States in 1837. The Dakota were paid twenty-five cents per acre. While this was vastly less than the land's worth, the Ojibwe got an even worse deal that same year: when they ceded the lands that adjoined the Dakota claim to the north the Ojibwe were only paid eight cents per acre.[105] The Dakota directly profited (and commanded a much higher price) from lands that were under effective Ojibwe control.

Following the precedent of the Dakota timber lease, Nena'aangabi and Moozojiid decided to make a similar agreement with Prairie du Chien entrepreneur Hercules Dousman as a way to bring goods and cash to their communities. Nena'aangabi and Moozojiid agreed to a ten-year lease with Dousman beginning May 1, 1836. The lease granted Dousman "exclusive privilege" to build a mill and cut timber within three miles of the Chippewa River from the boundary with the Dakota to ten leagues (a league is about three miles) above Chippewa Falls. Nena'aangabi and Moozojiid believed that "this arrangement will be of great and lasting benefit to their people and will materially benefit their white brothers." Under the agreement, every year the Ojibwe would get 400 pounds of tobacco, 300 pounds of powder, 2,000 pounds of lead, 1,000 gunflints, 50 knives, 75 bushels of corn, 150 pipes, and 150 gun screws.[106]

The contract Nena'aangabi and Moozojiid made with Dousman was an important historical moment and speaks directly to the motivation Ojibwe leaders had for making agreements with the federal government, including future treaties that ceded land. For Nena'aangabi and Moozojiid, the agreement brought goods into their communities, bolstering their own leadership positions. Both leaders knew that Dousman was only interested in cutting white pine, something that did not threaten Ojibwe livelihood. For the Ojibwe, the lease had the added benefit of circumventing the influence of fur traders, potentially ending their reign as the only place the Ojibwe could obtain outside goods. For the two ogimaag it provided a way to accommodate American interest in resources while retaining Ojibwe sovereignty. It was a nineteenth-century version of the mutually beneficial relationships that the Ojibwe had known with the French and British.

Under the Trade and Intercourse Act of 1790, federal law prohibits the direct sale or lease of Indian land to private citizens or corporations.[107] As a result, the lease required federal approval. Indian Agent Henry Schoolcraft recommended approving the lease to Lewis Cass, now the secretary of war and in charge of Indian affairs. However, Commissioner of Indian Affairs Carey Harris informed Dousman in December that the contract would "not be acted upon until a proposition for the purchase of the tract of country in question, which is now before Congress is finally disposed of."[108] Local politics played a role in the rejection of the Dousman agreement. Henry Dodge had been appointed governor of the newly formed Wisconsin Territory. Within the new territory was the Indian agency at Fort Snelling under Lawrence Taliaferro. Both men were appointees of Andrew Jackson and shared the president's goal of extinguishing all Indian title east of the Mississippi. Therefore, the contract with Dousman was ignored as both men lobbied for a land cession treaty the following summer.

The failure of the Dousman lease was the earliest example of how American colonialism worked against the Ojibwe of Manoominikaan. In this instance, Ojibwe leaders reached an agreement with a corporate interest that was mutually beneficial: the United States would gain access to Ojibwe timber, and the Ojibwe would get important goods. However, the federal government quashed the lease in favor of something much more threatening to the Ojibwe: a land cession treaty. Unfortunately, it was the beginning of a pattern that would repeat for the rest of the nineteenth century and into the twentieth. It was disorganization and conflict among the many facets of American colonialism including corporations, the federal government, and later state and municipal governments that threatened Ojibwe sovereignty. It is not that corporations were always respectful of Ojibwe sovereignty; in fact none of these entities were always good or bad for the Ojibwe. Instead what threatened Ojibwe sovereignty most directly was the presence of different groups with conflicting interests.

CONCLUSION

In 1831, Henry Schoolcraft visited Nena'aangabi and asked him to accept an American flag as a symbol of alliance and acceptance of the president's wishes to end Ojibwe-Dakota warfare. Nena'aangabi thought hard about Schoolcraft's offer and the next day made a dramatic appearance. According to Schoolcraft: "He had thrown the flag over one arm, and held the war club perpendicular in the other hand. He said, that although he accepted the one, he did not drop the other; he held fast to both."[109] Nena'aangabi's achievement in defending and maintaining an Ojibwe community at Manoominikaan was a major accomplishment, allowing more Ojibwe families to utilize the rich resources of the area, which led to the ogimaa becoming the most influential of the Lac Courte Oreilles Band. Even though Nena'aangabi believed alliance with the United States was beneficial to the community, he could not consent to stop fighting the Dakota, since it was the basis of his influence as a leader.

Nena'aangabi had a complicated relationship with American officials by the time of the first Lake Superior Ojibwe land cession treaty in 1837. While William Warren lamented "the evil ways of the whites" corrupting Ojibwe political institutions, the American presence in the region gave a charismatic leader like Nena'aangabi new ways to assert his influence and rise to prominence among Wisconsin Ojibwe leaders. He was a powerful leader American officials *had* to deal with. If Americans were to have access to the vast timber resources of the Chippewa Valley, let alone incorporate the territory into the United States in any meaningful way, Nena'aangabi and his young, growing community stood in the way.

CHAPTER 2

Nena'aangabi and the Language of Treaties, 1837–1855

At the 1855 annuity payment, Nena'aangabi told American officials about his understanding of the treaty that had transpired the year before where Lake Superior Ojibwe bands ceded iron-ore-rich lands in northeast Minnesota and retained reservations. In his colorful oratory, Nena'aangabi told government officials, "I swallowed the words of the treaty down my throat, and they have not yet had time to blister my breast."[1] The implication was that the longtime leader was dissatisfied with prior treaties and the relationship with the United States that had developed in the prior few decades. By 1855, Nena'aangabi was the most influential Ojibwe leader in Wisconsin. In 1837, the Ojibwe ceded lands in northern Wisconsin, including Manoominikaan. However, Nena'aangabi refused to sign the treaty. After the treaty, Nena'aangabi continued to assert his influence in defense of Ojibwe sovereignty. In 1847, he joined other Ojibwe leaders in protesting a treaty made that year that ceded Ojibwe lands in central Minnesota because it gave a greater share of annuity payments to Ojibwe bands in Minnesota (while the Minnesota Ojibwe still collected equal share of the annuities from sale of Wisconsin Ojibwe lands) and the treaty authorized persons of mixed descent who were not Ojibwe leaders to sell land. Tragedy struck Nena'aangabi's community and the rest of the Wisconsin Ojibwe in 1850 when Minnesota Territorial Governor Alexander Ramsey attempted to remove the Wisconsin Ojibwe to Sandy Lake, Minnesota. The events at Sandy Lake resulted in the deaths of four hundred Wisconsin Ojibwe, when the Wisconsin Ojibwe showed up at Sandy Lake with no provisions or annuities. As a result, Nena'aangabi and other Lake Superior Ojibwe leaders signed the 1854 treaty that secured reservations, including one for the Lac Courte Oreilles Band. However, in 1855, just weeks after Nena'aangabi told American officials the 1854 treaty had "not yet had time to blister my breast," the Dakota cut down the influential leader on the battlefield.

Accounts of how the Ojibwe understood treaties are found in a variety of surviving texts. In 1864, a delegation of Wisconsin Ojibwe presented Abraham Lincoln with a petition detailing unfulfilled treaty provisions. The delegation included Fond du Lac ogimaa Naagaanab, Lac du Flambeau ogimaa Aamoons, three ogimaag from the La Pointe Band, and Lac Courte Oreilles ogimaa Akiwenzii, the son and successor of Moozojiid. The petition was in both English and Ojibwe.[2] While other scholars have analyzed the English version of the text, scholars have not pondered the precise meaning of the Ojibwe text. The English text was not an exact translation of the Ojibwe and sometimes differs substantially. Analysis of the Ojibwe text reveals Ojibwe understanding of the treaties and that American officials explicitly told Ojibwe leaders that they were only purchasing rights to harvest certain resources and not purchasing title to the land itself, something borne out in other archival materials. Obtaining territory through outright deception is contrary to a just democracy and reveals how nineteenth-century American expansion was colonialism. Had Nena'aangabi lived even a few more years, the treaty of 1854 would no doubt have had time to blister his breast.

GAAWIIN WIIN OWIDI OJIIBIKAAWID GIBAGIDINAMOOSINOON: THE TREATY OF 1837

In the winter of 1836, Wisconsin Territorial Governor Henry Dodge and St. Peter's Indian Agent Lawrence Taliaferro lobbied the Jackson administration for a land cession treaty of Ojibwe pinelands in northern Wisconsin. Their efforts paid off, and Congress authorized a land cession treaty of Ojibwe lands in far east-central Minnesota and northern Wisconsin, including Manoominikaan. The treaty was held at Lawrence Taliaferro's agency at the confluence of the Minnesota (which was then called the St. Peters River) and Mississippi Rivers. Henry Dodge acted as treaty commissioner. The location made it easy for Ojibwe living on the Mississippi whose lands were not included in the land cession to attend, while geographical barriers made for a more arduous journey for the leaders of the Lac Courte Oreilles Band. This was by design, as Taliaferro knew that it would be easier to convince Ojibwe leaders along the Mississippi to agree to the cession, since he had a relationship with those leaders and they had nothing to lose and everything to gain by agreeing to the sale of territory they did not reside on.[3]

The treaty council began on July 20, 1837. As to be expected the majority of attendees were from Mississippi Ojibwe bands, as these bands lived in close proximity to the treaty site. The territory ceded included territory of the Mille Lacs, Snake River, St. Croix, and Lac Courte Oreilles Bands. When the treaty council began, these bands were represented by Negwanebi and Wazhashkokon from the Mille Lacs Band; Bayezhig, Noodin, and Zhaagobe from the Snake River Band; and Bizhiki from the St. Croix Band. Despite the fact that the Mille Lacs and Snake River Bands were well represented, no Lac Courte Oreilles Band ogimaag were present, nor were important St. Croix Band ogimaag Gabemabi or Ayaabens. One of the problems with the treaty that would plague subsequent treaties was that Treaty Commissioner Dodge dealt with all present as "the Chippewa Nation," with all having equal authority to sell land and collect annuities from sale of the land.[4] As historian Charles Cleland argues, "He thus created a political amalgam that had no reality for the Chippewa and plagued relations between both the Chippewa and the United States and separate Chippewa bands for years into the future."[5] Indeed, Dodge was anxious to get the treaty pushed forward, negotiating with Ojibwe leaders regardless of whether they resided in the territory or not. This contradicted the autonomy maintained by each individual Ojibwe band. On the third day of the treaty council, Leech Lake leader Eshkibagikoonzh (or Flat Mouth) expressed this concern:

> I am not the Chief of the whole nation, but only of my people or tribe. . . . I do not wish to take any further steps about what you have proposed to us, until the other people arrive, who have been expected here. They have not yet come; and to do so before their arrival, might be considered an improper interference, and unfair towards them. The residence of my band is outside of the country which you wish to buy from us. After the people who live in that country shall have told you their minds, I will speak.[6]

Nena'aangabi did not arrive until July 26; nearly a week after the negotiation had commenced. Akiwenzii, who had recently succeeded his father Moozojiid as ogimaa of the Lac Courte Oreilles village, joined him.[7] Both leaders refused to sign the treaty. Nena'aangabi's and Akiwenzii's names appear in the treaty text but were scratched out. The only ogimaa from the Lac Courte Oreilles Band who signed the treaty was Bakwe'aamo, leader of the village on Pacwawong Lake, near modern-day Seeley, Wisconsin.[8] This was the smallest village in the Lac Courte Oreilles Band. Other Ojibwe leaders of the Lac Courte Oreilles Band such as Gidagaa-bizhiw, long-time ogimaa of the village on Lake Chetac, and Gichi-Waabizheshi and Babaamikawe, who were ogimaag of villages on the Chippewa River, were not even in attendance.[9]

While there are no surviving accounts explaining why Nena'aangabi withheld his approval of the treaty, we do know some of the objections Akiwenzii and other Wisconsin Ojibwe leaders had to the treaty. One of the objections to the 1837 treaty the Ojibwe leaders had was the role played by leaders outside the territory ceded. This would be the beginning of a rift with Ojibwe bands living along the Mississippi River. The federal government was directly responsible for this by assuming a commonality of interests among Ojibwe people, when in reality each band exercised full autonomy from each other. In the 1864 petition, Akiwenzii and other leaders claimed that much of the negotiations of the 1837 treaty were not done by an ogimaa, but by Maajigaabaw, an individual from the Leech Lake Band, outside the territory being discussed: "Gaawiin wiin aw Anishinaabe wegimaawid ji-gii-giigidod apii bagidinaad onow zhingwaakwan Ogichidaa gaa-giigidod Maajigaabaw inaaban." The English version in this instance was a pretty faithful translation of the Ojibwe: "It was not the Chiefs that done the talking at the sale of the pine timber. It was done by a Warrior whose name was Madjigawbow."[10]

Non-Ojibwe accounts of the treaty echo the Ojibwe leaders' complaints about the influence of Maajigaabaw and others outside of the territory ceded. According to the treaty council minutes, Maajigaabaw was the only person who spoke on July 27.[11] Sault Ste. Marie Agent Henry Schoolcraft was left completely out of the loop, despite the fact that the territory in question was in his agency. In 1838, trader Lyman Warren visited Schoolcraft in Sault Ste. Marie:

> I took occasion to inquire into the circumstances of the cession of the treaty of the 29th of July, 1837, and asked him why it was that so little had been given for so large a cession, comprehending the very best lands of the Chippewas in the Mississippi Valley. He detailed a series of petty intrigues by the St. Peter's agent [Taliaferro], who had flattered two of the Pillager (Leech Lake) chiefs, and loaded them with new cloths and presents. One of these, Hole-in-the-Day, came down twenty days before the time. The Pillagers, in fact, made the treaty. The bands of the St. Croix and Chippewa Rivers, who really lived on the land and owned it, had, in effect, no voice. . . . Mr. Warren stated that the *Lac Courtorielle* band had not united in the sale, and would not attend the payment of the annuities; nor would the St. Croix and Lac du Flambeau Indians.[12]

While Schoolcraft erroneously identified the Gull Lake leader Bagone-giizhig the elder as a Leech Lake or Pillager chief, he was correct in his assessment that Ojibwe leaders residing outside of the territory ceded had too much influence over the proceedings. In his 1832 exploration of the sources of the Mississippi, Schoolcraft noted the influence of Maajigaabaw and his close association with Eshkibagikoonzh. Schoolcraft distrusted Maajigaabaw due to his alleged role in the murder of trader Robert Semple in 1816 in Winnipeg. Semple was a governor of territory claimed by the fur trade organization Hudson's Bay Company, while Maajigaabaw was loyal to the rival North West Company.[13]

Like subsequent Wisconsin Ojibwe land cession treaties, the federal government did not seek the land for immediate use by settlers, but instead sought resources, in this case pine. In their 1864 petition, Akiwenzii and the other leaders explained explicitly that they did not cede the land, but only timber rights:

> Aaniish go sa maa ninga-bagidinamawaa onow isa gegwejimijin zhingwaak-wan Gedako-minoga'igeyan, mii apii begidinamoonaan. Gaawiin wiin owidi ojiibikaawid gibagidinamoosinoon. Miinawaa maandan dekonamaan inin-aatig, miinawaa maandan mitigomizh miinawaa maandan bezhig mashkosiw dekonamaan, manoomin nindizhi-wiindaan maandan, gaawiin isa mamin gibagidinamossinoon.

The English text reads:

> Very well, I will sell him the Pine Timber as he requests me to, From (the) usual height of cutting a tree down and upwards to top is what I sell you, I reserve the root of the tree. Again this I hold in my hand the Maple Timber, also the Oak Timber, also this straw which I hold in my hand. Wild Rice is what we call this. These I do not sell.[14]

Clearly, Ojibwe leaders understood the treaty as only leasing the land for timber harvest. Furthermore, Ojibwe leaders understood that the lease only covered white pine and not hardwoods. Moreover, "I reserve the root of the tree" makes clear that the Ojibwe retained actual ownership of the land. Here is where the English text that was presented to President Lincoln diverges from the Ojibwe. The term "sell" in the English text is a misnomer. "Ninga-bagidinamawaa" means "I shall offer something to him," not "to sell." To sell something is the completely unrelated verb *adaawaage*. From the Ojibwe perspective, it was only natural to assume that the treaty was a lease of resources. There were practically no settlers moving onto the land. Also, the treaty made no mention of Ojibwe people moving onto reservations or removing outside the ceded territory. After all, why would the Ojibwe be allowed to stay on land that did not belong to them anymore? Finally, the Ojibwe made such an agreement with Hercules Dousman the year before that leased rights to harvest white pine but did not convey title to the land.

According to the 1864 petition, Ojibwe leaders were explicit that the resource rights were temporary, related to the mutual obligations of both the Ojibwe and the federal government toward each other:

> Gaawiin wiin gimiinisinoon, anishaa gidawi'in. Aaniish mii sa ezhinakwetoonaan noose. Gichi-apiitendaagozi maa aw nimishoomis, gaawiin dash niwii-aagonwetawaasii. Meshkwad dash wiin ninga-waabandaamin iw minik ba-izhi-waawiindamawiyan.

The English text reads:

> I do not make a present of this, I merely lend it to you. This is my answer, My Great Father is great, and out of respect for him I will not refuse him, but as an exchange of civility I must see and feel the benefits of this loan and the promises fulfilled.[15]

This is an instance where the Ojibwe and English texts align. "I merely lend it to you" is an important passage that makes clear the Ojibwe understood the treaty as not conveying title to the land. For Ojibwe leaders, the notion of equal exchange was foundational to their relationship to the United States. The Ojibwe were obligated to consent to the leasing of white pine rights, just as the Americans were obligated to provide the benefits they agreed to in the treaty.

Other sources echo this interpretation of the treaty of 1837. In 1929, the Lac du Flambeau Band held a special council for claims related to treaties. The council concluded: "the Chippewas, according to their understanding and memory, were asked by the United States emissaries to sell two kinds of timber, namely, Norway and white pine. . . . Can there be any doubt that a fraud and a great one was committed against the Chippewas?"[16] Historian Bruce White finds that this understanding of the 1837 treaty was also prevalent in the Mille Lacs community into the early twentieth century.[17] White also wrote that treaty commissioners misled the Ojibwe. In his 1894 autobiography, Benjamin Armstrong discussed the understanding of Ojibwe leaders of the 1837 treaty. Born in Alabama, Armstrong married a daughter of Bizhiki of La Pointe, had a close relationship with the influential leader, and was even adopted as a son by Bizhiki. According to Armstrong, the federal officials explicitly told Ojibwe leaders that their interests were for specific resources, not the land itself:

> He does not want your lands, it is too cold up here for farming. He wants just enough of it to build little towns where soldiers stop, mining camps for miners, and saw mill sites and logging camps. The timber that is best for you the great father does not care about. The maple tree that you make your sugar from, the birch tree that you get bark from for your canoes and from which you make pails for your sugar sap, the cedar from which you get material for making canoes, oars, and paddles, your great father cares nothing for. It is the pine and minerals that he wants and he has sent us here to make a bargain with you for it.[18]

While written some years after the treaty, this passage echoes much of what Ojibwe leaders recalled about the treaty: that the treaty constituted a lease of resource rights and not the sale of the land.

Translation played a role in the deception of the Ojibwe. According to Henry Schoolcraft: "The department is very much in the hands of ignorant and immoral interpreters who frequently misconceive the point to be interpreted."[19] Furthermore, linguist John Nichols argues that many of the words in the actual treaty were untranslatable, with meanings unique to Western legal institutions: "While the interpreters could have made up specific words to translate 'right, title, and interest,' it is very unlikely that these words (of which there is no record either in written sources or in the contemporary language) would have been understood by the Ojibwes present."[20] Historian Bruce White goes so far as to argue that for the Ojibwe "the idea of land alienation was completely foreign."[21] However, it is unlikely that Ojibwe leaders were unaware of the possibility that Americans purchased lands by treaty and dispossessed Native peoples. The year 1837 was the height of Cherokee removal in the South. Even closer to home, the Black Hawk War was fueled by broken treaty promises. Instead, evidence suggests that American officials went out of their way to convince Ojibwe leaders that the treaty was a lumber lease and distinct from what was occurring elsewhere.

Despite the fact that Nena'aangabi (and Akiwenzii) did not sign the treaty, it was ratified anyway. Article 5 guarantees the Ojibwe rights to hunt, fish, and gather within the ceded territory: "The privilege of hunting, fishing, and gathering the wild rice, upon the lands, the rivers and the lakes included in the territory ceded, is guaranteed to the Indians, during the pleasure of the President of the United States." The meaning of the phrase "the pleasure of the President" has been hotly contested in the years since the treaty and played a critical role in twentieth-century litigation of Ojibwe treaty rights. Linguist John Nichols argues: "If this phrase had been translated at all, a literal translation would not have been understood to have placed a limit on the activities."[22] Beginning in the late nineteenth century, the state of Wisconsin's enforcement of state regulations over Ojibwe people off-reservation was rooted in their interpretation of the phrase meaning that off-reservation treaty rights were temporary. Federal courts refuted this in both *Lac Courte Oreilles v. Voight* (1983) and *Minnesota v. Mille Lacs.* (1999).[23]

The treaty addressed the same points that all subsequent Ojibwe land treaties addressed: payments for territory, separate provisions for mixed bloods, and separate provisions for trader debts. These provisions were the direct result of the wishes of Ojibwe leaders. Article 3 provided $100,000 to persons of mixed descent, and Article 4 provided $70,000 of payment of Ojibwe debt to traders. Article 2 of the treaty provided $9,500 in money, $19,000 in goods, $3,000 for blacksmiths, $1,000 for farmers, $2,000 for provisions, and $500 for tobacco annually for twenty years.[24] The length of the annuities was hotly debated in the treaty council. As Eshkibagikoonzh eloquently stated: "If it were my land you were buying, I would, instead of an annuity for only 20 years, demand one from you as long as the ground lasted."[25] While there is no Ojibwe account of Eshkibagikoonzh's words, it is safe to assume that he also was under the impression that the treaty was not a land sale, and what was being purchased was the right to cut pine. Even in that context, Eshkibagikoonzh sought annuities for however long the federal government retained these rights. However, the United States acted as a colonial power whose primary goal was to extinguish Indian title as quickly and easily as possible. For the Americans, perpetual annuities were out of the question.

The treaty of 1837 and subsequent treaties with the Wisconsin Ojibwe reveal how Americans acted as a colonial power, rather than treating Native peoples as equals in a just or democratic manner. Important Ojibwe leaders like Nena'aangabi and Akiwenzii refused to sign the treaty. Federal officials actively misrepresented the treaty as being rights to cut pine rather than an actual sale of the land. Mere weeks after conclusion of the treaty, Pokegama Lake missionary Frederick Ayer forwarded a petition of Snake River Band leaders to President Martin Van Buren detailing how the Ojibwe there were unsatisfied with the treaty. Ayer wrote, "they as a body regretted sale of their land by the recent treaty." Snake River Band ogimaa Noodin, St. Croix Band ogimaa Bizhiki (not to be confused with prominent La Pointe Band leader Bizhiki), and seven others from the Snake River Band signed the petition. Both Noodin and Bizhiki signed the treaty of 1837. Among the objections the Snake River Ojibwe voiced was how Ojibwe leaders approved the treaty. Noodin argued, "I am an Indian and I do not know how to sign my name." Like Henry Schoolcraft, Noodin objected that Bagone-giizhig (the elder) had too much influence at the treaty. Noodin was extremely frank in his assessment of the Gull Lake leader: "But only one sold the land (the hole in the day). He does not own the land where I reside, he is a mere child." Noodin calling Bagone-giizhig a "child" illustrates how these treaties created tensions between Ojibwe leaders that would only worsen in subsequent treaties. Community members were upset with their leaders. Snake River Ojibwe leader Bwaanens told Ayer, "When I returned from St. Peter's last summer from attending the treaty where our chiefs sold the land, and told my wife and children what our chiefs had done they cried."[26]

GAAWIIN WIIN AKI NIMBAGIDINAMAWAASII: THE TREATY OF 1842

While Nena'aangabi withheld his approval of the treaty of 1837, he signed the next Wisconsin Ojibwe treaty in 1842. As in the 1837 treaty, the federal government sought extractable resources, rather than land for settlers. Specifically, the federal government sought the vast copper deposits of Michigan's Keweenaw Peninsula. In the treaty, Ojibwe people ceded lands along Lake Superior in Wisconsin and the western half of the Upper Peninsula of Michigan. The treaty was held in October at La Pointe, this time within the territory ceded. Robert Stuart acted as treaty commissioner. Stuart was a former American Fur Company trader who recently succeeded Henry Schoolcraft as Indian agent. Stuart twisted the meaning of the 1826 treaty to coerce Ojibwe leaders into signing the treaty: "Remember that you have already given permission by the Treaty of Fond du Lac, to have the minerals taken from your lands, which shall be done, whether you sell your lands or not."[27] Joining Nena'aangabi in signing the treaty from the Lac Courte Oreilles Band was Akiwenzii and Chippewa River ogimaag Gichi-Waabizheshi, Gwiiwizenzish (who succeeded his father Babaamikawe), and Bebookawe.[28]

Stuart continued the policy set forth in 1837 of dealing with the Ojibwe as a single nation. He told Ojibwe leaders: "Some of you have expressed a wish to treat *by bands*, & others to keep reservations, but I cannot sanction either—your Great Father will not treat with you as Bands, but as a nation."[29] However,

Stuart did distinguish between the Ojibwe bands living along the Mississippi River who had not ceded their lands and Ojibwe bands living along Lake Superior and directly inland who had ceded their lands (with the exception of the Fond du Lac Band and Grand Portage Band in northeast Minnesota, whose lands remained unceded and lived along Lake Superior). Acknowledging the tensions that had led Noodin to call Bagone-giizhig a "mere child" in 1838, Stuart told the Ojibwe "this will prevent future jealousies and allay the bad feelings which now exist among you."[30] It is important to remember that the federal government imposed these designations. The Ojibwe themselves did not use the terms "Lake Superior" or "Mississippi" prior to 1842.[31] Article 4 of the treaty stipulated a payment of $12,500 in money, $10,500 in goods, $2,000 in provisions and tobacco, $2,000 for blacksmiths, $1,000 for two farmers, $1,200 for carpenters, and $2,000 for schools annually for twenty-five years to the "Chippewa of Mississippi & Lake Superior."[32]

At this treaty, Ojibwe leaders were more emphatic about letting the ogimaag from the territory being discussed make the treaty. According to the 1864 petition, Fond du Lac Band ogimaa Zhingob told other Ojibwe leaders:

> Aaniish niijikiwenyidog, mii sa zhayiigwa ji-nakwetawag wa'aw Wayaabishkiiwed. Gaawiin giinawaa gidibendaasowiniwaa niwii-dazhindanziin niin isa go nindibendaasowin waa dazhindamaan. Aaniish nibagidinanawaa isa gimishoomisinaan maandan medwe-gagwejiminang.

The English text reads:

> Well my Friends, I shall give my answer to the White man. I shall not say anything about your property. I shall only answer for myself and speak of the property belonging to me. I comply with the request of our Great Father in what he expects from us.[33]

Again, analysis of the Ojibwe text brings a richer meaning to what Ojibwe leaders meant. While "I shall not say anything" is technically a correct translation of "niwii-dazhindanziin," use of the prefix "wii" is telling. The prefix "ga" is a more definite way to indicate what is going to occur at a future time, while "wii" is more indicative of what a speaker *desires* to happen. Thus, a more literal translation of Zhingob's words would be "I *wish* to not say anything." Moreover, use of the verb "dazhindan" is significant. It means to talk over something and can also mean to gossip. The verb for addressing someone is *gaagiigido*. Zhingob's use of the verb "dazhindan" may reflect how Ojibwe leaders viewed such interference into what they saw as the affairs of other leaders. Zhingob's hesitancy to speak about the territorial claims of other Ojibwe bands contrasts sharply with the role played by Maajigaabaw and Bagone-giizhig (the elder) in 1837. No doubt this had to do with the large numbers of Ojibwe leaders present from the territory. This also points to the ways that Americans were influencing Ojibwe political institutions. The bands that the federal government classified as the "Lake Superior" Ojibwe were starting to unify, aware of their common interests with regard to annuity payments.

According to the 1864 petition, the leaders in the territory being discussed did not consent: "Gaawiin dash ningod gii-ikidosiiwag ogow zhishodew bemi-inabijig ogimaag. Gaawiin gii-inendanziiwag." The English text reads: "It was all he said. The Chiefs along the Lake Shore did not say a word, not being able to sell or make any agreement."[34] Much like in 1837, while the English version of the text uses the term "sell," the Ojibwe text does not use any verb that means or even implies sell. Instead, "Gaawiin gii-inendanziiwag" literally means they did not think a certain way, or refused their consent. The lack of the term "sell" in the Ojibwe text reflects how Ojibwe leaders did not see the treaty as ceding title to lands, but instead that they were only leasing mineral rights. After Zhingob, the next speaker at the council was Lac du Flambeau leader Waabishki-gaagaagi, whose lands were included in the territory discussed. Waabishki-gaagaagi explicitly argued that Ojibwe leaders would only consent to leasing of mineral rights:

> "Noose gidizhi-nisidotoon bi-gagwejimiyan biiwaabik go sa maa. Ninga-bagidinamawaa aw isa nimishoomisinaan maandan biiwaabik medwe-gagwejimid aw nimishoomis. Gaawiin wiin aki nimbagidinamawaasii," gii-izhi-biibaagi gii-gwekitaad gii-ikidowaad, "Eh! Eh!"

The English text reads:

> "My Father I understand you to say that you want the Mineral, well then I will comply with the wish of our Great Father in asking me to sell him the Mineral which he wants. I do not give you the land, it is the Mineral only that I sell if there is any to be found on my land. I do not cede the Land," as he cried with a loud voice turning to his fellow Indians in which they all responded with, "Eh! Eh!" [an affirmative expression].[35]

When trying to decipher how the Ojibwe understood the treaty, it does not get any more explicit than "Gaawiin wiin aki nimbagidinamawaasii," "I do not offer the land," or as the English version reads, "I do not cede the land." The reaction of "Eh! Eh!" to Waabishki-gaagaagi's declaration from "all" the other Ojibwe leaders present shows the clear consensus of Ojibwe leaders that the treaty leased mineral rights (and only mineral rights: nothing is mentioned about timber or any other resource rights) and was not a cession of the land.

Other oral tradition supports this. Regarding the 1842 treaty, in 1929 the Lac du Flambeau Band special council claimed: "Only a portion of the iron range as well as the copper and zinc regions were sold by the Chippewas. . . . The Indians, not being able to read, did not discover the fraud perpetrated against them."[36] William Bigboy related his understanding of the treaties of 1837 and 1842 in the 1940s to the Works Progress Administration historical project at Bad River:

> In neither of these treaties did the Indians understand that they were ceding or signing away their lands. The Commissioners, in their eagerness to conclude the treaties, made promises that were never incorporated into the treaties. The Indians, depending on the verbal promises of the Commissioners and having no way of recording them, relied entirely on their memory of what transpired at these meetings. They understood that, in consideration for relinquishing their rights to the timber and mineral on their lands, they would be allowed to continue their hunting and fishing and enjoy the usual rights of occupancy, and that they would never be required to remove therefrom as long as they remained peaceable.[37]

Again, Benjamin Armstrong echoed this in his autobiography. Armstrong remembered, "No conversation that was had at this time gave the Indians an inkling or caused them to mistrust that they were ceding away their lands, but supposed that they were simply selling the pine and minerals, as they had in the treaty of 1837."[38]

In the treaty, the Ojibwe again retained rights to hunt, fish, and gather in the ceded territory. Other provisions were similar to those in the 1837 treaty, as money was provided for payment of trader debt ($75,000) and a payment for persons of mixed descent, although a substantially smaller amount of $15,000.[39] One aspect of the treaty that gave Ojibwe leaders pause was language in Article 2 that recognized the rights to hunting and other activities of traditional labor in the ceded territory, "until required to remove by the President of the United States."[40] A few months after the treaty, Lac Courte Oreilles Band ogimaa Gichi-Waabizheshi voiced concern about this provision: "when I touched the pen it was a condition that my relations were provided for [separate payment for persons of mixed descent] and that we should remain on the land, as long as we are peaceable."[41] According to the 1864 petition, when Ojibwe leaders raised questions to this provision Stuart quickly allayed their concerns:

> Mii dash miinawaa, gii-aazhidemigod, gii-igod dash, "Aaniish booch wiin igo geyaabi naanimidana-daso-biboon gigadabiitaan maandan aki, booshke bigo ningodwaak daso biboon gigadabiitaan maandan gidakiim, ezhi-dibendaman noongom ebiitaman. Aaniish gonimaa dash wiin ningoding giga-zagaswe'igowaa aw gimishoomisiwaa ji-gagwejimineg maandan gidakiim ezhi-dibendaman noongom ebiitameg."

The English text reads:

> Then he answered back, and told how he had the privilege of remaining on the land for Fifty Years, and even for a Hundred Years, as he owned and had possession of the land, he had a right to live on it. But then there may be a time that your Great Father will call you to a Council and ask you to sell him the land you live on.[42]

This not only indicates that Stuart did not intend for Ojibwe people to be removed for some time, but reinforces that the Ojibwe were told that they were only selling mineral rights. While prior passages of the petition illustrate how Ojibwe leaders understood the treaties to not impact land title, this was the federal government, presumably Stuart, explicitly telling Ojibwe leaders that the treaty was not a land sale: "Gidakiim ezhi-dibendaman noongom"; literally, "your land how you own it now." "Gidakiim" means "your land," "ezhi-dibendaman" is "how you own it," and "noongom" means "now."

Ojibwe leaders were not happy with the treaty. Bizhiki, the most influential leader of the Wisconsin Ojibwe and whose territory was in the heart of the land ceded, was emphatic about his disapproval of the treaty. Just weeks after the treaty council was concluded, he told trader Lyman Warren, "I tell you my friend, that I am ashamed of my treaty." Bizhiki went on to say, "the commissioner would not listen to us at all." A few months later, Bizhiki argued that Stuart coerced the Ojibwe to sign the treaty based on the treaty of 1826: "He spoke of the copper that is strewn along the shore of this Lake. He told us that we have given it away." In December, Waabishkigaagaagi recalled, "I did not want to sell anymore of my land, but I was told that it made no difference whether I did or not, if the majority of chiefs signed the treaty our grandfather would take the land."[43]

After the treaty of 1842, there was confusion as to the status of Isle Royale. While the treaty mentioned Lake Superior as a territory, "including all the islands in said lake," Ojibwe leaders were unsure if this included Isle Royale.[44] No small piece of real estate, Isle Royale is forty-five miles long and nine miles wide at its widest. Fifteen miles east of Grand Portage, today Isle Royale is a national park and classified as one of the world's most unique wilderness ecosystems. To clarify the situation, American officials made a "compact" with the Lake Superior Ojibwe affirming that the 1842 treaty included Isle Royale. While Nena'aangabi joined other Lake Superior Ojibwe leaders signing the compact, in the 1864 petition Ojibwe leaders claimed that it was a hard sell: "Ogow dash Anishinaabeg gaa-bizindamowaad maandan gaa-izhi-gagwejimindwaa, gii-ikidowag dash wii-bagidinanzigwaa ow minis. Baanimaa dash nesogwanagak ogii-bagidinaaanaawaa." The English text reads: "And when the Indians had listened and heard the proposition made to them, they said they would not sell the island. But on the third day the concluded to sell and did." However, once again while English text says "sell," the Ojibwe does not. In the Ojibwe text, the leaders "ogii-bagidinaanaawaa" or offered it. While the compact itself called for $400 of gun powder and $100 of beef, Akiwenzii and the other Ojibwe leaders claimed in 1864 that the Ojibwe were supposed to receive a one-time payment of $30,000. The failure to receive the money led the leaders to conclude, "Niwanitaas isa ganabaj," or as the English text reads, "Perhaps I have made a poor bargain and I am the loser."[45]

Ojibwe leaders continually protested the shoddy execution of treaty provisions by the federal government. Due to their location hundreds of miles inland from Lake Superior, the Lac Courte Oreilles and Lac du Flambeau Bands were isolated from the limited benefits that the treaties provided such as blacksmith shops for gun and spear repair. In 1843, Nena'aangabi and other Lac Courte Oreilles and Lac du Flambeau Band leaders petitioned the federal government for blacksmiths and that their annuities be paid at Chippewa Falls instead of La Pointe. At this time, Chippewa Falls had very few white settlers, while over a thousand whites and persons of mixed descent lived at La Pointe. The leaders echoed American reasoning for Indian removal nationwide: "If we go to Bad River we are near to the white men. . . . We do not wish to be near them. Whenever we are among white men we are sure to have trouble."[46]

THE LANGUAGE OF KINSHIP AND TRUST AT THE TREATIES

Kinship was central to Ojibwe diplomacy. However, the varying personnel involved with the treaties stood in stark contrast to the ways that Ojibwe people related to outsiders prior to the treaties, such as fur traders. This frustration was reflected in a speech by Fond du Lac Band ogimaa Naagaanab to

Commissioner of Indian Affairs George Manypenny, recorded by Benjamin Armstrong:

> When you talk we all listen, then we talk it over many times. In this way it was it is always fresh with us. This is the way we must keep our record. In 1837 we were asked to sell our timber and minerals. In 1842 we were asked to do the same. Our white brothers told us the great father did not want the land. We should keep it to hunt on. Bye and bye we were told to go away; to go and leave our friends that were buried yesterday. Then we asked each other what it meant. Does the great father tell the truth? Does he keep his promises? We cannot help ourselves! We try to do as we agree in treaty. We ask you what this means? You do not tell from memory! You go to your black marks and say this is what those men wrote down; this is what they said when they made the treaty. The men we talk with don't come back; they do not come and you tell us they did not tell us so! We ask you where they are? You say you do not know or that they are dead and gone.[47]

Naagaanab's speech reflected the frustration of nearly twenty years of shifting personnel and the inability of Ojibwe leaders to forge lasting relationships with American officials in the ways they had with French and British traders.

Alarming to modern readers are continual references by government officials in the treaties to Ojibwe people as children. However, as anthropologist Raymond DeMallie argues in his work on Plains Indian treaties, "Indian orators exploited the father-children metaphor to ask for important favors."[48] Scholar Russell Lawrence Barsh argues that Native leaders "did not imagine they were submitting to coercive laws, but rather accepting Europeans' desire to assume the burdens of leadership."[49] Historian Richard White argues that American use of "father" meant different things based on local context and was rooted in treaties between the United States and Native peoples in the eastern Great Lakes in the late eighteenth century. White argues that, for Native peoples, "A father was not a stern patriarch; a father was a generous friend."[50] Furthermore, White argues that the meaning of the language of kinship was contested prior to the arrival of Americans in the Great Lakes. However, White argues that the defeat of Tecumseh allowed Americans to create the fiction of Native peoples as children. White goes on to argue that this fiction was very damaging for Native people, as government policy makers understood the kinship relationship as paternalism.

A linguistic analysis of the 1864 petition shows how Ojibwe leaders did not see their relationship to the United States as paternalism. At the

1842 treaty, Ojibwe leaders employed vastly different kinship terms based on the context. While in the English text, the term used is merely "Father" or "Great Father," the Ojibwe text contains a variety of kinship terms. Waabishki-gaagaagi used the term "noose," which the English text has simply as "my father." *Noos* was the common term for father in the nineteenth century (today the Anglicized *nibaabaa* is more common), while *noose* was a way of saying "my father" similar to how a young child would plead for something. Later, the English text records Fond du Lac ogimaa Zhingob referring to "our Great Father," while the Ojibwe text says "gimishoomisinaan," or "our grandfather."[51] These variations in the Ojibwe text indicate that for the Ojibwe the kinship relationship with the American government was by no means standardized and paternalistic but fluid based on the particular context of the matter at hand. What was important to Ojibwe leaders was the notion of mutual responsibility that the relationship entailed. However, it is important to remember that at this time it really did not matter if federal officials articulated paternalism; the region was still controlled by the Ojibwe.

J. J. Ducatel, a visitor to La Pointe who later wrote about the 1835 annuity payment, witnessed Zhingob contest the meaning of kinship. At the annuity payment, Zhingob rebuked the paternalism of government officials:

> When I was a British Indian I was treated by the British agents like a man—they spoke well of me, which my young men heard, and they gave me presents, which my young men saw, and that caused them to respect me; but now that I am an American Indian, I am not noticed by the great father, and my young men think I am a child. I used to give them good advice, which they heeded; but now they don't listen to what I have to say. . . . It was not so when I was a British Indian; but now I am a child, and must expect to be treated like a child.[52]

According to Ducatel, after the agent admonished him, Zhingob retreated and shook hands with the agent. This incident reveals Ojibwe frustration with their still new relationship with Americans. Zhingob's preference for being a "British Indian" reveals that Ojibwe leaders were keenly aware of American goals for expansion in the region. It is likely that Zhingob was purposefully playing on American anxiety about British influence in the region in order to get better treatment from federal officials.

A different interpretation from White's would be to frame the contestation over this terminology within the historical development of the trust relationship. A discussion of trust is completely absent from White's exploration of the meaning of kinship terminology but is helpful as it speaks directly to the historical development of the trust relationship and informs American motives for utilizing kinship terminology. Indeed, the work of most historians does not include a consideration of the historical development of the trust relationship and how treaties shaped both Native and American understanding of trust. This may be a disciplinary divide, as legal scholars and historians are often exposed to different scholarly literature in their training. Regardless, the kinship terminology employed by federal officials and the notion of federal protection of Native nations is clearly informed by legal notions of trusteeship.

Trust is a foundational aspect of American relations with Native nations that was enhanced by treaty making. The American government initiated the trust relationship on its own and vowed to act in the best interest of Native nations. The trust doctrine is a moral obligation enshrined in the historical relationship between the US government and Native nations in congressional legislation and in treaties. While not explicitly constitutionally based, most scholars and legal decisions recognize the existence of some historically based form of trust. David Wilkins and K. Tsianina Lomawaima argue: "Common to many, but not all, definitions of 'trust' is the notion of federal *responsibility to protect or enhance* tribal assets (including fiscal, natural, human, and cultural resources) through policy decisions and management actions."[53] At the very least, the US government exercises very tangible limited trust with Native nations, the most notable example being management of allotment lands. Those lands are held *in trust* and thus cannot be sold or taxed. A more comprehensive vision of trust was articulated by the Supreme Court in 1942 in *Seminole Nation v. United States*: "In carrying out its treaty obligations with the Indian tribes the Government is something more than a mere contracting party. Under a humane and self imposed policy which has found expression in many acts of Congress and numerous decisions of this Court, it has charged itself with moral obligations of the highest responsibility and trust."[54]

More recently, the Supreme Court has back peddled, most notably in *United States v. Jicarilla Apache Nation*, where the court ruled that trust must be explicitly enshrined in statute.[55] However, the historical record reflects a broad definition of trust as it was articulated in the *Seminole* case. In the Lake Superior Ojibwe treaties, there are clear examples of American officials articulating an understanding of the moral responsibilities associated with trust. Likewise, Ojibwe leaders understood early that Americans had themselves pledged to act in a moral capacity. This is reflected in the speeches of Nena'aangabi and other Ojibwe leaders. Nena'aangabi had a clear vision of how relationship between the Ojibwe and the US government should be. At the annuity payment in 1855 at La Pointe, Nena'aangabi gave a stirring speech in which he chided government officials regarding their shoddy execution of treaty provisions:

> Five long winters have passed since I have received a blanket for one of my children. My father, what has become of your promise? You probably have sent what you promised to us, but where has it gone, is more than I am able to say. Perhaps it has sunk in the deep waters of the lake, or it may have evaporated in the heavens, like the rising of the mist—or perhaps it has blown over our heads, and gone toward the setting sun. Last year I visited our father who came here, and gave goods to a portion of his red children—but I could not get here in time—I got nothing. I turned round to some of our traders, no doubt who are standing among us here, and asked them for some clothing to take to my poor children, but they refused me. Therefore I had to retrace my foot-steps over a long road, with empty hands, to my home in the woods—just as I had come.[56]

Nena'aangabi clearly understood the moral component of American trust responsibilities to Native nations. Historians and other scholars need to think more about how nineteenth-century Americans and Native leaders thought about trust. This helps current policy makers and Native leaders to better understand federal trust responsibilities. Most notably, it provides better evidence in court cases. Practiced correctly, such as the articulation in the *Seminole* case, trust is one of the cornerstones of a just democracy, something that all American citizens could take pride in.

THE TREATY OF 1847 AT FOND DU LAC

Increasingly in the 1840s, hostility emerged between the Mississippi and Lake Superior bands as Mississippi bands collected an equal share of the annuities from the 1837 and 1842 treaties despite never having ceded any of their own territory. This tension erupted after the 1847 Treaty of Fond du Lac when the Ojibwe ceded lands in central Minnesota. The treaty occurred in August, and Isaac Verplank was treaty commissioner, with twenty-two-year-old William Warren acting as interpreter. The federal government intended to have the lands serve as a reservation for the Ho-Chunk, in one of a series of removal schemes the federal government inflicted on the Ho-Chunk. While the Lake Superior bands were already angered over the Mississippi bands collecting equal share of the annuities from sale of their lands, the poor planning and shoddy execution of the treaty of 1847 nearly brought these tensions to civil war. Some Ojibwe leaders arrived after the main group had, while Noodin of the Snake River Band and Bagone-giizhig the younger, son and successor of the prominent Gull Lake leader, signed the following day. This led to suspicion of coercion and cast an air of mistrust over the treaty proceedings. This was the first treaty where the charismatic and divisive Bagone-giizhig acted as an ogimaa, and Wisconsin Ojibwe leaders were nervous about the young upstart leader.[57]

Leaders from the Lake Superior bands were enraged when annuities were not evenly divided between the Lake Superior and Mississippi Ojibwe. The Mississippi Ojibwe were paid $63,000, and the Lake Superior Ojibwe were paid $17,000. When the Lake Superior bands sold their land in 1837 and 1842, annuities were evenly split. Now that the Mississippi bands were selling their lands for the first time, the Lake Superior bands were only entitled to less than a quarter of those annuities. In addition, there was no provision made for payment to persons of mixed descent. Instead, Article 4 of the treaty read:

> It is stipulated that the half or mixed bloods of the Chippewas residing with them shall be considered Chippewa Indians, and shall, as such, be allowed to participate in all annuities which shall hereafter be paid to the Chippewas of the Mississippi and Lake Superior, due them by this treaty, and by the treaties heretofore made and ratified.[58]

Furthermore, persons of mixed descent actually signed the treaty itself. These individuals had no political leadership role in Ojibwe communities. Most did not even reside in Ojibwe communities. For example, William Warren, who was also the federal government's interpreter, was termed a "chief." These provisions were stark breaks with prior Treaty precedents. Both provisions outraged the Lake Superior Ojibwe leaders, as they had explicitly argued for them in prior treaty councils. For example, in 1842, Gichi-Waabizheshi of the Lac Courte Oreilles Band urged US officials: "Our half breeds *must* be paid. . . . But our Great Father can better afford to pay them than we can."[59] The impact of this provision was immediate as people of mixed descent moved into certain Ojibwe communities in order to collect annuities. This had little impact on the community at Manoominikaan but did reshape the community at Lac Courte Oreilles. In 1850, Julia Warren Spears noted there were several families of mixed descent living at Lac Courte Oreilles.[60]

Nena'aangabi refused to sign the treaty. However, some ogimaag did sign the treaty. From the Lac Courte Oreilles Band, Akiwenzii, Gichi-Waabizheshi, and Gichi-binesi (new leader of the community on Pacwawong Lake, having succeeded Bakwe'aamo) signed the treaty. The Lac Courte Oreilles Band leaders represented on the 1847 annuity that did not sign the treaty included Gwiiwizenzish (who did sign the treaty of 1842), Ginoozhens (leader of a different community on the Chippewa River), and Omadaagami (leader of the Lake Chetac community). In the St. Croix Band, Gabemabi and Ayaabens signed the treaty, while Yellow Lake leader Gegwedaash (the son and successor of longtime Yellow Lake leader Bizhiki) did not.[61]

It was at this time that Nena'aangabi asserted a leadership role within the Wisconsin Ojibwe. Due to the suspicion and inconsistencies surrounding the treaty, Nena'aangabi and other Ojibwe leaders from the St. Croix and Mille Lacs Bands formally protested the treaty. At issue for Nena'aangabi and the other chiefs was that the treaty of 1847 gave a greater portion of annuities to the Mississippi bands while the treaties of 1837 and 1842 split annuities evenly between the Lake Superior and Mississippi bands. Also alarming for the leaders was the provision of the treaty authorizing persons of mixed descent who did not have any leadership role in Ojibwe communities to sign the treaty as "chiefs."[62] William Warren and Isaac Verplank both defended the treaty to Commissioner of Indian Affairs William Medill and claimed that Nena'aangabi and other Ojibwe leaders protesting the treaty were "minor figures" that were mere pawns of the American Fur Company. Both Warren and Verplank completely ignored the Ojibwe leaders' concerns about the annuity split with the Mississippi bands and did not explain why the American Fur Company would have any interest in this issue if the Ojibwe leaders were mere pawns of the company.[63]

At the very least, Warren's claim that they were all "minor figures" has little merit. Of the nine Ojibwe to sign the remonstrance, only three were not ogimaag. Aside from Nena'aangabi, the signers of the remonstrance included five other Ojibwe influential leaders with rather large communities. Just three years later Warren wrote his cousin George Warren and suggested organizing a delegation of the nine most important Ojibwe leaders from Wisconsin to go to Washington in order to convince the Wisconsin Ojibwe to remove to Fond du Lac. Warren's delegation included Nena'aangabi and St. Croix Band ogimaa Gegwedaash, two of the ogimaag he called "minor" in 1847.[64] Three of the ogimaag from the remonstrance, Negwanebi, Zhooniyaa, and Manoominikeshiinh, were not included not because they did not yield enough influence, but because the Mille Lacs and Snake River Bands were part of a different removal scheme that involved the concentration of the Snake River Band and St. Croix Band at Mille Lacs. Thus, just four years later, Warren in essence invalidated his own claim that the remonstrance was the work of "minor figures" being duped by the American Fur Company.

Shortly after the protest of Nena'aangabi and the other leaders who refused to sign the treaty of 1847, Snake River Band ogimaa Noodin rescinded his approval of the treaty in a letter to the president. Noodin was joined in his protest by Nena'aangabi and ogimaag Negwanebi, Gichi-Noodin, and Zhooniyaa. The reason that Noodin refuted his endorsement of the treaty was that the terms of the treaty were misrepresented at the council: "we now learn from those who can read the Paper we signed that it speaks words different from what we listened to and agreed to." The leaders placed the blame for this squarely on William Warren: "We do not blame you we blame the one who speaks our tongue!"[65] As a result, Commissioner of Indian Affairs Medill asked Verplank to address the issues raised by both documents. In his defense of the treaty, Verplank dismissed the remonstrance as solely the agenda of American Fur Company traders. Ignoring the interests of Ojibwe leaders and their possible objections, Verplank only noted how the treaty threatened the interests of the traders and did not discuss the specific complaints of the Ojibwe leaders. Verplank repeated Warren's earlier dismissal of the remonstrance and claimed that the traders "were only able to induce seven Indians claiming to be chiefs and two warriors to sign a remonstrance."[66] Despite the efforts of Nena'aangabi and other Ojibwe leaders, the Senate ratified the treaty on April 3, 1848.

GAAWIIN NINDAA-IKWABISII: ETHNIC CLEANSING AT SANDY LAKE

In 1848, Wisconsin became the thirtieth state of the union.[67] However, statehood did nothing to increase non-Ojibwe settlement in the vast northern one-third of Wisconsin: despite the declaration of statehood, it remained territory controlled by the Ojibwe. The vast majority of the population was Ojibwe, and very few white settlers lived there. Wisconsin Ojibwe people had little reason to think that they had sold their lands in 1837 and 1842, as white settlers did not move onto Ojibwe lands until decades later. Even the extraction of resources was something that occurred in small select areas and not across the entire territory. Little land in the territory passed into the hands of private individuals or timber companies.[68] The only exception to this was in the St. Croix River valley, where lumbering began on the southern fringes of the ceded territory, mostly due to the presence of sawmills at Stillwater, Minnesota.[69] Benjamin Armstrong noted, "After the treaty of 1837 lumbermen were in the habit of cutting choice pine timber wherever it was handy to get a market, without owning the land or getting permission to cut the timber. In other words, they were stealing it from the government."[70]

By 1850, the only white settlement that happened even remotely near the Lac Courte Oreilles Band was on the southern fringes of Ojibwe territory. Menomonie, Eau Claire, and Chippewa Falls were all more than sixty miles away from Ojibwe villages. Even here, though, the Ojibwe still vastly outnumbered whites. One example of this occurred at Chippewa Falls in 1849 when a Frenchman, Martial Caznobia, attempted to rape an Ojibwe woman. After entering the lodge and trying to force himself on her, Caznobia was stabbed by the woman's husband. The next morning a crowd gathered at the local saloon and decided to lynch the man who stabbed Caznobia. The crowd went to the man's lodge, dragged him out, tied a noose around his neck, hoisted him into a tree, and murdered him. However, at this time white settlers did not have the demographic advantage to get away with something like this. Soon, 1,500 Ojibwe warriors showed up at Chippewa Falls demanding that Caznobia and the murderers of the Ojibwe man be turned over to them or else they would burn every building in Chippewa Falls. This incident attracted Ojibwe leaders and warriors from hundreds of miles away including Gull Lake Band ogimaa Bagone-giizhig. Cooler heads prevailed. Leaders of the fledging settlement negotiated for the punishment of the perpetrators in American courts. However, the nearest police were at Prairie du Chien, over one hundred miles to the south. Ojibwe leaders insisted on a party of Ojibwe to accompany the perpetrators to Prairie du Chien to ensure that justice was served. Travel was by boat down the Chippewa River to the Mississippi. However, when the boat reached the Mississippi, the Ojibwe fled, fearing attack from the Dakota. When the group reached Prairie du Chien, there were no witnesses against the perpetrators, so they were released. However, neither the lynchers nor Caznobia returned to Chippewa Falls for fear of reprisal from the Ojibwe.[71]

This was the only tension between whites and the Ojibwe in the years following the treaty. The appearance of 1,500 Ojibwe warriors overwhelmed the small settlement and illustrated the fact that all the ceded territory was still effectively controlled by the Ojibwe. This reinforced Ojibwe understanding of the treaties conveying the lease of timber and mineral rights and not sale of the land. Ojibwe leaders were anxious to secure reservations, however, and avoid any chance of removal in the future. In 1849, a group of six Ojibwe leaders petitioned Congress for reservations. Naagaanab of the Fond du Lac Band, Oshkaabewis of the Lac du Flambeau Band, and Gezhiiyaash of the Lac Vieux Desert Band led the group. The reservations the leaders petitioned for were to be small village sites of a few sections.[72] While some federal officials had discussed removal of Wisconsin Ojibwe in the late 1840s, most federal officials saw no reason why the Ojibwe should move from Wisconsin. Things changed with the appointment of Alexander Ramsey as Minnesota territorial governor in 1849. Newly elected President Zachary Taylor appointed Ramsey. Ramsey had common interests with traders in Minnesota and saw an opportunity to enhance the economy of northern Minnesota by removing Wisconsin Ojibwe to Minnesota in order to bring the gold coin of annuities into Minnesota.

Later in 1849, Ramsey moved a resolution through the Minnesota Territorial Legislature petitioning Congress for the removal of the Ojibwe in Wisconsin and the western portion of Michigan's Upper Peninsula to Minnesota. The territorial resolution justified the removal in order to ensure "the security and tranquility of the white settlements."[73] However, as historian Charles Cleland argues, the number of white settlers living in northern Wisconsin was minimal. Except for the lower part of the St. Croix River, there were virtually no whites in northern Wisconsin. Furthermore, there were no complaints about the Ojibwe in Wisconsin. Cleland also points out that while states and territories commonly petitioned Congress and the president for removal of Native peoples out of their jurisdiction to another, it was a major violation of the authority of the state of Wisconsin by the upstart Minnesota Territory.[74]

Partisan politics trumped the law. Ramsey was an appointee of the president (governors of territories were appointed by the president and not elected by the people), and both men belonged to the now defunct Whig Party. Wisconsin's governor, Nelson Dewey, was a Democrat, as was Michigan's governor, John Barry. Accordingly, President Taylor acted on the territorial resolution by issuing an executive order on February 6, 1850, ordering the removal of the Ojibwe in Wisconsin and Michigan who were party to the treaties of 1837 and 1842. Ramsey planned to begin removal with the 1850 annuity payment. The agency at La Pointe was dissolved in 1850, a controversial move among missionaries and traders there, who saw Ramsey's motivation for removal based solely on greed. The payment would take place at Sandy Lake, in north central Minnesota, site of the new agency under John Watrous. Even more devious, Ramsey and Watrous hatched a secret plan to delay the annuity payment until after waterways had frozen and canoe travel was not possible, in order to trap Ojibwe families from Wisconsin and Michigan at Sandy Lake to ensure their relocation.[75]

The removal order perplexed Ojibwe leaders. In the 1864 petition Ojibwe leaders wrote: "'Why is this order from my Great Father' was the question among the Indians. I own the land yet, and I fail to see anything that I have done to my Great Father to deserve this punishment from him." Ojibwe leaders saw the removal order as a breach of the kinship duties that the Americans had cultivated with Ojibwe leaders. Additionally, it made no sense to Ojibwe leaders that they should have to remove from lands *they still owned*. The Ojibwe text contains the verb "nindibendaan" or "I own it." Ojibwe response to the removal order was decisive: "Gaawiin nindaa-ikwabisii, geyaabi isa nindibendaan maandan aki," or as the English text stated, "I will not remove and leave my lands, I own them yet."[76]

The role of Alexander Ramsey and the assertion of local interests in the guise of territorial law were part of a pattern that would reoccur to the Ojibwe again and again for the rest of the nineteenth century. From this point forward, American colonialism included not just federal power, but state and municipal governments, as well as corporate interests. This is what made American colonialism so threatening to Ojibwe sovereignty and survival. With Sandy Lake, the conflict that arose with the assertion of local government's power in violation of treaties and other federal law had disastrous consequences for the Ojibwe.

Due to the huge distance involved, Ojibwe people in Michigan and the Ojibwe village at Pelican Lake in far northeast Wisconsin refused to attend the payment. Ojibwe people from Wisconsin began arriving at Sandy Lake in late October, only to find Watrous not present. Ramsey and Watrous's removal scheme was foiled when only men of Ojibwe communities showed up, leaving their families in Wisconsin. Watrous would not arrive for six weeks, leaving thousands of Ojibwe at Sandy Lake with no ready food supply. Reports of Ojibwe deaths from starvation soon surfaced. When Watrous did arrive with the annuity on December 3, the remaining Ojibwe quickly collected their annuities and made the trip hundreds of miles back to Wisconsin on foot, resulting in hundreds more deaths.[77]

The actual number of Ojibwe people who died as a result of Sandy Lake has been the subject of an ongoing debate since 1850. John Watrous claimed that only 150 Ojibwe died at Sandy Lake.[78] However, in the midst of the crisis at Sandy Lake, the *Minnesota Chronicle and Register* suggested that at least eighty-five had died already by December 17, with five or six dying every night.[79] The *Chronicle and Register* reported that this total increased to at least 167 by December 23.[80] On January 8, Gull Lake Ojibwe leader

Bagone-giizhig addressed a crowd at the St. Paul Presbyterian Church, where he estimated that four to six Ojibwe died each day.[81] La Pointe missionary Sherman Hall claimed that at least seventy to eighty Ojibwe were buried at Sandy Lake alone with as many as nine dying per day during the removal attempt.[82] Wisconsin Ojibwe leaders asserted that 170 died at Sandy Lake with another 230 dying on the return trip home to Wisconsin.[83] Historians estimate these four hundred deaths represented 12 percent of the Wisconsin Ojibwe population.[84]

Annuity records suggest that the Ojibwe community at Manoominikaan was devastated by events at Sandy Lake. The population of the Ojibwe community at Rice Lake was 192 in 1847, while the first surviving record after Sandy Lake showed 161 people. Other Lac Courte Oreilles communities were hit even harder. For example, village at Lake Chetac decreased from 136 to 108, and the village at Pacwawong Lake under Gichi-binesi decreased from 99 to 62. Overall, the population of the Lac Courte Oreilles Band dropped by 126 people. Losses by the Lac du Flambeau Band were even worse: 167 people. Much of this population loss can be directly attributed to the events at Sandy Lake. While the Lac Courte Oreilles and Lac du Flambeau Bands showed population decreases, the population of the L'Anse Band in Michigan, who refused to go to Sandy Lake, *increased* in the same time period from 258 people in 1847 to 404 in 1857, an increase of 146 people. Furthermore, losses due to Sandy Lake might be even more than these numbers suggest. The provision of the treaty of 1847 that allowed persons of mixed descent meant hundreds of people collected Ojibwe annuities in 1857 that had not in 1847. Of the 849 people collecting annuities of the Lac Courte Oreilles Band in 1857, 124 had French or English surnames. Virtually all of these individuals collected annuities with Akiwenzii's community on Lac Courte Oreilles and a community on the Chippewa River under the leadership of Ginoozhens. This means that the population of these communities most likely decreased at the same rate as other Ojibwe communities that show a population decrease.[85]

William Warren wrote in 1851 that the Ojibwe "really supposed the whites intended to poison them off instead of removing them."[86] Despite the massive loss of Ojibwe life at Sandy Lake, the events of 1850 are largely unknown outside of Ojibwe communities. Few accounts of Minnesota history even mention the deaths at Sandy Lake. The events of Sandy Lake in 1850 constituted a deliberate act of ethnic cleansing worthy of inclusion in narratives of Minnesota history and American history. The four hundred Ojibwe deaths as a result of Ramsey and Watrous's actions are more than more widely known incidents such as the estimated two hundred Cheyenne massacred at Sand Creek in 1864 or the three hundred Lakota slaughtered at Wounded Knee in 1890.

Ramsey and Watrous persisted in 1851 with removal efforts, despite the refusal of the Wisconsin Ojibwe to go anywhere near Sandy Lake. Removal was further hampered with the death of Ramsey's patron President Zachary Taylor in 1850. Watrous put William Warren in charge of removal for the communities of the Lac Courte Oreilles Band.[87] Warren noted, "I have discovered that there is an extended league throughout the whole tribe (excepting only the St. Croix villages) not to remove. Pipes wampum and tobacco have been sent from village to village to effect this purpose."[88] As a result of Ojibwe resistance, recently appointed Commissioner of Indian Affairs Luke Lea suspended the removal order in August 1851. However, Ramsey and Watrous ignored Lea's instructions and instead hatched a new plan to get the Wisconsin Ojibwe into Minnesota by removing the Wisconsin Ojibwe to Fond du Lac and the St. Croix Band to Mille Lacs. Ramsey and Watrous were forced to back down from their removal plans as citizens in Wisconsin and Michigan were outraged due to Ramsey's role in the four hundred plus Ojibwe deaths at Sandy Lake. As a result, Ramsey relented on several points, including paying annuities in 1851 and 1852 at Fond du Lac, exempting Michigan Ojibwe from removal, and moving the agency from Sandy Lake to Crow Wing. In the meantime, La Pointe Band ogimaa Bizhiki, at the time over ninety years old, and young St. Croix Band ogimaa Oshoge, who had just assumed leadership after the death of his father, Gabemabi, began to organize a coalition of missionaries at La Pointe and Keweenaw Bay, citizens of Wisconsin and Michigan, and copper interests to oppose removal of Wisconsin and Upper Michigan Ojibwe. Most notably, copper interests in Michigan's Keweenaw Peninsula were staunchly opposed to Ojibwe removal, as their fledging operations were dependent on the Ojibwe for their food supply since there were no whites in the western Upper Peninsula besides miners. When Bizhiki and Oshoge traveled to Washington in 1852, they circulated a petition to present to the president, showing opposition to Ojibwe removal. Benjamin Armstrong noted: "From Ontonagon we went to Portage Lake, Houghton and Hancock, and visited the various copper mines, and all there signed the petition."[89]

Bizhiki and Oshoge were determined to see the president and end removal efforts through diplomacy. According to Benjamin Armstrong, much was at stake: "To give up this trip would be to abandon the last hope of keeping that turbulent spirit of the young warriors within bounds."[90] On meeting the president, Oshoge spoke for an hour to him, according to Armstrong. Armstrong recalled that regarding the treaties of 1837 and

1842 Oshoge "said that he did not understand that in either treaty they had ceded away the land and he further understood in both cases that the Indians were never asked to remove from the lands included in those treaties."[91] While scholars have questioned certain details about Armstrong's account of the trip to Washington, such as if the group met directly with the president, the trip illustrates the considerable political skill of Oshoge. While Bizhiki is often remembered in Ojibwe communities today, a close reading of Armstrong reveals that much of the skillful negotiation with American officials was done by Oshoge. This is not to take away from the role played by Bizhiki, but merely suggests that the great elder chief has overshadowed Oshoge. The young Oshoge was a rising star in Ojibwe politics. While he did not have the military success of Nena'aangabi nor was he in charge of a historically important community like Bizhiki, Oshoge's dazzling political skills in the wake of the disaster at Sandy Lake allowed him to ascend very quickly to great influence in Wisconsin Ojibwe politics.

At the same time that Bizhiki and Oshoge were in Washington, other events helped end the removal policy. Democrat Franklin Pierce took office in March 1853 and replaced Ramsey with Willis Gorman as Minnesota territorial governor. Meanwhile, the L'Anse Band brought charges of corruption against Watrous, leading to his ouster.[92] In 1853 annuity payments returned to La Pointe. In the meantime, American desire for another resource on Ojibwe land allowed Lake Superior Ojibwe leaders to secure permanent reservations.

THE 1854 TREATY AND RESERVATIONS

Federal officials had long eyed the vast iron-ore deposits of northeast Minnesota. This gave the Ojibwe of Wisconsin, northeastern Minnesota, and western Upper Michigan leverage in their demand to retain permanent reservations. Most Ojibwe leaders, including Nena'aangabi, agreed to the treaty of 1854, seeing it as the best way to finally end removal. Indian Agent Henry Gilbert served as treaty commissioner. Bizhiki worked diligently to secure reservations at the treaty. In 1937, Bad River elder Joseph Stoddard, who was a young man at the time of the treaty, related his memories of the events for the Bad River Works Progress Administration historical project. Stoddard was the grandson of La Pointe Band ogimaa Giishkitawag (not to be confused with Nena'aangabi's son and eventual successor), who signed the treaty and was one of the leaders who joined Akiwenzii in the 1864 bilingual petition. Stoddard remembered: "Mr. Gilbert stood at one end of a small writing table and Chief Buffalo on the other end, joining hands in a mutual grip of friendship."[93]

According to Stoddard, the treaty was to be Bizhiki's legacy: "Chief Buffalo worked so hard during the drafting of the treaty of 1854, that he suffered a general health break-down, and lived only a short time after the completion and signing of the document. The Chief felt highly elated after the work was completed, thinking that every word of the treaty would be carried out, affording permanence and security to his people." According to Stoddard, Bizhiki's faith in the treaty was based on what Gilbert explicitly told Ojibwe leaders, as the treaty commissioner "assured the Indians that the obligations of the United States under this treaty would be fulfilled to the letter." In a dramatic gesture, "Using the rolled treaty as a pointer, Mr. Gilbert pointed to the East, to the West, to the North and to the South. The gesture circumscribing the Great White Father's domain, explaining that the treaty just concluded was backed by the integrity of the U.S. and promising that the Great Father would see that the stipulations in the document would be taken care of at the time indicated." However, Stoddard claimed that the federal government changed the treaty from what was told to Ojibwe leaders: "Many of the most important provisions which were agreed upon at Madeline Island were stricken from the treaty. . . . the whole document was so changed that every provision leaned to the advantage of the United States."[94]

Other issues plagued the treaty. Anger persisted between Lake Superior and Mississippi Ojibwe as a result of the Treaty of 1847. According to Gilbert: "Much jealousy and ill will existed between them and the Lake Superior Indians and they could not even be prevailed upon to meet each other in council."[95] According to Benjamin Armstrong, the Mississippi bands arrived with traders from the American Fur Company and were opposed to any separation of interests of annuities from the 1837 and 1842 treaties.[96] To rectify the growing divide between Lake Superior and Mississippi Ojibwe over annuities, the federal government paid the 1854 land cession annuities to the Lake Superior Ojibwe only, pushed the Lake Superior Ojibwe to relinquish claims to lands west of cession, and agreed to pay the Lake Superior Ojibwe two-thirds and Mississippi Ojibwe one-third of future annuities due under the treaties of 1837 and 1842.[97]

Another disgruntled group at the treaty were traders. According to Armstrong, American Fur Company traders arrived armed in order to ensure a payment for traders in the treaty.[98] Despite their best efforts, there was no separate payment. In fact, the treaty explicitly forbade traders from collecting debt from the Ojibwe from the treaty. Article 6 read, "The annuities of the Indians shall not be taken to pay the debts of individuals." Persons of mixed descent were also not paid, although under the treaty of 1847 they were entitled to annuities if they lived in Ojibwe communities. While there was no payment for persons of mixed descent, the treaty provided off-reservation allotments of eighty acres.[99] This provision was the source of widespread corruption in the years following the treaty. For example, according to Benjamin Armstrong, La Pointe Agent Luther Webb ran a scheme in the 1860s that involved issuing mixed-blood allotments to young boys, obtaining the title for next to nothing, and selling the lands at a substantial profit.[100] The corruption prompted a House investigation in 1874.[101]

At the same time, Ojibwe leaders were ready for the treaty as well. Four thousand Ojibwe attended the treaty. Gilbert noted, "The Chiefs who were notified to attend brought with them in every instance their entire band."[102] No doubt much of the motivation to sign the treaty had to do with ending removal and securing permanent homelands. The treaty explicitly stated: "the Indians shall not be required to remove from the homes hereby set apart for them." In the treaty the Lac Courte Oreilles Band retained three townships in an unspecified location. Reservations were also established for the La Pointe Band at Bad River and Red Cliff, the Lac du Flambeau Band, the L'Anse Band, the Fond du Lac Band, and the Grand Portage Band.[103] Besides Nena'aangabi, all of the other Lac Courte Oreilles Band ogimaag signed the treaty, including Akiwenzii from the Lac Courte Oreilles village, Omadaagami from Lake Chetac, Gichi-binesi from Pacwawong Lake, and Ginoozhens, Gichi-Waabizheshi, and Ozhaawashko-giizhig, all ogimaag of separate villages on the Chippewa River.[104]

The acquisition of the territory of the Lake Superior Ojibwe was tantamount to robbery. Abundant historical evidence demonstrates that Ojibwe leaders were told they were merely selling resources (pine, copper, and iron ore) and not the land itself. Moreover, the compensation provided was a pittance compared to the wealth of the resources exploited by the US government in the nineteenth century alone. As historian David R. Wrone argues, the resources secured at these treaties enabled the expansion of the United States. Wrone estimated that the United States got 240 billion board feet of timber in the ceded territory of these treaties. From Michigan's Keweenaw Peninsula came 13.5 million pounds of copper with the 1842 treaty. By the end of the nineteenth century, the region supplied a large share of the world's copper. A more lasting industry was the steel industry, which flourished in the wake of the 1854 treaty and mining of the massive iron-ore deposits in Minnesota's Mesabi Range. Less sustainable but still significant was iron-ore production in Wisconsin's Gogebic Range during the late nineteenth and early twentieth centuries, which totaled four billion tons. Wrone argues that the acquisition of Ojibwe territory changed America:

> They provided several of the essential ingredients for the industrial transformation of late nineteenth-century and early twentieth-century America. The ores of the Mesabi enabled the steel mills of Pittsburgh to flourish, the copper of the Keewnanh [Keeweenaw] poured into wires made the telephone system possible. Power sites created paper mills, part of the industrial glory of Wisconsin. The lakes and fish offered a recreational paradise.[105]

WISCONSIN OJIBWE LEADERSHIP IN TRANSITION

By the time of the 1854 treaty, Nena'aangabi had been the chief at Manoominikaan for over two decades. At the 1855 annuity payment, Richard Morse described Nena'aangabi as "the favorite orator and chief" of the Wisconsin Ojibwe.[106] This was due to events that transpired since the 1854 treaty. Bizhiki of La Pointe had died within the year in his nineties. Tragically, Oshoge of the St. Croix Band died in 1854 of small pox. The death of the relatively young Oshoge was a severe blow to the political life of the Wisconsin Ojibwe. As Richard Morse noted "He was a young chief, of rare promise and merit; he stood high in the affections of his people."[107] Oshoge was clearly a leader with the potential to lead Ojibwe communities through the difficult decades of the second half of the nineteenth century. At the 1855 annuity payment, Richard Morse recorded the speech of a man from the La Pointe Band named Ja-ba-ge-zhick: "We had but one man among us, capable of doing our business for the Chippewa Nation; that man was O-sho-ga, now dead, and our nation now mourns."[108]

The deaths of Bizhiki and Oshoge left Nena'aangabi as the sole Ojibwe leader in Wisconsin with the abilities and experience to shape the Ojibwe relationship with Americans. *Rice Lake Chronotype* editor August Ender summed up Nena'aangabi this way: "Intelligent, fearless and a natural-born leader, the chief had the confidence of many smaller tribal leaders, and in dealings with the white man, was an outstanding figure."[109] Nena'aangabi's role in Wisconsin Ojibwe politics was still remembered at Lac Courte Oreilles in the 1940s: "There was one head chief who got the Indians seven reservations. His name was Nina'angebi—he was going to Washington to get a reservation for his people, but the Sioux killed him and his people were accepted here."[110]

In 1875, Ira Isham, who was married to one of Nena'aangabi's granddaughters, told the *Barron County Chronotype* that Nena'aangabi had made an agreement with Minnesota Senator Henry Rice to select six townships for a reservation: "Mr. Rice found them composed of six bands all under the control of Un-ga-ba as their principal chief. His immediate band claimed control of Rice Lake." This passage reflects the influence of Nena'aangabi within the Wisconsin Ojibwe. Like the oral tradition recorded in the 1940s, Isham claimed that Nena'aangabi was about to go to Washington to formalize the agreement: "The principal chief, Un-ga-ba had accepted the proposition of Rice viz: to select six townships out of the nine to be selected by the government, and was preparing to go to Washington when he was killed by the Sioux near Vance's trading post on Hay River."[111] Why Rice, a Minnesota senator, was interested in the affairs of Ojibwe in Wisconsin is unknown. Perhaps he was interested in timber harvest. Regardless, Nena'aangabi was cut down before he could make the trip to Washington.

In the fall of 1855, shortly after Nena'aangabi's impassioned speech at the annuity payment at La Pointe, he led a party of thirty-eight warriors into battle against the Dakota. The exact reason for the campaign is unknown. After leaving Manoominikaan, they caught sight of a much larger party of Dakota warriors. Sensing the vulnerability of their situation, Nena'aangabi made the decision to retreat. However, on their retreat, a second Dakota group ambushed the Ojibwe near the modern town of Prairie Farm. Nena'aangabi was carrying a heavy load and was vulnerable. The Dakota warriors killed Nena'aangabi while he was trying to unload his goods and get to his weapon.[112] According to oral tradition, Nena'aangabi's daughter Waabikwe played dead near the slain Ojibwe and then ambushed a group of Dakota that returned to collect the Ojibwe scalps. Waabikwe killed two Dakota.[113]

Nena'aangabi's was in his sixties or early seventies when he died. Sadly, Nena'aangabi left a child who was born after his death, Maggie White. The rest of Nena'aangabi's children were in their teens or in their early twenties when he died. Nena'aangabi left three sons and five daughters. Nena'aangabi's eldest daughter, Aazhaweyaa, was a noted warrior. His three sons were Waabizheshi, Ininiins, and Giishkitawag, later known to white settlers as Joe White.[114] Upon Nena'aangabi's death, Waabizheshi, the oldest son, ascended to leadership of the community. The task of securing a reservation at Manoominikaan would now fall to Waabizheshi. The deaths of Oshoge, Bizhiki, and Nena'aangabi within a year of each other could not have occurred at a worse time. The talent drain caused by the deaths of these three visionary leaders would impact Ojibwe communities in Wisconsin for the rest of the nineteenth century, a time when they faced unprecedented challenges to their sovereignty from federal officials, the state of Wisconsin, American settlers, and corporate timber interests.

CONCLUSION

In 1999, Supreme Court Justice Sandra Day O'Connor wrote in the majority opinion in *Minnesota v. Mille Lacs* about the court's interpretation of the treaty of 1837, "we look beyond the written words to the larger context that frames the Treaty."[115] At issue was whether the Mille Lacs Band (and by extension all the Ojibwe who ceded lands in the treaty) retained off-reservation treaty rights under the treaty of 1837. While Ojibwe in Wisconsin and Michigan practiced off-reservation treaty rights since the US Seventh Circuit Court of Appeals's 1983 decision in *Lac Courte Oreilles v. Voight*, the state of Minnesota was not bound to recognize the decision as it was outside their own federal court district, forcing the Mille Lacs Band to litigate. The Supreme Court found these rights to still be valid by a razor thin five to four majority, employing the canons of construction to reach the majority opinion. The canons include interpreting treaties the way that Native people at the time understood them and interpreting ambiguities in treaties in favor of tribes. Used since the 1970s in federal Indian law, the canons are not enshrined in statute and the courts are under no explicit obligation to employ them. However, O'Connor's use of the canons in the *Mille Lacs* case bolstered their importance.[116]

Employing the canons to look at larger issues in the treaty of 1837 brings many other legal issues to the fore. Nena'aangabi, the most important Ojibwe leader living in the area, refused to sign the treaty. Furthermore, there is overwhelming historical evidence from both Ojibwe leaders and non-Ojibwe that federal officials deceived Ojibwe leaders, telling them that the treaty merely gave the United States the right to harvest pine and did not impact title to the land. If we are to invest any significant meaning in the canons of construction, the cession of land in 1837 is not valid. If the United States is to live up to its promise of a just democratic society, it must recognize and rectify its colonial past of territorial acquisition through fraud in a meaningful way. The death of Nena'aangabi, along with the deaths of Oshoge and Bizhiki within the same year, changed Wisconsin Ojibwe politics. At the same time, the Ojibwe community at Manoominikaan faced unprecedented challenges in the years that followed. The treaties were just the beginning: American colonialism was more than just federal policy; it was state laws, local governments, corporate transformation of land, and white settlers. Waabizheshi's own leadership style was vastly different from his father's. As the United States expanded in the region, a new generation of Ojibwe leaders like Waabizheshi sought a more local response to these challenges.

CHAPTER 3

Waabizheshi's Vision of an Intercultural Community at Rice Lake, 1855–1877

In 1855, Waabizheshi assumed leadership of the Rice Lake community from his father Nena'aangabi following the influential leader's death on the battlefield. Waabizheshi inherited a thriving community, as well as an important political legacy, from his father, whom Richard Morse described in 1855 as "the favorite orator and chief" of the Lake Superior Ojibwe.[1] Lacking the raw charisma of his father, the exotic appeal of his warrior sister, or the tragedy that surrounded his brother Joe White's murder, Waabizheshi is overshadowed in the historical record. Nevertheless, his leadership was pivotal in the history of the community. Waabizheshi led the community for twenty-two years, and Ojibwe life at Rice Lake was vastly different by the end of those twenty-two years than it had been at the beginning. Beginning in the 1860s, timber companies leveled the region. Despite some initial benefits to Ojibwe life such as increased deer populations and employment in logging camps during the tough winter months, the dam building that accompanied clear-cutting destroyed rice beds throughout Ojibwe territory. In the midst of this ecological destruction, the strongest El Niño of the nineteenth century further reduced yields of wild rice and maple sugar in the 1870s. At the same time, white settlers moved into Rice Lake, quickly outnumbering the Ojibwe, while federal officials pressured the Ojibwe at Rice Lake to remove first to a reservation 50 miles northeast at Lac Courte Oreilles and later to the Bad River Reservation 120 miles to the north.[2]

Waabizheshi employed new strategies in response to these challenges. While Nena'aangabi's leadership was marked by engagement with federal officials and broad influence in Wisconsin Ojibwe political life, Waabizheshi virtually ignored federal officials and instead focused his efforts on building relationships with newly arrived white settlers in Rice Lake. Central to these exchanges was performance through speeches, gifting, and even dance. Performance was a central aspect of traditional Ojibwe political institutions that functioned as an important means of articulating policy. No evidence exists describing Waabizheshi himself formally articulating this as a strategy for remaining at Rice Lake. Instead these performances were a community effort. In 1858, Waabizheshi and other Lac Courte Oreilles leaders tried in vain to locate the reservation at Prairie Rice Lake. When federal officials refused and located the reservation at Lac Courte Oreilles, Waabizheshi virtually ceased to exert his influence among the Lac Courte Oreilles Band, let alone broader Ojibwe politics, and focused all of his efforts on building relationships with white settlers in order to avoid removal.

Scholars typically have focused on conflict when discussing the arrival of white settlers in Native lands. However, Waabizheshi strove for something much different, aiming to accommodate white settlers in Rice Lake while retaining Ojibwe sovereignty. Given the drastic demographic and ecological transformations that took place in the 1860s and 1870s, Waabizheshi and the rest of the community were no doubt keenly aware that things were never going to be the same again. Instead of acquiescing to segregation on reservation lands or attempting to repel the settlers through violence, Waabizheshi and the rest of the community sought to collaborate with the newcomers to create a new community rooted in mutual respect and Ojibwe sovereignty. The practice of treaty rights was central to Ojibwe survival under these new conditions. Armed with rights guaranteed in the treaty of 1837 and reaffirmed in the treaty of 1854 to hunt, fish, and gather throughout the ceded territory, the Ojibwe of Rice Lake made their living in the new community at Rice Lake by blending treaty-sanctioned traditional labor with wage labor in logging camps. In the process, the Ojibwe sought to accommodate the new conditions while at the same time asserting their sovereignty by continuing to practice traditional labor throughout the ceded territory. This was a subversive alternative to federal policy, which demanded total assimilation.

Waabizheshi's vision is important for a better understanding not just of Native history, but of American history as well. The Chippewa River valley was rich in white pine and supplied a sizeable amount of the timber that built America. As important as the area was to American expansion and growth elsewhere, Waabizheshi provides an important example of how Native leaders posed alternatives to colonial, race-based hierarchy and exploitation that were nonviolent and rooted in tribal sovereignty. Nonviolent alternatives to white supremacy are usually only talked about in twentieth-century American history. Waabizheshi and the Ojibwe at Rice Lake flatly rejected a segregated society in their refusal to be removed from Rice Lake and contained on the Lac Courte Oreilles Reservation.

What Waabizheshi instead strove for at Rice Lake was an intercultural alternative. While scholars of indigenous communities in North America have focused more on immediate conflict, scholars of indigenous communities in Latin America have been more attentive to the broader array of strategies employed by indigenous peoples in their struggles against colonialism. In her study of indigenous communities in Colombia, anthropologist Joanne Rappaport argues, "interculturalism fosters a broad field of intercultural exchange characterized by nonhierarchical relations."[3] Rappaport describes how indigenous communities in Colombia have posed alternatives in their relationship to the Colombian state emerging out of the context of dictatorship, violence, and civil war in the 1970s and 1980s. While the community at Rice Lake is seemingly removed by time and political conditions from the communities studied by Rappaport, interculturalism is a helpful way to think about how Waabizheshi's community sought to accommodate the presence of newly arrived white settlers by engaging them in processes of exchange that had marked Ojibwe interactions with non-Ojibwe for centuries. Waabizheshi was successful for twenty-two years in resisting removal. However, all of the stresses on the community culminated in violence when another Ojibwe murdered Waabizheshi in 1877.

THE RICE LAKE COMMUNITY UNDER WAABIZHESHI

Reconstructing Waabizheshi's leadership is a difficult task. In marked contrast to his father, there is no historical record of Waabizheshi's words. Waabizheshi's thoughts and ideas remain a historical mystery, and we are left to infer his leadership style by his actions. However, the very absence of material on Waabizheshi is telling. Waabizheshi, unlike his father, did not seek direct engagement with American policy makers or attempt to influence the broader arena of Ojibwe politics, leaving no direct accounts of the leader's thoughts or actions in federal records. Indeed, the only specific reference in federal records to Waabizheshi by name is merely his listing as the "chief" of the community in annuity records. Instead, Waabizheshi's political focus becomes clear by his inclusion in local historical materials. In the early twentieth century, *Rice Lake Chronotype* editor August Ender characterized Waabizheshi's leadership: "while not so popular with the whites as was his father, seemed to get along quite well with his own people."[4] Annuity records support Ender's contention. In 1857, Waabizheshi's community consisted of 161 people, and by 1874 the community had grown to 175 people.[5] This supports Ender's claim that Waabizheshi was able to maintain the popularity of his father's leadership within the community.

While Waabizheshi maintained a high degree of popularity in his own community, he did not seek the broader influence in Ojibwe politics or among American officials that characterized his father's leadership. Ender's assessment of Waabizheshi's leadership is helpful for thinking about changes in Ojibwe leadership during the mid-nineteenth century. In the wake of the treaty of 1854, Waabizheshi and other Wisconsin Ojibwe leaders increasingly turned inward, while in Minnesota leaders like Bagone-giizhig tried to build broad, multiband alliances as a way to resist American colonialism.[6] Following the failure in 1858 to secure the reservation at Prairie Rice Lake, Waabizheshi spent the next nineteen years leading his community in relative isolation, successfully resisting efforts to remove his own community to the Lac Courte Oreilles Reservation but making little to no effort to assert his influence in Ojibwe politics in Wisconsin or even within the Lac Courte Oreilles Band. It appears that Waabizheshi refused to participate in the selection of reservation lands at Lac Courte Oreilles in 1859. Moreover, Waabizheshi did not join Akiwenzii and other Wisconsin Ojibwe leaders when they visited Washington in 1864 to present the president with a bilingual petition detailing grievances against the federal government.[7] No evidence exists that shows Waabizheshi leading any effort to resist or accommodate American colonialism beyond what impacted his own community.

A major change for the Ojibwe community of Rice Lake occurred in 1862 when Dakota people were expelled from Minnesota and contained on reservations in the Dakotas and Nebraska following the Dakota War. Warfare shaped much of day-to-day life for Ojibwe in Wisconsin and Minnesota in the nineteenth century, especially for Ojibwe communities on the fringe of Ojibwe territory such as Rice Lake. Nena'aangabi rose to prominence through military success and was killed on the battlefield. With the removal of the Dakota from Minnesota, the extreme violence that had shaped the community for much of the nineteenth century vanished instantly. Despite repeated attempts by American officials to end the conflict throughout the nineteenth century, it was only the complete expulsion of Dakota from Minnesota that finally ended Ojibwe-Dakota warfare. So intense was Ojibwe-Dakota warfare by the 1860s that when local whites in Menomonie tried unsuccessfully to get the Ojibwe of Rice Lake to enlist in the Civil

War the local newspaper remarked, "They, however, express a willingness to enlist if the Government would send them to fight the Sioux."[8]

The Ojibwe could now participate in hunting and other traditional labor activities down the Red Cedar River without fear of Dakota attack. These areas were richer in game than the heavily wooded areas around Rice Lake and points north, as the open prairie lands provided much more food sources near the ground for deer. In the heavily wooded areas further north, deer struggled to find food sources, as old-growth forest canopy choked out sunlight that would enable food sources close to the ground to grow. In addition, these areas received less pressure from Ojibwe and Dakota hunters, as it was dangerous for both groups to venture into the area for fear of violence. However, this boon for Ojibwe quality of life was quickly offset by white settlement in this area. The lack of Native people in this "buffer zone" facilitated the movement of whites into the area in the 1860s and 1870s.

THE STRUGGLE TO DEFINE THE LAC COURTE OREILLES RESERVATION, 1858–1873

With white settlement moving north, leaders of the Lac Courte Oreilles Band were anxious to have the boundaries of the reservation set. The treaty of 1854 called for the Lac Courte Oreilles Reservation to consist of three townships in an unspecified location. In 1858, Lac Courte Oreilles leaders selected three townships that encompassed rice-heavy Prairie Rice Lake, about fifteen miles south of the Rice Lake community. In his seminal work *History of the Ojibway People*, William Warren noted that the wild rice harvested at Prairie Rice Lake could feed two thousand people per season.[9] For Lac Courte Oreilles leaders, it made sense to locate there in order to secure a plentiful food supply, as the Lac Courte Oreilles Band had a total population of 858 people in 1857.[10] The selection of the reservation at this location illustrates the central role wild rice played for Ojibwe survival in Wisconsin. When considering where to locate their permanent home, the Lac Courte Oreilles Band selected Prairie Rice Lake, deeming it the most vital place to ensure Ojibwe survival into the future. While the document containing the selection of the reservation at Prairie Rice Lake did not contain any information about the deliberations of the leaders of the Lac Courte Oreilles Band, it is likely that Waabizheshi played a central role in the selection as his community was the closest to the area and no doubt utilized the area more than the rest of the Lac Courte Oreilles Band.[11]

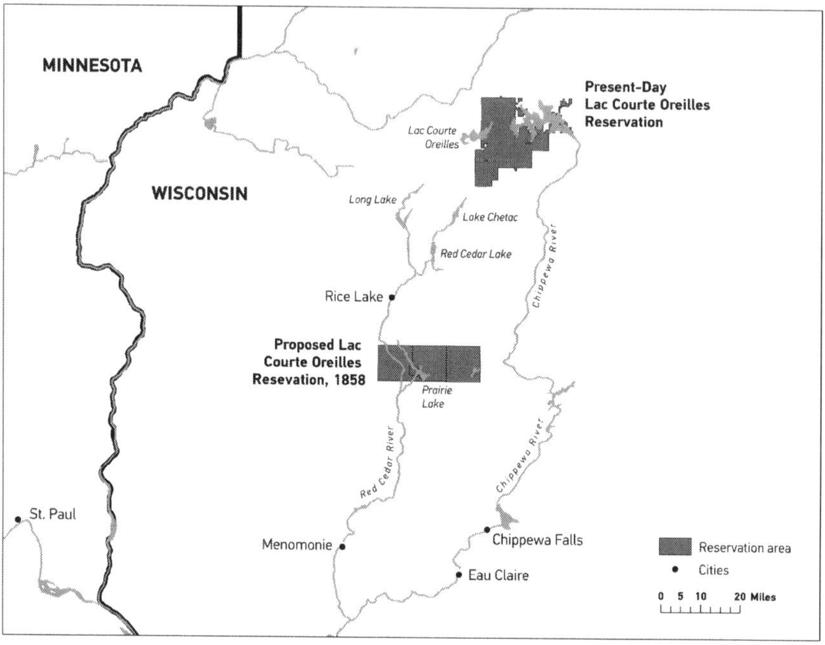

Proposed reservation, 1858.

After failing to secure the reservation at Prairie Rice Lake, Waabizheshi attempted to thwart federal efforts to remove and confine his community, an endeavor he succeeded at throughout his twenty-two years as leader of the Rice Lake community. In March 1859, Interior Secretary Jacob Thompson approved the plan of Commissioner of Indian Affairs Charles E. Mix to remove Ojibwe from Rice Lake to a reservation at Lac Courte Oreilles, including appointment of a special agent for removal.[12] In the summer of 1859, special agent Matthias Martin held a gathering of Lac Courte Oreilles Band leaders. While not actually engaged in removing all Ojibwe from Rice Lake, Martin's strategy for removal involved locating the reservation at Lac Courte Oreilles, and not Prairie Rice Lake. This was not an easy task for Martin: "I had great difficulty to induce the Indians to make their selection from the township designated by the Department their understanding being that they should have the lands about Red Cedar Lake, and Lake Chetek the place where many of them are located."[13] In fact, just as many people lived near Lac Courte Oreilles, but the rich hunting grounds south of Rice Lake and the rice of Prairie Rice Lake made even those at the flagship community at Lac Courte Oreilles willing to remove south if the reservation was there. In 1831, when discussing the Ojibwe population at Rice Lake, Henry Schoolcraft remarked: "it is evident that a very considerable additional population, particularly in men, resort there for the purpose of hunting a part of the year."[14] Unfortunately, no account of the deliberation survives, so we can never know exactly what the role of Waabizheshi was in resisting the effort to locate the reservation at Lac Courte Oreilles. However, the influence of Waabizheshi can be seen by the fact that a large number of Ojibwe lived under his leadership, and federal officials specifically targeted his community for removal.

On June 22, 1859, Lac Courte Oreilles Band leaders proposed their selections for the reservation under the direction of removal agent Matthias Martin. An oddly irregular shape, the proposed reservation encompassed the Ojibwe communities at Lac Courte Oreilles and Bakweyawaa and included several areas near these communities utilized for wild rice. Six of the seven leaders of communities considered part of the Lac Courte Oreilles Band signed the document. In addition, St. Croix Band ogimaa Ayaabens signed the document, as federal officials sought to remove his community, located on another Rice Lake directly west of Lac Courte Oreilles, to the new reservation, since no reservation for the St. Croix Band was provided in the 1854 treaty. A leader by the name of Waabizheshi signed the document, but it is highly likely that this refers to the long time ogimaa of the Ojibwe community on the Chippewa River. While we can never know for sure that Waabizheshi of Rice Lake did not sign the document, it is more likely that he abstained from signing the document and highly unlikely that Waabizheshi of the Chippewa River community would object since we know it was the Ojibwe at Rice Lake who were reluctant to remove and there is nothing in the historical record about the very small community on the Chippewa River objecting to the reservation being located at Lac Courte Oreilles.[15]

The selection of the reservation at Lac Courte Oreilles marks a watershed moment in the political career of Waabizheshi. There is nothing in surviving federal records about Waabizheshi following the failure to secure the reservation at Prairie Rice Lake. Not only did Waabizheshi not seek to extend his influence more broadly in Ojibwe politics like his father did, but after this point, Waabizheshi did not even seek influence within the Lac Courte Oreilles Band. Instead, the silence in the historical record suggests Waabizheshi's strategy was to focus solely on his own community at Rice Lake and thwart federal removal efforts. A central component of Waabizheshi's strategy for resisting removal to the reservation was forging relationships with the increasing number of white settlers in Rice Lake. Waabizheshi and his community sought an alternative to federal removal, striving to create a new, intercultural community at Rice Lake.

Despite the 1859 agreement to locate the reservation at Lac Courte Oreilles, it was still years before the reservation boundaries were set. In July 1863, the reservation was surveyed for the first time, four years after Lac Courte Oreilles Band leaders agreed to a preliminary reservation near Lac Courte Oreilles. Lake Superior Indian Agent Luther E. Webb instructed the surveyor: "You will consult with the Indians and as far as practicable carry out their wishes in the selection of the lands." After succeeding in preventing the reservation at Prairie Rice Lake, federal officials were open to whatever selections Lac Courte Oreilles Band leaders made in the area around Lac Courte Oreilles, which, unlike the areas around Prairie Rice Lake, was devoid of white settlers at the time. The surveyor reported, "I had council with Aw ke wen zee, head chief who claimed that he was appointed by the chiefs to represent them by designating to the surveyor the lands they wanted embraced in their Reservation in as much as they could not agree among themselves."[16] This reveals that selection of the reservation was highly contested. While there is no record of deliberations, it is likely that Waabizheshi played a role in the disagreement, given that the Ojibwe at Rice Lake were staunchly opposed to removal to Lac Courte Oreilles.

The selection of the reservation was an important moment in the political dynamic of the Lac Courte Oreilles Band. Unlike the treaty of 1837, where Nena'aangabi was the established influential leader and Akiwenzii the young upstart, by 1860, Akiwenzii was the senior chief. With the reservation located at Lac Courte Oreilles, Akiwenzii asserted a central leadership role. Federal officials came to Akiwenzii with decisions about internal affairs, such as the precise location of reservation boundaries. This bolstered Akiwenzii's influence, and he remained the most influential ogimaa in the Lac Courte Oreille Band right up until his death. In 1875 Ira Isham, who was married to Waabizheshi's niece, told the *Barron County Chronotype*, "Ac-quin-za of Court D'Orriella, became the leading chief, and he has been recognized by the bands for 10 years."[17] On the other hand, Waabizheshi withdrew from seeking influence within the band to focus on his own community at Rice Lake. This dynamic is reflected in the *Annual Report of the Commissioner of Indian Affairs for the Year 1863*, where Webb remarked, "the exterior boundary lines of the reservation have been defined and plainly marked, to the satisfaction of the Indians."[18]

Despite being marked, the 1863 survey was not formally declared as the boundaries by the federal government. In 1865 Lac Courte Oreilles Band leaders pressured the government to make the reservation boundaries official.[19] With little white settlement in the Lac Courte Oreilles area, federal officials were in no hurry to define reservation lands. However, Akiwenzii

Akiwenzii, 1884. (Courtesy Washburn Historical Society.)

was likely aware that settlement was pushing north and no doubt wanted the reservation defined when the settlers arrived. The boundaries were modified later that year, as swamplands were removed from the original selection and new lands were added to make up the difference.[20] Inactivity on the part of federal officials gave Waabizheshi opportunity to continue his opposition to locating the reservation at Lac Courte Oreilles throughout the 1860s. There is evidence that this led to friction between Waabizheshi and Akiwenzii. In 1868, new La Pointe Agent Asaph Whittlesey reported to the commissioner of Indian affairs that the annuity payment was executed without problems, "with the exception of jealousies existing among the chiefs of the Lac Courte Oreille bands, growing out of the unsettled condition of their reservation lines."[21] However, the reservation boundaries were still not declared by 1870 due to federal efforts to remove all Wisconsin Ojibwe to the Bad River Reservation on Lake Superior.

The 1854 treaty specified precise boundaries for the Bad River Reservation, while not specifying the boundaries for the Lac Courte Oreilles or Lac du Flambeau Reservations. Furthermore, the Bad River Reservation included six townships, compared to the three townships for Lac Courte Oreilles and Lac du Flambeau.[22] This suggests that treaty officials intended to concentrate all the Wisconsin Ojibwe on the larger Bad River Reservation in the future and not follow through with separate reservations for the Lac Courte Oreilles and Lac du Flambeau Bands. Immediately following the treaty, Treaty Commissioner Henry Gilbert wrote Commissioner of Indian Affairs George Manypenny about the Bad River Reservation, "I presume it will ultimately be the home of most of the Chippewas residing in that state."[23] The concentration of Wisconsin Ojibwe on one or two reservations was first mentioned by La Pointe Agent Luther Webb in 1863, who noted that the reservations on Lake Superior were better suited to agriculture and would provide a more sustainable living as game in the interior was declining. However, Webb argued, "In my judgment, the voluntary movement of these Indians to the reservations on the lake will be a work of time."[24]

Francis McElroy first proposed the concentration of Wisconsin Ojibwe at Bad River in 1864, noting the presence of educational facilities and agricultural instruction already on the reservation. McElroy argued that concentrating the Wisconsin Ojibwe (along with the Fond du Lac Band in Minnesota) on one large reservation would be the most efficient way to achieve assimilation of all the Wisconsin Ojibwe.[25] A few months later, Commissioner of Indian Affairs William P. Dole officially recommended removing the interior Ojibwe to the lake:

> the cost to the Indians of traveling to and from the agency at the annual payments is often nearly as much as the amount received. The best policy to be pursued would seem to be the abandonment, as soon as practicable, of these small reservations, and concentration of the Indians upon larger ones. The land this abandoned would furnish, on being sold, a considerable fund for the benefit of the Indians.[26]

Ojibwe leaders responded to this by journeying to Washington to meet with President Abraham Lincoln. Included in the delegation were representatives from two of the three reservations that federal officials sought to dispose: Naagaanab, a Fond du Lac ogimaa, and Aamoons, a Lac du Flambeau ogimaa, were joined by three ogimaag from Bad River.[27]

As a result of the proposed removal to Bad River, the group hastily left for Washington in January 1865, before Akiwenzii could join them. Eerily echoing his first encounter with federal officials in the treaty of 1837 when Minnesota Ojibwe leaders negotiated the sale of Lac Courte Oreilles lands before Akiwenzii even arrived, the leader fired off a letter to the commissioner of Indian affairs: "I wish the Commissioner of Indian Affairs not to make any arrangement or purchase that in any way effects my rights as chief of the Lake Courterille Band in Chippewa County as I wish to be present at the time of the sale and wish the whole matter be deferred until all the chiefs are present."[28] Waabizheshi was not present with the group, despite the fact that he led the most populous community of the Lac Courte Oreilles Band. Following the failure of the Lac Courte Oreilles to secure the reservation at Prairie Rice Lake, Waabizheshi's strategy for resisting removal was solely building relationships with local whites and not engaging with federal officials. As a result, there is not one single letter in the federal archives authored by Waabizheshi, whereas the historical record contains dozens from Akiwenzii. In fact, Akiwenzii signed his letter as "chief of the Corterille Bands residing on the Reservation."[29] This reflects the growing distance between Waabizheshi's community and the communities at Lac Courte Oreilles and Bakweyawaa. This separation would only increase in the coming years, as the communities on the reservation accommodated federal initiatives whereas Waabizheshi's community resisted federal authority. Furthermore, with his refusal to participate in the 1865 delegation, Waabizheshi did not join other Lake Superior Ojibwe leaders in broader strategies of resistance that characterized Nena'aangabi's leadership.

Akiwenzii caught up to the main group, and they met with President Lincoln. The group was successful in stalling removal to Bad River and in getting their next annuity paid in gold coin instead of paper currency.[30] The leaders also presented Lincoln with a bilingual petition, written by Joseph Gurnoe, a government official of mixed descent, detailing all the money the Ojibwe were due under prior treaties.[31] The success of the Washington delegation was fleeting, however, and federal officials persisted in their goal to remove the Wisconsin Ojibwe to Bad River. The very next year, new Commissioner of Indian Affairs Dennis Cooley argued: "Scattered as these bands of Chippewa are, it is difficult to do anything effectual for them in the way of education. Were they concentrated upon a single reservation, we might hope to do them some good."[32] In 1869, La Pointe Agent Whittlesey argued that annuities from the treaties would soon expire and that the Ojibwe would be more likely to agree to selling the reservations and removing to the lake.[33] Again in 1870, Superior Indian Agent John Knight (the La Pointe agency was temporarily relocated to Superior) wrote the commissioner of Indian affairs: "I cannot too earnestly urge upon you the great necessity of concentrating these Indians upon one reservation."[34]

In early 1872, new La Pointe Agent Selden Clark proposed all the Wisconsin Ojibwe remove to Bad River. At the time there were 3,500 Ojibwe in Wisconsin, and Clark argued, "The reservation of so much land for the comparatively small number of Indians is inconsistent with the rapid increase of the white population and the multiplication of railroads." Common to most justifications for removal, the agent noted that Lac Courte Oreilles and Lac du Flambeau were remote areas that made it difficult to enforce federal liquor laws banning sale of alcohol to Indians. Likewise, Clark argued that removal was necessary in order to Christianize the Ojibwe. Clark noted that removal would include the St. Croix Ojibwe, who did not secure a reservation in the 1854 treaty. Clark argued that timing was critical, as 1875 was the year of their last annuity, and the agent worried that greater poverty would result. Clark noted that both reservations were in the area of rich pinelands. The agent suggested the reservation lands be sold and the proceeds kept in an account managed by the federal government, the interest of which would fund education for the Ojibwe.[35] It is clear that Clark intended the sale to be before the harvesting of timber, and not after the lands had been cutover so the Ojibwe could reap the rewards of their timber profits.

After nine years and a cast of rotating bureaucrats, it was Clark's arguments that finally caused Congress to act. On May 29, 1872, the removal of the Lac Courte Oreilles, Lac du Flambeau, and Fond du Lac Ojibwe to Bad River was signed into law as part of the appropriation bill.[36] However, in June Secretary of the Interior Columbus Delano instructed Commissioner of Indian Affairs Francis A. Walker to secure the consent of each Ojibwe band prior to beginning removal.[37] The Lac Courte Oreilles flatly refused their consent.[38] This pushed the federal government to formally declare the boundaries of the Lac Courte Oreilles Reservation on March 1, 1873 based on the 1859 selections and modifications made in 1865.[39] This effectively ended the threat of removal to Bad River. Wisconsin Ojibwe were able to successfully resist removal to one large reservation at a time when Ojibwe in central Minnesota were fighting a very similar battle to avoid removal to the White Earth Reservation despite earlier treaties calling for reservations within the territory of the Minnesota bands. However, the Minnesota Ojibwe were not nearly as successful. The 1855 Treaty of Washington called for reservations at Mille Lacs, Rabbit Lake, Gull Lake, and Sandy Lake, yet today only the Mille Lacs Reservation remains, as the rest of these bands were removed to the White Earth Reservation in the late nineteenth century.[40]

While the Lac Courte Oreilles Band successfully resisted removal to Bad River, the band faced pressure to remove to and be contained on the reservation for the rest of the nineteenth century. The reservation boundaries only encompassed the communities at Lac Courte Oreilles and Bakweyawaa. In addition to Waabizheshi's community at Rice Lake, communities outside the reservation included Lake Chetac and Pacwawong Lake on the Namekagon River. Furthermore, even the two communities located within the reservation boundaries were impacted by federal efforts to contain the Ojibwe on the reservation. Ojibwe people rarely confined themselves to the village site. Seasonal labor activities such as hunting required large territory.

Even in the summer, Ojibwe people utilized a wide area for activities such as harvest of berries.[41]

Prior to the establishment of the reservation, the only federal officials were stationed at La Pointe, over 120 miles from Manoominikaan. Establishment of the Lac Courte Oreilles Reservation brought federal officials closer to the Ojibwe at Rice Lake. In accordance with federal assimilation policies of the time, the Bureau of Indian Affairs stationed an official on every reservation to teach Native people about agriculture and accordingly called the "farmer." At Lac Courte Oreilles and other isolated reservations within a larger agency, the farmer oversaw all federal directives on the reservation. One of the first acts of farmer Joseph Holt in 1873 was building Akiwenzii a house.[42] Akiwenzii's house was an important statement of federal goals of assimilation in the area. For federal officials, Ojibwe people belonged on the reservation. The relationship established between the farmer and Akiwenzii's community at Lac Courte Oreilles (and to a lesser extent the communities at Bakweyawaa) would distinguish these communities from those off the reservation, especially Manoominikaan. Increasingly, federal officials thought of the on-reservation Ojibwe as the "good Indians" and those stubbornly refusing to remove to the reservation, such as Waabizheshi and his community, as the "problem Indians."

The establishment of the reservation brought not just a farmer to Lac Courte Oreilles, but also a day school, opened in July 1873. One hundred ten students attended the school on and off the first school year, attendance being spotty as many students joined their families throughout the year for seasonal labor, something federal officials battled until the opening of the Hayward Indian School in 1901, which was a boarding school.[43] Nevertheless, the school represented yet another federal presence in the region. Despite this, establishment of the reservation did not spur removal of Ojibwe communities to the reservation. Instead, Lac Courte Oreilles Band Ojibwe would continue to remain in traditional areas to practice traditional labor activities for at least another two decades. Furthermore, Ojibwe participation in wage labor in the timber industry off-reservation acted to undermine the efforts to contain Ojibwe on the reservation.

AMERICAN COLONIALISM AND THE TIMBER INDUSTRY

In 1875, the last annuity payment from treaties was issued. This economic pinch on Ojibwe families was somewhat alleviated by economic opportunities in logging camps off-reservation. However, the short-term economic opportunities for work in timber operations were offset by the devastation the timber industry caused to wild rice throughout the ceded territory. The timber industry drove American expansion in the region. For the Ojibwe community at Rice Lake, the timber industry represented how Native people experienced American colonialism as a complex and contradictory process where opportunity and exploitation were inextricably linked.

Beginning in the 1860s, logging of ceded territory moved rapidly northward year by year. The production of lumber mills in Chippewa Falls exploded from 60 million board feet in 1860 to 436 million board feet in 1871.[44] The territory of the Lac Courte Oreilles Band is defined by the Chippewa River valley as all of the communities are either on the Chippewa River or on a waterway that empties into the Chippewa River: the outlet to Lac Courte Oreilles is the Couderay River, which joins with the Chippewa a few miles south of the reservation, and both Lake Chetac and Rice Lake are part of the Red Cedar River, which empties into the Chippewa River south of Chippewa Falls.

The treaty of 1837 that Nena'aangabi refused to sign was pivotal in American history. While the treaty brought few settlers in the mid-nineteenth century, America was literally built on the treaty, as Wisconsin white pine supplied new home and business construction on both the east and west coasts. Historian William Cronen saw the harvest of old-growth white pine in Wisconsin, Michigan, and Minnesota as critical to the development of the West: "Americans who contemplated the future of the Great West at midcentury understood that settling the western prairies meant cutting the northern forests." White pine was central to this; as Cronen put it, "they more than any other tree were lords of the north country."[45] White pine is the ideal wood for building construction, as it is light and easy to work with. Even more importantly, it easily floated down the many rivers of northern Wisconsin for processing in sawmills downstream. This was crucial in decades prior to railroads. While all Ojibwe lands in Wisconsin, Michigan, and Minnesota were rich with timber, the forests in the Chippewa River valley were particularly rich in white pine. The Chippewa River valley alone contained one-sixth of the white pine west of the Appalachians. Beginning near Chippewa Falls, logging operations moved north up the Chippewa River, clear-cutting forests and opening land up for white settlers to begin the enormous task of clearing cutover stump land for farms. While eventually all the old-growth white pine was cut, Wisconsin still led the nation in white pine production as late as 1900.[46]

An important moment in the history of Rice Lake occurred in 1853 when the Knapp, Stout Company was founded in Menomonie, sixty miles downstream on the Red Cedar River. The Knapp, Stout Company came into existence through the partnership of two small, struggling mills south of Menomonie, one owned by John Knapp and the other by Andrew Tainter. Lumber was processed at mills in Wisconsin, and the finished lumber was shipped by boat down the Mississippi to Dubuque, Iowa, where partner Henry Stout was in charge of distribution of the firm's products. Within a few years of its founding, the corporation became a juggernaut, amassing a fortune in Wisconsin's pine forests. Within a decade it was the largest lumber corporation in the state.[47] The Knapp, Stout Company had an important relationship with the Ojibwe at Manoominikaan. Waabizheshi, Ininiins, Giishkitawag, and dozens of other Ojibwe men were employed in Knapp, Stout Company lumber camps. Knapp, Stout Company officials such as Andrew Tainter, John Quaderer, James Bracklin, and Samuel Barker married and had children with Ojibwe women. Perhaps most significantly, however, were the dozens of dams the company built, including on Rice Lake and Prairie Rice Lake.

The site for the city of Rice Lake was logged in the 1860s. Most devastating for Ojibwe people, however, was the building of a dam on Rice Lake in 1864, which destroyed nearly all of the rice on the lake by significantly raising the water level. Today there is no rice in Rice Lake. This event, more than any other, would hinder the ability of the Ojibwe community at Rice Lake to support itself and avoid removal to the reservation. White settlement continued with the construction of a sawmill in 1871 and labor needed for the processing of timber at Rice Lake. The *Barron County* (later *Rice Lake*) *Chronotype* published its first edition on September 9, 1874, and the city of Rice Lake was founded in 1875.[48]

While clear-cutting of old-growth forest may seem horrendous to us today, logging actually enhanced economic livelihood for some Ojibwe families. Logging provided income for Ojibwe men in the harsh winter months, a time of the year when Ojibwe people struggled to survive. Furthermore, deer populations exploded in the ceded territory in the wake of clear-cutting, as the cutover provided much more food on the ground for deer in the form of forest litter from logging and plant growth on the forest floor that was no longer blocked out by the canopy of massive old-growth trees. According to wildlife biologist Robert Willging:

> The wholesale and rapid conversion of the mature northern forest into a vast area of "cutover"—a mess of stumps and slash prone to wildfire—had a great impact on whitetail numbers. As each new tract of big woods was logged and

> the trees carted off to the mills, new, young growth—shrubs, forbs, and young, succulent tree growth—replaced the big trees. Ironically the devastation of the pineries greatly improved deer habitat.[49]

Ojibwe people no longer had to travel long distances down the Red Cedar or Chippewa Rivers to more open areas to find deer.

Prior to clear-cutting, the Ojibwe modified the environment through controlled burns in order to increase deer habitat. On his trip though northwest Wisconsin in 1831, Henry Schoolcraft noted the presence of controlled burns on the Namekagon River:

> The country as we descend assumes more the appearance of upland prairie, from repeated burnings of the forest. The effect is, nearly all the small trees have been consumed, and grass has taken their place. One result of this is, the deer are drawn up from the more open parts of the Mississippi, to follow the advance of the prairie and open lands towards Lake Superior.[50]

When Schoolcraft reached the portage between the Namekagon River and Lac Courte Oreilles the agent noted: "It is open as far as the eye can reach."[51] The area around Lac Courte Oreilles was much more wooded than the area around Manoominikaan. These dense woods had less deer habitat in them, causing the Ojibwe to set controlled burns in the area. When Schoolcraft traveled to Lac Courte Oreilles in 1831, he noted that the area "had a proportion of prairie or burnt land, caused by the ravages of fire."[52]

Fire was also a useful tool for the creation of blueberry habitat. In the Bad River Works Progress Administration (WPA) historical project, Marie Livingston described an area near Gordon, Wisconsin: "My father had come across a patch of berries which was approximately one mile square. It had originally been part of a Jack Pine forest through which a raging fire had swept through two years previous and made it a real Eldorado for berry seekers."[53] This was the case throughout Ojibwe territory. Also in the Bad River WPA historical project, Florenia Denomie wrote about blueberry picking near the Keweenaw Peninsula in Michigan: "The berries were found on a 'burning' about two years old, near a swamp. What he pocketed probably constituted the first crop of 'burnt-over' land."[54]

However, despite the increase in deer and blueberries in Ojibwe country, the destruction of rice beds through the creation of dams by the timber industry posed an unprecedented threat to Ojibwe sovereignty and quality of life. Dams were central to timber operations prior to railroads, as logs were transported down rivers to sawmills in Chippewa Falls, Menomonie, and after 1871, Rice Lake. Logs were moved to lakes by horses and oxen where they were cached over the winter until spring thaws moved the logs downstream to the sawmill. Dams were built on most lakes that were connected to rivers to raise water levels so that the lake could hold more logs.[55] The use of rivers to transport logs meant that all of the lakes that were attached to the Red Cedar River, including Rice Lake and Prairie Rice Lake, were flooded by timber operations to move logs down the Red Cedar to Menomonie.

Dams devastated rice crops. In the 1864 bilingual petition, Akiwenzii and the other Ojibwe leaders explained that, at the council for the treaty of 1837, Ojibwe leaders were explicit that timber harvests should not interfere with traditional Ojibwe labor, of which ricing was central: "ji-nishiwanaajitoosiwan maandan manoomin"; "That you may not destroy the rice in working the timber."[56] In 1921, Lac Courte Oreilles tribal member Jim Bennet testified about the devastating impact the flooding from dams has on wild rice:

> It is very tender at that time, the roots are tender, and if there is a sudden rise of water it pulls out the rice straws from the bottom or else after the flood goes down it is so weak that it falls over. Any disturbance of high water on the rice at certain periods when it is tender, before it is ripe, has usually the effect of either the roots pulling loose or the rice falling over.[57]

While Bennet's testimony was in a hearing about the building of a dam on the Chippewa River that created the Chippewa Flowage in 1923 and destroyed wild rice beds on the reservation, the destruction of wild rice that Bennet described was the same in the nineteenth century.

By the summer of 1864, the Ojibwe were very nervous about the increasing dams on the Red Cedar. Menomonie's weekly newspaper, the *Dunn County Lumberman*, reported:

> It is said that the Indians along the Red Cedar and adjacent streams, are very indignant against the dams that have been built to facilitate the bringing out the logs. They represent that the high water will prevent them from gathering their annual supply of wild rice, and they threaten to make a "fuss" if they cannot have an opportunity to gather their rice. They say they may as well be killed in a row as to die next winter from want of rice.[58]

These fears proved correct that fall when the Knapp, Stout Company built a dam on Rice Lake. Despite the devastating blow to Ojibwe survival that the dam at Rice Lake posed, surviving historical evidence suggests that Waabizheshi and the Ojibwe at Rice Lake pursued a pragmatic, nonviolent approach. Writing in 1922, Newton S. Gordon noted in his *History of Barron County*, "When the dam was built at Rice Lake, late in the sixties, raising the water and flooding the rice fields, the Indians were much incensed, and for awhile danger was threatened, but the excitement in time died down."[59] A more detailed account came from early Rice Lake settler Horace Drake, who remembered in 1928, "the Indians were furious and threatened to kill the settlers here and tear out the dam. The Indians from a large territory gathered in the neighborhood and the settlers in the vicinity were terrified."[60]

In order to avoid violence, the Knapp, Stout Company was forced to enter into a treaty with the Ojibwe. Drake did not recall the exact terms of the treaty, but it included food provisions such as flour and pork to make up for the rice that was destroyed. The fact that the Knapp, Stout Company had to enter into a treaty with the Ojibwe reveals the degree of sovereignty the Ojibwe exercised at this particular moment. According to the text of the treaty of 1837, the Ojibwe ceded Rice Lake. However, twenty-seven years later, American claim of ownership on the area was mere rhetoric. The treaty that Drake claimed the Knapp, Stout Company made with the Ojibwe does not survive, and no other references to the treaty exist.[61] The treaty was not mentioned in an account left by Knapp, Stout Company superintendent James Bracklin. Bracklin, Rice Lake's first mayor, was married to Waabizheshi's sister Aazhaweyaa in the 1860s, and the couple had three children. According to Bracklin, "we had consulted with the old Chief several times and tried to settle matters with him, but without coming to any understanding that was satisfactory to him."[62] In this account, taken down shortly before Bracklin's death in 1900, Bracklin did not identify the "old Chief" as Waabizheshi or mention his marriage to Waabizheshi's sister. Bracklin's family relationship to Waabizheshi may have been the reason the Ojibwe at Rice Lake did not commit violence when the rice in Rice Lake was flooded. Bracklin linked the events to the disappearance of two Stillwater lumbermen while on an expedition near Balsam Lake, Wisconsin, in June 1864. Over the summer of 1864, searchers looked for the men in vain. By late August hundreds of Ojibwe from many bands were camped at Rice Lake and Prairie Rice Lake for ricing. It was then that the "old Chetek Chief," presumably Waabizheshi, heard a rumor that troops were coming up the Red Cedar from Menomonie to investigate the matter.

Motivated by the rumor of the impending troops, Waabizheshi requested that Bracklin and Samuel Barker, a trader who operated a store just north of Rice Lake at a logging camp named Louseburg, meet him at Prairie Rice Lake. According to Bracklin, "the Chief thought a great deal of Barker." Meeting near Prairie Rice Lake "out in the jack pines in a secluded place," Waabizheshi confirmed Bracklin's suspicion that two Ojibwe men murdered the lumbermen. Waabizheshi claimed that the murders were motivated by money, as one of the victims was carrying $1,500 on his person. To put this amount of money in the perspective of its value in the nineteenth century, the last annuity payment the Lac Courte Oreilles Band received in 1874 was $1,032 for the entire band of 1,074 people. Waabizheshi called the meeting with Bracklin and Barker because, "as his band did not have anything to do with this murder he wanted us to protect his band and tell the commander of the troops that they were good Indians." No doubt with the events of the Dakota War just two years prior in mind, the rumor about the troops motivated Waabizheshi to avoid violence in order to protect his community. Waabizheshi's strategy to accomplish these ends was to draw on his apparently good relationship with Barker, someone who had the potential to articulate Ojibwe interests to outsiders. This would have been sound diplomacy, except for the fact that Bracklin was purposefully lying to the Ojibwe: there were no troops coming. Bracklin wrote, "We knew that there were no troops coming, and that there was no danger in that direction to the old Chief, but told him that we would look after his interests."[63]

Shortly after Bracklin and Barker's meeting with Waabizheshi, one of the murderers showed up at Louseburg. According to Bracklin, there were seventy-five to one hundred Ojibwe camped at Louseburg. Barker sent for Bracklin, and the pair decided to capture the man themselves instead of waiting for backup from Chetek. Barker lured the murderer into his store, and when the man realized he was about to be captured, he lunged for the door. Barker grabbed him by the wrist, and then Bracklin grabbed the man by the hair and pulled him back into the store. Then some of the Ojibwe camped there broke the door down, grabbed the man by the legs, and essentially played tug-of-war with Bracklin and Barker. This went on for an hour. By the end of it, the man himself was injured and unable to escape on his own. Bracklin and Barker were aided by Barker's size. At six foot, he was described by Bracklin as "a giant in strength, and brave as a lion."[64] Having reached an impasse, the Ojibwe there sent for reinforcements from the Yellow River of the St. Croix Band. Given that the murder occurred near Balsam Lake (which is still today the home of a St. Croix Band community) and Waabizheshi's assertion that the murderers were not associated with his community, it is likely that the man was from the St. Croix Band.

In any case, when the Ojibwe from the Yellow River arrived, they demanded the release of the prisoner. Bracklin and Barker refused, saying he would be sent to Stillwater for trial. They then snuck out a messenger to go to Menomonie for troops. The messenger was shot at by the Ojibwe but made his escape. The rest of the day was a tense standoff. However, rumors of as many as twenty-five wagons of troops moving north circulated among the Ojibwe at Louseburg. With troops apparently on the way, the Ojibwe smuggled a gun to the murderer. After visiting his mother and sister (a moment Bracklin characterized as "very touching"), the prisoner sang a death song and then shot himself around nine that evening. The next day Bracklin met the troops at Rice Lake: "The Indians there wanted protection from the army, but the army came and there were only seventeen men, and so we sat around and visited and talked the matter over that night and they went back."[65]

Major violence was avoided that day at Rice Lake through the diplomacy of Waabizheshi. Writing decades later, Bracklin, now the mayor of Rice Lake, saw it as a watershed moment: "I tell you that after we got started in that scrape we had to stay in it, or else there would have been no living in that part of the country. If they had got that Indian away from us, we could not have stayed there."[66] The murder of the two Stillwater lumbermen by St. Croix Ojibwe is important for understanding why Waabizheshi did not lead the community to war when Rice Lake was flooded. The threat of troops motivated Waabizheshi to use diplomacy over violence. A dam was built on Prairie Rice Lake shortly thereafter. Even less is known about the events surrounding this event or why the Ojibwe did not rise to violence to prevent the dam. The heightened water levels destroyed nearly all of the rice. The lake that William Warren claimed could feed two thousand people in the nineteenth century is now called Prairie Lake, as white settlers renamed the lake since there was no rice there anymore.

Armed resistance would have been a viable option for the Ojibwe in the 1860s. Nena'aangabi's success as a leader was built on military achievement: the growth and increased importance of the community and its leader were sustained only by the ability to defend it. In 1831, Henry Schoolcraft wrote: "I found at Rice Lake a band of Chippewas, most of them young men, having a prompt and martial air, encamped in a very compact form, and prepared, at a moment's notice, for action."[67] Only two years after the Dakota were removed from Minnesota, the Ojibwe at Rice Lake were effective and experienced warriors. In the 1860s the white population of Rice Lake was still less than the two hundred Ojibwe in the immediate area, let alone the one thousand more of the Lac Courte Oreilles Band. Furthermore, most of the whites at Rice Lake in the 1860s were single laborers without families or an individual economic stake in the area, such as a farm. Despite this, Waabizheshi and the community saw exchange as a better alternative to violence as a strategy for remaining at Rice Lake.

It cannot be overstated how devastating the flooding of rice beds was to Ojibwe livelihood. Wild rice was the main food source for Native people in the region as it could be stored throughout the harsh winter months without spoiling. For the Ojibwe community at Rice Lake it was the destruction of rice beds at Rice Lake and Prairie Rice Lake by timber corporations that most weakened the community by threatening the very survival of its members. Likewise, a notable aspect of the treaty that Drake claimed was made by the Knapp, Stout Company was the payment of pork and flour in lieu of the wild rice that the Ojibwe lost. The direct substitution of pork and flour for wild rice is another way colonialism impacted the Ojibwe by introducing cheap, unhealthy food to Ojibwe communities instead of healthier, traditional foods. Less healthy goods such as pork and flour were common staples of government commodities to the present day. The destruction of wild rice illustrates how American colonialism in the nineteenth century continues to impact Ojibwe communities today as we struggle with high rates of diabetes and other health problems.

TRADITIONAL LABOR AND CLIMATE

In the midst of dramatic ecological transformations due to logging, the Ojibwe at Rice Lake also had to contend with unusual climatic events. Extreme climate is a fact of life in northern Wisconsin, but extreme weather in the 1870s and 1880s illustrated how American colonialism impacted everyday life for Ojibwe families in indirect and unintended ways. Unstable climate further limited wild rice production immediately following the destruction of rice stands on Rice Lake and Prairie Rice Lake by dam building, deepening Ojibwe poverty and dependence on outside sources of income. In 1870, Superior Indian Agent John Knight reported to the commissioner of Indian affairs, "Owing to the heavy cold rains of the summer and fall of 1869 the rice was destroyed, and has not appeared in quantities heretofore found."[68] Later, the strongest El Niño of the nineteenth century occurred during the late 1870s, resulting in extremely mild winters throughout the western Great Lakes, the warmest occurring in 1877–78. During this winter, Minneapolis (one hundred miles away, the nearest location to Rice Lake with surviving climate records) recorded high temperatures in the fifties during the week of Christmas, farmers in southern Minnesota began planting in February, and lakes in southern Minnesota did not freeze over.[69] Even in far northern Minnesota the climate was abnormally mild. In January, La Pointe Agent Isaac Mahan was frustrated at the inability to get annuity goods to the Bois Forte Band by sled due to the complete lack of snow on the ground.[70]

The impact of abnormally warm weather on Ojibwe labor activities was mixed. While mild temperatures may have made life during the winter more bearable, extreme climate variations can be devastating to yields of Ojibwe mainstays. Maple sugar is vulnerable to temperature change, as sustained periods of high temperatures just above freezing during the day results in a high yield. Likewise, if spring comes too early, and temperatures get too warm right away, the effect on maple sugar production is devastating, as the sap only runs for a few days and then quits.[71] Wild rice is a somewhat different story, as there are many variables that can make a good or bad rice crop. Aside from temperature fluctuations, extremes in precipitation devastate rice yields. Furthermore, there is variance by body of water: a good year on one lake does not necessarily mean a good year on another.[72]

The mixed impact of the mild El Niño weather was apparent in a July 1877 account of the Ojibwe in the *Barron County Chronotype*:

> From recent information we learn that the Indians on the Lac Court de O'Reilles reserve are in rather a pitiful plight many of them being on the verge of starvation. Last year their wild rice crop was a total failure, and they were only able to get half a crop of sugar. This supply gave out early in the spring and they were obliged to depend entirely on hunting and fishing for their subsistence. This year they have had another very poor sugar season, many families securing but 125 pounds who in a good season put up 500 pounds. During the month of June and this far in July the weather has been so stormy on the reserve, that for days at a time they were unable to either hunt or fish. . . . Some of the Indians have a little money, but the distance that would have to be traveled to obtain food is so great that their families would starve while they were gone. This year they have the promise of a very large wild rice crop, and the rice will be ripe one month earlier than was ever known to the oldest Indian.[73]

This account provides a detailed description of the impact of mild El Niño conditions on maple sugar and rice yields. Many whites tended to view Ojibwe labor activities as primitive and inferior to white labor activities, in particular agriculture. This resulted in many descriptions of Ojibwe labor that cited fluctuations in seasonal yield as proof that Ojibwe people needed to give up traditional labor and adopt agriculture. However, this quote is somewhat more balanced in its assessment of the impact of the El Niño on Ojibwe seasonal yield. Warm weather clearly devastated maple sugar yields in northwest Wisconsin in 1876 and 1877. It is not clear what impact the El Niño had on the failure of the wild rice crop in 1876. It may have been abnormal precipitation during that summer that led to the wild rice failure. However, in 1877, the mild winter led to the earliest rice crop in memory.

Just a few years later, the climatic pendulum swung the other way. The winter of 1880–81 was known as the "Long Winter" in the upper Midwest, immortalized in Laura Ingalls Wilder's book of that name detailing the struggles her family faced that winter while living in eastern South Dakota.[74] During the "Long Winter" there was heavy snowfall recorded at St. Paul every month from October to April.[75] The presence of snowfall for such an extended period indicates freezing temperatures to maintain that snowfall, meaning that the above-freezing conditions needed to begin maple sap runs would have occurred in April at the earliest. Spring spearing of spawning walleyes would have been delayed as well, as walleyes spawn when the ice has gone off lakes, a process that takes many days of above-freezing weather. Wild rice harvest was likely impacted as well. The result of such a long winter in all these labor activities was likely reduced yields, as all of these staples require sustained periods of gradual warming for productive harvest. Abrupt warming from colder than normal weather to typical seasonal temperatures often results in reduced yields. For example, when spring temperatures get too warm too quickly, walleye spawns only last a few nights and tend to occur in all places at the same time, making the spring spearing season short and yields greatly reduced.

While the Ojibwe had always dealt with variations in climate, the weather of the 1870s and 1880s was extreme and could not have occurred at a worse time as it coincided with man-made ecological devastation such as the destruction of rice beds at Rice Lake and Prairie Rice Lake. At the same time, white settlers were eager to contain the Ojibwe on the reservation. This is an important aspect of colonialism to bear in mind. From time to time life is more difficult due to things like climate and other factors completely outside of our control. Colonialism exacerbates these events. For the Ojibwe at Rice Lake, colonialism deepened the devastation caused by extremes in climate.

However, the Ojibwe remained at Rice Lake throughout the 1870s and 1880s despite these hardships. During this time, the Ojibwe village site at Rice Lake was at Howard's Point on the west side of the lake, where archeological excavations revealed gardens just to the north. In 1879 and 1880, residents of the city of Rice Lake were uneasy when large *Midewiwin* ceremonies drew hundreds of Ojibwe from across the region.[76] Ricing continued in areas less affected by dam construction, such as Little Rice Lake south of Rice Lake. At Prairie Rice Lake, some rice remained, and archeological excavations unearthed a rice camp on the east side of the lake that white settlers claimed was used by the Ojibwe after 1870.[77] These many sites provide evidence that for Ojibwe people, the community was not just one fixed location of a village site but encompassed a very large area. Traditional labor required large areas to be utilized, something that clashed with increasing white farms.

While the increasing presence of white settlers created tensions, it also meant new markets for surplus goods. The Ojibwe of Rice Lake gathered blueberries at Louseburg on the Red Cedar River, a few miles downstream from Rice Lake. Early Rice Lake settler J. A. H. Johnson remembered: "each day during the berry season, birchbark canoes could be seen, headed downstream loaded with blueberries going to market to Menomonie and other down-river points and other canoes headed up stream with articles of trade such as ammunition, calico, beads, etc."[78] By participating in trading relationships with whites, the Ojibwe sought to maintain their presence at Rice Lake, rooted in centuries of exchange with the French and British.

OJIBWE MEN IN THE TIMBER INDUSTRY

While the Ojibwe at Rice Lake struggled to continue to practice traditional labor in the area, Ojibwe men worked as wage laborers in timber operations, alleviating seasonal poverty during the harsh winter months. The Ojibwe were crucial to logging operations. In the 1940s, Lac Courte Oreilles Ojibwe Prosper Guibord recounted his life in the logging camps to anthropologist Robert Ritzenthaler and claimed, "Indians were the best loggers—caught on to the job easily & very seldom got hurt."[79] Dan Morrison echoed this in the Bad River WPA historical project: "In the logging days, all work requiring skill and experience was filled by Indians."[80] Most Ojibwe men in the Rice Lake community participated in timber operations. According to early Rice Lake settler Paul Kirkendall, Knapp, Stout Company typically employed about five Ojibwe men in each camp.[81] While early logging camps consisted of about a dozen men, by the 1880s camps were made up of at least sixty men.[82] In Waabizheshi's own family, men were active in the timber industry. The ogimaa's brother Ininiins was working for Knapp, Stout Company in 1877 when he heard of Waabizheshi's death, and his other brother Giishkitawag was working at an off-reservation lumber camp prior to his 1894 death.[83] Participation in the lumber industry was one of the ways Ojibwe people began to acquire English names, as whites in charge of logging camps were unable to pronounce Ojibwe names. Sometimes, these were translations of Ojibwe names, other times not.[84] Ininiins was referred to as John White and Giishkitawag became known as Joe White. However, the Ojibwe were slow to use English names. In an 1878 census of all the Lake Superior Ojibwe, a column was provided for English names. Neither Ininiins's nor Giishkitawag's English names appeared.[85]

The participation of Ojibwe men in the timber industry and the income they provided, however meager, changed gender dynamics in Ojibwe communities. The traditional labor activities that were most threatened by ecological transformation and climate extremes during this time, maple sugaring and wild ricing, were solely the work of women. The participation of Ojibwe men in the timber industry came at a critical moment that gave new importance to male labor. Similar dynamics occurred in Ojibwe communities during the eighteenth century, when the fur trade and men's role in trapping transformed male labor.[86] The legacy of Ojibwe participation in the timber industry remained even after old-growth forests were long gone. Historian Brenda Child describes how during the Depression men quickly began participating in ricing, maple sugaring, and other forms of traditional labor that were previously only done by large collectives of women.[87] Today, ricing is mostly a male activity. While these changes were likely a direct result of male participation in Depression-era federal work programs, the lineage of this shift dates back to men's participation in the timber industry in the late nineteenth century.

While providing Ojibwe families with income during lean winter months, work in the timber industry was dangerous and provided little pay. Paul Kirkendall's description of white laborers is useful, as it illustrates how the timber industry did not provide sustaining employment. Describing the time after the winter season, Kirkendall noted: "In Rice Lake many, many of them staggered around the streets for several days and left for home broke."[88] Furthermore, while local newspapers portrayed drunkenness as exclusively a problem of the Ojibwe community, Kirkendall's account suggests that the culture of Rice Lake and of work in the timber industry centered on single men in physically demanding jobs that paid very little. Both Ojibwe and white laborers were impacted by these harsh conditions.

Ojibwe men were forced to work in mostly white logging crews and be away from their families for long periods of time. Lac du Flambeau Ojibwe Tom Badger described labor in the winter:

> The same winter I went to work in a logging camp at Land O'Lakes. That was my first job. I had a job sawing and cutting logs. I had to leave my wife at home and go live in the camp. But I went home every Saturday and spent Sunday at home. . . . There were about fifty men there, mostly white men. . . . We worked all day for only $2.50 a day. They charged us for meals at the camp. I also bought food at the camp to take home to my wife and her folks. There wasn't much left of my wages by the next pay day. It was the same every time. We couldn't save nothing.[89]

After logs were cut in the winter, the logs were floated down to sawmills in the spring with the melting snows. According to Badger, labor was even more dangerous and difficult in the spring:

> Sometimes I had to ride logs down the river. It was dangerous, but I never got hurt. . . . While we were going down the river on the drives there were no weekends off. . . . I never slept. I was working so hard, moving about so much, that I never felt sleepy. We worked for nearly a month on the river.[90]

The work was seasonal, and Ojibwe men returned home in late spring to participate in traditional Ojibwe labor activities. Badger recalled:

> Then I went home again. We worked on the garden at my father-in-law's place, made it a little bigger. We planted potatoes and corn. . . . We went to make the canoes at Black Oak Lake. . . . We stayed there for two or three weeks, working everyday. After we'd made three canoes, we took them home. We used these canoes for fishing, hunting, and shining deer. Whenever we had a good catch of fish, we'd sell it at ten cents a pound at Phelps. We sold meat there too at ten cents a pound.[91]

A falling tree later killed Badger's father, vividly illustrating the danger of working in the timber industry.[92] These were the dangers faced by Ininiins, Giishkitawag, and other Ojibwe men throughout Wisconsin.

Both white and Ojibwe workers were exploited in the timber industry, yet the logging era is still celebrated as part of the collective heritage of the northwoods of Wisconsin, Minnesota, and Michigan. The irresponsible clear-cutting of the old-growth forest of the ceded territory by timber corporations for immediate profit created massive wealth, but it was not a sustainable industry. Furthermore, waste characterized the early years of timber harvest in northern Wisconsin. Technology was part of the waste: wide-blade circular saws chewed up inches of each tree into sawdust. Had the companies used thinner band saws over circular saws, it is estimated an additional billion board feet of white pine would have been produced. In the woods, trees were cut high, leaving tall stumps to rot. Old-growth hemlock, the focus of timber harvest after 1900 when most of the old-growth white pine was gone, was cut for bark in the nineteenth century and left to rot.[93] As historian William Cronen stated: "the people of plenty were a people of waste."[94]

As a result of clear-cutting and timber industry waste, once lush old-growth forests were replaced by a bleak, barren landscape, fueling many fires in the late nineteenth century throughout Wisconsin, Michigan, and Minnesota, including major fires that destroyed Peshtigo, Wisconsin, in 1871 (killing 1,500 people) and Hinckley, Minnesota, in 1894 (killing over 400). What grew in the wake of clear-cutting and fire were largely species of trees that were less profitable. While white pine itself grew quite well following fire, this could only occur when some of the old-growth trees survived, the heat of the fire opening cones that contained the seeds of the towering trees above in the scorched earth below. Because of clear-cutting, there were no longer seeds to produce a new generation of trees. What did thrive in the wake of clear-cutting was aspen, which grew fast and could grow from roots. While this species gave rise to the paper industry in the twentieth century, this was a far less lucrative industry than nineteenth-century saw log production. As a result of this shortsighted approach, the economy of northern Wisconsin was underdeveloped in the twentieth century, resulting in poverty for Ojibwe and whites alike.[95]

Colonialism in Wisconsin, while not as violent as the military campaigns against Native people in the West, involved squandering of forest resources by corporations for short-term profit and resulted in crippling poverty. Also indicative of how colonialism replicates and sustains itself, this shortsighted exploitation of forest resources fueled American expansion and Native dispossession elsewhere on the continent. There were alternatives: state regulation might have provided a more sustaining resource. As James Willard Hurst's exhaustive study *Law and Economic Growth: The Legal History of the Lumber Industry in Wisconsin* makes clear, the law instead functioned to create short-term wealth that had real long-term costs to both the national and regional economies.[96] Nevertheless, as a result of the decline of the timber industry, northern Wisconsin's population growth in the late nineteenth century halted by the beginning of the twentieth and in many areas declined as the century went on. However, despite the sparse overall population, whites still vastly outnumbered Indians in northern Wisconsin after the late nineteenth century. If the Ojibwe were to avoid removal to the reservation and remain at Rice Lake, it was up to Waabizheshi to form new relationships with them.

WHITE SETTLEMENT AND WAABIZHESHI'S INTERCULTURAL VISION

As the region around Rice Lake was logged, settlers came seeking to farm cutover lands. Despite the land of northwest Wisconsin being sold in 1837, the federal government did not dispose of the lands until decades later. Federal land laws were designed for turning lands acquired in Indian treaties into individual 80- or 160-acre farms. As historian Robert Fries argued, this system was not well suited to northern Wisconsin, where timber companies were forced to buy outright thousands of small 80- or 160-acre parcels rather than merely leasing the timber rights. After timber companies clear-cut the timber, they had no use for the land. Cutover lands were then sold by the company itself or went tax delinquent and reverted to county ownership and eventual auction. In many areas close to the reservation, these lands became the basis of national, state, or county forestlands.[97] However, the areas near Rice Lake had soils better suited to agriculture, and white settlers began acquiring cutover lands throughout the 1870s and 1880s.

Ojibwe people attempted to forge relationships with the newcomers, just as they had with traders and government officials earlier in the nineteenth century. By forging these relationships, the Ojibwe at Rice Lake sought to position themselves in a new, intercultural community where there was a place for both whites and Ojibwe. This was highly subversive, as federal policy sought to create a northern Wisconsin that was segregated, with Indians confined to reservations. One of the ways Ojibwe people attempted to forge relationships with the new settlers was through a dance, termed by anthropologists as the "begging dance." Historian Brenda Child argues this is a misnomer, as the performance of Ojibwe music and dancing for outsiders was a reciprocal exchange, not begging.[98] Performance of the dance was part of an exchange rooted in friendship and affection that Ojibwe had used for centuries to forge relationships with outsiders.

Historical evidence shows that performance of the dance was central to how the Ojibwe forged diplomatic relationships with American officials earlier in the nineteenth century prior to the arrival of white settlers.[99] For example, during the 1835 annuity payment of all the Lake Superior Ojibwe held at La Pointe, J. J. Ducatel noted:

> During the period of the payment the performance of the pipe-dance, together with the war-dance, is a frequent exhibition with them; and as they resort to it for the express purpose of levying a contribution upon the merchants and traders of Lapointe, it has been more significantly called the "begging dance." Accordingly they make great preparation for its coming off with effect—such as anointing their limbs, painting their bodies in the most fantastical manner, and, barely saving decency, appear almost naked. After promenading the village, they assemble before the agency house, and other places where they expect to be treated, and commence their performances.[100]

For the Ojibwe, receiving annuities every year was more than just a monetary transaction. It was the renewal of a relationship built on exchange. In that context it was appropriate for the Ojibwe to expect gifts in return for performance. Exchange was the basis of how Ojibwe people formed their relationship to Americans for decades following the treaties.

The Ojibwe continuously based exchange and the "begging dance" in their relationship with Americans throughout the treaty period. Twenty years later, the dance was still central to Ojibwe relationship to Americans. In 1855, Detroit physician Richard Morse noted that the dance was a central aspect of the annuity payment he witnessed. Morse noted that the dance was "instituted for the benefit of the widows and orphans of the poorer bands."[101] Like Ducatel twenty years before, Morse noted that the dance was most effective when taken to the extreme: "At least one hundred warriors dressed in the most eccentric and fantastic style that the imagination can conceive."[102] The performers circled the most notable Ojibwe. This time, an Ojibwe from Manoominikaan played a central role in the dance. Morse described how Waabizheshi's sister, Aazhaweyaa, attracted the attention of Americans due to her exploits in war. In order for the dance to be effective and American officials to donate goods, Aazhaweyaa was showcased: "Inside the circle were the musicians and persons of distinction, not the least of whom was our heroine, who sat upon a blanket spread upon the ground."[103]

Later, when white settlers moved into Manoominikaan and other places in Ojibwe territory, the Ojibwe attempted to maintain a relationship rooted in exchange. Accordingly, the *Barron County Chronotype* reported on a performance of the "begging dance" in October 1876. While the language of the account reflects white stereotypes of Native savagery, it suggests that some local whites tried to understand the dance as an exchange:

> About forty hungry Chippewa's from the upper camps came marching into town last Saturday with drums beating and armed with war clubs and other

> implements of savage warfare. They were all elaborately painted and decked out with eagle feathers. Their mission was a peaceful one. They proceeded to the Hay Scales in front of K.S. & Co.'s [Knapp, Stout & Company] store where they held a dance of about an hours duration. After making their wants known they were bountifully supplied with pork, flour, tea and other kinds of goods. The pipe of peace was then lighted and passed around everybody present taking one pull at it. The head chief made a speech of thanks and assured the white people that everything was lovely. J.H. Ives Esq. was made a chief in return for his liberality and joined in the wind up dance. After visiting several other places of business and favoring each with a dance in return for which they received many presents, the party went on its way rejoicing. Many timid ones were not a little alarmed on the first appearance of the Indians, but there were no grounds for any fears.[104]

While Waabizheshi is not mentioned by name in the account, it is safe to assume that he is the "head chief" mentioned. While Waabizheshi's speech was an important part of the exchange, equally important was the performance of the dance, illustrating how performance was essential to Ojibwe political institutions. Many white settlers were newcomers to the region, and their ideas about the Ojibwe were informed by stereotypes of Indians from elsewhere. The dance succeeded then, as Waabizheshi was able to convince local whites "that everything was lovely" and "there were no grounds for any fears." It is significant that the dance took place at the Knapp Stout company store, the center of American power in the region. For the Ojibwe at Rice Lake American power rested not so much at the federal level, but with a corporation. This presented new challenges to Waabizheshi, as Nena'aangabi's performances were strictly for federal officials in far-off La Pointe who interacted with the community once a year during annuities. Twenty years later, American presence in Rice Lake was an everyday reality.

The dance performance is the best expression of Waabizheshi's vision of Rice Lake as an intercultural community, with relationships between Ojibwe and whites equal and not founded on a race-based hierarchy. This was a historically rooted alternative to federal removal efforts, which were characterized by Ojibwe confinement to the reservation and economic and social marginalization of the Ojibwe. It was expression of Ojibwe sovereignty, as not only did it make clear that whites and Ojibwe at Rice Lake were autonomous from one another, but it was the Ojibwe themselves who directed how Ojibwe and whites would relate to each other. Waabizheshi's vision of Rice Lake as an intercultural community was highly subversive in the context of American colonialism and its race-based hierarchy of exploitation.[105]

Dancing was only one way the Ojibwe at Rice Lake attempted to create a new, intercultural community at Rice Lake. Ojibwe people also attempted to forge relationships with whites they worked with in timber operations through gifting. Early Rice Lake settler Paul Kirkendall remembered his father's relationship with Ojibwe loggers when his father worked for Knapp, Stout Company:

> They were really decent Indians. They would give you things of their own if they took a liking to you. My dad, like I said, was always good to them and they kept him in buckskin gloves, jackets and moccasins, etc., and me, too.[106]

Similarly, early Long Lake settler Arthur Hovey remembers Niikaanis, an Ojibwe headman at Long Lake, visiting Hovey's family:

> He and his wife were frequent visitors at my grandmother's home, where they were given coffee or tea with cookies and cake for lunch, and at times a package of smoking tobacco. In return they would brings gifts of Indian rice, maple sugar, and sometimes venison.[107]

Ojibwe seasonal celebrations and dancing aroused the interest of some settlers. Hovey remembers his uncle attending Ojibwe celebrations at Indian Point on Long Lake that lasted three days, and Hovey himself attended in 1892.[108] In these examples, Ojibwe people successfully forged relationships with white settlers, defying federal efforts at removal and confinement to the reservation.

Likewise, logging camps were sometimes places where evidence suggests that the relationship between the Ojibwe and whites in the timber industry was harmonious. In the 1940s, Lac Courte Oreilles Ojibwe Prosper Guibord recalled his days working in the logging camps: "Indians & whites got along well—little fighting."[109] In some instances, white loggers learned from how the Ojibwe interacted with the land. In the 1940s, anthropologist Robert Ritzenthaler interviewed Lac Courte Oreilles spiritual leader John Mink about his time working in the timber industry in the late nineteenth century:

> John says that in logging camps when they would be driving logs across the lake & a headwind would come up they would give tobacco to an old man who had that wind for his spirit & could control it & he would stop that wind until the logs were across the lake. They often did this. Even the lumber companies would give big piles of goods to those old fellows to help them their way.[110]

This is an important example of how contradictory colonialism could be. While the lumber industry was responsible for inundating rice beds, logging camps were important places for cultural exchange.

VIOLENCE AT RICE LAKE

The success of the community at Rice Lake in resisting federal removal efforts and continuing seasonal labor for two decades was a major accomplishment of Waabizheshi's leadership. However, by the last years of the 1870s, there were many stresses on the community. Seasonal labor itself was a precarious endeavor even without the ecological devastation brought by American colonialism, as weather fluctuations resulted in massive variations of Ojibwe food supply. However, the destruction of the rice beds at Rice Lake and Prairie Rice Lake by timber corporations was devastating to the Ojibwe community. The destruction of these resources weakened the Ojibwe at Rice Lake, as white settlers soon became the majority in the area. The stress put on the community began to manifest itself in violence. In his study of violence among Native peoples of the Great Basin in the eighteenth century, historian Ned Blackhawk argues that intertribal violence was a result of colonialism even when outsiders were not directly involved.[111] Tragically, this dynamic played out at Rice Lake as the 1870s drew to a close.

In 1875, a young woman in the community stabbed another young woman to death. The *Barron County Chronotype* claimed alcohol was involved in the incident.[112] Though the *Barron County Chronotype* report in 1875 did not specify the names of the individuals involved, in *The First Fifty Years: Rice Lake, Wisconsin, 1875–1925*, Alvah Axtell claimed the victim was Waabizheshi's sister Minotaagoz.[113] We know that Minotaagoz, who was the mother of spiritual leader Steve Grover, died in the 1870s; however, these sources do not specify how she died.[114] Regardless of whether or not the victim was Minotaagoz, violent incidents increased in the community. In September 1877, the *Barron County Chronotype* reported a drunken fight between Giishkitawag's wife and his sister, identified in the article as "Poskin." The *Chronotype* alleged "Poskin" sustained injuries when Giishkitawag gashed her above the eye with a hatchet. The *Chronotype* used the incident to argue for enforcement of laws banning sale of liquor to Native people.[115] The *Chronotype* cast the incident in stereotypical tropes of Indians consuming too much alcohol, and in fact "Poskin," the first wife of Knapp, Stout Company founding partner Andrew Tainter, was not Giishkitawag's sister. Regardless of specifics, the incident suggests how greatly the community was experiencing the stress of American colonialism.

Violence within the community was inextricably linked to American colonialism, as manifested by logging, the flooding of rice beds, and pressure to remove to the reservation. That same fall a more serious incident of violence within the community occurred when Waabizheshi was stabbed and killed. Tensions grew in the community that fall leading to a disagreement between one member of the community, Bidad, and Waabizheshi. The historical record does not indicate whether the tensions were political or personal in nature, but it is likely external pressures created tension in the community.[116] Historical accounts claim that Bidad had been consuming alcohol when he stabbed and killed Waabizheshi at Long Lake. However, Ojibwe behavior is often oversimplified in the historical record. Surviving accounts written by whites tend to cast complexities within the Ojibwe communities as mere "drunken quarrels." In his study *Deadly Medicine: Indians and Alcohol in Early America*, historian Peter C. Mancall analyzed numerous accounts and critiques of Native consumption of alcohol and wrote "Colonists' descriptions became formulaic."[117] Furthermore, white settlers themselves were heavy drinkers. In the late eighteenth century, the average American consumed the equivalent of seven shots of liquor a day.[118] While no studies exist that estimate alcohol consumption in northern Wisconsin in the nineteenth century, taverns were ubiquitous in Rice Lake and other lumbering towns.

The violence continued when Ininiins heard of his brother's murder. Ininiins ran over ten miles from Red Cedar Lake, where he was employed at a Knapp, Stout Company logging camp, to Long Lake. Ininiins was rash and immediately sought out Bidad on his arrival at Long Lake. Ininiins threw open the entrance to Bidad's lodge, but Bidad was armed and waiting for him. As soon as Ininiins opened the entrance to the lodge Bidad blasted Ininiins in the chest. Ininiins shouted, "I am dying!" and fell over dead.[119] Ininiins's attempt to take Bidad's life was likely justified, if not well thought out. Under traditional Ojibwe criminal justice, the victim (or their family if it was murder) was responsible for punishment. Ininiins was responsible for seeking retribution for Bidad's killing of Waabizheshi, as his spirit could not move on to the next realm until this was done. Retribution could happen one of two ways: Waabizheshi's family could agree to compensation of money and goods from Bidad, or they had the right to kill Bidad. It was the decision of Waabizheshi's family.[120]

Following Waabizheshi's death, Giishkitawag became the new ogimaa of the community. It was now up to the new ogimaa to seek retribution for the murder of both his brothers. Bidad and his sons fled the community after shooting Ininiins, relocating to the St. Croix River. Unlike Ininiins, Giishkitawag was more careful in seeking out Bidad. In June 1878, Bidad surfaced at a social gathering at Lac Courte Oreilles. Bidad departed the event in a group of five. The group left the event walking in single file. Giishkitawag carefully waited and fatally shot Bidad as he was leaving.[121] While the *Barron County Chronotype* characterized the incident a "deadly feud," Ojibwe protocols of criminal justice functioned for centuries and were arguably more humane and just than American forms of criminal justice of the time.

CONCLUSION

Waabizheshi's ability to resist federal removal efforts was a major achievement in the twenty-two years he led the Ojibwe community at Rice Lake. Without question the ability to resist removal contributed to an enhanced quality of life and economic well-being for Ojibwe people of Rice Lake. Furthermore, it demonstrated Ojibwe sovereignty during a period of immense pressure from American colonialism. The Ojibwe at Rice Lake were able to resist American colonialism by actively striving to create an intercultural community at Rice Lake in an era when federal law and policy strove for a segregated society. The ability of Ojibwe people to remain at Rice Lake and the surrounding area for over two decades while white settlers became the majority illustrated the continuing vitality of Ojibwe sovereignty. Many narratives of Native American history ignore the years of struggle to avoid removal to the reservations of important leaders such as Waabizheshi. Many studies simply portray Native groups as signing treaties and immediately moving to the reservation, implying that the movement of Native people to reservations was inevitable. In contrast, Waabizheshi's tenure as leader of the community was not a small amount of time. It represents a major portion of the lifetimes of the individuals of the community: in this time span children became adults and had children of their own. The Ojibwe of Rice Lake did not see removal as inevitable during these twenty-two years. Waabizheshi's ability to resist federal removal efforts for this long was a triumph over colonialism and an important demonstration of Ojibwe sovereignty.

At the same time, Waabizheshi's failure to directly engage American institutions as his father did or to seek broader influence in Ojibwe politics may have had serious repercussions for his community in the longer term. Henry Schoolcraft noted in 1831 that Nena'aangabi was a powerful leader "whose influence is entirely of his own creation."[122] Waabizheshi inherited the legacy of his father's influence and was able to maintain the number of people in his own community over two decades. These two factors would have allowed him broad influence in Ojibwe politics in Wisconsin. It can be argued that he squandered this potential and the opportunity for a broader Ojibwe resistance to American colonialism. This united resistance may have been more effective in the long run. Instead, in the years after Waabizheshi's death, the Ojibwe at Rice Lake under Giishkitawag faced mounting pressure from local governments to remove as well as state prosecution of off-reservation treaty rights. In the twentieth century, this would result in confinement to reservations, poverty, and suppression of off-reservation treaty rights until the 1980s. A chance for a broader opposition to American colonialism was an opportunity Nena'aangabi would not have missed. After Waabizheshi's death, his brother and successor Giishkitawag would meet these new challenges with a different style entirely.

CHAPTER 4

Aazhaweyaa and Ojibwe Women in Transition

"My mother actually fought to protect the Chippewa Indians in their land rights"

—THOMAS BRACKLIN TO CATO SELLS, NOVEMBER 10, 1915

In 1915, Thomas Bracklin wrote a letter to Commissioner of Indian Affairs Cato Sells requesting an allotment on the Lac Courte Oreilles Reservation for himself and his children. Bracklin, then around fifty years old, cited the rich legacy of his family, telling the commissioner, "I believe that if the true history of my ancestors was better understood by the Indian Office, there would be no hesitation in granting my application."[1] Bracklin was the firstborn son of Aazhaweyaagiizhigokwe, commonly known as Aazhaweyaa, eldest daughter of Nena'aangabi. In the 1850s, Aazhaweyaa became a venerated warrior, celebrated throughout Ojibwe territory. However, the mid-nineteenth century was a time of transition for her family and for all the Ojibwe. In 1859, the federal government denied the request of Lac Courte Oreilles Band ogimaag, led by her brother Waabizheshi, to locate the reservation at Prairie Rice Lake. This led to the creation of a reservation instead at Lac Courte Oreilles and efforts by federal, state, and local authorities to remove the Ojibwe of Rice Lake to the reservation. Aazhaweyaa's life provides a vivid example of how Ojibwe women experienced these changes. Aazhaweyaa went from being a highly venerated warrior to being the wife of lumber baron James Bracklin, the first mayor of Rice Lake.

WARFARE

Aazhaweyaa was the firstborn daughter of Nena'aangabi and Nigooyoo. She was born sometime in the mid-1830s.[2] We know very little about Aazhaweyaa's early life. However, Aazhaweyaa's life changed drastically when she had a vision during a fast. Like in traditional Ojibwe families today, Ojibwe girls in the nineteenth century went out fasting after their first menstruation, something that marked their transition into adulthood. We do not know if Aazhaweyaa's vision occurred during her puberty fast or if it occurred during a fast later in her adolescence. Regardless, in her vision, Aazhaweyaa accompanied Nena'aangabi on a war party against the Dakota and then returned with a Dakota scalp.[3] The fact that the young girl had such a vision was unique. In traditional Ojibwe culture, people who sought to step outside traditional gender roles were honored when it was sanctioned by a vision or other spiritual intervention.

However, despite the spiritual significance of Aazhaweyaa's vision, Nena'aangabi and Nigooyoo were vehemently opposed to Aazhaweyaa joining a war party.[4] Nena'aangabi and Nigooyoo were likely concerned for their daughter's safety. The fact that Aazhaweyaa's vision was remarkable speaks to how rare and unique it was for women to directly participate in war. Aside from Aazhaweyaa, there are no other surviving accounts of Ojibwe women warriors in the nineteenth century, and the written accounts of Aazhaweyaa make clear that she was the only Ojibwe and Great Lakes Native woman who participated directly in warfare in the nineteenth century.[5]

However, Aazhaweyaa was persistent with her parents. Eventually they relented, and Aazhaweyaa joined a military campaign led by Nena'aangabi. The party crossed the Mississippi River and spent just over ten days deep in Dakota country but was consistently eluded by the Dakota.[6] By the mid-nineteenth century the days of large-scale military campaigns that expelled one tribal group from its territory were gone. The vast majority of time in warfare was mundane, as nineteenth-century Ojibwe-Dakota warfare was marked by brief but violent encounters.[7] Without any success, Nena'aangabi ordered his warriors to return to Rice Lake. However, when they recrossed the Mississippi, the Ojibwe encountered a lone Dakota man in his birchbark canoe, whom they ambushed.[8] Aazhaweyaa then scalped the Dakota and ran directly to Rice Lake.[9] We do not know where exactly on the Mississippi Aazhaweyaa took the scalp, but the shortest distance from the Mississippi River directly to Rice Lake is just under one hundred miles, although it was likely much farther.

Aazhaweyaa's fame as a warrior was rooted in her running ability. As Richard Morse noted: "On foot she is the fleetest of her race. It was said that she offered her life in servitude to any man, who, giving her one rod the start, could catch her in the race."[10] Running was central to Ojibwe warfare, as the speed of the retreat was often the difference between life and death. Therefore, it was not just the taking of the scalp but Aazhaweyaa's quick return to Rice Lake that cemented her reputation as a skilled warrior. According to Johann Georg Kohl, Aazhaweyaa "had run straight home for several days, thus bringing the first news of the victory, which greatly augmented her renown."[11] Aazhaweyaa's vision and subsequent return with the scalp made her famous throughout Ojibwe country. As Richard Morse explained: "Thus was the prophecy of the prophetess realized to the letter, and herself, in the esteem of all the neighboring bands, elevated to the highest honor in all their ceremonies."[12]

In subsequent campaigns, Aazhaweyaa built on her already famed exploits. Just prior to the 1855 annuity payment, Nena'aangabi had a close call with death. Nena'aangabi was sleeping on his back when a group of Dakota warriors brazenly came into the Ojibwe encampment. A Dakota warrior snuck into Nena'aangabi's lodge and fired at the ogimaa. Incredibly, the Dakota shooter missed, despite the close proximity. The musket ball grazed Nena'aangabi's nose, leaving only a scar. Aazhaweyaa instantly grabbed her father's already loaded rifle and led a party of Ojibwe warriors in pursuit of the Dakota. Aazhaweyaa killed one of the Dakota, and another Dakota was killed in the campaign. Except for Nena'aangabi's scar, the Ojibwe suffered no casualties. When Aazhaweyaa returned to her father's lodge with the Dakota scalp, it only fueled her already growing renown and fame in Ojibwe territory. When Aazhaweyaa arrived at the annuity payment at La Pointe in the fall of 1855, she was a celebrity. The annuity payment drew several thousand Ojibwe, hundreds of persons of mixed descent, traders, and federal officials, including Commissioner of Indian Affairs George Manypenny. German ethnographer Johann Georg Kohl reported: "At La Pointe she walked in procession through the village, the scalp being borne before her as a banner. She was pointed out to everyone as the heroine of the day and of the island."[13]

Aazhaweyaa's role as a warrior was unusual but did occur in other Native cultures. In her study of gender roles on the Plains, anthropologist Beatrice Medicine noted, "Thus through institutionalized dreams or visions both sexes could assume other roles without seriously damaging their social acceptance or self-esteem."[14] While Aazhaweyaa was unique because she participated directly in warfare, historical evidence suggests that women sometimes had a supporting role in warfare. In the Bad River Works Progress Administration (WPA) historical project, Angeline Cedaroot discussed what her grandmother (*nokomis*) told her about women's role in warfare:

> they would be in the thick of the battle themselves. Nokomis would take a gun into battle and by her mere presence won many battles, the Sioux being frightened by the presence of an "Amazon" in the Chippewa ranks. In a battle that would have taken place near St. Paul with the Sioux, the Sioux immediately surrendered when they saw No-ko-mis with the Chippewa. They were dreadfully afraid of a woman warrior.[15]

In other realms of Ojibwe life, women were free to participate in roles that were overwhelmingly practiced by one gender. While ogimaag were nearly always men, women were not prevented from occupying positions of leadership in their communities. In 1827, the wife of prominent Lac du Flambeau Band leader Giishkiman attended the Treaty of Butte des Morts in place of her ailing husband. According to Henry Schoolcraft: "She was treated with the respect due to the character she represented, and ample presents were directed to be given to her; among other things a handsome hat."[16] Among the Plains Ojibwe, John Tanner's mother, Nednaakwe, was an ogimaa.[17] Women also took on leadership roles in ceremonies as well. Kohl reported: "Women become full members of the Mide order, dance with the men in the temples, sing with them, have like them the mysterious bag, and perform miracles."[18] Women also held other ceremonial roles dominated by men outside Midewiwin, such as acting as a *jaasakiid*. A *jaasakiid* is a spiritual leader who communicates with spiritual entities through a ceremonial lodge, sometimes referred to as a shaking tent, that the spirits enter, informing the *jaasakiid* of desired knowledge. This duty was held mostly by men but was not closed off to women. For example, one of the granddaughters of famed eighteenth-century La Pointe Band ogimaa Waabojiig was a *jaasakiid*.[19]

While women were free to become warriors or assume other duties dominated by men, Aazhaweyaa's skill as a warrior gave her problems in finding a marriage partner in Ojibwe communities. Richard Morse reported: "No warrior nor brave need presume to win her heart or to gain her hand in marriage, who cannot prove credentials to superior courage and deeds of daring upon the war-path, as well as endurance in the chase."[20] Finding a marriage partner was difficult for Aazhaweyaa, as few Ojibwe men desired a woman who was a superior warrior. Ojibwe oral tradition supports this. In "Weak of Heart—Strong of Heart," told by Jim Littlewolf, an Ojibwe warrior in Minnesota is camped with his wife when the Dakota attack the village. When a Dakota warrior comes into their wigwam, the Ojibwe warrior reacts this way:

> Ogichidaa wayaabamaad, bazigonjise, ezhi-aazhawigwaashkwanid imaa boodawaadenig, YAAY bangishing. Mii waabamaad aw mindimooyenh, onawadinaan

> giiwenh waagaakwad, gaa izhi-niiwanaskindibe'waad iniw—iniw bwaanan—mii zaagijiwebinaad.
>
> When the brave saw him, he stands up, and jumps across the fire and falls. The old woman sees him, grabs the axe, and, when she'd clubbed him on his head—that Dakota—throws him outside.[21]

The leadership of the village then met to decide on a course of action regarding the incident. The council decided:

> Mii gii-shaagode'ed nawaj aw ogichidaa; Iniw wiiwan nawaj zoongide'ewan. HAA Gaawiin geyaabi da-ogichidaawisiin. Wa'aw mindimooyenh—wiiwan—mii aw ge-ogichidaawid.
>
> It was this brave who was the more weak of heart; His wife was the more strong. He will be brave no more; This old woman—his wife—will be the brave.[22]

While women were able to step outside their assigned gender roles, this story makes clear that marital relations were altered when they did so. While Ojibwe women were not ostracized for taking on male gender roles, this story suggests that the men they were married to did suffer social stigma when their wives took on male gender roles.

GENDER ROLES IN SEASONAL LABOR

Finding a marriage partner was essential for both Ojibwe women and men in the nineteenth century. Ojibwe gender roles were complementary in seasonal labor, and both men and women were dependent on each other for survival. Ojibwe life in the nineteenth century was hard. Cold temperatures and deep snowfall in northern Wisconsin, northern Minnesota, Upper Michigan, and southwestern Ontario made the task of feeding families during the winter months, which ranged from November through March, difficult. Benjamin Armstrong harshly noted:

> Their food was game, no great quantities of which could be preserved. . . . The best fed Indians were never as well provided for in any respect as the poorest families of white working-men. . . . The Indians lived a hard life with but little sunshine to it.[23]

Likewise, Henry Schoolcraft noted: "The truth is, the calls of hunger are often so pressing to these northern Indians that anything in the shape of animal fibre, that will keep soul and body together, is eaten in times of their greatest want."[24] Schoolcraft also noted: "Seasons of scarcity and want are the ordinary occurrences of every year; and a mere subsistence is the best state of things that is looked for."[25]

At the end of fall, Ojibwe villages would split up into small family groups to better facilitate winter hunting. While men were away on long hunting forays, women would tend to household duties and snare small game as well as attending to all domestic tasks related to families. During this time, men would also spearfish though the ice and hunt for fur to trade, as beaver and other small game furs taken in winter were the most valuable because the pelts were the thickest during the cold winter months. Life during the winter months was hard, and hunting took up much time, as Ojibwe men often had difficulty finding enough game in order for their families to survive. While living in eastern North Dakota, John Tanner described the struggle to survive:

> This is but a fair specimen of the life in which many of the Ojibbeways of the north lead during the winter. Their barren and inhospitable country affords them so scantily the means of subsistence, that it is only with the utmost exertion and activity that life can be sustained, and it not unfrequently happens that the strongest men, and the best hunters, perish of absolute hunger.[26]

Survival in this harsh environment required a large degree of movement, for which women provided the primary labor. The rugged terrain of northern Wisconsin, northern Minnesota, Upper Michigan, and southwestern Ontario made movement difficult. While transportation was mostly by canoe in rivers and lakes, portages between waterways required Ojibwe women to carry hundreds of pounds of cargo through swamps and woods. One of the most difficult portages in Ojibwe territory was the area between the St. Louis River and Sandy Lake, which linked Lake Superior and the Mississippi River. In 1831, James Allen led a party of US Army soldiers while accompanying Indian Agent Henry Schoolcraft. Allen described the difficulties faced by his party through the portage:

> The portage road continued a little, narrow, crooked path, with bushes crowding it on either side, winding round trees, through marshes, over ridges, and across ravines, and presenting all the irregularities and inconveniences of a ride trail through difficult woods. There has been little or no cutting to clear it out, and all the bridging consists of a few small poles, laid in the length of the path, which serve to annoy rather than assist the passenger. No idea can be formed of

> the difficulty of this portage without witnessing it. The men, with heavy loads, are sometimes forced to wade through a swamp of half a mile, full of roots and bushes, and over their knees in mire at every step. And where the road is dry, it is generally over a hill, or across a gulley, the steep banks are worse to pass than the swamps.[27]

After describing the wretched conditions of his soldiers after the portage, Allen noted:

> I had four or five Indian women, and as many Indian men, carrying for me, and without these I would not have made half the distance. The Indian women carry better than the men, being less indolent, and more accustomed to it. I saw a small young Indian woman, at the close of the day, carry a keg of one thousand musket ball cartridges, for a distance of one mile, without resting, and most of the distance through swamp that was frequently over her knees; this too after having carried heavy loads all day, and when, with less exertion than she had made, my strongest men were exhausted.[28]

Whites were amazed by the hard work of Ojibwe women. Here, for example, is fur trader George Nelson's description of Ojibwe women: "To see the loads these poor wretches carry upon their backs, the drudgery, trouble & misery that some of them undergo is really astonishing."[29] Writing in 1825, Commissioner of Indian Affairs Thomas McKenney noted:

> The women, in fact, are expected to labor at everything. From the building of a lodge, to the boiling of the kettle; and from the making of their husbands moccasins, to the construction of their canoes, and to the gumming and sewing them when they require it, is a woman's employment. . . . They are literally the pack horses too—for, on a journey, these poor creatures have heaped upon them heavy burdens, whilst the man encumbers nothing but his rifle.[30]

Writing in 1855, Johann Georg Kohl came to similar conclusions when discussing the construction of lodges:

> This is the business of the women, like all the work, heavy or light, always with the exception of hunting. . . . In fact, their hands are much harder to the touch than those of the men; and, indeed, their entire muscular system is far more developed, and they are proportionately stronger in the arm, for the men do not do much to bring out the muscle. It is a general remark that the male Indians have a soft, aristocratic hand, which is evidence of their freedom from toil.[31]

Benjamin Armstrong noted with less judgment: "the women's duty in those days was to do all the labor in moving camps, pitching them in new places, and doing all the work attached to camp duty."[32] Late in the nineteenth century women continued to practice difficult labor. Early Rice Lake settler Paul Kirkendall recalled often seeing Ojibwe women cutting logs with a crosscut saw in subzero temperatures.[33]

Historian David D. Smits detailed in "The 'Squaw Drudge': A Prime Index of Savagism" how, beginning in seventeenth-century Virginia, Europeans often described Native men as idle and lazy and Native women as overworked. According to Smits, these observations were rooted less in actual Native labor practices than in European goals of conquest. For Europeans, taking the land from Native people was justified, as European agriculture resulted in greater productivity than could ever be achieved by idle Native men.[34] Many observers of Ojibwe labor were no doubt influenced by the biases that Smits described. However, there is overwhelming evidence that Ojibwe women worked extremely hard and that the division of labor was somewhat unequal.

One example of how the division of labor was unequal was in movement. It cannot be overemphasized how much work Ojibwe women did in moving villages, including transporting structures and implements needed for the Ojibwe seasonal living cycle. While women carried hundreds of pounds of cargo, men carried only their guns. This was so men could provide protection. However, this occurred in all Ojibwe communities, regardless of how real the threat of attack was. While fear of attack was a legitimate concern in areas such as Manoominikaan, the Dakota did not attack communities to the north and east of Manoominikaan in the nineteenth century. In his discussion of Bizhiki of the La Pointe Band, Benjamin Armstrong noted that Bizhiki "never went on the warpath and would only agree to fight when it became absolutely necessary to repel an invasion."[35] Richard Morse also noted that in 1842, Bizhiki claimed that he had never taken scalp.[36] In 1832, US Army Lieutenant James Allen characterized the La Pointe Band as being "at peace."[37] It was not just the La Pointe Band or the influence of Bizhiki that made the area adjacent to Lake Superior peaceful. Allen also noted that the Ontonagon Band engaged in no warfare with the Dakota due to their far proximity from Dakota communities.[38]

This is not to suggest that Smits is incorrect in his critique of written accounts that claimed Ojibwe men were lazy. However, just because Ojibwe men were not idle does not necessarily mean that the workload was equal between genders. This inequity in workload was enforced by social pressure. In the Bad River WPA historical project, Jerome Arbuckle claimed,

"For a man to do these tasks would have subjected him to ridicule from the men and particularly the women of the tribe."[39] Even so, Ojibwe women still experienced less oppression than women did in the United States and Europe. For example, American and European legal institutions discriminated against women seeking divorce whereas Ojibwe women could dissolve their marriage at any time and retained all property. Indeed, Ojibwe men and women were both dependent on their spouses to provide for the family, as it was extremely difficult for an adult of either gender to survive without a spouse.

OJIBWE WOMEN, MAPLE SUGAR PROCESSING, AND CHANGE

The running of sap in maple trees in the early spring brought Ojibwe people back into larger groups, with families relocating to camps adjacent to maple groves. Maple sap was not typically boiled down into syrup, but instead sap was boiled down into granulated sugar, which was eaten as candy or used as seasoning for a variety of foods.[40] Producing maple sugar is hard work requiring constant boiling, as it takes roughly thirty-five gallons of sap to make one gallon of syrup. Ojibwe oral tradition as told by Lac Courte Oreilles elder Jerry Smith provides an explanation for why maple sugar production is so labor intensive. Wenaboozhoo, the most prominent figure in Ojibwe oral tradition, was instructed by the spirits to teach Ojibwe people how to produce maple sugar. At first the syrup that came from the trees was pure:

> When he tasted the pure maple syrup, it was good and sweet. Winaboozhoo thought to himself, "If this syrup comes way too easily, the people will not appreciate it and they will waste it." Facing west Winaboozhoo then called upon the binesee (the Thunderbirds) to bring rain. When the rain came, it mixed with the pure maple syrup, turning it into the sap water it is today. Now Winaboozhoo liked it. "Now," he said, "to make maple syrup and maple sugar, the Indian people will have to work hard for it. They will have to cut and haul wood and also haul the sap water." This would teach the Ojibwe people to be hard working, industrious people.[41]

Like most Ojibwe seasonal labor outside of hunting and spearfishing, women did all of the labor directly associated with maple sugar production. In the nineteenth century, trees were tapped by gashing the tree with an axe and stuffing the gash with a wood chip so the sap would drip into birchbark containers called *makaks*.[42] Next, women collected thousands of gallons of sap from hundreds of trees and carried the sap to large kettles for boiling. Women ran sugar camps. However, evidence suggests that men were responsible for important supporting roles. Alexander Henry observed an Ojibwe sugar camp in Michigan in the mid-eighteenth century: "the men were not less busy in cutting wood, making fires, and in hunting and fishing in part of our supply of food."[43]

When men were off hunting or trapping, women were responsible for finding food. In the Bad River WPA historical project, Florenia Denomie recalled how as a girl she went hunting for food in her family's sugar camp near Keweenaw Bay. The family was out of meat, and Denomie came upon a porcupine, which she tried to kill. Denomie brought the animal back to sugar camp, and her grandmother finished the kill and roasted the porcupine over an open fire. A first kill ceremony was held for Denomie, and her grandmother used the quills of the porcupine to make a design on a birchbark basket.[44] This incident illustrates that, while women were often dependent on men for the supply of game, oftentimes women and even girls had to function independently from men to feed their families.

Maple sugar was utilized as the most common flavoring in food. Writing in 1855, Johann Kohl explained: "They are fond of mixing their meat with sweets, and even sprinkle sugar or maple syrup over fish boiled in water." Sugar was so prominent in the Ojibwe diet in the nineteenth century that American traders could not sell salt or salted meats to the Ojibwe. Kohl claimed: "They have a perfect aversion for salt, and I was often told they could not digest salt meats, and were taken ill if they lived on them for any time."[45] Salt was also unpopular among non-Ojibwe living in Ojibwe territory. J. J. Ducatel wrote in 1835: "This disrelish for salt, or perhaps it might be better stated, this indifference to the use of it, is equally remarkable amongst the half breeds, and even with the Canadian *voyageurs* of Lake Superior."[46] Kohl echoed this: "A similar distaste for salt is noticeable among European traders who have lived with the Indians."[47] The use of a table condiment may seem trivial but in fact speaks to the cultural hegemony the Ojibwe exercised over non-Ojibwe well into the mid-nineteenth century.

The influence of white settlers led to an increase in the use of salt as a condiment in Ojibwe communities in the late nineteenth century. However, even into the 1940s, maple sugar remained the preferred condiment among an older generation of the Ojibwe. In the Bad River WPA historical project, Jerome Arbuckle wrote: "Many of our own time have never acquired the taste for salt and do not use it as a seasoning; others use it sparingly. . . . There are a few of the old Chippewa who still follow the custom of seasoning their food with maple sugar."[48] Change also occurred in gender roles. Increasingly in the late nineteenth century, making maple sugar was an activity of the entire family, with men more directly involved in the processing of maple sugar.[49] This, like the increase in the use of salt, was part of broader changes in Ojibwe culture that were the result of American colonialism in the region. While neither use of salt nor men participating in the processing of sugar were actively encouraged by federal officials, both trends reflected American cultural influence that was inseparable from increased American power in the region.

Another aspect of women's labor in sugar camps was making pictographs with one's teeth out of small pieces of birch bark. After working throughout the day, women would relax in the evenings by folding small pieces of birch bark, biting them to make a pattern, and then holding them up to light to illuminate them. The thin pieces of birch bark used in the pictographs are easiest to work with during the early spring. This was an art form practiced exclusively by women and common in other Algonquian speaking communities. Patterns were varied and included geometric designs, flowers, animals, and people.[50] While many women bit birch bark during sugar camps, certain woman were renowned for their skills. In the mid-nineteenth century, German ethnographer Johann Georg Kohl visited one such artist, Angelique Marte, near Sault Ste. Marie, who only had one intact tooth to make her bitings.[51]

The oral tradition concerning the origin of birchbark transparencies speaks directly to the importance of women's labor. During the maple sugar season, a man who lived with his parents noticed they were getting old and realized they would not be able to help him much longer, so he decided to marry. At the sugar camp, the man sent his new wife to collect birch bark to make containers to collect the sap. The wife was gone all day, and she returned at night with a large bundle of birch bark. The man was happy with his new wife, until she opened the bundle and revealed she had been biting the birch bark all day instead of making containers with the birch bark. The man was devastated: "The man was so ashamed that he hung his head and died. He could not bear to have people know that he had brought home such a good-for-nothing wife."[52]

American colonialism in the late nineteenth century resulted in change in the practice and prevalence of birchbark biting. While Ojibwe women still made them in the early twentieth century, according to ethnographer Frances Densmore, the quality of the pieces suffered tremendously. According to Densmore,

> A woman never copied one pattern from another—it was an original work, and a peculiarity was that the pattern was clear in the mind of the worker before she made the first fold. . . . Some women of middle age undertook to make the transparencies as they had seen the older women fold and bite the bark, but they lacked the *mental concept* and their work was not *art*. . . . The old, *clear thinking* had gone, and nothing can take its place.[53]

Anthropologist Ernestine Friedl wrote in 1943 that one of her informants at Lac Courte Oreilles claimed that she remembered participating in birchbark biting as a child as a family activity during the winter months.[54] Regardless of when exactly Ojibwe women stopped making birchbark transparencies, by the mid-twentieth century, nobody at Lac Courte Oreilles (or other nearby Ojibwe reservations) made them anymore.[55]

OJIBWE WOMEN'S LABOR IN THE SUMMER

As maple sap stopped running, men speared fish when walleye and other larger fish congregated in more shallow waters to spawn for a few short weeks in the spring. By this time, Ojibwe people were concentrated into larger villages for the summer. Due to this increased concentration of people, Midewiwin and other ceremonies were held in May, often lasting around three weeks. Midewiwin ceremonies were also held at more irregular intervals as circumstances required.[56] Summer activities such as berry picking, netting, and gathering of birch bark were all the responsibility of women. Birch bark was an essential item for Ojibwe labor. It was gathered in June, as this is when the bark most easily separates from the tree. Canoes, lodges, containers, and torches for spearing were all made from birch bark.[57] Prior to contact and the use of kettles, birch bark was also utilized for cooking. Despite its ability to easily burn, when filled with liquid birch bark is not as combustible.[58]

In the nineteenth century, Ojibwe communities of the Lac Courte Oreilles Band also had substantial gardens. The production of gardens varied among Ojibwe bands based on location. In late July of 1831, Henry Schoolcraft noted the prominence of gardens in the small Ojibwe community on Pacwawong Lake on the Namekagon River:

> We found eight large permanent bark lodges, with fields of corn, potatoes, pumpkins, and beans, in fine condition. The lodges were cleanly swept, giving

> the premises a neat air. The corn fields were partially or lightly fenced. The corn was in tassel. The pumpkins partly grown, the beans fit for boiling. The whole appearance of thrift and industry was pleasing.[59]

In midsummer, Ojibwe men began deer hunting again when fireflies began to appear, as oral tradition teaches that this is when deer are healthy again following the long winters. Summer was also the time when both women and men collected medicines.[60]

OJIBWE WOMEN AND WILD RICE

Gathering wild rice was the last major activity of the summer before families again split off into small family groups for hunting. The importance of wild rice to the survival of Native people in the western Great Lakes cannot be overstated. Rice could be easily stored in caches throughout the year without spoiling.[61] Processing wild rice is an extremely labor-intensive activity. During the nineteenth century, women did nearly all the work in gathering and processing wild rice. Ricing, more than any other activity of the Ojibwe seasonal labor cycle, illustrates how the division of labor by gender was fundamentally unequal.

In the nineteenth and early twentieth centuries, Ojibwe people would begin ricing by binding the rice together with *wiigob* (or a twine made of the inner bark of basswood trees) a few weeks before the rice was ripe. Binding rice greatly increases the yield when gathering rice, as more rice falls into the canoe. This is illegal today under state and tribal law as rice is an annual, and the grain that falls back into the water provides the seed for next year's crop. Binding rice also keeps small birds, or *manoominikeshiinyag*, from eating the rice. Another benefit to binding rice is that the rice is protected from wind and heavy rain when it is in the latter stages of ripening. Lastly, binding eases the harvest of rice as it provides lanes through the thick rice stands for canoes. When the rice ripened, Ojibwe women would gather it by having one woman in the front of the canoe poling through the shallow rice fields and another woman in the rear of the canoe knocking the rice with two sticks. Then the rice was parched in order to warm the kernel so the husk would separate more easily. The next step was to have a young boy "dance" on the rice, essentially stepping on it to separate the warm kernel from the husks. Henry Schoolcraft wrote in 1831: "A man then treads out the grain. This appears to be the only part of rice making performed by the men. The women gather, dry, and winnow it."[62] This was the only part of the process women did not participate in due to Ojibwe beliefs that women could not step over food without contaminating it due to women's power.[63] One way around this was the use of a *bootaagan*, where women could accomplish the same thing by utilizing a mortar to apply pressure to the rice and separate the husk from the kernel. The final step was winnowing it, where women placed the rice in a large birchbark basket and shook it rapidly in order to separate the empty husks from the kernel. Even at this stage, not all kernels were separated, making several repeats of the process necessary and ending in individual hand cleaning of each kernel.[64]

Ojibwe women processed thousands of pounds of rice every year throughout the nineteenth century. Aside from ethnographic evidence, we know that Ojibwe women did all of the gathering of rice in the nineteenth century based on surviving implements used for harvesting rice. For example, one pair of cedar ricing sticks in the collections of the Minnesota Historical Society collected by ethnologist Frances Densmore in the 1930s in Grand Portage are slightly shorter than twenty-five inches long.[65] Today, one would be hard-pressed to find twenty-five-inch ricing sticks. The current maximum length for ricing sticks under state and tribal law is thirty-eight inches, reflecting men's role in harvesting wild rice. Like other changes in Ojibwe labor, men increasingly were more directly involved in the harvest of wild rice in the late nineteenth century. Early Long Lake settler Arthur Hovey remembered: "This wild rice harvest was a whole family affair, each family moving down with all their possessions."[66] The length of ricing sticks provides evidence of the changes in gender roles in Ojibwe seasonal labor that indirectly resulted from American colonialism and the influence of American gender roles on Ojibwe communities.

OJIBWE FAMILY LIFE

Despite the inequality of the division of labor in the nineteenth century, Ojibwe women endured these hardships for the benefit of their families and communities. Complementary roles were also common to Ojibwe childrearing in the nineteenth century and actually served to equalize labor workload. According to Joseph Nicollet:

> In reference to matters of education, advice, scoldings, punishments, permissions, etc., the father is in charge of the sons, the mother of the daughters. If the

> father wishes to inform his daughter of something that might be to her benefit, he will only do it through the intercession of the mother and vice versa. It is a matter of tradition, separation of duties in the family, and not a matter of one sex having power over another.[67]

This separation helped ease the labor workload of women, especially when men were off on long hunting forays during the winter. This meant that during these times, women were only responsible for the labor of childrearing associated with their daughters. According to Nicollet, "As soon as the son is able to follow his father, you will never see the latter without the former."[68] According to J. J. Ducatel, Ojibwe men were slow to physically punish their sons: "When the men are too much annoyed by them, they knuckle them on the head, but never recourse to flagellation."[69]

Much like their central role in feeding Ojibwe communities through their labor in the production of wild rice, Ojibwe women were the anchors of Ojibwe family life in the nineteenth century. This was related to the actual amount of domestic labor performed by Ojibwe women, but also reflected their devotion to their families. According to Thomas McKenney:

> So far as I am able to learn, and judging from what I see, there are no people who love more affectionately, or with greater constancy than do these Chippewa women. Their attachments to their husbands and their children, are strong, ardent, and lasting; and lead them to endure privations and sufferings for them, and all manner of self-denial while alive, and to mourn for them when they die.[70]

J. J. Ducatel expressed similar sentiments: "A very remarkable trait in the character of the Indian mother is her excessive fondness for her children, who are indulged in every way, are never chastised, and whose loss is bewailed with great demonstrations of sorrow."[71]

CHANGES IN OJIBWE MARRIAGE

Marriage was foundational to women's roles in family life and seasonal labor. The structure of marriage reflects women's agency in the nineteenth century. While there were many arranged marriages, both men and women were able to separate from these arrangements. According to John Tanner:

> The match is agreed upon by the old people and when their intention is made known to the young couple, they commonly find, in themselves, no objection to the arrangement, as they know, should it prove disagreeable mutually, or to either party, it can at any time be broken off.[72]

Benjamin Armstrong described a marriage ritual where a man would bring game, usually deer or moose, to the lodge of his desired bride. The woman then chose whether to accept his offer: "If the girl does not like his appearance she remains where she is, but if he is agreeable to her fancy she takes a knife and proceeds to skin the animal and take charge of the meat, after which the suitor takes his leave."[73] This same power to refuse an arranged marriage extended to the right of either party to dissolve the union. Usually in instances such as this, the property stayed with the wife, and husbands were forced to leave and return to their families. This may have protected women from physical abuse and other mistreatment: unlike in European and American society, Ojibwe women were able to leave an abusive husband at any time. However, this power was somewhat negated by the overwhelming gender imbalance in Ojibwe villages. In a council on Lac Courte Oreilles that included the communities of Moozojiid, Bakwe'aamo, and Gichi-Waabizheshi of the Chippewa River, Henry Schoolcraft noted, "The assemblage of Indians was large, but I was struck by the great disproportion, or excess, of women and children."[74] Schoolcraft noted that at the Lac Courte Oreilles village led by Moozojiid there were eighteen men and forty-eight women and at the village of Pacwawong Lake on the Namekagon River led by Bakwe'aamo there were eighteen men and thirty-eight women.[75] When Aazhaweyaa was a young adult at the age to marry in 1857, the annuity record found thirty-five men and fifty women at Manoominikaan.[76]

The gender imbalance in Ojibwe villages was partially due to warfare. Commonly when a woman's husband died, a brother would marry her.[77] One result of this was the prevalence of polygamy. According to Johann Kohl in 1855, polygamy was not practiced arbitrarily, but under certain conditions:

> it is considered highly honorable to be in the position to support several wives. The cleverer and more fortunate a hunter is, the more wives does he have. . . . Usually they take their wives from one family—frequently a whole row of sisters. The first wife, however, always remains at the head of affairs. . . . They, however, rarely have more than three wives.[78]

Henry Schoolcraft argued that polygamy was not as common among the Ojibwe as among other Native peoples. Schoolcraft noted how polygamy was related to the survival of Ojibwe families and cited as an example one Ojibwe man, Metaakozige, married to a mother and daughter.[79] Lac Courte Oreilles ogimaa Moozojiid had three wives.[80] John Tanner's mother was one of his father's three wives.[81] In the WPA historical project at Bad River, Jerome Arbuckle wrote that polygamy was not to enhance the status of successful hunters, but instead was driven by more practical considerations: "the old Chippewa claim that a man who was a good hunter considered that one woman was not capable of caring for all the meats, hides, gardens, lodges, etc. and therefore, he took another wife as an assistant."[82]

Another result of the demographic inequity between men and women was that husbands were in great demand, which may have negated some of the ability that women had to get rid of abusive husbands.[83] However, families mitigated the circumstances that allowed men to abuse their wives. This was especially true in cases of traders marrying Ojibwe women. Benjamin Armstrong described an 1847 incident that involved one of the daughters of Snake River Band ogimaa Bayezhig. Bayezhig's daughter was married to a white whiskey trader, and when her family showed concern about his character, they moved their lodge close to his store. The husband responded by demanding that she not see her parents, threatening to shoot them if she did. When she left for her parents lodge, the man shot through the wigwam. An associate of the husband seized his rifle, and Bayezhig then shot this man, believing him to be the husband. The husband then fled and was killed a short time later over a bad business deal.[84]

Despite the fact that women did nearly all of the work in the Ojibwe seasonal living cycle, neither men nor women could survive without each other. Men could not survive without the food produced by women's ricing and the labor of women in processing food. Women could not survive without the food produced by men's hunting, especially in the winter. The demographic imbalance in Ojibwe villages facilitated women's dependence on men, which may have contributed to the unequal division of labor in Ojibwe seasonal labor.

MARRIAGE AND AMERICAN COLONIALISM

The lives of Ojibwe women changed dramatically in the mid-nineteenth century as a result of broader changes in Ojibwe communities. At Manoominikaan, the destruction of rice at Rice Lake and Prairie Rice Lake, clear-cutting of old-growth forests, and increased white settlement all brought sweeping changes to the community. These years coincided with Aazhaweyaa's early adulthood. Marriage to white men was one strategy the Ojibwe employed to develop a relationship with whites at Rice Lake. Marriage between Ojibwe women and non-Native men was nothing new. Indeed, scholars have argued that the fur trade was shaped to a large extent by marriages of Native women and French or British men.[85] However, unlike many Ojibwe communities (including the community at Lac Courte Oreilles), marriage with non-Ojibwes was rare at Manoominikaan prior to the 1860s. Aazhaweyaa's generation marked a major turning point as Aazhaweyaa and all four of her other sisters married white men. However, this strategy yielded mixed results. Instead of such marriages linking white and Ojibwe communities, white men often abandoned their Ojibwe wives as soon as more white women moved into the region.

By the late 1850s, Aazhaweyaa was famous throughout Ojibwe territory. *Rice Lake Chronotype* editor August Ender claimed that Aazhaweyaa "had many suitors."[86] Aazhaweyaa's role as a warrior was critical in how she related to men in the community. A story of unknown origin in the papers of anthropologist Robert Ritzenthaler attests to this:

> One time (this was before I got married) about a hundred of us set out on a war expedition against the Sioux. Our leader was nena'angebi. Near the banks of the Mississippi R. nena'angebi called a halt & gave each one a piece of maple sugar & told them why he had brought his daughter along (she was the only woman in the party). He said that she had had a dream & she was to do this. That the first person to reach a dead or wounded Sioux was to marry her. (He used maple sugar instead of tobacco).
>
> When they got to the Miss. R. they saw a Sioux way out in the middle in a dugout. One of the men osagi shot at him, & the Sioux looked over & pointed his paddle at the Chippewa & they thought he had a gun & ducked. Then they shot & wounded him & then went to borrow a canoe to get him, but before they got one he had paddled across & got away. He probably was sheltered by some white farmers who lived there. There was a big party of Sioux on the other side & when they heard the shooting they ran. The expedition was a failure all the way around & the daughter didn't get married![87]

Marriage to another Ojibwe was likely difficult for Aazhaweyaa, as success in war defined much of men's roles. Few men were superior warriors. In addition, Aazhaweyaa was the daughter of a very important and influential ogimaa. By the 1850s, many marriages of daughters of important leaders served a political function. Some children of high-profile leaders were married off to children of other influential leaders. Even more commonly, the daughters of ogimaag were married to traders or government officials, whose kinship could benefit the community by securing access to goods.

Accordingly, Aazhaweyaa's first marriage was to a person of mixed descent, Joe Koveo of Taylors Falls, Minnesota. It is likely Koveo was involved in lumbering on the St. Croix River. Lumbering was the new industry in the region, which in the 1850s was focused in the St. Croix River valley, as the lumber industry in the Chippewa River valley was not yet the powerhouse it would become. Like prior relationships with fur traders, kinship with lumber company officials allowed the Ojibwe to have greater access to goods. However, Nena'aangabi and Nigooyoo were reluctant to give up their eldest daughter. Eventually they did consent, and Aazhaweyaa and Koveo were married in a large ceremony at Long Lake that included the exchange of gifts.[88] The exchange of gifts illustrates how exchange was central to Ojibwe marriage, especially in the context of marriage to those outside the Ojibwe community.

While we do not know for certain, sources imply that the couple went to live at Taylors Falls. This was a break with typical marriage arrangements, as Ojibwe newlywed couples typically resided with the bride's family. The couple had a daughter, Ogimaabinesikwe, known in English as Julia. Sadly, Aazhaweyaa and her daughter returned to Rice Lake a few months later. Apparently, Koveo was already married.[89] Little is known about Koveo following his marriage to Aazhaweyaa. However, there is no evidence that suggests he had any further contact with Aazhaweyaa or his daughter.

The annuity payment for 1859 was much different for Aazhaweyaa than the 1855 annuity payment. In 1855, Aazhaweyaa was paraded around La Pointe, a celebrity. In 1859, she was noted on the record of the payment as the head of household with her one child.[90] Between these two annuity payments, things changed drastically for Aazhaweyaa and the Ojibwe at Rice Lake. Her father, Nena'aangabi was dead. Also in 1859, the federal government denied the request by Waabizheshi and other Lac Courte Oreilles Band leaders to locate the reservation at Prairie Rice Lake. In 1862, the Dakota were expelled from Minnesota, ending Ojibwe-Dakota warfare. By 1865, dams destroyed the vast rice beds at both Rice Lake and Prairie Rice Lake. The world where Aazhaweyaa came of age and made her fame was disappearing.

The Ojibwe of Rice Lake responded to these changes by trying to forge relationships with the lumbermen coming into the region. As it had been in the prior two centuries with fur traders, marriage was central to this strategy. Aazhaweyaa was no different: a single mother, she did not marry an Ojibwe to support herself and her daughter. Instead, she married a Knapp, Stout Company official, James Bracklin.[91] Bracklin was born in 1839 in Patten, a town in northern Maine. Bracklin's parents were immigrants from Ireland who left Ireland for the United States on the day they were married. From Maine, the Bracklin family moved to Pennsylvania before finally settling at a farm near St. Anthony's Falls in what is today the city of Minneapolis. James Bracklin left the family farm at age nineteen for Menomonie to work for the Knapp, Stout Company in 1858. Bracklin quickly rose through the ranks of Knapp, Stout to become one its top officials. By 1891 he supervised a workforce of 1,200 men.[92]

It is not known how their romance developed, but in the early 1860s the couple married. Like her marriage to Koveo, the couple was married in Ojibwe custom. Soon after their marriage the couple had a daughter, Nellie.[93] The couple then had a son, Thomas, in 1864.[94] However, Bracklin left Aazhaweyaa and moved to Eau Claire to work for the Northwestern Lumber Company. In 1868, Bracklin married a white woman, Julia Vance, and had five children with his new wife. However, this was not the end of Aazhaweyaa and Bracklin's relationship. A few years after Bracklin's marriage to Julia Vance, Aazhaweyaa gave birth to James Bracklin Jr.[95] The impact that this had on his marriage to Vance is unknown.

Bracklin returned to Rice Lake to work for Knapp, Stout in 1876.[96] According to James Bracklin and Aazhaweyaa's great-granddaughter Sylvia Bracklin, James Bracklin took active role in the lives of his children with Aazhaweyaa. Bracklin took their children from their mother and tried to keep them at Rice Lake, as he was adamant they were to be educated. However, Aazhaweyaa traveled from the reservation to Rice Lake on foot to retrieve them. This pattern repeated itself a number of times.[97] In his Bureau of Indian Affairs personal record, Thomas Bracklin stated "I attended public school in Menomonie, Wisconsin."[98] This is reflected in annuity records, which show that Aazhaweyaa's children with James Bracklin did not always live with her. For example, in 1868, Aazhaweyaa's family had no boys.[99] In 1873 and 1874, Aazhaweyaa was listed as the head of household in a family that consisted of herself, another woman (likely her daughter Ogimaabinesikwe, at this time grown), and one boy and one girl.[100] However, by this time, Aazhaweyaa had a boy and a girl with her new husband.

James Bracklin remained married to Julia Vance until her death in 1886. The following year Bracklin married Minnie Russell. He had two more children with his new wife. Neither George Forrester's *Historical and Biographical Album of the Chippewa Valley*, published in 1891, nor Newton S. Gordon's *History of Barron County*, published in 1922, mentioned his marriage to Aazhaweyaa or their children together in their biographies of James Bracklin. Bracklin served as Rice Lake's mayor intermittently in the late nineteenth century and died in 1900 during one of his terms as mayor. His obituary in the *Rice Lake Chronotype* mentioned his marriages to Julia Vance and Minnie Russell and listed his seven children with these women as survivors but featured no mention of his marriage to Aazhaweyaa and did not list Nellie or Thomas Bracklin as survivors.[101] White historians simply erased Bracklin's past ties to the Ojibwe.

Aazhaweyaa's next husband was another Knapp, Stout lumberman, Samuel Barker. Barker was a midlevel official in the company, who worked as a trader in the company store. It is unknown how the romance between Aazhaweyaa and Barker began, but Barker worked under James Bracklin and the two were close friends. Barker had a reputation for working well with the Ojibwe. Alvah Dewey eulogized Barker shortly after his death: "During the most turbulent times he had the confidence of the Indians."[102] According to James Bracklin, Waabizheshi "thought a great deal of Barker."[103] Barker was born in 1844 in New York. It is unclear why he migrated to Wisconsin, but he was one of the first white men to permanently settle in Barron County. Barker's relationship with the Ojibwe was defined in part in an 1858 incident. Barker ran a lumber camp in southern Barron County when the Ojibwe, presumably Waabizheshi, asked him to join a war party against the Dakota. Barker responded by joining the war party in full Ojibwe regalia and even painted his face.[104]

Aazhaweyaa had two children with Barker: Edward Barker, born 1871, and Mary Barker, born in 1873.[105] However, Barker, like Bracklin, abandoned his Ojibwe family. In 1873, Barker married Susan Hickok. Barker died shortly thereafter in 1876.[106] As more white women settled in northern Wisconsin, early pioneers like Bracklin and Barker quickly left their Ojibwe families to begin families with white women. A notable exception was Benjamin Armstrong, who was married to a daughter of famed La Pointe Band ogimaa Bizhiki. In his account *Early Life among the Indians*, Armstrong summed up the situation: "The abandoned women have, in many cases, lived to see their former husband married to white women, too proud to even speak to their wife or child of a few years before."[107]

We do not know the specifics of the relationship between Aazhaweyaa and James Bracklin and what role personality conflict played. However, the atmosphere of racism and discrimination against the Ojibwe in Rice

Lake almost certainly played a role in the dissolution of their marriage. In this environment, marriage to Ojibwe women was not something that helped men like Bracklin and Barker expand their political and economic power. White women were viewed by most at Rice Lake as more respectable. Another example of this was Knapp, Stout Company founding partner Andrew Tainter. Tainter's first wife was an Ojibwe woman, Mary Poskin, and in 1861 the couple had a child, Thomas Tainter.[108] Tainter left Poskin and went on to marry a white woman. In 1892, George Forrester described Tainter as "the wealthiest man in the whole Chippewa Valley."[109]

John Quaderer was another Knapp, Stout Company official who married an Ojibwe woman. Quaderer, however, remained married to his Ojibwe wife. Born in Switzerland in 1829, Quaderer immigrated in 1852, making his way to Dubuque, Iowa, and securing work at Knapp, Stout Company headquarters the year of its founding. The company sent Quaderer up the Red Cedar River north of Menomonie in 1854, where he founded the city of Barron. In 1872, Quaderer married an Ojibwe woman, Mary Ross, and the couple had five children. Mary Quaderer died in 1884, and a few years later Quaderer married another Ojibwe woman, Margaret Redmon. The couple had six children. In addition, Redmon had a son from a previous marriage, Joseph Parent.[110] However, despite the fact that Quaderer remained married to Ojibwe women, they resided in the white community of Barron and not in an Ojibwe community. It was only later when Quaderer's son John Quaderer Jr. married Aazhaweyaa's daughter Ogimaabinesikwe and the couple moved to the reservation that the Quaderer name became part of the Ojibwe community.

In the *History of Barron County*, Newton Gordon wrote: "For many years after the opening of Barron county the presence of these Indians was tolerated. Some of them were related to the lumberjacks by marriage, for such prominent leaders as Capt. Andrew Tainter and John Quaderer and others took brides of Indian blood."[111] This quote suggests that intermarriage helped the Ojibwe avoid removal in the short term. However, the dissolution of the marriages between Ojibwe women and white men determined the course of the relationship between Ojibwe and Americans as much as the flooding of wild rice stands or the murder of Aazhaweyaa's brother Joe White by state game wardens. When white men left their Ojibwe wives for white women (or in the case of John Quaderer, resided in white communities with their Ojibwe wives), they were complicit in the creation of a segregated society that sought to diminish Ojibwe sovereignty. Marriage was foundational to the relationship the Ojibwe (and other Native nations of the Great Lakes) built with the French and later the British. The exchange between cultures that marked Ojibwe relationships to outsiders for nearly two centuries was over.

CONCLUSION

In 1929, the Senate Committee on Indian Affairs convened hearings in Wisconsin to assess the failures of federal assimilation policies following the release of the Meriam Report from the Department of the Interior the previous year. At sessions at Lac Courte Oreilles, the committee got an earful about Ojibwe poverty and Ojibwe understanding of the treaties of 1837, 1842, and 1854, as well as complaints about enforcement of state game laws in violation in Ojibwe treaty rights. In the midst of the hearings, an old man hobbled up to testify and plunked down a large silver medal on the table in front of the senators. The medal was engraved with George Washington's signature and dated 1789. The old man was Aazhaweyaa's son Thomas Bracklin. According to the *Milwaukee Journal*, "Spectators, both brown and white, flocked about Bracklin. Such a hub-bub of motion and chatter set up that Senator La Follette was obliged to rap for order."[112] Bracklin then testified before the committee: "I want to speak for the tribe, I want the Indians to speak for them, because I am their chief: I want the Indians to see that this is the medal presented to me by my great-grandfather, the chief of the Chippewa tribe."[113]

Thomas Bracklin's testimony and the reception it received speak to the legacy of leadership of his family. Bracklin himself was the product of unprecedented changes that reshaped the political, social, and cultural institutions of the Ojibwe community at Manoominikaan and throughout Ojibwe territory. Bracklin's mother, Aazhaweyaa, along with other Ojibwe women, experienced these changes in different ways. Roles in families, traditional labor, and even food consumption changed in a process that was not always driven by direct coercion. The Ojibwe internalized broader changes that were rapidly occurring in the 1860s and 1870s in very different ways. The response of political leaders like Aazhaweyaa's brothers Waabizheshi and Giishkitawag to changes brought by American expansion in the region is an important part of the story but not the only significant one. The efforts of women like Aazhaweyaa to forge relationships with important lumber company officials through marriage was another important way the Ojibwe sought to create relationships that were deeply rooted in Ojibwe sovereignty. This was consistent with the historical experience of Ojibwe people with

French and British traders. Aazhaweyaa's marriages and the abandonment of Ojibwe women are important for understanding how American colonialism functioned to exploit Ojibwe people and broke with past relationships that were rooted in and driven by Ojibwe sovereignty. As American colonialism challenged Ojibwe institutions directly and indirectly, Giishkitawag emerged as the ogimaa of the Ojibwe community at Rice Lake. Giishkitawag met these challenges with more aggressive and confrontational strategies that were a direct result of the failure to create a relationship with Americans that was based on exchange and Ojibwe sovereignty.

CHAPTER 5

Giishkitawag Confronts Removal, 1879–1894

In 1877, Giishkitawag, at age thirty-eight, became ogimaa of the Ojibwe at Rice Lake following his brother Waabizheshi's death. The seventeen years of Giishkitawag's leadership were difficult ones. Federal, state, and local governments all challenged Ojibwe sovereignty. The Barron County Board petitioned the federal government for removal of the community to the reservation, and the white population of Barron County boomed. While Giishkitawag did not seek a military solution to avoid removal, historical evidence suggests that Giishkitawag was much more aggressively defiant in resisting removal to the reservation than his brother. Where Waabizheshi avoided federal officials and solely focused on building relationships with local white settlers, Giishkitawag marched up to the reservation, demanded federal rations and other goods for his community, and then returned to Manoominikaan. When federal officials objected to his continued presence off-reservation, Giishkitawag threatened their safety and called the Ojibwe that chose to stay on the reservation cowards. At the same time, Giishkitawag skillfully manipulated federal policy. In the 1880s, allotment of reservation lands to individuals brought the opportunity of income from timber sales. Ironically, while federal officials saw allotment as a way to contain the Ojibwe on the reservation, Giishkitawag tried to use the policy to provide supplemental income to the community as a means for sustaining the continued presence of his community off-reservation.

However, the wealth from sale of allotment timber was short-lived. The federal government failed to provide an effective and sustainable management plan for reservation forest resources, resulting in corruption and poverty. As much as assimilation policy robbed the Ojibwe of income through mismanagement of forest resources, a much more direct threat to Ojibwe safety and survival was the law. As federal officials suppressed Ojibwe legal institutions, at the same time they failed to provide the Ojibwe equal protection under American law. For the Ojibwe of Rice Lake, this manifested itself both off-reservation and on-reservation. Off-reservation the Ojibwe were not protected from violence perpetrated by local whites. On-reservation, individuals had little protection against timber trespass and forms of corruption on their allotments. Furthermore, by the 1890s, the state of Wisconsin was intent on enforcement of its game laws on the Ojibwe. State game laws were a direct violation of Ojibwe treaty rights, which were federal law that had never been extinguished. However, federal officials did not assert the supremacy of federal treaty law over state game laws. This made remaining off-reservation increasingly dangerous for the community and its defiant leader.

LOCAL GOVERNMENT, FEDERAL GOVERNMENT, AND REMOVAL

In January 1878, just months after Giishkitawag assumed leadership of the Ojibwe community at Rice Lake, Barron County officials responded decisively to the efforts of his brother Waabizheshi and other Ojibwe at Rice Lake to create an intercultural community. The Barron County Board petitioned the federal government for the removal of the Ojibwe at Rice Lake to the Lac Courte Oreilles Reservation. In 1878, Barron County was changing. As old-growth timber was being cleared from the land, white settlers were coming to Barron County to farm. In many cases, these new settlers' ideas about Native people were informed by stereotypes of Indian savagery and not the centuries-long historical experience of relations between the Ojibwe and outsiders. Their economic livelihood was not based on cooperation with the Ojibwe as fur traders, who supplied traders with the raw materials that they shipped to Europe. Likewise, the timber industry was made up of single white men, many of whom were temporary seasonal workers and not threatened by the Ojibwe. In fact, Giishkitawag and hundreds of other Ojibwe men worked alongside whites in logging camps. Farming was different. Whites sought to make Barron County a land of individual farmsteads. The solution for white settlers was to separate Indian and white communities by containing Indians on the reservation. Ironically, this came at a time when federal officials based in distant La Pointe had eased their efforts to make the Ojibwe at Rice Lake remove to the reservation.

In their petition to federal officials, the Barron County Board repeated many of the themes common to removal efforts nationally since passage of the Indian Removal Act in 1830, illustrating the influence this law had for decades following its passage. The petition read:

> that the presence of said Indians in Barron County is greatly injurious to the moral, social, and pecuniary interests of the general community, and also detrimental to their own best interests for the following reasons, to-wit:
>
> 1st. In violation of our statutes large number of deer are killed annually by fire hunting during the summer on our streams, by these Indians.
>
> 2d. The greater portion of the deer are wantonly wasted by the Indians; the skins are secretly bartered by them, not for clothing or food, but for intoxicating liquors which are drank by nearly all regardless of age or sex.
>
> 3d. That while thus intoxicated these Indian have brutally murdered several of their own number including, recently, by horrible burning, a helpless babe; and in addition thereto, have in numerous cases molested, and even jeopardized the lives of white citizens of this county.
>
> 4th. If these Indians were removed to their reservation, in addition to their being free from the use and influence of intoxicating drinks they would, for the fruits of their chase, receive clothing and food and, greater yet, would enjoy the benefits of education in the schools which the government so generously furnishes.[1]

Like whites throughout the nineteenth century seeking to segregate Native communities from their own, the county board cited exposure to alcohol as a corrupting influence on the behavior of the Ojibwe at Rice Lake. There is no historical evidence that corroborates the charge that an infant was burned as a result of intoxication. In fact, the only instance of violence within the community in the historical record is Giishkitawag's killing of Bidad, which was consistent with Ojibwe protocols of criminal justice. Nevertheless, the killing shook local whites, who portrayed it as "murder" throughout Giishkitawag's tenure as ogimaa. Also common to removal tropes was the notion that Native exposure to growing white communities was "detrimental to their own best interests" as the federal government could better provide education away from white communities in a less populated area, in this case the Lac Courte Oreilles Reservation. Yet the petition also noted that the presence of Ojibwe in Barron County was "greatly injurious to the moral, social, and pecuniary interests of the general community." This was a direct repudiation of the intercultural Rice Lake that Waabizheshi sought to achieve as the white population of the city grew. Instead, the county board and most of their constituents saw the presence of the Ojibwe in Barron County as something that was detrimental to both whites and Ojibwe (mostly whites though).

The petition also reveals another theme common to nineteenth-century Native history: the prioritizing of state statute over federal treaty rights. Despite treaties being the "supreme Law of the Land," the county board noted that the Ojibwe at Rice Lake killed deer during the summer "in violation of our statutes." This privileging of state statute over federal was foundational to state and local attempts to undermine the sovereignty of Native nations, as by this time recognition of tribal sovereignty was entrenched in federal law through treaties, as well as executive orders, congressional acts, and judicial rulings. Moreover, the petition illustrates the threat that state and municipal governments posed to tribal sovereignty. The Barron County Board directly challenged Ojibwe sovereignty by seeking to restrict the movement of Ojibwe people and enforcing state game laws over federal treaty rights. For the Ojibwe at Rice Lake, the impact of these measures on day-to-day Ojibwe life and sovereignty rivaled the impact of federal policies of allotment of reservation lands and education of Native children at boarding schools.

The county board's claim that "the greater portion of the deer are wantonly wasted by the Indians" was a common justification for suppressing Ojibwe treaty rights. In the Bad River Works Progress Administration historical project in the 1930s, Joe Stoddard, then in his nineties, articulated one of the clearest and most powerful rebuttals to the notion that the Ojibwe "wasted" resources:

> They claim that the fish and game have to be preserved; that the Indians are notorious slaughters and wasters of game and fish, and that they should be subjected to the same laws that affect the white men in regard to the taking of game and fish. I can state with authority and certainty that the arrival of the white men in this region marked the decline of the wild life of the forests and waters and the virtual and complete extinction of many species.[2]

Although Stoddard was speaking of fishing on Lake Superior, Stoddard came of age during the same era in the late nineteenth century that saw the attempted arrest of Giishkitawag for violating state game laws. The ability to manage resources was central to both American colonialism and Ojibwe sovereignty. In many ways, colonialism was about waste. Whites sought the power to determine what was wasteful and to be wasteful themselves. With the rampant waste of Wisconsin's timber industry at this time, whites charging the Ojibwe with being wasteful reveals the hypocrisy of colonialism. Interestingly, the petition and the 1894 arrest warrant for Giishkitawag were for deer hunting and not fishing. A century later, after federal courts found that Ojibwe treaty rights were never extinguished, non-Indian groups focused their opposition to treaty rights around spearing fish.

Evidence of the impact that state and municipal governments had on Ojibwe sovereignty is found in the federal response to the county board's petition. Writing to Commissioner of Indian Affairs Ezra Hayt, La Pointe Agent Isaac Mahan said of the Rice Lake Ojibwe, "They have caused myself and the employees (of the agency) considerable trouble. They are a worthless lazy drinking and fighting set of people, *but who makes them so*?" Mahan then went on to firmly place the blame on Barron County's elected officials for allowing sale of liquor to the Ojibwe and then angrily declared: "if the community in which alot of Indians live make such beds they should be *made to sleep in them*." Mahan saw whites in Barron County as contributing directly to the alcohol-related dysfunction they decried: "as soon as any man makes an attempt to stop the sale, the whole whiskey selling and drunken community, Indians and all oppose him for any office in the County, and almost every man in the County is either a candidate or expects to be before he dies." The last comment would make Mahan enemies among the local press in Barron County, beginning the personal animosity that many in Barron County held toward the agent. Mahan responded to the commissioner's instructions to remove the Rice Lake Ojibwe to the reservation by noting: "It can only be done by force and at considerable expense." Mahan argued that the agency had no such funds for the removal, and no Ojibwe in the entire agency received rations of any kind to feed the Ojibwe during and after the removal.[3] This last point is an important one: for this brief window, from the last annuity payment in 1874 to the beginning of timber sales on individual allotments in the mid-1880s, no Ojibwe at Rice Lake received any support from the federal government. In other words, the community was completely independent and autonomous from the federal government. In that context, what incentive was there for the community to remove to the reservation?

Mahan's response to the county board's petition and the growing animosity between the agent and Barron County residents personalize the struggle between the federal government and state and local governments. While Mahan was less than tactful in his characterization of white residents of Barron County, his response is still rooted in federal interests, which in this instance worked to uphold tribal sovereignty. Mahan's harsh indictment of the "entire drunken community" at Rice Lake reveals the extent to which white communities in northern Wisconsin were dysfunctional places at this time, burdened with the same problems that white settlers claimed were rampant in Ojibwe communities. It wasn't just Mahan who had this view of white communities in northern Wisconsin. In 1882, Mahan's successor William Durfee wrote that the seven Ojibwe reservations in his agency had "less lawlessness than in the adjacent white communities."[4]

Following the petition of the county board, many whites were unbending in their resolve to remove the Ojibwe. In August, the *Barron County Chronotype* reported that when three women and a small dog showed up a meeting of the county board it "produced a panic" and that members of the board "skedaddled for home."[5] Earlier in the summer, a much more serious incident illustrated white hostility to the Ojibwe. In June, Mahan traveled to Barron County and found that the week prior an Ojibwe was killed in Rice Lake when a group of Ojibwe, allegedly intoxicated, attacked two whites. The man who killed the Ojibwe claimed he was defending himself, and it is unclear whether the two men were intoxicated also. Mahan attempted to intervene in the matter: "I asked the authorities to investigate the matter, but the feeling against the Indians is so not spoken and unvoiced that no one would do anything."[6] This incident illustrates the central role of the law in American colonialism. Now the demographic minority in Rice Lake, the Ojibwe were unable to employ their own legal institutions against whites who committed crimes against them. At the same time, white residents and elected officials were unwilling to extend the protection of American law to Ojibwe people. More than federal policy, the lack of any legal system to protect the Ojibwe threatened their safety and very existence.

Likewise, Mahan reported that state courts were equally reluctant to prosecute those who sold liquor to the Ojibwe. Selling liquor to the Ojibwe was illegal under Article 7 of the treaty of 1854: "No spirituous liquors shall be made, sold, or used on any of the lands herein set apart for the residence of the Indians, and the sale of the same shall be prohibited in the Territory hereby ceded, until otherwise ordered by the President."[7] The Lake Superior Ojibwe were not unique in this regard; many treaties contained such provisions. As legal scholar Felix Cohen argued in the *Handbook of Federal Indian Law*, the right of Congress to regulate alcohol sales to Native people on- and off-reservation regardless of state lines was constitutionally based, as the commerce clause gives the Senate exclusive right to regulate commerce with Native nations.[8] Accordingly, Mahan reported: "it seems of no use to prosecute these people in the State Courts the only relief we have is in the US Courts."[9] Mahan's frustration at the inability to prosecute violence against Ojibwe people and his desire to prosecute in federal court those who sold alcohol to Ojibwe people in Barron County indicate that the federal government was willing to accommodate continued Ojibwe presence at Rice Lake and illustrate that by the late 1870s pressures to remove the Ojibwe to and contain them on the reservation emanated more from state and local governments.

Later in the year Mahan's report to the commissioner of Indian affairs regarding the petition of the Barron County Board was made public. The county board responded by firing back another petition to the commissioner of Indian affairs that answered Mahan's report. First, the county board argued that jurisdiction to prosecute those who sold alcohol to the Ojibwe was not vested in the county board. This deferring of responsibility is appropriate, as the county board itself was not charged with federal law enforcement. The county board argued that Mahan's characterization that alcohol sales to the Ojibwe were openly allowed was "a libel alike on the peace officers of our county and law observing residents thereof which your memoralists most indignantly resent." The county board answered Mahan's attack that "almost every man in the County is either a candidate for office or expects to be before he dies" by saying that it was "too ridiculous for notice." However, most significantly the county board disputed Mahan's argument that removal to the reservation would be too costly. The county board argued: "the fear of falling into the hands of the law works a powerful influence on the Indian mind, that the known determination of the government to insist upon the removal to their reservation of said Indians, will effect, with but little expense, the desired result."[10]

Despite the strategy proposed by the Barron County Board to remove the Ojibwe of Rice Lake to the reservation, the federal government did not take any further direct action regarding removal. The main outcome of the battle between Mahan and the Barron County Board was fallout in the local press. In June 1879 the *Barron County Chronotype* noted that Mahan "went to the reservation by the way of Rush City (Minnesota), giving this country a wide berth. He evidently doesn't like the recommendations he receives at Washington from the County Board of Barron County."[11]

In the fall of 1879, fifteen white settlers north of Rice Lake on Red Cedar Lake petitioned Mahan. The Red Cedar Lake petitioners argued that the Ojibwe were "very troublesome to the settlers and citizens here and an absolute nuisance no longer to be tolerated by us." The settlers demanded "immediate attention and remove them from here or the citizens will take the matter into our own hands and clear them out at once." However, this bravado was absurd: it was highly unlikely that fifteen settlers could remove a community of over two hundred people that had demonstrated military success right up until the Dakota were removed from Minnesota in 1862.

After all, if these settlers had power to remove the Ojibwe, they wouldn't need to petition a low-level bureaucrat located over a hundred miles away on the shores of Lake Superior. This time, federal inefficiency actually helped the Ojibwe, as Mahan told Commissioner of Indian Affairs Hayt that he would be leaving his post soon and that he could do nothing.[12] No doubt Mahan was sick of the complaints of settlers over a hundred miles away about just one of the seven reservations under his agency.

GIISHKITAWAG AND JOSEPH GURNOE

While Giishkitawag was successful in his efforts to avoid removal from local whites, the ogimaa departed from the strategies employed by his brother Waabizheshi. While Waabizheshi refused to participate in any type of relations with federal officials in far-off La Pointe, Giishkitawag engaged with federal officials more aggressively than his brother or father. In 1880, Joseph Gurnoe was appointed the farmer of the Lac Courte Oreilles Reservation at age sixty-seven. Formerly an interpreter at La Pointe, Gurnoe was of mixed descent.[13] Gurnoe had a rocky relationship with Giishkitawag and the other Ojibwe who refused to remove to the reservation. In 1881 Gurnoe wrote, "The Indians living off the reserve *very very* seldom visit the Indians on the reserve. They will come at payment time and promise to move on the reserve but as soon as the payment is over, they are gone and laugh at the Agent and Chiefs whom they have duped and deceived."[14]

In March 1882, Giishkitawag led a delegation of Ojibwe from Rice Lake to demand its share of government rations. No doubt Giishkitawag sought to supplement the community's food supply toward the end of the lean winter months. Giishkitawag, in the prime of his powers at age forty-three, was tough on the old man: "If I would not willingly give it to them they would take it, and if I interfered he (the headman a murderer) would put an end to me." While not mentioned by name, the "headman" no doubt was Giishkitawag, especially given Gurnoe's labeling him a "murderer," likely a reference to Giishkitawag's killing of Bidad in 1878 on the reservation. Gurnoe told the delegation he could not issue the rations and if the group took them by force the government would punish them. When the group demanded enough flour and pork that they could carry back with them, Gurnoe relented. Just as Gurnoe thought he had appeased the group, Giishkitawag persisted in his protests: "This appeared to satisfy them, when the headman the murderer once again broke out again making threats. Finally they went off, he growling and threatening still."[15] The entire episode was in stark contrast to the leadership style of Waabizheshi, who did not even warrant a reference in any federal records during his twenty-two years of leadership.

This encounter reveals the cultural gap between Gurnoe and the people of Lac Courte Oreilles. Gurnoe's labeling Giishkitawag a "murderer" is particularly telling. While this was no doubt partially an attempt to convey to his superior how dangerous his job could be, it also speaks to Gurnoe's cultural identity. Giishkitawag was justified in taking Bidad's life under traditional Ojibwe legal institutions, and most if not all in the community shared this belief. However, many persons of mixed descent during this time saw Ojibwe institutions and beliefs as barbaric and placed their faith in Catholic and American institutions. Many persons of mixed descent lived in distinct communities from Ojibwe people. Despite kinship ties to Ojibwe people and ability to speak Ojibwe, these individuals saw themselves as distinct from Ojibwe people, based on their practice of Catholicism, ability to speak French and sometimes also English, and making a living through some aspect of the fur trade and not traditional labor. This certainly was true of Gurnoe who, after all, was an employee of the US government. As the nineteenth century drew to a close, individuals in communities of mixed descent either migrated to the reservation or intermarried into the white population and took on a white identity. Persons of mixed descent who moved to the reservation sometimes clashed with traditional Ojibwe in the early twentieth century, as Gurnoe did at Lac Courte Oreilles.[16]

While Giishkitawag successfully resisted the removal efforts of Gurnoe, the community was challenged more directly by increasing white settlement in Rice Lake. The population of Rice Lake skyrocketed to 2,130 people in 1890. In 1870, the population of all of Barron County was 538, with most of that population focused to the south of Rice Lake in Barron and Chetek. However, things had changed by 1890, when the population stood at 15,416.[17] The role that the influx of these settlers had on the Ojibwe at Rice Lake and their ability to remain there cannot be overstated. The transformation of this space was drastic: instead of one highly mobile Ojibwe community, Barron County now consisted of roughly five white communities fixed in one location. Outside of these population centers, whites living in the county were likewise fixed in one location. It was not just the vast outnumbering of Ojibwe people but different approaches to engaging the land that threatened Ojibwe resistance to removal. As a result, the community under Giishkitawag spent more time at Long Lake, which had a lower white population, and attempted to build cordial relationships with white settlers there. Long Lake had always been an important site for the Rice Lake community to practice seasonal labor. Early Rice Lake settler Paul Kirkendall remembered attending an Ojibwe celebration of the rice harvest on the west shore.[18] When white settlers set up the Nobleton School on Long Lake in 1888, many Ojibwe children living in the area attended.[19]

ALLOTMENT AND REMOVAL

Despite the failure of the Barron County Board to remove the Ojibwe, what did spur the removal of the Ojibwe at Rice Lake was allotment of the Lac Courte Oreilles Reservation. The 1854 treaty, which created reservations for the Lake Superior Ojibwe Bands, called for the reservations to be eventually allotted (at the discretion of the president) into eighty acres to each head of family or person over twenty-one.[20] The Lac Courte Oreilles Reservation was surveyed into eighty-acre parcels in 1876, something that produced opposition among many young men at Lac Courte Oreilles and Bakweyawaa. According to the *Barron County Chronotype* these young men persuaded many on the reservation, "by threats of violence from occupying or taking possession of the lots assigned them."[21]

In 1878, the federal government first called the Ojibwe to select their allotments. By September 1878, 160 allotments had been selected, and the number grew to 205 by August 1880.[22] However, selection of an allotment meant nothing until a patent was issued. A patent legally conveyed title of allotment selection. Patents were slow in coming, leading to conflict within the Lac Courte Oreilles Band, in which Giishkitawag's community was directly involved. B. Cornell of Chippewa Falls petitioned Secretary of the Interior Carl Schurz in 1879 protesting the close relationship between the Giishkitawag's community and the Knapp, Stout Company and how this would impact allotment. Cornell noted "selections were promptly made for them by Agents of the above company. In this way the claims of the Red Cedar Indians cover a large portion of these most valuable lands." Cornell argued that the Knapp, Stout Company employed many in Giishkitawag's community (on the Red Cedar as Cornell identified them).[23] It is unknown what Cornell's interest was; likely he was associated with a Chippewa Falls lumber interest competing with the Knapp, Stout Company.

Giishkitawag attempted to utilize the new policy as a way to sustain the community off-reservation. This led to another tense standoff with Gurnoe. At this point the Giishkitawag's community (on Red Cedar as

Gurnoe identified them) were joined by the Lake Chetac community in resisting removal: "The Red Cedar and Shetek Indians are strongly averse to living on the reserve, averring that it is cowardly to be kept on the reserve by the government." Giishkitawag claimed an area of the reservation called Meadow Creek, a meadow on the reservation where he planned to cut hay. In the meantime, federal officials allotted the area to Ojibwe living on the reservation. Giishkitawag told other Ojibwe at Lac Courte Oreilles: "no man will come out alive who dared cut the grass on his allotment." According to Gurnoe, Giishkitawag had agreed to sell the hay to an unnamed merchant for pork and flour.[24]

Gurnoe petitioned La Pointe Agent William Durfee for four or five government troops to protect the pasture and the "good and working Indians" as they harvested the hay. In addition, Gurnoe requested that Durfee make a personal appearance to Giishkitawag's community to tell them the government would not tolerate harassment of Ojibwe on the reservation. Gurnoe pleaded with Durfee, arguing that Giishkitawag had already "murdered one of the tribe with impunity," another reference to Giishkitawag's killing of Bidad in 1878, and thus would have no problem making good on his threat. Gurnoe also sought circulation of regulations about trade among local vendors in the area to thwart transactions that were unapproved by the federal government like Giishkitawag's selling hay in exchange for pork and flour.[25]

Three weeks later, Gurnoe had heard no response from Durfee. Elsewhere on the reservation, Gurnoe reported that some allottees at Bakweyawaa were complaining that hay was being cut on their allotments. Gurnoe again complained to Durfee about Giishkitawag and his community: "You can not reason with them. They say the allotment scheme has failed and it is of no account, therefore they have a perfect right to cut hay wherever it is found."[26] With the allotment policy, Giishkitawag saw an opportunity to provide for his community. For Giishkitawag, using the allotment policy for resources was consistent with sustaining the community off-reservation. While Giishkitawag may at first seem radical and unbending, it is important to think about the broader context of Gurnoe's characterization of the leader. While he was more confrontational than Waabizheshi and even Nena'aangabi, this stance was confined to his relationship with federal officials. While he was downright tough on Gurnoe, Giishkitawag was not opposed to the presence of whites in northwest Wisconsin. After all, the hay being sold from the allotment he claimed was likely going to white cattle farms. Like Waabizheshi, Giishkitawag knew that alienating white settlers would bring violence. It is likely he targeted Gurnoe because he was keenly aware that Gurnoe was a lone sitting duck, with an overworked and underfunded superior a hundred miles away in La Pointe, with seven other reservations to worry about. Gurnoe could not even get the half dozen troops he requested.

The first patent on the Lac Courte Oreilles Reservation was issued March 11, 1881. By August 1882, 186 patents had been issued at Lac Courte Oreilles.[27] The following year, 188 additional patents were issued and another 77 by August 1884.[28] Giishkitawag received a patent for his allotment near Whitefish Lake on June 20, 1881.[29] Aazhaweyaa also received a patent that same day for her allotment, also near Whitefish Lake.[30] Thus, Giishkitawag, Aazhaweyaa, and hundreds of other Ojibwe at Lac Courte Oreilles, Bad River, and Red Cliff received patents to their allotments a full six years prior to passage of the Dawes Act, the legislation making allotment national policy.[31] Individuals submitted their selection to the agent, who approved them. This process was often highly contentious, as many had made claims earlier during the survey in 1876 that they thought were official.

Allotment was instrumental in the formation of new communities on the reservation. The reservation boundaries already encompassed villages at Lac Courte Oreilles and Bakweyawaa. The residents of the village on Lac Courte Oreilles took their allotments in close vicinity to where they were already living, and this community, which held the farmer and first school, became known as Reserve. Likewise, people from Bakweyawaa took their allotments in the area, and this community became known as Post, after trader Thaddeus Thayer's trading post. The communities off-reservation also tended to take their allotments together, forming the basis of what would become new communities on the reservation. Giishkitawag's community took their allotments on Whitefish Lake, on the western edge of the reservation, a few miles west of Reserve.

Allotment in the 1880s was the beginning of the Ojibwe of Rice Lake creating a new community at Whitefish. Increasing white settlement in Barron County and Wisconsin's enforcement of its game laws also contributed to this. Federal officials pushed individuals to remain on the reservation by cutting hay for cattle and growing crops such as potatoes on their allotments. However, what brought the Ojibwe to Whitefish was not so much agriculture, as federal officials hoped, but sale of timber on their allotments. This was the case for all the Lake Superior Ojibwe. In 1887, La Pointe Agent James Gregory submitted census data to the commissioner of Indian affairs and explained the population increases on reservations throughout the agency: "This is due to the fact that many are moving onto the reservations to get pineland, who have never lived there before."[32] However, many in Giishkitawag's community continued to spend much of their time at Long Lake and engage in seasonal labor activities near Rice Lake.

WILLIAM RUST AND THE THEFT OF LAC COURTE OREILLES TIMBER

Ojibwe allotments were private property that held valuable stands of old-growth timber. Allotment land was and still is held in trust, thus protected from alienation and taxation. Because the allotments on the Lac Courte Oreilles Reservation (and the other reservations of the Lake Superior Ojibwe) were allotted under the treaty of 1854 and not the Dawes Act, this trust never expired. As soon as Ojibwe received their allotments, they were anxious to begin timber harvest to provide much needed income. However, this was complicated by the history of timber harvest on the reservation in the 1870s. Federal policy based on racism and colonialism coupled with lack of federal oversight of timber corporations operating on the reservation resulted in the outright theft of millions of board feet of reservation timber from the Lac Courte Oreilles Band.

Prior to allotment, the Ojibwe at Lac Courte Oreilles were anxious to gain income from timber harvest on communally held reservation lands. In 1872, a year before declaration of the reservation boundaries, the Lac Courte Oreilles people petitioned for sale of their timber to provide income. A contract was made with William Rust of Eau Claire for sale of timber on the Lac Courte Oreilles Reservation for $50,000 over five years, to be paid in equal installments of $10,000 annually. The contract allowed Rust to harvest all the white pine on the reservation within three miles from any lake or stream that could float a log. The first season in 1873–74, Rust harvested fourteen million board feet of pine, amounting to $1.00 per one thousand board feet. This amount was extremely low: during the 1887–88 timber season at Lac Courte Oreilles the rate paid was $7.00 per one thousand board feet. When government officials realized their mistake in approving a contract that amounted to near robbery of the reservation's forest, the contract was modified to include $75,000 more to be paid in equal annual installments of $5,000 for fifteen years.[33]

In its very first year, the Rust contract was threatened by a Supreme Court decision. In October 1873, the Supreme Court ruled in *United States v. Cook* that Native people could not harvest timber on their lands, except in cases approved by the federal government in order to promote cultivation of lands. The case originated on the Oneida Reservation in Wisconsin, when under the direction of Oneida leadership, tribal members began cutting timber of reservation lands held in common. The logs were sold to lumberman George Cook, which prompted the federal government bring suit against Cook for recovery of the timber. The Supreme Court cited *Johnson v. McIntosh* (1823), and the infamous discovery doctrine, where Chief Justice John Marshall ruled that Native title to land was that of mere occupancy and title to the land resided with the European "discoverers" and the American government as their successors. Therefore, the court found, the Oneida had no right to harvest timber on the reservation, since their title to the land was that of strictly occupancy, and the right to sell timber belonged to the government alone.[34]

In their analysis of *Johnson v. McIntosh*, scholars David Wilkins and K. Tsianina Lomawaima argue that the decision did not reflect the historical reality of how the French and British saw Native title to lands in the seventeenth and eighteenth centuries but instead was the result of the expansionist goals of the United States at the time of the decision. At the time of Marshall's decision in *Johnson*, the government sought to dispose of Native title in the southern Great Lakes and elsewhere as quickly as possible to meet the demands of increasing numbers of settlers in the region. Wilkins and Lomawaima argue that historical evidence indicates that the French and British understood discovery to not in any way impair Native title. According to Wilkins and Lomawaima, the French and the British only understood discovery rights to mean the exclusive right to first purchase of Native lands.[35]

The *Cook* decision was a clear example of American colonial efforts to assert total control over Indians, even on reservations. The Supreme Court effectively barred the Oneida (and all Native nations) from managing their own timber resources on their own lands. This was a direct attack on tribal sovereignty with tragic results, as federal management of reservation forests was often marred by corruption. The court's decision in *Cook* was not based on legal precedent or how Native nations used timber resources on their lands. Instead, the court's ruling in *Cook* can be better understood in the context of assimilation-era federal policies of the late nineteenth century, such as allotment and boarding schools. The court's ruling in *Cook*, that the only exception where timber could be cut was for agricultural improvements, was in keeping with the direction of federal policy that sought to transform Native economies from traditional labor activities to agriculture. The court ruled that even removing dead and down timber was illegal, as timber on tribal lands was property of the United States because the discovery doctrine made the government true owners of even reservation lands. Native people could not legally cut dead timber on their own reservation lands until Congress passed the Dead and Down Timber Act of 1889.[36] Internationally, Ojibwe in Canada faced similar restrictions as their Ojibwe relatives in the United States in terms of cutting green timber on reserve lands. Canada allowed only harvest of dead timber by permit.[37]

As a result of the *Cook* decision, the Rust contract was voided, and Rust was ordered by La Pointe Agent Isaac Mahan to cease operations in the upcoming harvest season. Rust did not. During the winter of 1874–75, Rust removed an undetermined amount of timber from the Lac Courte Oreilles Reservation without *any* compensation to the Lac Courte Oreilles Band.[38] Federal officials took no action against Rust in the outright theft of reservation timber. Rust's theft of Lac Courte Oreilles timber and federal officials' unwillingness to take action graphically illustrates how corporate interests were able to exploit federal policy for their own profits due to the fact that most reservations are located in isolated areas with little or no federal oversight. At the local level was where American colonialism was the most dangerous to tribal sovereignty: disorganization, bureaucratic ineptitude, and neglect allowed policy, no matter how well intentioned, to be exploited for profit at the expense of Native peoples. Rust went on to become a very wealthy man and influential politician: first as a state senator, then as mayor of Eau Claire.[39]

ALLOTMENT AND TIMBER HARVEST

In the 1940s, Lac Courte Oreilles spiritual leader John Mink told anthropologist Robert Ritzenthaler that allotment was "The worst thing that ever happened to the Indian. Timber companies really established the reservation. They wanted timber rights and pushed the setting up of a reservation through."[40] Mink's sentiments speak to the result of federal mismanagement of reservation timber that resulted in massive corruption. There was an alternative: tribal sovereignty. Had Ojibwe leaders been more directly involved in the management of their own forest resources, the theft and corruption of the Rust contract and sale of allotment timber would have been avoided. Elsewhere in Wisconsin on the Menominee Reservation, tribal leaders dictated the harvest of reservation timber using what would today be called sustained yield forestry. This provided employment for tribal citizens for a much longer duration. Profitable timber operations continue on the Menominee Reservation to the present day, more than a century after the surrounding white communities and other reservations in Wisconsin were stripped of valuable old-growth timber.[41]

While individual allottees pushed for sale of their timber as a way to provide income to their families, allotment presented a whole new set of issues in regard to the harvest of reservation timber. Unlike reservation lands held in common, allottees were private property owners. Both allottees and timber companies pressured the federal government to allow allotments to be open to timber harvest.[42] La Pointe Indian Agent William Durfee (who succeeded Mahan in 1881) responded in 1883. Under the Durfee Plan, allottees were allowed to sell three-fourths of their timber and required to leave one-fourth remaining for future use, such as for fuel or fencing. The Indian agent made contracts on behalf of individual allottees with outside contractors. Additionally, non-Indians were not allowed work on timber harvesting, as Durfee wanted to supplement Ojibwe income as well as provide Ojibwe men with experience in the timber industry so they could work in lumber camps off-reservation. It was a well-thought-out plan that sought to provide the Ojibwe with much needed income. However, like most federal initiatives, corruption and lack of oversight robbed Native people.

During the first winter of 1882–83, 3,302,880 board feet of pine were sold from Lac Courte Oreilles, with the figure increasing to 31,391,950 board feet in 1883–84 and 25,260,760 board feet in the 1884–85 season. The 1885–86 season brought a marked increase in production to 46,510,156 board feet. Lac Courte Oreilles was the focal point for timber production in the La Pointe Agency (which included Bad River, Red Cliff, and Lac du Flambeau in Wisconsin and the Fond du Lac, Grand Portage, and Bois Forte Reservations in Minnesota) with 72 percent of all lumber in the La Pointe Agency in the 1885–86 season coming from Lac Courte Oreilles.[43] As impressive as these totals were, they produced wealth that was not sustainable.

In keeping with federal paternalism, money earned from sale of allotment timber did not go directly to the Ojibwe: it was paid to the agency, who then paid individual allottees. As a result, the federal archives from the mid-1880s are filled with thousands of requests from Ojibwe people wanting their money from the agent. Allottees were private property owners, and yet there was a third party dispersing monies that came from the sale of timber on private property. This illustrates how much American colonialism was rooted in white supremacy. After all, private property ownership was a cornerstone of the American ideal that federal policy makers were pushing Native people to assimilate to. However, Native people were not allowed to manage their own private property. Even more appalling, this is still the case today: those having shares in allotments have no say when timber harvest occurs or who the contractor is. The Bureau of Indian Affairs (BIA) makes all of these decisions. The contractor pays the BIA following the timber harvest, not the owner directly.

Although the Durfee Plan did have guidelines, federal officials failed to ensure proper compliance. As a result, corruption was rampant. Allottees at Lac Courte Oreilles had little legal recourse when they were defrauded of their timber through timber trespass. However, the same was not true of trader Thaddeus Thayer. Thayer, a non-Indian, married an Ojibwe woman and started his trading post at the Bakweyawaa community on the Chippewa River in 1865.[44] This Ojibwe community soon became known as Post, so named after Thayer's trading post. In February 1881, Thayer purchased logs from the allotments of Biidaanakwad and Chiz-ai-aw. Both cut the logs and delivered them to Thayer. Thayer paid Biidaanakwad $504.60 and Chiz-ai-aw $59.95. On April 29, 1881, on orders from the Indian agent, General Land Office Agents George A. Henry and Benjamin F. Millard seized Thayer's logs and sold them to Stockings and Savings for $809.20, which went to the federal government. They moved the logs behind Thayer's dam on Pokegamon Creek to float them downstream for transportation, in the process inflicting $200 worth of damage to Thayer's dam.[45]

Thayer brought suit, and in 1885 the US Court of Claims ruled on the case. In its decision, the court ruled "that the government is not responsible for the wrongful acts of its officers. It is liable only for the money which it received on consequence of those wrongful acts."[46] Therefore, the court denied Thayer damages done to his dam during the trespass of the agents but awarded Thayer $809.20 from the sale of the logs. In the decision, the court cited *United States v. Cook* that allottees could cut timber for improvement and cultivation of the land with the approval of the government.

Foundational to American colonialism was how the law only protected whites. Thayer, a non-Indian, had the means to seek redress in the courts, something few Ojibwe had the means to do. Instead, all the Ojibwe could do was complain to the agent, a bureaucrat, who himself could only complain to his superiors, even if he were so inclined. Most of the time, these complaints went unanswered. This was a matter that affected Ojibwe people as individual property owners, not as a collective Native nation. Yet Ojibwe people at Lac Courte Oreilles were not given the same legal protection that other individual property owners received. This is yet another example of how Ojibwe quality of life was impacted by the failure to extend equal protection under the law, which impacted Ojibwe life as much if not more than federal policy.

There were other issues of corruption under the Durfee Plan. In particular, enforcing the provision that called for only Indian laborers in timber operations proved to be a difficult task. In 1886, twenty-one timber operators petitioned Durfee's successor James Gregory claiming they had made every effort to employ Indians in their operations on the reservation but had failed. According to the petitioners, economics played a large role: "Indian sawyers will not work for less than from 40 to 45 dollars per month. White men are working on the outside for 22 to 26 dollars." According to the petition, the reason for this was scarcity: "Indian labor at any price is scarce."[47] Not all the parties to the petition were outsiders. Among the signers were persons of mixed descent such as John Quaderer, Ira Isham, Joseph Gurnoe, and John LaRush. In addition, Giishkitawag's nephew Thomas Bracklin was among the signatories.

That same winter the new farmer, William Rusler, was left to police each camp at the height of timber harvest: "As to the matter of white men I find some of them in each camp (besides the teamsters cooks and foreman), and have had those not allowed here discharged at each camp I visit, but as there are so many camps not a few of them go to other camps and find work." Rusler went on to claim: "I find the Indians who want to work are all employed, and a disposition on the parties running these camps to give them the preference every time. The wages given the Indians are from $26 to $45 per month and the whites who have been working averaged from $26 to $35 per month."[48] While Ojibwe laborers were able to get slightly higher wages, Rusler's assessment also reveals how local whites took advantage of federal Indian policy to bolster the local economy. This was no different than Alexander Ramsey's plan to move Wisconsin Ojibwe annuities to Minnesota in 1850. Like so many federal policy initiatives, the lack of oversight meant local whites were able to exploit federal policy to enrich themselves.

These difficulties pushed La Pointe Agent James Gregory to modify the Durfee Plan without authorization of the commissioner of Indian affairs. Gregory began approving contracts with many large timber companies beginning with the 1886–87 harvest season and ignoring Durfee Plan provisions requiring Ojibwe labor. Gregory believed provisions requiring Ojibwe labor promoted Ojibwe absenteeism on the job and that Ojibwe laborers could demand exorbitant wages. As a result of allowing white workers on the reservation, the pine harvest increased dramatically from 46,510,156 board feet during the 1885–86 harvest season to 78,069,770 board feet in the 1886–87 harvest season. The 1887–88 harvest season brought a further increase to 88,347,340 board feet. During this season, the price of $4.75 to $7 per one thousand feet of pine brought Lac Courte Oreilles allottees $218,671. The figure of $7.00 per one thousand feet of pine contrasts sharply with the $1.00 per one thousand feet paid the Lac Courte Oreilles in 1873–74 under William Rust. During this massive year for timber harvest, a number of contractors worked on the reservation, including Dobie & Stratton; England, Thomas, & Clark; Valley Lumber Company;

D. F. Carroll; and Charles Bergeson. All of these contractors violated Durfee Plan provisions requiring Ojibwe labor.[49]

The massive amount of timber being removed from Lac Courte Oreilles by non-Native contractors prompted a Senate investigation, which resulted in a halt in all timber operations on all the reservations in the La Pointe Agency until new regulations were approved. As to be expected, the Senate investigation found widespread violations of the Durfee Plan, concluding:

> That a plan designed to benefit the Indians by giving them for many years useful employment and reasonable sums of money while removing from the reservations only trees which could be judiciously spared and leaving the rest suitably preserved and located, had been perverted into a system under which greedy contractors have rushed upon the reservations; have aroused the desire of the Indians to obtain money without work; have made contracts practically unlimited as to the number of trees to be cut; have brought in swarms of lumbermen to do the work; have already denuded the finest timber tracts, and are stripping the allotments so rapidly, that it is probable that within two or three years the pine lumber of the reservations will all be gone, and that not long after the temporary and delusive prosperity of the Indians will cease, and the Government will be asked for appropriations for their support.[50]

Beyond the issue of individual allottees being defrauded of timber and using white laborers in the lumber camps, the findings of the Senate committee bring another issue to the fore: how the reservation timber resource was managed. Once Durfee Plan provisions requiring Ojibwe labor were ignored under James Gregory, old-growth white pine at Lac Courte Oreilles was stripped within a couple of years. Had Ojibwe leaders had a voice in determining how the resource was harvested, as happened on the Menominee Reservation, reservation timber could have provided Ojibwe families income for a longer duration. This would have benefitted the federal government as well. As the Senate committee noted, sustainable forest management would have made the Lac Courte Oreilles (and other Lake Superior Ojibwe) more self-sufficient, and thus less in need of federal aid.

The massive clear-cutting on the Lac Courte Oreilles Reservation as a result of the abuses of timber operations under Gregory left the Lac Courte Oreilles timber resource devastated. Furthermore, the clear-cutting made the reservation a tinderbox, and fires raged throughout 1889. After one fire in the summer wiped out six million board feet of remaining pine, new La Pointe Agent M. A. Leahy recommended that the remainder of pine on the Lac Courte Oreilles Reservation be cut immediately to prevent more loss of timber due to fire. However, these suggestions were met with no response from Washington. In the meantime, Ojibwe men had to go to lumber camps off-reservation to find winter work. New regulations came in 1893 with the La Pointe Plan, which stipulated awarding a contract to one contractor who received a monopoly on reservation timber harvest. The contractors themselves set prices for allottees, had to process the timber at sawmills on the reservation, and were required to adhere to regulations, including use of Ojibwe laborers. With just one contractor, the task of ensuring regulations were being followed was easier than under Gregory, when five different contractors were running rampant on the Lac Courte Oreilles Reservation alone.[51]

The La Pointe Plan was enacted on an experimental basis on the Lac du Flambeau Reservation (which had much more pine intact than Lac Courte Oreilles) for the 1893–94 season. After it proved a success there, the other reservations began contracting with a single contractor beginning in 1894. At Lac Courte Oreilles, Turrish Lumber Co. of Rhinelander was awarded the contract under the La Pointe Plan. In the first season in 1894–95, 13,469,410 board feet of pine were harvested. This increased the following season when an additional 118 allotments were made at Lac Courte Oreilles, resulting in twenty-two million board feet harvested in 1895–96. The timber harvest was suspended in 1896–97, and in 1897–98 the 3.5 million board feet of pine harvested by Turrish was the last of the standing old-growth pine on the Lac Courte Oreilles Reservation.[52]

ALLOTMENT TIMBER HARVEST AND REMOVAL

Despite corruption, allottees still received hundreds of thousands of dollars annually from the sale of allotment timber from 1886 to 1888. During the peak of season of production in 1887–88 Lac Courte Oreilles allottees received $218,671. To put this in perspective, in 1874 the Lac Courte Oreilles Band received $1,032 during the last treaty annuity.[53] The income received by allottees for sale of timber dwarfed annual payments received for land cession treaties. Income from timber sales on allotments served to supplement the Ojibwe standard of living in the wake of the destruction of wild rice beds in northwest Wisconsin. On the Lac du Flambeau Reservation one hundred miles east of Lac Courte Oreilles, Tom Badger described the prosperity enjoyed by some allottees: "Most of the Indians there had houses—log houses and frame houses. At that time some of the Indians had a lot of money which they got from selling timber on their land."[54] While allottees may have enjoyed an increased standard of living, this was only for a few fleeting years in the late 1880s at the peak of the timber harvest. At the end of this time, Ojibwe timber resources were devastated, most traditional areas for ricing were destroyed, and Wisconsin increasingly enforced its game laws on Ojibwe people. All of this resulted in poverty for the Wisconsin Ojibwe throughout most of the twentieth century.

Furthermore, the wealth from sale of allotment timber was not distributed evenly. Examination of the 1887–88 harvest season illustrates this. Giishkitawag's timber was worth $146.86. This was on the low end of the sixty-two allottees who sold timber that season. The high was Harriet Duprie, whose timber was worth $4,325.81. There were twenty allottees whose timber was worth more than a thousand dollars, including the author's grandfather's grandmother Sophia LaRush, whose timber was worth $1,491.51. Only seven of the twenty allottees receiving more than one thousand dollars had Ojibwe names. Since at this time Ojibwe people had Ojibwe names, this may suggest that persons of mixed descent were able to manipulate the system more effectively. The reason for this wasn't just the amount of timber cut: price paid for stumpage varied widely from $6.25 to $1.25. Giishkitawag only got $2.00.[55]

The promise of this prosperity drew Ojibwe to the reservation, as life became tougher off-reservation by increased enforcement of Wisconsin game laws and pressure to remove from white settlers. The account of Tom Badger on the Lac du Flambeau Reservation sheds light on Ojibwe motivation to move onto the reservation. Allotment at Lac du Flambeau began five years later than Lac Courte Oreilles, in 1886.[56] The first time Tom Badger came onto the Lac du Flambeau Reservation was in 1897 when he was in his twenties to apply for his allotment. Badger's motivations for securing an allotment shed light on Ojibwe motivations for securing allotment and eventually moving onto reservations:

> We had no money at the time, but the paper we had with us to give old Herrick was to let Herrick have the right to cut timber on our land when we got it. The storekeeper took a piece of paper and wrote out the allotment number that was on the paper we were to give to Herrick. Then we went back to the Farmer's Office again. They took some things down and then sent for a map showing these two allotments. Then we went down to Herrick's office and handed our papers over to Herrick, who gave them to the clerk. They had alot of maps on the wall.[57]

From there, Badger and his family visited the Ojibwe community on Lac du Flambeau. While not remaining on the reservation full-time at this point, taking an allotment began a period of spending an increasing amount of time on the reservation for Badger's family, which culminated with Badger permanently settling on the reservation in the 1910s.

Some of the Ojibwe community under Giishkitawag moved to the reservation in the early 1880s. For example, Giishkitawag's niece Mary Dingley moved to the reservation with her husband Ira Isham in 1881.[58] However, most in the community remained at Long Lake throughout the 1880s. For reasons not specified in historical sources, the community left the village site on Indian Point at Long Lake in 1892. According to early Long Lake settler Arthur Hovey, the Ojibwe community at Long Lake split after the summer of 1892. Some moved to the reservation, while others moved to a new site a mile and a half north called Bakerville, after Joe Baker, a resident of the community. The obituary of Giishkitawag's son Charles White reported that he left Long Lake and moved to the reservation in 1892.[59] Once the final old-growth white pine was harvested in 1898, the value of allotment timber was drastically reduced. Since allotment failed to create sustaining income, even the Ojibwe on the reservation needed to practice seasonal labor off-reservation. Movement was facilitated by new modes of transportation. Early Long Lake settler Arthur Hovey remembered:

> Soon after school started, the Indians started coming down the lake to the old landing below our home on their way to Bear Lake for their annual rice harvest. They came from two villages on Long Lake, from Lake Sissabagama, Sand Lake, and from the Reservation. Some came by canoe and others came in light wagons and in almost anything that had wheels.[60]

However, even for those who moved to the reservation, Ojibwe cultural ties to traditional areas kept the Ojibwe coming back. For example, early Long Lake settler Lena Larson remembered Ojibwe returning to leave spirit dishes for deceased relatives at gravesites after moving to the reservation.[61]

However, the state of Wisconsin became an increasing threat to the presence of Ojibwe off-reservation. Again, the law, rather than policy, was the primary tool for making this happen. Throughout the ceded territory, Wisconsin game wardens increasingly sought to enforce state game laws in the 1890s. Lac du Flambeau Ojibwe Tom Badger described losing his birchbark canoe when his brother-in-law borrowed the canoe while fishing off-reservation in the late nineteenth century. Badger's brother-in-law was forced to leave the canoe behind in order to flee from a game warden. The game warden seized the canoe, which Badger could not retrieve since they were off-reservation.[62]

As dire as the situation was for Ojibwe in the United States, the situation in Canada was worse. Ojibwe there were subject to dispossession not only by whites seeking farmland, but also by the government seeking lands. The protected one million acre "wilderness" of Quetico Provincial Park we know today was achieved by expelling the Sturgeon Lake Ojibwe Band in 1913. Forest rangers destroyed Ojibwe trap lines and cabins and forced Ojibwe families out at gunpoint. Furthermore, in 1914, off-reserve hunting was criminalized throughout Ontario. As in the United States, Canadian Ojibwe treaty rights were outright ignored in the prosecution of the Ojibwe for violation of provincial game laws. In their excellent study on Ojibwe removal in northwest Ontario, Leo G. Waisberg, Joan A. Lovisek, and Tim E. Holzkamm describe the ordeal of Ojibwe Pierre Hunter of Lac Seul. Hunter was convicted for possession of moose meat, imprisoned at Port Arthur, two hundred miles away, for thirty days, then released with no means of transportation home. After four weeks, Hunter died, since killing game to eat would have put him back in jail. Ontario officials denied any responsibility for the incident, and no immediate changes to Ontario game laws resulted.[63]

The suppression of Ojibwe treaty rights had real impact on Ojibwe quality of life. As the state of Wisconsin increasingly prosecuted tribal members for hunting and fishing off-reservation, the Ojibwe had less access to traditional food such as wild rice and venison. The void was filled with less healthy, Western food such as flour and pork obtained through government commodities. In his study of Lake Superior Ojibwe demographics in the nineteenth and early twentieth centuries, historian James Oberly found that the population of the Lake Superior Ojibwe reached its lowest point in 1900, a full decade after the Native population reached its lowest point nationally. However, Oberly's research found that birthrates for the Lake Superior Ojibwe during this time did not decline, and in fact were higher than the overall Wisconsin population. The reason for the population decline was a horrific infant mortality rate: in 1890, out of 152 births only 72 babies survived their first year. Oberly attributed this decline to a lack of access to nutritious foods, which was the direct result of Wisconsin's suppression of off-reservation treaty rights.[64]

CONCLUSION

Much has been written about the role of federal policies such as boarding schools and allotment and their adverse effect on tribal sovereignty during the closing years of the nineteenth century. However, for the Ojibwe of Rice Lake, American colonialism was broader than just federal policy during these years. Even the impact of federal policy diverges from common ideas about Native history. For example, what had an adverse effect on Ojibwe family income wasn't so much allotment itself as the inability of the Ojibwe to effectively manage forest resources on their allotments. There was a model for this: despite a turbulent history, today the Menominee Reservation forest in northeast Wisconsin still stands as an example of how old-growth forest can be sustainably managed using select cut principals.

Despite the corruption, the income from timber sales on allotments brought Giishkitawag and the Ojibwe community of Rice Lake to the reservation. Giishkitawag's leadership was characterized by his confrontational stance that yielded some success. Giishkitawag successfully resisted the removal efforts of Barron County officials in 1879. Likewise, Giishkitawag successfully defied reservation farmer Joseph Gurnoe by threatening him and securing supplies for his community. However, growth of the white population made Rice Lake an increasingly hostile place to the Ojibwe in the 1880s, as a white population of a couple thousand by 1890 vastly outnumbered the Ojibwe community of a couple hundred. The Ojibwe responded by spending more time in less populated areas of Barron County such as Long Lake. However, state enforcement of its game laws provided the greatest pressure on the community yet to remove, more than federal policy, local governments, and increasing white settlement. The reason was Wisconsin's willingness to employ the law and even violence to achieve its goals. This represented the greatest danger to the community and especially to its defiant leader. This produced an environment where Giishkitawag could be legally murdered.

CHAPTER 6

The Murder of Joe White and the Culmination of Removal

"I KNEW THE FACE WELL. BLOOD WAS RUNNING OUT OF HIS EARS. A crack in his skull. His right shoulder all mashed up. Next I saw a bullet mark," commented Joe Baker, providing an eyewitness testimony during the arraignment of two Wisconsin game wardens who murdered Giishkitawag, or Joe White. At the time of his chilling account in 1894, Baker and the rest of his community at Bakerville still lived off the reservation in wigwams, four decades after the Treaty of La Pointe had created the Lac Courte Oreilles Reservation. Among their Ojibwe friends and relatives, the villagers of Bakerville were in the minority by choosing to live on traditional Ojibwe lands not included in the reservation. In many ways, Baker and his community, who had been part of the larger Ojibwe community led by Giishkitawag, embodied the late ogimaa's resistance to removal to the reservation.

Michigan Supreme Court Justice John Voelker (using his pseudonym Robert Traver) wrote in his classic 1958 novel *Anatomy of a Murder*, "a trial was after all a savage and primitive battle for survival itself."[1] Voelker's dramatic words refer to the high stakes involved in every trial, but they ring even truer for American Indians involved in courtroom battles at the turn of the century. Through the trial of Joe White's killers, two lawmen of the state of Wisconsin, the Ojibwe would once again experience the extension of American colonialism into their everyday lives. Scholars may dwell on federal Indian policy as a way to understand Native history, but it is also important to remember how local history and smaller legal stories and events, including the trial of Joe White's killers, have also determined the shape of broader policy initiatives, including Indian removal. An acquittal for Martin and Hicks, the two Wisconsin lawmen, meant that local whites were willing to accept violence when extending their authority over American Indian people, even condoning murder in the process.

Joe White exercised his legal right by killing a deer, but he had also resisted removal to the reservation. Both of these acts challenged the authority of the state of Wisconsin over Indian lives. By the time of Joe White's murder and the trial of his killers, the experiences of white settlers with Ojibwe people varied greatly. Some settlers saw the Ojibwe strictly as savage obstacles to civilization while others had deep connections to them based on exchanges that included goods and even kinship. The individuals involved in the trial of Joe White's killers, including their level of interaction with the Ojibwe, were critical to the verdict. In Wisconsin in 1894, that verdict was by no means inevitable.

THE MURDER OF JOE WHITE

On Thursday, December 13, 1894, Deputy Game Warden Horace Martin and his assistant Josiah Hicks were sent to serve a warrant issued by Rice Lake Municipal Judge Franklin Angel for the arrest of Joe White, fifty-seven, for hunting deer out of season. Journeying the road from Rice Lake to Long Lake (today County Road M), the pair traveled twenty-five miles to the head of Long Lake where Joe White was working at a logging camp. On their arrival at the camp, Martin and Hicks learned that Joe White had just left for the reservation. The game wardens caught up to White not far from the logging camp.

White was traveling with a group that included his wife Ikwewidog, forty-seven, one of his daughters, and his son Charles, age eighteen. The group also included another man from Whitefish later identified as "Wabasha," and five other women and children.[2] At gunpoint the game wardens separated Joe White from the group, disarmed the ogimaa and the other Ojibwe, and tossed all firearms out of their reach. According to all witnesses, when Martin and Hicks confronted White, he agreed to go willingly but then stepped back when Martin tried to handcuff him. Martin and Hicks claimed that Joe White then brandished a knife. Regardless, all eyewitness testimonies agreed that White was then beaten: first Martin struck White with handcuffs on the head and then Hicks struck White with a gun on the shoulder and head. The coroner noted that White's skull was fractured as a result of the trauma from the cuffs and gun. When White got up and fled, he was fatally shot in the back by Hicks, a fact confirmed by all eyewitness testimony (including Martin and Hicks) as well as the coroner. As the ogimaa lay wounded, his teenage son Charles ran to his side, only to hear his last words, "I am killed. I cannot live."[3]

Contrary to how law enforcement officers should perform their duties,

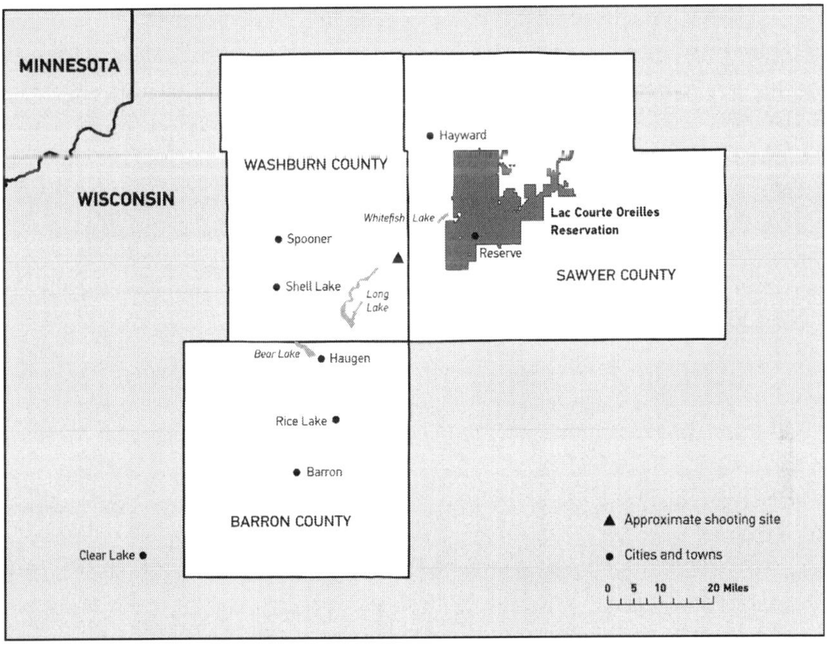

Important places in the trial for the murder of Joe White.

Martin and Hicks fled the scene on foot, leaving Joe White's dead body at the scene. Surviving documents do not specify exactly when the body was taken for autopsy. The game wardens arrived in Rice Lake at 1:00 a.m. The next day, December 14, Washburn County prosecutor William Knapp went to Rice Lake to meet with Martin, who agreed to be questioned the following day in Shell Lake. After traveling with the prosecutor to Shell Lake, Martin told Knapp that White resisted arrest, pulled a knife, and attempted to cut him. According to his own admission, Martin struck White in the head and White started to run away. Martin then ordered Hicks to shoot him. Evidently, Martin felt his actions were justified, as Knapp later remarked, "He made these statements to me without being solicited in any way to do so."[4]

The *Spooner Register* reported that on December 18, La Pointe Indian Agent Lieutenant William A. Mercer was in Duluth gathering evidence about the case. The paper argued: "The federal authorities will also demand jurisdiction on the grounds that the Indian had a right to hunt where he did." The article also noted that the state had jurisdiction on the basis of the crime occurring off-reservation.[5] Nothing in existing federal records explains why the federal government never assumed jurisdiction in the case. The only reference to the incident in the federal archives is a December 14 handwritten Western Union telegram from Horace Martin to the Sawyer County Sheriff reading: "Notify Indian Agent Joe White Indian shot about 12 miles south La Courte Oreilles Reservation Long Lake Road while resisting arrest." The telegram accompanied a letter from Sawyer County District Attorney John Riordan to Agent Mercer stating that the state would have jurisdiction if the crime was committed off-reservation. What neither Riordan nor Mercer (nor Martin apparently) knew at the time was that the crime occurred in adjacent Washburn County and a different county district attorney would prosecute the case once it was clear the federal government was not going to assume jurisdiction.[6]

The failure of the federal government to assert jurisdiction in the case reveals much about the nature and practice of American colonialism at the close of the nineteenth century. The unwillingness of federal officials to assert jurisdiction in the case was not surprising and was consistent with federal policies that had assimilation as their objective. While Ojibwe treaty rights were, as all treaties, "the Law of the Land" according to the Constitution, promoting treaty rights and tribal sovereignty ran counter to efforts to assimilate Native people. Existing laws that recognized and sought to enhance tribal sovereignty were meaningless if they were not enforced. Failure to enforce laws enacted to protect tribal sovereignty was just as effective as federal policies that directly attacked tribal sovereignty, such as allotment or boarding schools.

At the local level, it was up to Indian agents to protect tribal sovereignty when states violated treaty rights. However, most Indian agents were overworked bureaucrats drawn from the military with little to no experience in Indian affairs and even less sympathy for Native people. Legal scholar Sidney Harring argues that Indian agents were not interested in enforcement of the law, but instead acted as stewards of assimilation goals: "the BIA created a substantial system of policing and punishment that was administrative rather than legal, therefore effectively beyond the reach of federal or state courts."[7] At the same time, Harring also found that increasingly in the late nineteenth and early twentieth centuries the federal government ceded jurisdiction to states for efficiency's sake.[8] This legal environment explains the failure of the federal government to defend Ojibwe treaty rights.

MARTIN AND HICKS

Martin and Hicks both came of age during the dispossession of Ojibwe people from important areas that sustained Ojibwe communities of the region in the nineteenth century. Josiah Hicks was born in Chetek in 1861, the son of Irish immigrants.[9] Three years prior to Hicks's birth, Waabizheshi sought unsuccessfully to locate the Lac Courte Oreilles Reservation at Chetek, as the massive rice beds of nearby Prairie Rice Lake sustained not just the Ojibwe at Rice Lake but most of the Lac Courte Oreilles Band. Horace Martin was born in Maine in 1866, but his family migrated to Clear Lake, Wisconsin, when Martin was a young boy. While Martin's father was born in Maine, his mother hailed from Ireland. Martin's father was a farmer, and it is likely that he moved the family to the area for access to cheaper and better land.[10] The challenge of farming on recently cutover lands was something Martin's father likely had experience with in Maine. As a young adult, Martin left the family farm in Clear Lake and moved forty miles northeast to the larger town of Rice Lake.

Colonialism was not just policy or laws that functioned independently, but instead was the result of the decisions of people. While Martin and Hicks had motives unique to their individual personalities, the environment in which they were raised shaped the decisions they made. Martin and Hicks both inhabited a world where more economic opportunities were made possible because of Ojibwe dispossession. Both men's parents were either immigrants or from another part of the country who migrated to two locations, Rice Lake and Chetek near Prairie Rice Lake, vital to Ojibwe survival. Their families, and others like them, did not have any type of economic relationship or any other ties to Ojibwe people. These two factors directly shaped their hostile view of Indians, especially a leader like Joe White who defiantly resisted removal. In fact, after the murder, Martin wrote a jailhouse letter to the editor of his hometown *Clear Lake Mirror* detailing how Joe White's political standing was enhanced by his resistance to removal and how this justified his killing of White. Later, at the trial, the wardens made Joe White's hostility to white settlers the entire basis of their defense. The environment in which Martin and Hicks were raised shaped the choices they made. Accordingly, the two game wardens made a choice that December day to shoot down the Indian leader who most embodied resistance to removal.

FRIDAY, DECEMBER 21: INQUISITION

An inquisition was held on Friday, December 21, over a week after the murder, at the scene of the crime. A jury of six was convened to determine whether Martin and Hicks would be charged. District Attorney Knapp, Justice of the Peace Andrew Ryan, the witnesses, and the six jurors journeyed to the home of town of Long Lake Chairman William Todd. From there the group walked ten miles to the scene of the crime.[11] Shell Lake physician George Barker testified that White died from a bullet that entered his right buttock and passed through his pelvis and that the wound was sufficient enough to cause immediate death. Barker also testified that the head injuries Joe White received as a result of the beating would also cause death, although not immediately. Next, White's employer, Nicholas Abrahamson, identified the body of Joe White. Abrahamson's testimony spoke directly to the interaction of the Ojibwe and whites in lumber camps: "I have known him for nine years. I always considered him a peaceable man. I have had dealings with him and been closely acquainted with him for the last six years." From the local Ojibwe community at Bakerville, Joe Navaosh also identified White's body, saying he knew him for forty years, since he was a child.[12]

Next, Joe White's son Charles testified. Charles White's testimony was the most extensive of the inquisition. According to the boy, Martin and Hicks did not present a warrant to Joe White: "They read no papers to Joe White and showed him none." Charles White disputed Martin's claims that Joe White stabbed him: "Joe White had no knife, not even a pocket knife." Charles White added, "Joe White did nothing only to run away. He was willing to go to Rice Lake with them, but did not want to be handcuffed." According to Charles White, he was also threatened: "The game warden said to me to get away or he'd shoot my head off. When they pointed their guns at White, he was about so close to them that they nearly touched him and Joe White started and ran away." Charles White then testified that after falling from Hicks's rifle shot, his father knew he was going to die: "He said for me to run and tell my mother to come. I am killed, I cannot live."[13]

With the awareness of basic principles of forensic science among Americans today through the prevalence of crime procedurals on television, it may seem strange that the inquisition at the scene of the crime was held a week after the murder. Indeed, when people of color fail to receive the same rights and protection of law that whites have in trials, it is often during the processing of evidence. In *The Trial of "Indian Joe,"* historian Clare McKanna analyzes the prosecution of Jose Gabriel (or "Indian Joe" as he was known in the local press), a Borjeno farm laborer who in 1892 allegedly murdered the white couple he worked for at their farm outside San Diego. Gabriel maintained his innocence throughout the trial but was found guilty and executed by the state of California. McKanna argues that shoddy processing of the crime scene played a role in the guilty verdict. McKanna demonstrates how racial prejudice led those at the crime scene to not conduct a thorough investigation.[14] However, in Joe White's murder, this was not the case. Examination of the crime scene was thorough and offered evidence of the wrongdoing of Martin and Hicks. For example, at the trial crime scene examiner Henry Mitchell offered testimony that refuted Martin's and Hicks's claims about Joe White's proximity to weapons that was the basis of legal justification for their actions.

In the presence of Justice of the Peace Andrew Ryan, six jurors concluded that Joe White died by a gunshot from Hicks, acting under orders from Martin. As a result of the inquisition, criminal complaints were made to Justice Ryan that Horace Martin and Josiah Hicks did "willfully, feloniously, and with malice aforethought, kill and murder one Joe White, against the peace and dignity of the state of Wisconsin."[15] A warrant was then issued for the arrest of each. Interestingly, the person making the complaint was Joe Baker, from the Long Lake Ojibwe community that bore his name. Baker, thirty, spoke English and was of mixed descent. While his mother was Ojibwe, his father was from Canada, either French or of mixed French and Native ancestry. Baker was also a US citizen, which may have given him the standing to make the complaint.[16] On Sunday, December 23, Washburn County Sheriff Peter Mills arrested both Martin and Hicks. Martin was arrested at Rice Lake, and Hicks was arrested at Chetek. The next day both were arraigned in Shell Lake and pleaded not guilty. The arraignment was scheduled to be continued December 27, meaning both Martin and Hicks had to sit it out in jail during the interim.[17]

THURSDAY, DECEMBER 27: ARRAIGNMENT

At the arraignment, witnesses were called and cross-examined. Barron attorney Clarence Coe appeared for the defense. Charles White was the first witness called, and Ellen Thomas was sworn in as interpreter. White testified that he knew Hicks but not Martin. How Charles White knew Hicks is not specified in court documents. Charles White testified that when Martin and Hicks approached the group, "They did not say they were officers of the law." According to Charles White's testimony, his father was compliant when confronted by the wardens: "Joe White told me to take the ponies and stuff and that he would go to Rice Lake."[18]

According to Charles White's testimony, he was standing right next to his father when the wardens began beating him. Martin hit Joe White with handcuffs, and Hicks struck Joe White with a gun three times, once on his shoulder and twice on his head. According to Charles White, the attack was completely unprovoked: "Joe White was doing nothing when they struck him with the handcuffs." After Charles White went to gather the ponies, he saw his father run away and get shot. Charles White did not see if it was Martin or Hicks that shot Joe White, but when the shots were fired the boy ran back to his father and, as he had testified at the inquisition, witnessed his father die.[19]

A critical issue for the defense was that Joe White had weapons on his person. Their contention was that his character demonstrated that he intended to use them against the wardens. Charles White's testimony directly refuted the defense claims that Joe White tried to stab the wardens: "Joe White had no knife—I would have known if he had any." Then Charles White laid out the physical proximity of the group's guns: "At the time those men came we had no guns. They were on the other side of the road. The old man White had a shotgun. I had a gun. It was a Winchester. Joe White's gun was a muzzleloader. It was not loaded." Charles White added: "He did not run towards the guns. He ran in the other direction. White did not try to get his guns at all."[20]

Not surprisingly, defense counsel Clarence Coe pressed Charles White about this issue:

Q: Where were you when you first saw those men on that day?
A: They were on the other side of the road, about as far across as the room.
Q: How many guns were there?
A: There were about four. The white men had two and we has three.

As adept as Charles White was as a witness when examined by the prosecution, he was just as effective when cross-examined. The teenager did not get tripped up when Coe, an experienced attorney, pressed Charles White further in an attempt to prove that Joe White was attempting to secure a weapon:

Q: While you were running down the hill did Joe White take the gun away from the other White man?
A: I did not see him. I saw him all the time.
Q: What was he doing while this man was going down the hill with you?
A: Nothing.
Q: Was the other White man touching the Indian?

A: Yes, he hit him with the gun.
Q: How many times did he hit him with the gun while you were going?
A: Three. I did not see the other man hit him with the gun. I was present all the time.

The fact that a teenager could hold his composure in a courtroom a mere two weeks after witnessing his father's violent murder is astonishing. Coe repeatedly attempted to cast doubt on the young boy's contention that his view of the events was unobstructed. However, Charles White yielded no ground, repeatedly stating his continued presence as an eyewitness to the events:

Q: When you went down the road that time wasn't the big Indian with you?
A: The other Indian was ahead of me. I don't know how far. I could not see him. I was not looking at the other Indian. I was looking at the one they got a hold of.
Q: When you was going away did you walk backward?
A: When I was going away from the other fellow I did. I had no gun. My gun wasn't with my packs. They were broken. The other fellows broke them.[21]

It is clear from this testimony that Charles White was a remarkable young boy. Charles White was not rattled under the intense scrutiny of Coe's cross-examination and stated with precision how he was able to maintain his view of the events.

Following Coe's cross-examination, District Attorney Knapp was allowed to question Charles White further in response to Coe's cross. Knapp's redirect focused on the incident of the beatings and Joe White's response. Charles White testified: "The white men did not point the gun at him before they struck him with the hand cuffs as I could see." Then the young boy added: "I did not see White do anything immediately after he was struck with the gun." This was in direct response to Coe's contention that the game wardens were not only justified in killing Joe White, but they were also justified in beating him. Next, Coe was allowed to cross-examine Charles White a second time. In the second cross-examination, Coe pressed the boy about the "big Indian" who was present, who at this point in the proceedings was still unidentified. Coe no doubt sought to establish that this person also presented an imminent threat to the wardens. Again, the young boy's testimony gave the defense little to argue:

> The big Indian camped with us the night before. The first time I saw him was a week before I was away to a little store and he was to the camp when I came

> back. They call him "Ooshkoshur." The last time I saw him was last week on Friday, he was at White Fish. I think he is at White Fish now. I don't know where he lives. He was alone when he came to our camp. There were in our party at the time of the trouble there were eleven but part of them were ahead about as far as from here to that White House (pointing to a house on another street). My Mother, Sister, a Brother younger than me and the balance smaller there, no other grown people.[22]

With this testimony Charles White was able to defuse any notion that the wardens were vastly outnumbered by a party of warlike Indians. The only adult on the scene besides Joe White and his wife was the "big Indian," identified at this time as "Ooshkoshur," later identified at the trial as "Wabasha."[23] With earlier testimony the young boy had firmly established that neither Joe White nor "the big Indian" had immediate access to weapons of any sort (gun or knives). With this fact irrefutable, the defense was forced to argue that the wardens were vastly outnumbered, something they had not tried to establish until now, with the weapons defense shattered. However, once again Coe's defense was torpedoed by the testimony of a teenager.

The testimony of Charles White during Coe's second cross-examination reveals the important role of Indian removal in the murder of Joe White. Charles White's testimony showed how his community was not confined to Whitefish on the reservation. In the course of one day, Joe White and his family moved back and forth from Whitefish on the reservation to an off-reservation logging camp on Long Lake, a distance of over thirty miles. However, Joe White and his family group were not just aimless, wandering nomads. Instead, the group's travels were the direct result of the actions of federal policy makers. In 1894, federal officials had failed to make Whitefish a permanent home for Joe White's community. This failure was due to the lack of sustaining income on the reservation. The community's presence off the reservation was not based solely on its federally based treaty rights to hunt, fish, and gather off-reservation, although this alone was subversive. Ojibwe movement off-reservation was rooted in the community's historical presence at Long Lake and sustained by employment opportunities off-reservation.

At the same time, Ojibwe presence off-reservation was extremely risky, something the murder of Joe White made clear. This was the conundrum Indians faced at the close of the nineteenth century: federal policy had failed them on the reservation, while off-reservation Indians encountered state laws and the hostility of local whites. This was American colonialism in Wisconsin. Many local whites were fed up with the presence of Indians off the reservation. This, more than the statutory scope of justifiable homicide, played a role in how potential jurors saw the case.

The next witness at the arraignment was Dr. George Barker, who conducted the examination of Joe White's body. According to his testimony, Barker graduated from Bowden Medical College in Maine in 1884 and had practiced medicine in the ten years since. While he was a general practitioner in Shell Lake, Barker testified "I have had some experience in autopsies." According to Barker's testimony, he did not know the defendants. Barker's testimony regarding cause of death differed little from the doctor's testimony at the initial inquest, stating again that the bullet entered Joe White's right side above the buttock, passed through the abdomen, and exited two inches below his naval. Barker testified, "The bullet was severe and sufficient enough to cause death in a short time." The doctor offered more extensive testimony regarding the beating. Barker testified:

> I found a scalp wound about an inch long over the right ear. Through the scalp with a slight depression of the bone. Blood in the right ear. Rest of the head and face clean. Scalp clean. This led me to think that blood issued from ear after he was washed. Discoloration on right shoulder. A blow like that would have the tendency to stun or daze a person. If it received proper care it would not necessarily cause death.[24]

Regardless of the medical impact of the beating on the actual cause of death, this testimony made it difficult for the defense to claim justifiable homicide when prior to being shot Joe White had received injuries that would "stun or daze a person." After all, how could one be in imminent danger from someone who was stunned or dazed?

On cross-examination, the defense did not waste any time in getting to the beating, most likely in order to argue that in terms of the cause of death, the beating was not relevant. However, Barker testified with some uncertainty: "I pressed my thumb into the opening and probed the wound on the shoulder. Was not serious. I don't think." Regarding Joe White's head injuries, Barker's testimony was also marked with a degree of uncertainty: "From my examination of the skull I think that the outer plate only was damaged." In terms of the gunshot wounds, Barker's testimony failed to help the defense and only served to reiterate that Joe White was running away from the wardens when he was shot: "The bullet seemed to take an upward course as if the deceased was leaning or running." Building on this and earlier testimony, Barker added, "It came out about an inch higher than where it entered."[25]

The next witness was Joe Baker, who testified in English without a translator. Despite his appearance here, Baker would not appear as a witness at the trial. Baker testified that he knew Joe White seven years and did not know Hicks. Baker then went on to describe Joe White's injuries, which differed little from his testimony at the December 21 inquisition at the crime scene. Interestingly, on cross-examination, the defense questioned Baker about Joe White's status as the chief.

> Q: Was he a regular Chippewa?

This must have been unclear to Baker, because at this point District Attorney Knapp interceded and asked the next question.

> Q: Was Joe White a chief?
> A: He was. He wasn't the highest but he was a chief. The second highest chief.[26]

It is strange that this was brought up by the defense, since it indicated a political motive for the killing. However, neither the defense nor the prosecution made a connection at any stage in the proceedings about how Joe White's political position shaped the defendants' motives.

It was not in the defense's best interest to discuss this as a motive, as it went directly against their claims that the murder was mere self-defense. However, the prosecution never asked the defendants if Joe White's political position was motive for their actions. For Native people, seeking justice in American courts had its limitations, as the courts were part of the very system that was attempting to suppress tribal sovereignty. If the prosecution had linked the murder of Joe White to the desire of local whites to contain Ojibwe people on the reservation or the state of Wisconsin's goal to suppress Ojibwe treaty rights they would have been forced to argue that these actions were unlawful. This was something that would not play well with potential jurors as most locals directly benefited from the dispossession of Native people. The defense, however, had much more latitude to exploit these issues, implicitly building into their case the local whites' fear of Indians.

The next witness was Joe Navaosh, forty-four, who testified in English without a translator. Like Joe Baker, Navaosh also testified that Joe White was a chief. Navaosh went on to testify that he lived at Long Lake, knew Joe White his entire life, and did not know Hicks. The cross-examination consisted solely of Coe asking where Navaosh knew Joe White, to which Navaosh responded: "I first knew him at Long Lake."[27] This small bit of testimony skirted around the issue of Ojibwe presence off-reservation. The defense never explicitly argued that the mere presence of Ojibwe people off the reservation justified the shooting, but slyly implied it throughout the proceedings. Navaosh was part of the Bakerville community at Long Lake that did not remove to the reservation. In the minds of most local whites Indians belonged on the reservation. It is important to remember how in this instance federal law diverged from the desires of local whites. In fact federal statute supported Ojibwe presence off-reservation, since Ojibwe treaty rights to hunt, fish, and gather off-reservation had never been extinguished.

Christian Sorstead was the next witness. Sorstead lived at John Mc Cullum's logging camp at the head of Long Lake, a few miles south of Nick Abrahamson's camp where Joe White worked, and also knew Hicks. Importantly, Sorstead's testimony spoke directly to the issue of premeditation. According to Sorstead's testimony, Martin and Hicks stopped at John Mc Cullum's camp while on the hunt for Joe White: "I heard them tell John Mc Cullum that they was after the Indians because they tried to shoot white men on Bear Lake. They said they were after Joe White." Later Sorstead added: "Mr. Hicks did not say he was going to arrest Joe White. He said he was after him." The defense chose not to cross-examine Sorstead.[28] Sorstead was the pivotal witness in these proceedings. Sorstead's testimony made clear that the murder was premeditated: Hicks saying he was "after" Joe White could be interpreted to mean that he merely wanted to bring him into custody, except for Hicks explicitly saying he did not intend to just arrest him. Sorstead's testimony was crucial in the context of the late nineteenth-century courtroom: here was a white man under oath testifying that Josiah Hicks planned to kill Joe White prior to encountering him. For many whites, the testimony of a white man was what mattered, no matter how many Indians testified.

At this point Dr. George Barker was recalled by the prosecution and testified that a blunt instrument would have caused a skull wound. On cross-examination, Barker testified that he could not say with absolute certainty if the wound was caused by handcuffs only a "heavy instrument." The timing of this redirect is strange, since Sorstead's testimony was not about the beating. The next witness was Horace Martin. Martin testified to knowing Joe White prior to the incident. On cross-examination, Martin produced the warrant for Joe White's arrest, which was entered into evidence. Martin then testified that he informed Joe White of the warrant and arrest. Martin did not offer any testimony about the killing of Joe White.

Based on the weight of the testimony, Washburn County Justice of the Peace Andrew Ryan ruled: "I find that the crime of manslaughter has been committed and that there is probable cause to believe the defendant guilty."

The trial date was set for March. Ryan set bail for each of the defendants at $3,000. The case records do not indicate why Martin and Hicks were charged with manslaughter instead of murder. No evidence exists indicating that District Attorney Knapp sought this charge or whether this was Justice Ryan's decision alone. Perhaps Knapp felt that manslaughter would be easier to sell to a jury. Had the District Attorney charged the wardens with murder, he would have to prove to a jury beyond a reasonable doubt that the killing was premeditated. In the context of the late nineteenth century, this would have been difficult, despite Christian Sorstead's testimony that the wardens planned to kill Joe White and not arrest him. If the game wardens were charged with murder, the prosecution would have to delve more deeply into the motives of Martin and Hicks, namely that the murder happened because Joe White was an Ojibwe leader who resisted removal to the reservation and enforcement of state game laws in violation of Ojibwe treaty rights. These were issues that most potential jurors had little sympathy for. With the manslaughter charge, the prosecution instead made their case against the game wardens as an abuse of duty. Joe White's political position, resistance to removal, even that he was Indian, figured little in the prosecution's case.

While the arraignment testimony was entered into evidence as exhibit "C," a jury never sat and listened to this testimony. The jury had access to the transcript of this testimony during the trial, but it is not known how closely it was read by the jurors, or if it was read at all. The next day, December 28, Horace Martin was released on bail. Martin, M. T. Howard, S. A. Peterson, and William Dietz provided the $3,000. Dietz was a former Barron County deputy who would testify later at the trial as a character witness for the defense. Hicks had to sit it out a few more days. Hicks was released on December 31 on bail provided by Hicks, Walter Speed, E. G. Slayton, C. F. Munseas, John Kleve, T. H. Apkes, and P. A. Moe.[29]

THE CASE IN LOCAL NEWSPAPERS

As the trial date approached, rumors swirled around the towns of Washburn and Barron Counties. In Washburn County, the two largest towns were (and still are today) Shell Lake, the county seat, and Spooner, five miles to the north. Both places had weekly newspapers, the *Shell Lake Watchman* and the *Spooner Register*. Local newspaper coverage, in particular the *Shell Lake Watchman*, was hostile to Joe White and favored the defendants' perspective of the case. For example, in reporting the initial facts of the case in its

December 20 issue, the newspaper printed Martin and Hicks's version of the events as fact. The *Watchman* reported, "White drew a knife and made a vicious stab at Martin, wounding him slightly in the hand." Following the beating the *Watchman* claimed, "White made a rush for his gun." When this was disputed and later convincingly refuted at the trial, the *Watchman* did not print a retraction. The *Watchman* went on to say that White "is a 'good Indian' now," a reference to the saying "the only good Indian is a dead Indian." In addition, the *Watchman* highlighted White's supposedly bad character in patronizing, racist terms: "He has been a terror among the Indians for years, and no one will miss his departure for the 'happy hunting grounds.'" The *Watchman* went on to report an unsubstantiated account of White's attempt to rob a cook shanty in the nearby village of Haugen.[30] Closer to the reservation, when the *Hayward Republican* reported Joe White's death, it added "his death will be no loss to this section."[31]

By the end of January, the local media saturated the readers with news about the murder. The *Watchman* noted: "The readers of the different newspapers of this locality have no doubt become somewhat weary of reading of Joe White." Most of the coverage blamed the victim for his own demise due to alleged incidents prior to the murder with little focus on the details of the crime. The *Watchman* directly took up the issue of Joe White's character: "A large number of people will testify that he was a quiet, peaceable man, while as many more say he was one of the most desperate characters in this section." This report went on to say that Thomas Bracklin would be a character witness in the trial, identifying Bracklin as "one of the camp foreman for the Knapp, Stout & Co.," and made no mention that Bracklin was Joe White's nephew.[32]

The *Clear Lake Mirror* published a letter to the editor from Horace Martin, which appeared in its January 20 edition. Martin was born in Clear Lake and likely had family still living there. Four days later, the *Watchman* reprinted Martin's letter. The letter contained wildly unsubstantiated claims justifying his actions, which would be the center of his trial defense. First Martin attacked District Attorney Knapp: "The district attorney who has been prosecuting this case was drunk when he received the information, and he was posted in the saloons though the city of Shell Lake." Martin argued that he did not try to conceal his actions following the killing: "we walked thirty-eight miles after dark to report this matter to the proper authorities." Next Martin claimed that they sent telegrams to any authority with power to investigate, a claim supported by the telegram in the federal archives that Martin sent to Sawyer County authorities. According to Martin, all the authorities agreed with the killing "except the ambitious district attorney of Washburn County, who wished to get his name in the paper."

Martin then went on to attack the character of the deceased: "Joe White has done nothing but steal and murder all his life." Martin backed this claim by pointing out that Joe White killed Bidad and another unnamed Indian in Rice Lake. No existing historical evidence proves Joe White killed anybody in noncombat besides Bidad. Martin argued that Joe White's killing of Bidad and harassment of whites bolstered his political standing within his community: "All that was required of White the time he killed Petud was to stay away from the reservation a few months, and on his return he was held so high in the estimation of his tribe, by cutting and shooting several settlers in the vicinity of Barron and Sawyer counties." Martin's letter gave no other reason for his actions than White's alleged bad character or provided any direct explanation of his shooting of White.[33]

There is nothing in the historical record that supports or refutes Martin's claims that Joe White harassed individual settlers in and near Rice Lake. If this was true, it is very likely that Martin was correct in claiming that this enhanced Joe White's political standing. Joseph Gurnoe and other federal officials on the reservation made similar claims. Unlike Gurnoe, white settlers had no superiors to report to and therefore did not leave detailed records of their interaction with the Ojibwe. Regardless of the truth of Martin's claims that Joe White harassed white settlers, he believed it to be the case. Martin's letter demonstrates that the wardens' shooting of Joe White was not about enforcing the law, but instead it was to silence Joe White and his resistance to removal specifically because he was a chief and had the potential to influence other Indians.

The *Spooner Register* was more balanced in its coverage of the murder. The paper published a letter from District Attorney Knapp, where Knapp attempted to answer many of the rumors regarding the case and to argue the legality of charging Martin and Hicks.[34] Interestingly, Knapp lived in Shell Lake, and the paper there did not print anything from the district attorney. The *Register* also featured an article in its December 22 edition where Long Lake town chairman William Todd reported that popular opinion in Long Lake tended to be against Martin and Hicks.[35] The *Register* reported this again the following week: "The feeling of the people in the neighborhood where the killing was done appears to be entirely in favor of White and bitter against Martin and Hicks."[36] It is likely this was the result of relatively harmonious relations between the Ojibwe at Bakerville and white settlers at Long Lake.

The *Register* also discussed Ojibwe treaty rights, something completely absent in coverage of the case in the *Shell Lake Watchman* and other local papers. In an article about the failure of the federal government to take over jurisdiction, the *Register* noted, "When the lands were ceded by the Indians they reserved the right to hunt and fish whenever and wherever they pleased so long as the president did not withdraw such reservation. The president has never interfered, and so White was apparently doing what he had a right to do at the same time he was killed, though off the reservation."[37] No other newspaper recognized that Ojibwe treaty rights were still the law of the land. Not even the prosecution at the trial argued that the warrant issued for Joe White's arrest for hunting out of season violated federal laws and the game wardens had no right to arrest White.

Likewise, the *Shell Lake Watchman* only once made a passing reference to Joe White's political position.[38] The *Spooner Register* more frequently referenced Joe White's role as leader of the community but did not seriously discuss it as a possible motive or if the game wardens targeted Joe White for that reason. On December 29 the *Register* ran the front-page headline "The Slayers of Joe White," with a subtitle underneath in smaller letters, "The Indian Chief."[39] In their coverage of the trial proceedings the *Register* again referred to Joe White as "the Indian chief."[40] However, even the more sympathetic *Spooner Register* did not go so far as to explicitly say that Joe White was targeted because he was the chief who led resistance to removal to the reservation.

THE DEFENSE TEAM

As the trial date neared, Martin and Hicks rounded out their defense teams. In addition to Coe, Martin retained Lewis Mead of Shell Lake and Charles Stark of Rice Lake. Henry Ellsworth of Barron defended Hicks.[41] These men, like Martin and Hicks, benefited from the dispossession of Ojibwe people from their lands in Barron County as their careers were shaped by the new opportunities as the region came under American authority. Lewis Mead was forty-one at the time of the trial. He was born in Marshall in southern Wisconsin. At age nineteen, Mead lost his right hand in a farming accident, after which he began to study law at a Madison law firm and was admitted to the bar in 1882. For a year he practiced law in Hudson, in west-central Wisconsin on the Minnesota border, before moving north to Shell Lake. Mead was elected to the Wisconsin State Assembly in 1888 as a Republican, serving through 1893. Mead was next elected Washburn County district attorney in 1896.[42]

Clarence Coe was born in 1864 on a farm outside of Sterling, Illinois. According to Newton S. Gordon's *History of Barron County*, "His parental ancestry in America has been traced back to the year 1631, when the first Coe arrived in New England among the early Puritan settlers."[43] Coe graduated from high school in Sterling in 1884 and came to Barron immediately after graduating to work in his cousin's law office. Coe graduated from the University of Wisconsin–Madison law school and passed the bar in 1888, returning to Barron to practice law. That fall he was elected Barron County district attorney and in 1892 became a municipal judge, a position he held for eight years. Later, Coe was elected for a single two-year term in the Wisconsin State Assembly as a Republican in 1918 but was defeated in 1920. Coe had two children, one of whom, Robert, followed his father's footsteps by getting a law degree at the University of Wisconsin–Madison and eventually practicing law in Rice Lake.[44]

Charles Stark was a relatively recent arrival to Barron County. He was born in 1854 in Randolph, a town in southern Wisconsin. Stark graduated from the University of Wisconsin–Madison with a law degree in 1878, setting up a law practice in Randolph. In 1887, Stark moved to Rice Lake to practice law. Later in his career, Stark was appointed second municipal judge of Rice Lake in 1919.[45] Hicks's attorney, Henry Ellsworth, was born in Oregon, Wisconsin, a town in southern Wisconsin about ten miles south of Madison. His parents were natives of New York. Ellsworth grew up on a farm, and after college at the Platteville Normal School (today called the University of Wisconsin–Platteville) and law school at the University of Wisconsin–Madison, was admitted to the bar in Wisconsin in 1881. In 1890, Ellsworth left southern Wisconsin for Cumberland in Barron County. In November of that same year, Ellsworth was elected district attorney of Barron County, the first Democrat to hold that office.[46]

What these men had in common is that they were all legal professionals who furthered their young careers by achieving elected offices in the developing white communities of Barron County. These men, like the other white settlers of various occupations who made the population of Barron County explode between 1870 and 1890, moved onto Ojibwe homelands in hopes of a better life than they could achieve where they came from. Indeed, all of these men enhanced their economic and social standing by moving to what had been Ojibwe territory. Indians were an obstacle to their economic and social mobility. They were actively a part of the very process that Joe White was resisting. While these men were all deemed important enough to be included in the *History of Barron County* and other early local histories, Joe White appeared in none of these publications.

MARCH 19, 1895: JURY SELECTION

A major shift in the case occurred when Webster Goss succeeded William Knapp as Washburn County district attorney in early 1895. Goss was elected in November prior to Joe White's murder. Goss, a Republican, was elected district attorney during a Republican landslide that gave Republicans control of Congress and brought Republicans to the Wisconsin governorship, State Senate, and State Assembly districts.[47] Goss's presence as prosecutor was marred by conflict of interest. This shaped the first day of the trial. Before jury selection commenced, the defense introduced several affidavits that the defendants had retained Goss during the preliminary examination. According to the *Spooner Register*, this "created a sensation."[48] Goss reacted by quickly filing his own deposition stating that when Martin was first arrested he sought Goss as his attorney. Goss claimed that he told Martin he could only serve as Martin's attorney if the federal government asserted jurisdiction, but that he informed Martin he could not serve as his attorney if the state charged Martin. Complicating the matter was the fact that Martin paid Goss's expenses to accompany him to Martin's initial hearing at Shell Lake. Goss stated that his appearance with Martin was not as his attorney of record and he received no compensation for appearing, and it would not interfere with his duties as prosecutor if the state chose to charge Martin.[49] Amazingly, the judge agreed, and Goss was allowed to continue prosecuting the case.[50] Goss's conflict of interest would not have been permitted in most courts and underscores how courts in the late nineteenth century failed to extend protection of the law to Native victims of violent crime.

Once the matter of District Attorney Goss's conflict of interest was settled, jury selection began. Jury selection was a challenge. The *Spooner Register* noted that the saturation of local press coverage about the case was a serious obstacle to the selection of impartial jurors. According to the *Register*, the defense was concerned "that the reports in the county papers were so impartially made as not to create any prejudice toward the defendants." Another aspect of jury selection that the *Register* commented on was that many of the prospective jurors were recent immigrants.[51] Many of these newcomers had little direct interaction with Ojibwe people themselves. Instead, they were exposed to common stereotypes of Indian savagery that contrasted sharply with the historical experience between Ojibwe people and outsiders. On the other hand, Washburn County was not just Shell Lake and Spooner.[52] As the *Spooner Register* reported, many in Long Lake were sympathetic to Joe White.

Then there was the northern part of the county: newly established towns such as Minong (an Ojibwe word meaning "good place"), Trego, and Springbrook. Settlers from these communities may have had a much different view of the case based on actual interaction with Ojibwe people. For example, a pioneer resident of Springbrook was Joseph Trepania, a French Canadian. Trepania had left Quebec for Prairie du Chien and then took a farm in Chippewa Falls. After a brief stint in Rice Lake, Trepania moved his family to Springbrook in 1880, where he operated a store and saloon on the Chicago, St. Paul, Minneapolis and Omaha railway that ran from the Twin Cities to Ashland (today US Highway 63). Trepania was first married to a Lac Courte Oreilles woman, Niizhoodenh, a cousin of Akiwenzii, and then to a woman named Gekek, one of Akiwenzii's nieces. Trepania had a child with each of these two women. Then Trepania married and had two children with Margaret De Marie, a mixed-blood Cree woman from Chippewa Falls. Even after Trepania married Margaret De Marie, he still raised his children from his prior marriages, and they all lived in Springbrook. Trepania's son Alfred himself had two wives from Lac Courte Oreilles, first Maggie LaRonge and then Elizabeth Greeley, and had three children with each of these women, all of whom also resided in Springbrook.[53] Men such as Trepania and the many members of his family living in Springbrook were all potential jurors with significant ties to the Ojibwe.

Jury selection consumed the entire first day and the morning of the second. By the end of the first day, the defense had used thirty-eight challenges and had ten remaining, while the prosecution had used ten and had two remaining. In all Judge Marshall examined 115 jurors.[54] The fact that many potential jurors were recent immigrants from Scandinavia and that many in Long Lake were sympathetic to Joe White and perhaps Ojibwe people in general were two factors that had the potential to sway the verdict in either direction. However, none of the jurors were from Long Lake or any area outside Shell Lake or Spooner and many were recent immigrants.

The eldest juror and the foreman was Oliver Purdy, sixty-three. Purdy lived in the township of Bashaw, to the west of Spooner and Shell Lake. A Civil War veteran from Elbridge, New York, Purdy came to Washburn County to farm in 1882.[55] John Arnquist, thirty-eight, was a native of Sweden, as was Ole Errickson. Both lived in the township of Shell Lake. Also from the township of Shell Lake was Millage Irwin, thirty-three, a native of Canada, and Charles Blair, forty-one, who was born in New York but whose parents were French Canadians. The last juror from the township of Shell Lake was John Lynch, twenty-eight, who was born in Wisconsin but whose parents hailed from Ireland.[56] Artemus Crandall, fifty-two, lived in the village of Shell Lake. Crandall was from New York, and both his parents were also from the northeast.[57] Jurors from the village of Shell Lake also included Charles Mitchell and William Bergin. Two jurors lived in the town of Spooner, A. C. Buxton and Albert Stratton.[58]

No jurors were included from the northern part of the county or from Long Lake. Unlike many settlers from these areas, the jurors selected had little direct relationships with Ojibwe people. However, like Martin and Hicks and the legal professionals involved with the case, these men too were recent arrivals who came to the region specifically to enhance their economic and social status. None of the jurors left journals or letters. There are no surviving written accounts documenting how any of these jurors felt about Indians. Unlike many Long Lake settlers, there is no evidence that they chose to develop any type of relationship with the Ojibwe. This made it much more likely they had a hostile view of Indians in general and a leader like Joe White in particular, who sought a continued presence off the reservation. They had much more in common with Martin and Hicks than Joe White.

The reason for this was more than merely ethnic background or immigration status. There was a sharp distinction between the type of labor practiced by white settlers in and near Shell Lake and Spooner and other parts of the county. This is still evident today, as the southern part of Washburn County is much more agricultural than the northern portion or the area along Long Lake where the murder occurred. This difference had a profound effect on settler's relationships with the Ojibwe. The men selected for the jury were farmers. Their labor and profit was solitary and derived from land they themselves owned. Whites in the lumber industry were wage laborers for large corporations on lands owned by the corporation. They worked alongside Joe White and hundreds of other Ojibwe. The witnesses at the trial bear this out: Christian Sorstead was just as Scandinavian as the jurors, yet held a favorable opinion of Joe White and Ojibwe people in general based on working with them.

MARCH 20, 1895: THE TRIAL, DAY ONE

The trial commenced on March 20 at 10:00 a.m. with the opening arguments of the state. In his opening, District Attorney Goss argued that the jury should not consider that Joe White was an Indian and made a direct reference to the heritage of the jurors: "when the Maker created us he recognized all men as equal—it makes no difference whether the unfortunate be an Indian or a Scandinavian." In reference to Martin, Goss claimed, "I have known him since he was a small boy; it is no matter of pleasure that I stand here to prosecute him but it is a matter of duty."[59]

Goss then called Charles White as the first witness for the state. Ira Isham, who was married to Joe White's niece, was sworn in as interpreter. Charles White testified that he was in a party of eleven, with the only adult males in the group being Joe White and another Ojibwe man, now identified as "Wabasha." The rest of Charles White's testimony was similar to his arraignment testimony that Martin attempted to handcuff Joe White but White told him it was not necessary and he would go with them, but Joe White pulled back when Martin attempted to handcuff him. Martin then struck Joe White with the handcuffs on the head. Hicks also beat Joe White with the end of his gun landing three blows, including one on his shoulder and two on his head. Charles White testified that when his father ran away Hicks shot him in the back, under direct orders from Martin.[60]

After the noon lunch break, Goss called Dr. George Barker. The doctor testified that the bullet entered Joe White's right side and exited on his left just below his navel. Two other local physicians corroborated Barker's testimony. Barker testified that the cause of death was the gunshot wound. Crime scene examiner Henry Mitchell testified next. Mitchell offered precise testimony that contradicted Martin and Hicks's version of the events. According to his testimony, Joe White fell 412 feet from the site where Martin and Hicks beat him. Hicks shot White from a distance of eighty-five feet. All of this corroborated Charles White's testimony. Christian Sorstead took the stand after Mitchell and testified, as he had at the arraignment, that Martin and Hicks stopped at John Mc Cullum's camp and told him that they were "after" White for shooting at a white man at Bear Lake, in northeast Barron County. Goss then recalled Charles White, asking the boy how much English he could understand. After an examination, it was determined he could understand most of what was being said.[61]

The next witness for the state was Wabasha, who was not a witness at the arraignment and there was identified as "the big Indian." Wabasha offered the most detailed testimony. Through Isham's interpretation, Wabasha testified that he was with Joe and Charles White when Martin and Hicks approached them. According to Wabasha, one of the wardens grabbed Joe White while the other attempted to handcuff him. When Martin began beating him with the handcuffs, Joe White stepped back. Martin then ordered Charles White and Wabasha to step back, which they did. Hicks then began beating Joe White with his gun, while Martin picked up Joe and Charles White's guns and threw them away. Oddly, Martin then patted Wabasha on the shoulder and told him "you are a nice old man." Wabasha then started to leave the scene but turned around when he heard a shot and saw Joe White fall. Wabasha then ran to Joe White and picked up the wounded leader and carried him a few feet before laying him on the ground. According to Wabasha's testimony, a few short moments later, Joe White was dead. There was a brief interlude of humor in the courthouse when Goss asked Wabasha if he was the one who shot Joe White. Wabasha replied with a quick "gaawiin" (no). The judge suppressed the laughter throughout the courthouse, and Goss had nothing else for Wabasha. On cross-examination Wabasha testified that Martin forced him up the road by gunpoint, warning him and Charles White to stay back.[62]

Martin's words to Wabasha, "you are a nice old man," were noteworthy. We do not know if Martin said these words to Wabasha in English or Ojibwe. Wabasha testified through an interpreter, but he may have been able to understand some English even if he could not speak it very well. We do not know if Martin would have had to say those words in Ojibwe. We do know that Wabasha understood what Martin said to him, since it came from Wabasha's testimony. Either way, this statement is significant. In Ojibwe, referring to someone as an old man or old woman is not pejorative as it is English. Instead, it is a term of deference and respect. It is possible that Martin may have understood that Wabasha would interpret it this way, which shows that Martin would have had contact with Ojibwe people before. The other possibility is that Martin saw Wabasha as a good, passive Indian, in contrast to Joe White who, as trial testimony would prove, was viewed by many at Rice Lake as a dangerous, problem Indian.

Joe Navaosh was called as the next witness. Navaosh was sworn in, climbed to the witness stand, and then unexpectedly pulled out a billy club. The jurors and the capacity crowd were whipped into a frenzy, stunned to see an Indian on the witness stand with a weapon. It took several minutes to calm the gallery. After calling for order, the judge demanded an explanation. Navaosh claimed he took the club from the crime scene. He went on to testify that he knew of no Indian who had access to such a weapon and that the weapon was left by Martin or Hicks. This meant that Martin and Hicks were in possession of firearms, handcuffs, and a club after they disarmed Joe White. Barker was then recalled and testified that the wound indicated that White was bent over while he ran. On cross-examination, the doctor was closely questioned about the wounds to White's head and whether the doctor's medical examination conformed to Charles White's and Wabasha's testimony regarding the beating. The doctor's testimony confirmed the beating according to Charles White and Wabasha and generally supported the case of the state.[63]

Following Barker's testimony, the state rested its case. Henry Ellsworth then opened for the defense, arguing that the killing was justifiable self-defense: "Gentlemen, the only thing that stood between these men and death was Hicks' gun. Such was the judgment of both of them. Had not this shot been fired Hicks' wife would be a widow and his children without a father." Ellsworth told the jury that witnesses for the defense would demonstrate that the homicide was justifiable, painting a picture of the two wardens as fearful of being overwhelmed by dangerous Indians. The defense claimed Joe White drew a knife on Martin before he beat him with the handcuffs and that Hicks then shot Joe White because White was going for his gun and Wabasha was trying to join him in resisting the officers. Ellsworth further argued that the defense would prove that Joe White was a dangerous person, who had just days before shot at a white man. The state objected to the defense counsel introducing new evidence of specific acts that indicated Joe White's bad character. This objection was sustained, and the court adjourned for the day.[64]

MARCH 21, 1895: THE TRIAL, DAY TWO

The doors to the courtroom opened the following day at 8:30. The *Shell Lake Watchman* reported that attendance in the courtroom was less than the prior day. The defense presented their character witnesses who would each testify that Joe White was reckless and dangerous, thus proving their case of justifiable homicide. The first witness of the day was former Barron County deputy William Dietz of Rice Lake. Dietz testified about an 1883 incident when as Barron County deputy Dietz attempted to arrest Joe White and shot at the Ojibwe leader to no avail. Dietz was prepared to elaborate on his encounter with Joe White when the state objected, which was sustained. The judge only allowed Dietz to state his opinion regarding Joe White's character and barred him from relating any specific incidents. In the testimony he was able to deliver, Dietz claimed that Joe White's character was very bad; however, this testimony could not have been too convincing without any specific incidents to back it up.[65]

Judge Franklin Angel took the stand next. Angel was municipal judge of Rice Lake and issued the warrant for Joe White's arrest that was served by Martin and Hicks. Like Dietz, Angel was barred from relating any specific incidents of Joe White's alleged bad character and did not provide any reason why he issued the warrant. Angel testified that he told Martin and Hicks to be careful, that Joe White was dangerous. The state did not cross-examine

Angel.[66] The failure to cross-examine Angel was a critical factor in the trial and illustrates how Goss failed to provide the jury with important information that pointed toward the game wardens' guilt. Goss could have questioned Angel about why he ordered Joe White's arrest. Specifically, Goss did not question Angel as to why he issued an arrest warrant when the Ojibwe still retained rights to hunt off-reservation. Even the *Spooner Register* had acknowledged Joe White had a right to hunt off-reservation.

After Judge Angel, the defense provided a parade of witnesses describing Joe White's alleged bad character and how he posed a real danger to the wardens. Harry Anderson of Haugen testified that Joe White had shot at him just days before his death. Anderson also testified to Joe White's bad character and claimed that he was usually armed. The next witness for the defense was Ole Brane who warned Martin of Joe White's bad character. Hans Peaborgen of Rice Lake also warned the wardens of Joe White's bad character, calling him "blood-thirsty." C. O. Nass of Rice Lake, a former deputy US marshall, testified next that Joe White had "an aversion to being arrested."[67] Nass's testimony reveals the depth of prejudice against Ojibwe people at the time. The parade of witnesses the defense produced claimed that Joe White was a dangerous person based on rumors with no specific incidents to back up these claims. The absurdity of it all peaked with Nass. After all, who, white or Indian, *doesn't* have "an aversion to being arrested"? Only in an environment of extreme racism would the flimsy testimony of these witnesses be seen as credible.

Horace Martin then testified in his own defense. According to Martin, the game wardens informed Joe White he was under arrest and then White pulled a knife. Martin testified:

> When [Joe] White drew the knife, I struck him with the handcuffs, which flew out of my hand. Charlie [White] tried to get behind me and I pushed him back and drew a revolver on the big Indian, Wabasha, and told him I would kill him if he did not go on. I followed him down the road a short distance. When I came back, I was running and White tried to get Hicks' gun away from him. I picked up the handcuffs and when White saw me coming he struck at me with his knife, but struck over Hicks' gun and I struck him, but not hard. He then ran up the road and we after him. I was close to him and struck at him. He jumped over a fallen tree and then turned back and ran towards the gun. Hicks was close after him. When I saw what White intended to do I called to Hicks to "stop him for God's sake! Shoot him in the leg." I told Hicks to get the handcuffs and put them on. Hicks went to the Indian and said he was shot through the leg.[68]

Martin then testified that he and Hicks left the scene and arrived back at Rice Lake at one in the morning. Martin claimed eight men warned him that Joe White was dangerous. The warden also testified that Wabasha had a gun, and not being able to speak Ojibwe, he was unable to tell Wabasha to put his gun away, causing him to draw his own.

The last witness for the defense was Sarah Kelly of Rice Lake, the only woman to testify. Kelly claimed she had witnessed Joe White brandish a knife on another Indian. The defense then rested their case at 10:40 a.m. The state spent half an hour on rebuttal witnesses. First was Andrew Ryan, Washburn County justice of the peace, who offered testimony based on the December 21 inquisition at the crime scene. Ryan's findings directly refuted Martin's testimony in two ways. First, the trajectory of the fired round disproved Martin's testimony regarding where Hicks stood when he fired. Second, Ryan's testimony of the location of two pools of Joe White's blood indicating the beginning and end point to White's path when he ran away from the wardens also refuted Martin's testimony. Ryan's testimony was significant as the defense claim of justifiable homicide was based on Joe White running toward the firearms. Yet evidence at the crime scene in the form of the pools of blood proved that Martin was lying, and Joe White was not running toward the firearms. Ryan's testimony regarding the location of the shooting was supported by Nick Abrahamson's eyewitness testimony. Abrahamson further testified that he had known Joe White nine years and had always known him to be a peaceable man.[69]

Next, the prosecution recalled Henry Mitchell, deemed "the smoothing iron" by the *Shell Lake Watchman* because Mitchell's testimony spoke directly to the facts. This time, the prosecution questioned Mitchell about Joe White's character. Mitchell testified White was "about the ordinary run of the Indians in character." After Mitchell, Goss bumbled by calling John Harrington, a Knapp, Stout foreman, who did not help the prosecution when he testified that he saw Joe White shoot at a man several years ago. Despite this misstep, Goss recovered by recalling Wabasha, who testified that Joe White had no knife. At 11:10 a.m. Goss offered his closing argument, ending just before noon.[70]

Defense counsel Lewis Mead offered his closing argument on behalf of Martin, which lasted almost two hours. The *Watchman* gave Mead's closing glowing reviews:

> One of the most able efforts ever made in this county. He was not only eloquent in his oratorical flights, but was so sympathetic and earnest in his appeals in behalf of his client and his right as an officer in the discharge of his duties that

> he deeply impressed everyone with the force of his logic and the vindication of officers of the law in the discharge of their duties in defense of the rights of the public and their own individual protection.

Even the more balanced reporters of the *Spooner Register* concurred, albeit more briefly, referring to Mead's closing as "an eloquent impressive plea." Henry Ellsworth then offered closing on behalf of Hicks, which the *Watchman* called "a very touching address." Ellsworth's argument centered on Joe White's alleged prior misdeeds and the fact that the defense maintained Joe White reached for his gun.[71]

Following closing arguments, Judge Marshall instructed the jury as to what legally constituted justifiable homicide and that since Martin had instructed Hicks to shoot both were equally liable. Marshall also instructed the jury as to the scope of the rights of an officer carrying out an arrest for a misdemeanor offense. Within the original case files is an unlabeled page of precedent cases that may have served as jury instructions, as they closely follow newspaper accounts of jury instructions given by Judge Marshall prior to deliberations. The four cases include an Arkansas case, *Smith v. State*, that found that an officer could only kill or seriously hurt a suspect for a misdemeanor if his own life was in danger. Also included was an Alabama case, *Karr v. State*, that found that defense was justifiable if the deceased was a violent man. The last two cases drew from Wisconsin case law. In *Clifford v. State* a defendant was excused from guilt if they acted from "reason and honest conviction" at the time of the killing. *State v. Nett* allowed the defendant to offer evidence that the slain was "a man of great physical strength and was a desperate, fighting, ruffianly man," and provided the defendant knew this prior to the killing.

None of these cases, nor the documented instructions given by Judge Marshall, spoke to premeditation, something clear in Christian Sorstead's testimony that the game wardens were not going to arrest Joe White but were "after" him. Furthermore, the defense's case and the jury instructions were based on the assumption that the wardens' actions were justifiable because their lives were in danger due to Joe White's possession of or intent to use a weapon. However, no knife was ever found or entered into evidence. Moreover, Martin's testimony that Joe White was running toward his gun was a lie based on Justice of the Peace Andrew Ryan's examination of the crime scene, which clearly demonstrated that Joe White was running away from the wardens and the guns. Even if the jury chose to disregard the testimony of two Indian eyewitnesses, Charles White and Wabasha, the testimony of two upstanding white citizens of Shell Lake made it clear that the murder was premeditated and Martin and Hicks were in no imminent danger and had no right to shoot Joe White according to existing case law. It didn't matter though. The jury retired at 4:00 p.m. and returned over an hour later with a verdict of not guilty.[72]

SYMPATHY WAS IN FAVOR OF THE PALE FACES

The reason for the not guilty verdict is readily apparent when one considers the fact that many jurors were recent immigrants whose view of Ojibwe people was rooted in fear, based on stereotypes of Indian savagery that contradicted the historical experience of Ojibwe relations to outsiders. For over two centuries, the relationship between Ojibwe people and non-Ojibwe traders was marked by economic cooperation and cultural respect.[73] However, by the end of the nineteenth century, the majority of residents of northern Wisconsin were either recent immigrants from northern Europe or Euro-Americans. The makeup of the jury reflected this. These new arrivals to northern Wisconsin had no desire for cooperative relationships with Ojibwe people and wanted Ojibwe people segregated on the reservation. The *Spooner Register* explained the prosecution's dilemma this way: "having to rely almost entirely on the testimony of Indians, against whom, in this case especially, exists a great deal of prejudice in the whole county." The *Register* further noted that the verdict

> was rather a surprise as the weight of testimony seemed to be on the State's side. Sympathy was in favor of the pale faces. The verdict appears to be entirely satisfactory, though not thought to be in accordance with the testimony.[74]

Typically, the *Shell Lake Watchman* had a different take:

> There was a few who discented with the jury, but we believe it safe to say the ninety percent of all who listened to the evidence thought the verdict was right. It was well brought out by the evidence that Joe White, the dead Indian, was a dangerous, blood-thirsty character.[75]

The following week the *Watchman* went even further by praising the murderers: "The Watchman feels at liberty to say that their course has not only been highly honorable, but they have showed a considerable amount of grit. . . . The boys are made of good stuff, and have served the state faithfully and deserve a good deal of credit for what they have done for law and order."[76] Even more shocking than the reaction of the general public and the local press to the acquittal was District Attorney Goss's reaction to the verdict: "I expected it. I have done my duty to the state, but personally I feel glad that Martin got clear."[77]

Back in Rice Lake, the *Chronotype* had a brief notice of the result of the trial. After reporting the acquittal of Martin and Hicks in a scant two sentences, the *Chronotype* went on to say:

> The Chronotype has no desire to discuss the unfortunate affair, as it believes that justice has been done to all concerned, with the possible exception of the tax-payers of Washburn county who have had a needless expense saddled upon them through the medium of incompetent officials who listened to the old grannies at Shell Lake and forced a trial when an intelligent investigation of the killing at the time of its occurrence would have clearly demonstrated, what the trial has now done, that the taking of Joe White's life was not only justifiable, but an imperative necessity.[78]

It is not insignificant that the Rice Lake paper called the murder of Joe White "an imperative necessity." It was "an imperative necessity" for whites at Rice Lake in order to finally remove Ojibwe people from Rice Lake. This is clear when one considers the facts of the case. It was the municipal judge of Rice Lake that issued the arrest warrant for Joe White, who was not in Rice Lake or Barron County at the time. Why was the warrant not issued from Washburn County where Joe White was actually hunting? Even more telling, one of Rice Lake's own, Horace Martin, ordered his assistant to murder the community's leader. While some families of the Ojibwe community of Joe White would remain near Long Lake into the twentieth century, most Ojibwe people were contained on the reservation. The *Chronotype* and the citizens of Rice Lake had no need to discuss the "unfortunate affair" at length: their judge and their game wardens had, in violation of federal law, went out of their way to eliminate the Ojibwe from Rice Lake by killing their leader. They could now look forward to the future having fully achieved their goal of eliminating the Ojibwe from their community.

CONCLUSION

Historian Ned Blackhawk argues that violence was central to American colonialism: "Violence enabled the rapid accumulation of new resources, territories, and subject peoples."[79] In his work, Blackhawk sees violence in the Great Basin as an unwieldy force emanating from colonial disruptions, whether perpetrated by whites against Native people or by Natives themselves against other Natives. For Blackhawk, regardless of its source, violence resulted in Native dispossession. Things were much different in Wisconsin where Ojibwe sovereignty was most threatened not by large campaigns of violence but by smaller events like the murder of Joe White and the failure of the law to effectively protect Native people. The decades-long struggle of Joe White and his family to resist removal ended not on a battlefield but in a courtroom.

For the Ojibwe of Rice Lake and their leader, violence was perpetrated not by the federal government but by the officials of the state of Wisconsin. While there were no federal military campaigns against the Ojibwe, the murder of Joe White achieved much the same result. State policies such as Wisconsin's enforcement of game laws and the resulting tragedy that ensued on that cold December day in 1894 were more destructive to Ojibwe people and their sovereignty than the federal policies of allotment or boarding schools. The violence that Giishkitawag was a victim of tragically illustrates this point. Giishkitawag was successful in defying federal efforts to remove the Ojibwe for more than a decade. Likewise, the policy of allotment failed to keep Giishkitawag and other Ojibwe on the reservation. In the end, it was the determination of whites of Rice Lake, emboldened by state laws, to end the leader's resistance by ending his life.

The Indian Removal Act passed Congress in 1830. However, it took sixty-four years, two game wardens, and twelve jurors to give the law any real meaning for the Ojibwe of Rice Lake. These men were recent arrivals to Wisconsin, many directly from Scandinavia. They came to Wisconsin in an environment of Ojibwe dispossession, which enhanced their social and economic status. These men had little sympathy for an Ojibwe leader who resisted this. This, in turn, led to an environment where premeditated murder was legal. It mattered little that there were laws on the books protecting Ojibwe treaty rights and sovereignty. In Wisconsin, colonialism was a local affair, achieved by the selective enforcement of the law.

CHAPTER 7

Maggie Quaderer, Steve Grover, and the Creation of Community at Whitefish, 1894–1920

In 1900, most of Giishkitawag's community lived at Whitefish on the reservation. While there was still a significant number of holdouts living off the reservation at Bakerville on Long Lake, the majority of the community, including all of Nena'aangabi's surviving children and grandchildren, lived on the reservation. No one succeeded Giishkitawag as ogimaa. Like almost all Native people at this time, colonialism undercut traditional political institutions. The farmer at Lac Courte Oreilles and the Indian agent at La Pointe effectively directed much of reservation life, down to dispensing money from sales of timber on allotments, a major source of Ojibwe income. There were areas where the Ojibwe did exercise autonomy, such as deciding who was entitled to allotments. In the decades during which Waabizheshi and Giishkitawag resisted removal, these decisions were made by ogimaag at Lac Courte Oreilles and Bakweyawaa, who had formed a relationship with the Indian agents and created a place for themselves in the political life of the reservation. However, by 1900 these leaders (who had signed the treaty of 1854 creating the reservation), such as Akiwenzii and Ozhaawasho-giizhig, were dead, replaced by a Business Committee comprised primarily of assimilated individuals of mixed descent.

However, the descendants of Nena'aangabi found new ways to take a leadership role in reservation life. In 1900, one of Aazhaweyaa's grandchildren, Maggie Quaderer, was walking to school in Whitefish. In the middle of her walk, the eight-year-old experienced a vision where she was instructed about how to carry out *Chi-dewe'igan*, or Big Drum ceremonies. Big Drum was not new to the reservation. It came to Ojibwe communities in the late nineteenth century. However, Quaderer's vision added new elements to the ceremony and stressed prohibition of alcohol and gambling. Quaderer was also told that the leader of these ceremonies should be her cousin Steve Grover, who was the son of one of Nena'aangabi's daughters. Grover was forty years old at the time of his younger cousin's vision and was not involved in Big Drum ceremonies on the reservation. However, in the months prior to the vision, Grover was becoming more interested in the ceremonies. After Maggie Quaderer had her vision, Steve Grover began leading Big Drum ceremonies at Whitefish. These ceremonies began to draw hundreds from Native communities as far away as Oklahoma. Grover's ceremonies were unique and were controversial among followers of Big Drum elsewhere on the reservation. However, Steve Grover emerged as a different kind of leader, building on the rich legacy of leadership in his family.

Scholars have typically characterized the years of the late nineteenth and early twentieth centuries as ones of cultural decline for Native peoples due to federal policies of boarding schools and allotment. Many narratives of Native history are driven by policy and do not have Native leaders at their center. Therefore, it seems inconceivable that Native people could sustain their traditions, let alone create new ones, during this time. Beginning in the late 1870s, Ojibwe and other Native communities throughout the Great Lakes integrated Big Drum into their community life. Big Drum required major time and labor commitments among its many followers to adhere to its many complex ceremonial protocols. While there were many drums at Lac Courte Oreilles, Whitefish became a major center for Big Drum after 1900, due in no small part to the charismatic leadership of Steve Grover. With federal, state, and local governments seeking to curb Ojibwe sovereignty, Grover became a regionally prominent leader of a spiritual movement rooted in tradition. The early years of Big Drum at Lac Courte Oreilles reveal the creative and transcendent power of traditional culture for Native peoples during what is commonly characterized as the darkest time for Native culture and traditions. In this context, traditional culture was an avenue both for Steve Grover to assert a leadership role and for Ojibwe people more broadly to resist colonialism and demonstrate their sovereignty.

OJIBWE POLITICAL INSTITUTIONS IN THE EARLY TWENTIETH CENTURY

By 1900, the original ogimaag who signed the treaties had passed on. Nationally the Bureau of Indian Affairs (BIA) sought to curb traditional Native political institutions. At Lac Courte Oreilles, the BIA consulted a Business Committee to make internal decisions about resources on the reservation. The Business Committee included six members (one from each community on the reservation), a chairman, a clerk, and an interpreter. Representing Whitefish was Charles Diamond, who was married to Eliza Diamond, one of Nena'aangabi's grandchildren.[1] However, the scope of the Business Committee's power was not defined, and the Indian agent made all final decisions. The Business Committee's power was limited to internal issues such as timber contracts and inheritance. Even there, when the committee attempted to assert itself it came into conflict with federal officials. In 1913, farmer David Jacobs sent off a frustrated letter to his superior, La Pointe Agent Samuel Campbell:

> I would respectfully state that after about two months of workin with the Business Committee, I got them togather again yesterday and then they did not get around untill three OK then the same old storry, first wanted to know about thier pay, I tould them just as soon as they passed on what we had I would order on the contractiors, which had been arangeed by you and one of the contractiors when you were here last but I could see that they did not entend to do any thing, I then requested them to resign, and after a long talk they stated they would not do so as a council of Indians had appointed them and would not resign unless tehy had a council.[2]

This passage reveals the depth of American colonialism during this time. Instead of a committee of Native leaders appointed by tribal council, the reservation was governed by Jacobs, a man who couldn't even spell. The Business Committee was merely a rubber stamp for the agent. Particularly telling was Jacobs telling the committee they would be paid "as soon as they passed on what we had." When the committee protested, Jacobs threatened to disband the committee or withhold its pay.

Nena'aangabi's grandson Thomas Bracklin attempted a more direct approach. Bracklin, the son of Rice Lake Mayor James Bracklin and Aazhaweyaa, was educated in public schools in Menomonie at his father's insistence. However, Bracklin returned to Whitefish to live by his mother and take an active leadership role on the reservation. With the power of the traditional political leaders waning and the Business Committee pawns of the federal government, Bracklin chose another route and tried to work as a government official. In 1915, Bracklin applied to be the government farmer at Red Cliff. When he was appointed by the commissioner of Indian affairs, Red Cliff Agent John Dady fired off an angry letter to Hayward Indian School Agent William Light, who oversaw affairs on the Lac Courte Oreilles Reservation: "When the position was made vacant last year I advised the Office that I did not want an Indian."[3] Assistant Commissioner of Indian Affairs E. B. Meritt reduced Bracklin's annual salary to $720, from $840. Even Red Cliff Agent Dady, who had earlier protested against the appointment of a Native person, sent a letter to Commissioner of Indian Affairs Cato Sells on Bracklin's behalf. About Bracklin's reduction in pay, Dady argued, "this is not a living wage in this district."[4]

Not surprisingly, Bracklin's career was short, and within a year Assistant Commissioner Meritt demanded his resignation.[5] Meritt effectively blackballed Bracklin from the BIA. Meritt was adamant that Bracklin not be allowed to transfer and instead demanded "action be taken immediately toward compliance with the wishes of the Office as to his separation from the service."[6] The BIA was clearly not interested in promoting Native leaders with ties to traditional political institutions, even when they were well educated like Bracklin. However, Bracklin continued to assume a leadership role through informal channels, using his education to be a staunch advocate for people on the reservation right up until his passing in 1950. For example, in 1934 Bracklin authored a petition in response to the proposed Indian Reorganization Act that advocated for much greater autonomy for tribal governments. Bracklin ended his petition with this plea to the federal government: "REMEMBER THAT THE WHOLE WORLD IS RIGHT NOW WATCHING YOU EVERY MOVE YOU MAKE. WILL YOU STAND THE TEST?"[7] It was this uncompromising stance that was the legacy of his grandfather Nena'aangabi and his uncles Waabizheshi and Joe White and made Bracklin too threatening to be a part of the federal governmental structure.

DEMOGRAPHIC CHANGES

Just as the influx of whites to Barron County hastened the removal of the Ojibwe at Rice Lake to the reservation in the 1860s and 1870s, so too did the changing demographics of areas outside the reservation impact the Ojibwe at Lac Courte Oreilles in the 1890s and 1900s. The non-Native population of the area surrounding the Lac Courte Oreilles Reservation grew rapidly in the last years of the nineteenth century. Sawyer County was created in 1883, from the vast northern portion of Chippewa County. By 1890, Sawyer County had a population of 1,977 people. By 1905, this figure had swelled to 5,044. Also in 1905, townships were formed, including the township of Reserve, which shared boundaries with the entire Lac Courte Oreilles Reservation.[8]

The expanding of railways fueled the non-Native settlement of the area. In 1878, the Northwestern Railway extended its line from the Twin Cities to Turtle Lake, Wisconsin, to Barronett (the route of modern US Highway 63). A year later it was extended ten miles to Shell Lake and a few years later to Spooner. At the same time, the Chicago, St. Paul, Minneapolis, and Omaha Railroad extended their line from Eau Claire to Spooner. In the early years of the twentieth century, rail tracks crisscrossed northern Wisconsin.[9] In 1905, the "blueberry" line reached Reserve, providing daily service to Rice Lake.[10]

THE LAST OF THE OLD-GROWTH TIMBER

With valuable old-growth pine gone, a second phase of timber harvest began on the reservation and throughout northern Wisconsin, this time focused on hardwoods, which were in less demand since they were not utilized in home construction.[11] The first phase of timber harvest centered on white pine as it was the most valuable species in old-growth forests and it floated down Wisconsin's vast network of waterways. Hardwoods do not float. However, the extension of railroads into northern Wisconsin made possible the harvest of the remaining old-growth timber. In 1902 a contract with Signor, Crisler & Co. of Rice Lake was approved under the La Pointe Plan, which stipulated awarding a contract to one contractor who received a monopoly on reservation timber harvest. Fifty-three contracts with allottees were approved that year and two sawmills built on the reservation. From 1903 to 1908 Signor, Crisler & Co. harvested hardwoods, mostly from southern and eastern parts of the reservation.[12] This harvest of old-growth hardwoods led to the short-lived boom of the community of Signor in the southern part of the reservation.[13]

Contracts during this second era of timber harvest were just as controversial as before. In 1904, a contract was approved for Signor, Crisler & Co. to cut timber on Aazhaweyaa's allotment. The year before, the reservation Business Committee had determined that Mary Barker, Aazhaweyaa's youngest surviving child, was the sole heir to the allotment. However, the Signor, Crisler & Co. contract did not sit well with Barker's brother Thomas Bracklin. He complained to the agent in La Pointe, and on December 27, 1904, the Business Committee met and determined that all Aazhaweyaa's surviving children, Ogimaabinesikwe, Thomas Bracklin, Nellie Bracklin, and Mary Barker, were the heirs to the allotment. Farmer David Jacobs then instructed Signor, Crisler & Co. to begin cutting timber. However, Thomas Bracklin was not happy with the price and felt that a bid should be made with another contractor. Bracklin had years of experience in the lumber industry with Knapp, Stout Company. According to Jacobs, when the Signor, Crisler & Co. crew began work, Bracklin "said thare would be shooting don if they did not stop work."[14]

The second wave of old-growth timber harvest was riddled with many of the same issues as the first. Charges of corruption circulated about La Pointe Agent Samuel Campbell working with lumber interests to defraud the Ojibwe. Furthermore, Campbell angered many Catholic officials by forcibly removing students from St. Mary's Catholic School on the Bad River Reservation and placing them in off-reservation boarding schools. This led Progressive Republican Wisconsin Senator Robert "Fighting Bob" LaFollette to call for a Senate investigation in 1909.[15] Despite specific concerns about Campbell and the Ojibwe, the Senate committee traveled to all the reservations in Wisconsin. The committee even held a hearing in Shell Lake where they heard witnesses from the landless St. Croix Band.

At Lac Courte Oreilles, witnesses testified to numerous instances of timber trespass by Signor, Crisler & Co. Witnesses also complained that Ojibwe employees were paid in coupons that could only be redeemed at the company store, which charged exorbitant prices, or be cashed at a bank in Eau Claire, over one hundred miles away. Company head James Signor testified that a black market developed, where whites (who had better access to transportation to Eau Claire) would pay the Ojibwe for coupons—for a 10 percent charge. More abuses were revealed at the Bad River hearings.[16] Remarkably, Campbell was able to hang on until 1912, when an audit of Campbell's records ordered by the commissioner of Indian affairs found that the agent embezzled $54,771 from funds owed to the Ojibwe from timber sales on allotments.[17]

By 1910, the Lac Courte Oreilles Reservation was left mostly cutover and burned. Forest fires raged throughout the reservation. That same year, Signor, Crisler & Co. went out of business, leaving allottees not fully compensated. In 1911, M. H. Bekkedal of Westby received a contract under the La Pointe Plan to harvest the few remaining hardwoods left on the

Thomas Bracklin and Mary Barker. Thomas Bracklin was Aazhaweyaa's son from her marriage to Rice Lake mayor James Bracklin, and Mary Barker was her daughter from her marriage to Knapp, Stout official Samuel Barker. (Courtesy Lac Courte Oreilles Ojibwe Community College Library.)

reservation. During the 1911–12 season, 3.5 million board feet were harvested with 4,268,050 board feet the following season. Logging continued on a small scale on the reservation under Bekkedal, with operations formally ending in 1925.[18] Old-growth timber was gone from the reservation and the rest of northern Wisconsin, leaving mostly less lucrative, fast-growing new-growth species such as aspen and basswood. Instead of sale of old-growth timber for saw logs, Wisconsin's vast forests now were almost solely harvested for paper production. The jobs and wealth produced by northern Wisconsin's fifty-some-year timber boom were a thing of the past, leaving the entire region economically marginal and poor.

THE TRANSFORMATION OF INDIAN EDUCATION

One of the major benefits of removing to the reservation touted by federal officials both at Lac Courte Oreilles and nationally was that Indian children could be educated in order to achieve greater material success. Back in 1873, the first school was opened on the reservation during Waabizheshi's struggle to remain at Rice Lake. To encourage the Ojibwe to permanently remain on the reservation, the federal government opened multiple day schools in the largest communities on the reservation. A school was opened at Post in 1881. In 1883, another day school was opened in the Round Lake community. In 1895, the fall after Joe White was murdered, education came to Whitefish when a twenty-four-by-seventy-foot schoolhouse was completed. A person of mixed descent from Bad River, William Denomie, was the teacher. Denomie came to Lac Courte Oreilles as the teacher at Reserve earlier in the year.[19] The school averaged about fifteen students per year.[20]

Federal officials hoped the school would keep the Ojibwe at Whitefish. However, because the federal government mismanaged reservation timber resources, the Ojibwe had no way to make a living on the reservation. Federal records from the time period are filled with letters from frustrated educators writing to the agent at La Pointe complaining that their efforts came to a screeching halt as students had joined their parents for traditional labor and work in logging camps off-reservation. In 1899, five years after Joe White's murder, Denomie reported to La Pointe Indian Agent Samuel Campbell that Ojibwe families at Whitefish were still leaving the reservation for logging camps:

> During the month four families from this settlement have taken their children out of school and have moved away to the logging camps located about fifteen miles from the school. This caused a loss of ten pupils. I understand that another family is to leave this week. The men of these families work in the camps during the winter. They will all be back to the reservation in the spring. They can hardly be blamed for going away as there is no work on the reservation. It is a case of work or go hungry.[21]

Whether engaged in traditional labor or working in lumber camps, for the families at Whitefish and the rest of the reservation, leaving the reservation was about survival. As local whites and state game laws pressured the Ojibwe to remain on the reservation, the federal government provided little opportunity for the Ojibwe to make a living on the reservation.

At the same time as federal officials at La Pointe authorized the construction of day schools to keep the Ojibwe on the reservation, federal officials in Washington pursued a policy focusing on the growth of large boarding schools located far from reservations with a student body made up of many tribal groups. This policy had its origin in the work of US Army Lieutenant Richard Henry Pratt, an officer directly involved in combat against Native peoples in the West. Pratt's philosophy of Indian education was summed up in the famous quote attributed to him: "kill the Indian, save the child."

Pratt began his efforts at Indian education in 1878 at the Hampton Institute in Virginia, an educational institution for African Americans. The following year he founded the Carlisle Indian Industrial School in Pennsylvania. Other large boarding schools were founded on Pratt's model in the following decade including Flandreau in South Dakota, Haskell in Kansas, and Tomah in southern Wisconsin. The Ojibwe enrollment of these institutions was often high. Historian Brenda Child notes that by the time Carlisle closed in 1918, Ojibwe students were the majority.[22] Of the fifty-one Ojibwe students who attended Hampton while it educated Native students (1878–1923), nine were from Lac Courte Oreilles, including Akiwenzii's great-grandson Michael Wolfe.[23]

By the end of the nineteenth century, local policy and larger national federal policy merged with the creation of a boarding school at Hayward designed specially to educate all the Ojibwe at Lac Courte Oreilles (and from the landless St. Croix communities) off-reservation and avoid the attendance problems described by Denomie and other educators. The school was completed in 1901 and began taking students that fall. The Whitefish School was closed, along with the day schools at Post and Round Lake. The only day school that remained open was a Catholic day school at Reserve, which remained open after fifty-four tribal members (mostly of mixed descent) petitioned the federal government against its closing.[24] Students were housed year-round at the facility. Despite the fact that the new school was located only fifteen miles from the reservation, the lack of quick and affordable transportation for most tribal members meant that access to their children was limited. While some students from Lac Courte Oreilles Ojibwe attended national boarding schools prior to the building of the Hayward Indian School, the new school brought the boarding school policy to nearly every family on the reservation.

By design, the school alienated children from their families and traditional Ojibwe culture. However, alternatives for parents were just as bleak. In off-reservation day schools in Hayward and Winter (which services the southern part of the reservation), students faced daily discrimination, as the vast majority of students were white. Lac Courte Oreilles tribal member Rose Martin remembered one family who would torment her and her siblings during their years in elementary school in Winter in the 1920s: "All we heard out of them was that we were dirty Indians."[25] On the reservation, nuns who took a less than tolerant approach to traditional Ojibwe culture ran the Catholic day school at Reserve. Most families at Lac Courte Oreilles lived in extreme poverty during this time, and despite the problems associated with these institutions, many had no better choice but to send their children there. As historian Brenda Child points out, even after federal policy shifted away from boarding schools in the 1930s, enrollments still increased, as many poor Ojibwe families were dependent on these institutions to feed and clothe their children.[26] Likewise, in her study of Hampton Institute, Paulette Molin Fairbanks found that eventually the school was receiving double the number of applicants of its enrollment cap of 120.[27]

The overall effectiveness of boarding schools has been the subject of scholarly debate. In her study on the Mount Pleasant boarding school in Michigan (a school that largely served Ojibwe and Odawa students), Alice Littlefield argues that the boarding school achieved not assimilation but proletarianization of the student body. Littlefield argues that the skills taught to Native students were appropriate for entry into the larger local economy. To support her argument, Littlefield points out that by the 1920s Mount Pleasant primarily served very poor students and orphans.[28] Scholars have also noted the importance placed on team sports at boarding schools as a means of teaching Western values to Native peoples, one result of which was the high number of Native athletes in the early history of professional sports. Prominent Ojibwe athletes included pitcher Charles Bender from White Earth, who is enshrined in the Baseball Hall of Fame, and quarterback Gus Welch from nearby Spooner.[29] This seems to point toward an intention, however flawed, to train Native peoples for success in local economies by instilling students with working-class values of teamwork and cooperation in a Western context.

However, Ojibwe people themselves articulated a different reality at the Hayward Indian Congress. When the federal government sought to transform its relationship to Native people in the 1930s under Commissioner of Indian Affairs John Collier, Native delegates from Wisconsin, Michigan, and Minnesota were anxious to know how the federal government sought to rectify the many wrongs brought about by federal assimilation policies, including boarding schools. Lac du Flambeau Ojibwe delegate Thomas St. Germaine offered a potent critique of the failure of boarding school education:

> The bill provides that the young people must reveal a capacity for higher education in order to be sent to large institutions, but how are they going to develop this capacity? Are they just going to jump right into it? If the Indian schools can prepare the youth up to the point of entering the University of Wisconsin, or Yale, or some other large school, all well and good, but it does not prepare the youth up to that point. Why do we have a Dr. Roe Cloud or a St. Germaine or perhaps one or two others who are graduates of these big schools? Why do we

> have so few of them? Because the system of education has been so faulty, so low in grade that it does not prepare for entrance in to higher schools.[30]

While some Native people did benefit from their boarding school education in higher educational institutions or, in the case of Bender, as professional athletes, it was clear by the 1930s that the "low in grade" education offered at boarding schools did not equip Ojibwe people to build better lives. Most Ojibwe lived in dire poverty. Conversely, the boarding schools did much to erode traditional culture and language. Most Ojibwe people paid a high cultural cost for little to no improvement in their household income.

TRADITIONAL CULTURE AS A RESPONSE TO ASSIMILATION POLICY

Ojibwe people responded to these assaults on their sovereignty and ability to make a living in many ways. Many turned to Catholicism. Catholic churches at Reserve and Post became increasingly important in the lives of people on the reservation, and by the 1940s the majority of people on the reservation were Catholic. Catholicism had much success in Ojibwe communities during this time. Benjamin Armstrong claimed that Catholics provided more tolerance and less corruption than other denominations on Ojibwe reservations.[31] However, the community at Whitefish followed a different path with the establishment of a Presbyterian church. The church became increasingly important to community life at Whitefish, and Christian belief had a major impact on many in the community. For example, when anthropologist Robert Ritzenhauler asked Whitefish store owner John Quaderer Jr. about the origin of Ojibwe people in the 1940s, he reported, "He went out and got a bible and started to look it up said they must be descended from Cain and Abel."[32]

However, this wasn't the whole story. Many Ojibwe people responded to the rapid changes of this era by maintaining and renewing their traditional culture. Scholars have only recently begun to complicate narratives of Native history with stories of how Native people innovated traditional culture in the late nineteenth and early twentieth centuries. Historian Brenda Child argues that the advent of the Jingle Dress Dance in Ojibwe communities was a response to the Spanish influenza epidemic that ravaged the United States during the World War I era. Child notes that the Jingle Dress tradition came about as a result of the vision of an Ojibwe father whose daughter was suffering from Spanish influenza. The father made a dress based on a vision. The dress in his vision had many rows of metal cones that would make a rattling noise based on the dancer's movements. The father instructed his daughter to dance springlike, which meant one foot was never to leave the ground. Slowly, the daughter began to dance, which aided in her recovery.

From this first dancer, the Jingle Dress Dance spread to other Ojibwe communities and then to other Native communities. Child sees the spread of the Jingle Dress Dance as an important response of traditional culture to the stresses of the time: "They designed jingle dresses, organized sodalities, and danced at tribal gatherings, large and intimate, spreading a new tradition while participating in innovative rituals of healing."[33] Child argues that the spread of the Jingle Dress Dance was a direct response not just to the Spanish influenza epidemic of 1918, but also to health threats posed by tuberculosis and trachoma.[34] Like the spread of Big Drum, the spread of the Jingle Dress Dance illustrates the agency exhibited by Native people during the assimilation era, as Native communities innovated traditions as a response to the stresses in Native communities of the time.

The growth of Big Drum at Lac Courte Oreilles and Whitefish was the subject of much anthropological attention. While there is a lack of historical literature about the Lac Courte Oreilles Ojibwe, the community has been the focus of much anthropological study. Numerous anthropologists focused their studies on the community in the early twentieth century. University of Minnesota anthropologist Albert Jenks did field work at Lac Courte Oreilles included in his 1897 *The Wild Rice Gatherers of the Upper Lakes: A Study in American Primitive Economics.*[35] Milwaukee Public Museum Director Samuel Barrett's 1911 "The Dream Dance of the Chippewa and Menominee Indians of Northern Wisconsin" is based largely on extensive fieldwork at Lac Courte Oreilles and, despite its title, actually includes little information on the Menominee Reservation.[36] Barrett came to the Milwaukee Public Museum from the University of California, where in 1908 he became the first person to earn a doctorate in anthropology from an institution west of the Mississippi River.[37]

In the 1940s, an anthropology student from Colombia University, Robert Ritzenhauler, conducted extensive fieldwork at Lac Courte Oreilles over three summers. In each of these summers, a different graduate student colleague from Colombia joined Ritzenhauler. In 1941 Joseph Casagrande joined Ritzenhauler, Ernestine Friedl the following year, and Victor Barnouw in 1944.[38] Following brief publications about their time at Lac Courte Oreilles, Casagrande and Friedl changed research focus after graduate school.[39] Casagrande moved on to fieldwork among indigenous people in Ecuador, and Friedl went on to study Greek women. Ritzenhauler and Barnouw, however, continued to write about Wisconsin Ojibwe communities throughout their careers. Barnouw spent most of his career at the University of Wisconsin–Milwaukee and in 1977 published *Wisconsin Chippewa Myths & Tales and Their Relation to Chippewa Life*.[40] Ritzenthaler went on to become curator of anthropology at the Milwaukee Public Museum, and his fieldwork at Lac Courte Oreilles formed the basis of *The Woodland Indians of the Western Great Lakes*.[41] More recently, many of anthropologist Thomas Vennum's numerous works were strongly influenced by fieldwork at Lac Courte Oreilles, specifically his relationship with Lac Courte Oreilles elder Bill Baker.[42]

This relatively abundant anthropological literature about Lac Courte Oreilles has shaped ideas about historical change in the community. In the 1980s, James Clifford and other postmodern anthropologists leveled a critique at the methodological basis of classical ethnography. Noting the distance between the ethnographer and subject, Clifford and others pointed out the links between classical ethnography and colonialism.[43] While anthropologists working at Lac Courte Oreilles during the first half of the twentieth century were generally much more sympathetic toward Ojibwe culture and people than other anthropologists at the time, tropes of the inevitable decline of traditional cultures shaped how these scholars saw traditional Ojibwe culture.[44] After all, all of these scholars were trained in an era that portrayed Native cultures as static.

Bringing a historical perspective to the cultural life at Lac Courte Oreilles produces an alternative narrative. By the mid-twentieth century, anthropologists were quick to point out the decline of Big Drum ceremonies at Lac Courte Oreilles. To support this claim they pointed to the smaller number of attendees at ceremonies and those on the drum not fully adhering to ceremonial protocol. However, the anthropologists failed to historically contextualize the emergence of Big Drum. If they had, they would have noted the emergence of a dynamic cultural tradition during a time when Native people were supposed to be suffering from cultural decline due to the onslaught of assimilation policies. However, this conclusion was near impossible for these anthropologists as their discipline and training was built on assumptions of the inevitable decline of non-Western cultures. For example, Samuel Barrett contextualized the decline of Native culture at Lac Courte Oreilles as a linear narrative of steady, inevitable decline, despite the fact that his study was about Big Drum, a tradition that only recently emerged: "They have in fact lived under these conditions for many years past and this long association with the white has yielded the inevitable result: the whole mode of life of the people has been greatly altered."[45] Despite Barrett's sympathetic (for the time) depiction of Big Drum ceremonies, his training in anthropology could not let him move beyond the notion of essential cultural traits, despite what was right in front of him.

THE GROWTH OF BIG DRUM CEREMONIES

Problems with the studies of Big Drum by anthropologists begin with the name with which they identified the ceremony. Referred to as the "dream dance" in numerous works, this term has no currency among contemporary Ojibwe people (or Ojibwe people historically) and was a term utilized by anthropologists and no one else. In his study, Thomas Vennum noted that Ojibwe people utilized the term "Big Drum" when referring to the ceremonial drum due the difference between larger drums introduced to Ojibwe communities in the late nineteenth century from Plains cultures and hand drums indigenous to Ojibwe communities.[46] Among the Ojibwe, the ceremony was first called *bwaaniniimi'idiwin. Bwaan* is the Ojibwe term for Dakota people and reflects the ceremony's Dakota origins. Despite this, scholars throughout the twentieth century persisted in referring to Big Drum ceremonies as the "dream dance."

The origin of Big Drum ceremonies was a direct response to American expansion in the nineteenth century. While varying in detail, a common thread to the various oral traditions about the origin of Big Drum is the role of a Dakota woman, Tailfeather Woman, forced to flee from US soldiers and hide in a lake. During this hiding she experienced a series of visions, hence the moniker of "dream dance" imposed by anthropologists. In her visions, Tailfeather Woman was instructed about a ceremony that would bring peace to Native communities. After four days, she emerged and instructed the men in her village about the ceremony.[47] Tailfeather Woman told the men how to make the drum and related the elaborate ceremony in order to transfer drums to other communities. These drums were large, as Tailfeather Woman had been instructed in her vision that smaller drums were no longer adequate to deal with the problems faced in Native communities.[48] A central aspect of Tailfeather Woman's vision was that the drum be shared among neighboring communities as a way to promote peace among Native people. Communities receiving a drum were to learn the songs and ceremonial protocol, practice the ceremony, and then in turn introduce the drum to neighboring communities.[49]

This was a seminal event in Ojibwe history, as Ojibwe-Dakota warfare had raged in central Minnesota and west-central Wisconsin until the US-Dakota War in 1862, just a few years prior to the introduction of Big Drum ceremonies in Ojibwe communities. While Americans had inadvertently stopped Ojibwe-Dakota warfare when they expelled the Dakota from Minnesota in 1862, Big Drum institutionalized the end of centuries of conflict between the Ojibwe and Dakota. In this way, Big Drum was a major cultural innovation in Ojibwe communities as nearly all people in Ojibwe communities had been impacted by Ojibwe-Dakota warfare, the 1855 death of Nena'aangabi being just one example.

The oral tradition usually does not specify the precise date or location of the origin of Chi-dewe'igan. In the 1920s, an intense debate raged in the pages of *American Anthropologist* over the origin of the drum between anthropologists Truman Michelson (who completed the edits of Mesquakie linguist William Jones's *Ojibwa Texts* following Jones's premature death) and Alanson Skinner, former curator of anthropology at the Milwaukee Public Museum. It began with a 1923 article where Michelson cited Benjamin Armstrong's account of the origin of Chi-dewe'igan ceremonies in Wisconsin in 1878.[50] Armstrong even claimed to have met Tailfeather Woman, who he claimed told him she experienced her visions while fleeing Custer's soldiers on the Little Bighorn River in May 1876.[51] Skinner retorted in the very next issue that he believed the origin of Chi-dewe'igan ceremonies in Wisconsin to be in 1862. Skinner cited Menominee "informants" who stated to him that Big Drum ceremonies were central to an 1862 incident on the Menominee Reservation where federal troops were called in out of fear of the ceremony.[52]

Michelson then published a piece in *American Anthropologist* in the spring of 1924 claiming there was no documentary evidence in military or Indian affairs records of troops being called into the Menominee Reservation in 1862 nor any connection or mention of Big Drum. However, Michelson pointed to mention in records of the Indian Affairs Office of Big Drum ceremonies causing alarm among federal officials in Wisconsin in 1878.[53] The following year in a piece entitled "Final Observations on the Central Algonkian Dream Dance," Skinner noted that there was no military record of engagement of Custer's troops with anyone in May 1876, and Custer's troops were stationed in North Dakota throughout the month, debunking Armstrong's claims.[54] It appeared Skinner's inclusion of "final" in his title would be the last word, but this was not meant to be. Skinner's 1925 death in an automobile accident meant that Michelson's next piece, "Final Notes on the Central Algonkian Dream Dance," was truly the final word in the debate between the two anthropologists.[55] While Michelson was forced to concede Skinner's point regarding Armstrong's claims about Tailfeather Woman being pursued by Custer in May 1876, he went on to cite an "informant" from the Bad River Ojibwe Reservation who corroborated Armstrong's claim of 1878 being the introduction of Big Drum ceremonies in Wisconsin.[56]

Regardless of when exactly Big Drum arrived in Wisconsin, it moved from its Dakota origins in the west throughout Ojibwe communities east. In the 1940s, Lac Courte Oreilles Ojibwe tribal member John Bisonette explained the movement of the drum east to anthropologist Robert Ritzenthaler. According to Bisonette, the drum moved west to east in Ojibwe communities in Minnesota and Wisconsin, then to Potawatomi and Menominee communities, then to the Ho-Chunk in central Wisconsin, then to the Mesquakie in central Iowa, then to the Prairie Potawatomi in Kansas who spread it to the Oklahoma Potawatomi where it spread to other Algonquian-speaking communities in Oklahoma.[57] The spread of Big Drum did not (and has not to this day) supplant Midewiwin, or Medicine Lodge. The two ceremonies each have a different focus, with Midewiwin being focused more on medicines to benefit the health of the individual, while Big Drum has a more community focus. Historically, there was a large amount of people who belonged to both, although not all Midewiwin members belonged to Chi-dewe'igan and vice versa (the same holds true today).[58]

This is important to remember when thinking about the role of Big Drum in Ojibwe communities. In *The Death and Rebirth of the Seneca*, anthropologist Anthony F. C. Wallace argued that the Handsome Lake spiritual movement was a direct response to stresses such as being forced onto reservations.[59] Wallace wrote, "A revitalization movement is defined as a deliberate, organized, and conscious effort by members of a society to construct a more satisfying culture."[60] However, the Ojibwe at Whitefish already had a traditional culture. There is no evidence that they found it unsatisfying. The Ojibwe integrated Big Drum ceremonies into their existing spiritual life. It did not replace anything. This was not a case of broken people revitalizing a dying culture. Instead these were traditional people who chose to innovate their culture as their ancestors had done for centuries, demonstrating Ojibwe cultural sovereignty.

Archival sources document some of the early hostility of federal officials to the spread of Big Drum ceremonies. In 1878, La Pointe Indian Agent Isaac Mahan visited the reservations in his agency in an attempt to understand the spread of the ceremonies. Mahan concluded, "the new Sioux dance which is said to be a religious institution introduced about a year since among the Mille Lacs Indians and by them brought over among my Indians." Mahan was concerned about the interaction of people from Mille Lacs and Lac Courte Oreilles leading to hostility against federal officials: "at this council it was reported that the Mille Lacs Indians had demanded an ox, and the Lac Courte Oreilles Indians decided to call upon the farmer, and if he refuse they intended to take possession of the ox, and have a feast." Despite the resolve of some Lac Courte Oreilles people to have the ceremonies, some in the community refused, including Bakweyawaa ogimaag Ozhaawasho-giizhig and Ogabebinens. Mahan reported: "The Pacawong chiefs, 3 in number, refused to have anything to do with the dancing."[61]

Federal officials were so alarmed by the rapid spread of the ceremony among the Ojibwe in northwest Wisconsin that Commissioner of Indian Affairs William Leeds was moved to report to the secretary of the interior about the matter. Leeds wrote: "there were evidences of an alliance for hostile purposes between the Sioux and the Chippewas."[62] These rumors were completely unfounded. In fact, the origin of Big Drum was to bring peace. By the 1890s, Big Drum ceremonies had been accepted by most at Lac Courte Oreilles. By this time, federal officials had realized the ceremonies posed no threat to the federal government. In 1890, Round Lake school teacher Susie Daughtery complained to La Pointe Indian Agent M. A. Leahy that the ceremonies were draining her classroom of students: "We commenced school this week, but as the 'Sioux Dance' which has *just been* adopted by all of the Indians here (with the exception of Kagigabie, the headman, and his son who refuse it) threaten to seriously interfere with the average attendance of the scholars."[63]

Big Drum ceremonies emerged in a similar historical context as the Ghost Dance, which spread from the Great Basin to the northern Plains in the late nineteenth century. Like Big Drum, the Ghost Dance was an innovation of traditional culture that responded to American colonialism. Despite the similarities in the way the two ceremonies emerged and were practiced, there is no connection between them or evidence that one influenced the other.[64] Unlike Big Drum, fear of the Ghost Dance among federal officials was constant, culminating in the massacre of over two hundred Lakotas at Wounded Knee in 1890.[65] In the early years of the spread of Big Drum ceremonies, it was often confused with the better-known Ghost Dance.[66] While Big Drum ceremonies may have produced some anxiety and unease among federal officials and missionaries in its first years, this subsided by the early twentieth century.[67] Historian Jeff Ostler characterized the Ghost Dance as an "anti-colonial movement" due to the Ghost Dance's goal of destruction of the present world and creation of a new one.[68] In contrast, the vision of Tailfeather Woman was based on peace with the

US government and among different tribes. Furthermore, the American flag was (and still is) a fixture at Big Drum ceremonies.[69] Eventually, federal officials even supported Big Drum ceremonies. For example, at the July 1911 Big Drum ceremony at Whitefish, the superintendent at the Hayward Indian School donated a sizeable portion of beef for the ceremony.[70]

The adoption of Big Drum ceremonies in Native communities constituted a major cultural innovation that flourished as federal policies sought to eradicate traditional Native culture. The ceremonial protocols of Big Drum were difficult to learn and maintain and required a major time and economic commitment by its adherents. In 1940 there were three drums at Lac Courte Oreilles. Furthermore, each drum had over a dozen positions.[71] Each drum required knowledge of forty to fifty songs.[72] Some of these songs were unique to a particular drum.[73] These songs corresponded to different positions on the drum and different stages in the ceremony.[74] In addition, the drum itself is seen to be a living entity and required special attention from the drum owner. Frances Densmore noted the rigid protocol of Big Drum ceremonies:

> The ceremonies of the Mide are not marked by extreme ritual exactness and some latitude is allowed the leaders in the choice of songs as well in the text of their discourses, but in the ceremonies connected with the drum certain songs and no others must be sung, and dancing once begun must be continued the prescribed length of time regardless of conditions. The central idea of the "drum religion" is that of peace, yet mingled with this idea is law, rigorous and inflexible.[75]

Likewise, giving of drums to neighboring communities was an elaborate process. In 1940, John Bisonette described the gifting of a drum to the Ojibwe community at Lac du Flambeau:

> Years ago when they gave away Drums to Lac du Flambeau they would have a horse and buggy to take the Drum, but most of the people going would have to walk. It took them about three or four days to get over there, and each night where they camped they would have a dance with the Drum and sing that special Drum Presentation Song and all would dance and point to the east in the direction of Flambeau with their drumsticks.[76]

The difficulty in maintaining these ceremonies during the height of the assimilation efforts of the federal government suggests a degree of agency not typically represented in historical literature in this time period. The fact that Big Drum grew and thrived in Ojibwe communities during this time causes us to rethink ideas about the linear decline of traditional Native cultures.

A MECCA FOR THOSE WHO EMBRACE THE DREAM DRUM FAITH

While Ojibwe practice of Big Drum was a major cultural innovation throughout Ojibwe communities, after 1900 the Whitefish community on the Lac Courte Oreilles Reservation became a major center for Big Drum ceremonies. There were several drums at Lac Courte Oreilles, and Big Drum ceremonies had been practiced for at least twenty years when Steve Grover took a leadership role in them.[77] Around 1900, Grover started experiencing a series of visions. Prior to this, Grover was not a devout follower of Big Drum. These visions were not taken seriously until Grover's cousin, eight-year-old Maggie Quaderer, had a series of corresponding visions. Quaderer was a student at the Whitefish School, and one of her visions occurred on her way to school when she claimed she was transported to heaven, where the Great Spirit gave her instructions as to the proper practice of Big Drum ceremonies.[78] Central to Quaderer's visions was the prohibition of alcohol and gambling for the devout, the presence of a large red cross in the dance ring (which was to be venerated), and the leadership role of Steve Grover.[79]

Maggie Quaderer was the daughter of John Quaderer Jr. and Ogimaabinesikwe, or Julia Quaderer.[80] Ogimaabinesikwe was the eldest child of Aazhaweyaa. Like those of her famous grandmother, Maggie Quaderer's visions changed her community. After attending the nine-day summer ceremony in 1911 at Whitefish, Milwaukee Public Museum Director Samuel Barrett noted the centrality of Quaderer's visions in the Drum at Whitefish:

> The dream dance had been for many years practiced . . . by the Indians in the vicinity of Whitefish, and bore no particular features. . . . However, from the visions of a little girl . . . there were certainly created entirely new features in this ceremony, which have rendered Whitefish more or less a Mecca for those who embrace the dream dance faith. In fact it not infrequently happens that Indians come from various other localities, even as far distant as Oklahoma, to attend one of these ceremonies.[81]

What is noteworthy about the Drum at Whitefish is not so much the particulars of Maggie Quaderer's vision, but how it enriched community life at Whitefish with a traditional ceremony, something typically not discussed in narratives of Native history during the early twentieth century.

Steve Grover was born in 1860, the son of Minotaagoz, one of Nena'aangabi's five daughters.[82] We do not know as much about Minotaagoz

John Quaderer Jr. and daughters. Maggie Quaderer is pictured on the left. (Courtesy Lac Courte Oreilles Ojibwe Community College Library.)

as her famous sister Aazhaweyaa or even her sister Waabikwe. Minotaagoz died sometime in the 1870s at Rice Lake. Grover's father was a white man.[83] Sources emphasize that Grover was charismatic. The ceremonies at White-fish were well attended. Grover cultivated relationships with followers from many Native communities. In the 1980s Grover's daughter Susie Levake remembered: "My dad became friends with some Sac and Fox Indians (from Oklahoma) and they wrote back and forth." Levake remembered that her father would host visitors at their house during the ceremonies.[84] At the 1911 ceremony at Whitefish, Barrett recorded speeches that reiterated the feeling of the positive innovation of Big Drum ceremonies in general for Native people of the time and the central role of Whitefish in particular:

> One visitor at the dance at Whitefish, for instance, recounted how he had traveled over a great part of the middle west and had danced in many different localities and with many different tribes, and how he found in all these localities the same ceremony, how its principals were the same wherever he had encountered it, and what a great benefit it was proving to the communities in which its devotees resided. He took occasion to mention especially the importance of Whitefish as a center of this creed, and delighted the people of Whitefish by recounting the fact that he had danced at a point far towards the west, in the Sioux country, to the music of a drum which had been made by the Whitefish

> people and which had been presented by them to another community toward the west and which had eventually found its way to this comparatively remote region.[85]

The Big Drum ceremony at Whitefish that Barrett attended was an elaborate ceremony filled with strict protocols, the violation of which could bring negative consequences. Like other Big Drum ceremonies of the time, the ceremony itself constituted a major time commitment for participants. The Whitefish ceremony attended by Barrett in 1911 was nine days long. Given the strictness of the ceremonial protocols and the high stakes for violating them, it should be no surprise that they were a source of contention among members of the Drum. On the fourth day, one of the head members gave a speech criticizing the other members for not following ceremonial duties according to Tailfeather Woman's instructions. These criticisms included omission of certain songs, the ceremony not being conducted in the correct order, failing to set apart a day for each of the two drums, and failing to set apart a day for Steve Grover. So serious was the man's conviction that he offered to step down from his position if people felt he was wrong. After his speech another of the head members spoke, claiming that the ceremony had been conducted according to the instructions he received when the community first received the drum. The original speaker then spoke again, reiterating his position. Barrett noted:

> No reply was made to this speech, but a strong feeling of tenseness and suspicion was in the air, and from the looks on the faces of the participants there was certainly a question as to what the outcome of this controversy might lead to. It was, of course, not a personal matter between the directors, but a matter which concerned the whole people and their religion and might therefore lead to grave misunderstandings in the whole community. The situation was, however, greatly relieved after a few minutes by the fact that one of the drummers started a tune. He was immediately joined by the rest of the drummers, with the result that all the dancers joined heartily in the dance that followed. This was said to be a silent expression of good will, the purpose of which was to smooth over the recent unpleasantness.[86]

Participants were to wear their best cloths, a consistent aspect of the ceremony from its inception, but one that was emphasized in particular in Maggie Quaderer's vision. This was apparent on the sixth day of the 1911 Whitefish ceremony, when a young man from the Round Lake community on the reservation showed up without a shirt and was attired in body paint.

The young man intended to pay homage to traditional Ojibwe dress of the nineteenth century. Ojibwe men had not worn body paint in this manner for decades, since around the time of the creation of the reservation. A member of the drum then made a speech about why the young man's lack of shirt was wrong and emphasized his belief that the young man's ignorance was not intentional. As a gesture of good will, the older man provided the younger man with a new shirt, and two other older men then followed the example, providing the younger man with gifts.[87]

The careful handling of this incident was done so that spirits presiding over the ceremony would not be offended and no harm would befall the participants. It illustrates the intricate responsibilities entailed with holding a position on the drum. A similar example illustrating the strict protocol of the ceremony occurred the same day when one of drummers took a seat on the wrong drum. This was rectified by a speech of an older man and tobacco being distributed on the drummer's behalf in order to not offend the spirits.[88] Likewise, on the seventh day of the ceremony a young boy stubbed his toe and fell in the dance circle. This was considered a bad omen, and to rectify the situation, the boy's father made a speech and conducted a giveaway.[89] Similarly, when a drum head was broken on the eighth day, gifts and tobacco were offered followed by a feast the next day.[90]

Despite the serious nature of much of the ceremony at Whitefish, Ojibwe humor played a role as well. Barrett noted the reverence and respect paid ceremonial objects but at the same time observed: "Frequently the dancers purposely do various things to create a laugh, and now and then a speaker purposely makes some remark which causes a great outburst of applause or laughter."[91] Indeed, Barrett's presence as a visitor and his purpose in writing about the ceremony were dealt with by a mixture of careful speech-making to ensure Barrett's presence was not offensive to the spirits, but also genuine warmth in the reception of the speech discussing Barrett's presence and articles he was gifted.[92] Barrett's account of the Whitefish ceremony underscores how adhering to traditional life was the most effective way for the community to remain functional in the face of the economic and social devastation caused by American colonialism. Conducting oneself in a kind manner was an explicit aspect of traditional life. Failure to do so would bring dire consequences. Therefore, adherence to traditional values promoted community in a time when American colonialism actively sought to destroy it. Barrett put it this way:

> They are at all times helpful one to another and never let pass an opportunity to do an act of brotherly kindness, regardless of whether the recipient of this

benefaction is a member of their own cult or not. In fact it is even immaterial whether he is a member of their own race.[93]

Big Drum ceremonies served a number of important functions in the social life of the community. On the eighth day of the ceremony, Barrett reported a feast of thanks to the drum for its power in healing a young child who had been sick. Medicine men had tried to heal the boy when his father had a vision that the drum could heal the child. Barrett noted the boy was recovered and a feast was given.[94] During the ceremony, Barrett noted there was a divorce song, where any man wishing to divorce his wife could dance. This was subject to approval, and a man could speak for the woman to be divorced to give her consent. Barrett reported that only one old man danced during the song, and he simply wanted to ensure there was at least one dancer.[95] Likewise, on the final day of the ceremony, a feast was given by a man to honor a vision he had to marry a widow and provide for her two children.[96] The political life of the community was also brought up in the ceremony. When a speech was made on behalf of a young man who was too ill to work, it was suggested that the town of Reserve (the local municipality that matched the boundaries of the reservation) could provide financial assistance to the young man. One of the board members was present and indicated that the town was in debt due to construction of roads but suggested the young man go to the agent on the reservation.[97] Finally, there was a speech by Maggie Quaderer's father, John Quaderer Jr., who served on the board of a neighboring township, who pledged to keep liquor sales out of the jurisdiction of his township.[98]

Women had a somewhat complicated place in Big Drum ceremonies. In some respects, women did not have the same standing as men in the ceremonies. Unlike the Midewiwin, where women could achieve the same positions as men, women could not attain any position on the drum or dance. Instead, women had an entirely separate category as drum women or *ogichidaakwewag*. The *ogichidaakwewag* were charged with assisting with food preparation, maintaining dance grounds, and keeping the drum in good condition. In addition, while not allowed to sit at the drum and sing, Ojibwe women would sit near the drum and provide vocal accompaniment for the male singers, a tradition predating the arrival of Big Drum in Ojibwe communities.[99] Because of the fact that women could not dance during Big Drum ceremonies, a separate Woman's Dance developed, usually taking place the last day of Big Drum ceremonies.[100] The Woman's Dance had a more secular focus and was quite popular in the early twentieth century at Whitefish. However, by the midcentury the Woman's Dance drums had been given away to neighboring communities as attendance at Chi-dewe'igan ceremonies declined.[101] Today, there are no Women's Dances at Big Drum ceremonies at Lac Courte Oreilles. While at first glance the role of women in Big Drum may seem more restrictive than Midewiwin ceremonies, it should be remembered that the role of women in the ceremony includes the reverence for Tailfeather Woman as the messenger of the Great Spirit. Likewise, it is important to remember that the Whitefish ceremony under Steve Grover originated with the visions of Maggie Quaderer.

At the same time, Steve Grover was a polarizing figure. One controversial aspect of the ceremony under Grover was the presence of a cross in the dance ring and Grover's use of Christian ideas. The cross in the dance ring was unique to Big Drum ceremonies at Whitefish under Grover. The cross was located in the center of the dance ring, and tobacco and other offerings were made to it.[102] The cross is a prominent feature in photographs taken by Barrett during the July 1911 Chi-dewe'igan ceremonies. Anthropologist Thomas Vennum argued that the cross was also used in Midewiwin and that its use in Midewiwin ceremonies was independent from Christian iconography.[103]

One adamant critic of Steve Grover was Lac Courte Oreilles spiritual leader John Mink. Mink was skilled in applying powerful medicines, and although he claimed he never used medicines to hurt people, others on the reservation disputed this. Maggie Quaderer's father, John Quaderer Jr., claimed Mink targeted him. In 1941, Quaderer discussed his run-in with Mink with anthropologist Joseph Casagrande:

> John Mink used medicine on him seven years ago and poisoned him—made his right leg and arm semi-paralyzed. He went with his old woman to get medicine and he fell in a ditch unconscious—the sky kept getting smaller. He couldn't talk, only shake his head. Some white men came and asked him if he was drunk. They took him home. He saw John Mink four times in succession in his dreams, so he knew it was he who poisoned him.[104]

For John Mink, Grover's use of Christian ideas was unacceptable: "Had a cross during the time of Steve Grover, but they didn't like the way he talked—of God and Jesus like a Catholic priest. He wore a red cross braided on the back of his vest." The "they" in this critique is consistent with traditional Ojibwe ways of criticizing. Rarely would older traditional people directly criticize others in the first person, instead saying that it was others that were talking about the person. Casagrande went on to note: "Steve Grover didn't live long after that—some say the old fellow [Mink] killed him. John Mink says that is why he didn't live long—because he was lying." Casagrande's interpreter was Prosper Guibord. About the circumstances of Grover's death, Casagrande wrote, "Prosper says he knows better—the old fellow [Mink] killed him."[105]

While these contestations over the meaning of tradition may appear at first to be dysfunctional, in actuality they reveal the health and vitality of Ojibwe traditions at this time. Whatever the particulars of Grover's ideas about tradition and how we view them today, he was asserting his ideas within the framework of traditional ceremony, the mere practice of which was highly subversive during this time. Likewise, John Mink's animosity toward Grover was the result of his convictions about the meaning of tradition and shows how important and contested traditional culture was to the Ojibwe at Lac Courte Oreilles during this time. This sharply contrasts with the characterization of this time period as one of cultural decay and decline.

CONCLUSION

In *Decolonizing Methodologies*, Maori scholar Linda Tuhiwai Smith argues that recovery of traditions is only the first step for indigenous communities to true indigenous self-determination.[106] By doing so, Smith challenges common notions about tradition as stagnant and argues that indigenous traditions are creative, always changing, and transcendent. Many narratives of Native history cast the decline of traditional cultures as linear, thus implicitly casting indigenous traditions as static. The story of Big Drum in Ojibwe communities tells us something different. Not all Native people turned away from traditional beliefs and Native languages at the height of the assimilation era. Moreover, it is vital for us as Native people to know more about those persons who made the difficult sacrifices to retain traditional ways in the face of massive institutional pressure from American colonialism and social pressure from Native people within their own communities. It is due to the efforts of these persons that we have the cultural inheritance we possess today.

While polarizing and controversial, Steve Grover was such a person. Grover built on his family's legacy of leadership in a different arena. With the BIA seeking to suppress traditional Native political institutions, Grover and individuals like him served important leadership roles within the community that were rooted in tradition. This speaks to the complex ways that assimilation policies actually worked to strengthen Native culture and community life. The Ojibwe at Whitefish and Native people elsewhere did not stop functioning as leaders just because the BIA told them to.

Thinking about tradition as transcendent is a major shift from more Western-based ideas about tradition. As Ojibwe scholar Anton Treuer argues, tradition can help us transcend many of the problems our communities face. In his discussion about successful language revitalization efforts among the Maori in New Zealand and Native Hawaiians, Treuer argues:

> Both groups have enjoyed not only a revitalization of their traditional languages and cultures but also a major boost to community cohesion, pride, and solidarity. They've also seen the first meaningful declines in gang activity and drug and alcohol abuse in their histories. The Ojibwe could pursue the same goals in Minnesota.[107]

When Ojibwe in the early twentieth century faced allotment, boarding schools, and denial of treaty rights, many turned to Big Drum ceremonies to keep their communities strong. Much of the dysfunction in our communities today is the direct legacy of the poverty created by assimilation policies of the early twentieth century. Once again traditional culture may hold the key for us to transcend these issues and build stronger communities.

Conclusion

Charles White appears to not have talked much about his father's murder, based on what little we know about the murder from his descendants.[1] For Charles White, the murder of Joe White was not just an attack on Ojibwe sovereignty but also robbed a boy of his father. The world in which Charles White grew up was directly shaped by events such as the murder of his father. These were dark times for Native people, as most Native people lived in dire poverty while American institutions were attacking their traditional culture. Federal policy used education as a tool to separate Native children from their families in order to eradicate Native traditions, including the practice of traditional labor. The community at Whitefish that Charles White grew up in was no exception. The day school at Whitefish was followed by the Hayward Indian School, a boarding school built specifically to keep Lac Courte Oreilles children in school instead of out with their families gathering maple sugar, fishing, harvesting wild rice, and hunting. At the same time the Ojibwe struggled to continue these activities off-reservation, as the murder of Joe White showed how far the state of Wisconsin was willing to go to enforce its laws. It took almost a century after White's murder for federal courts to decisively assert that Wisconsin's denial of Ojibwe treaty rights was illegal.

LIVING AND WORKING OFF-RESERVATION AFTER JOE WHITE'S MURDER

Both federal educational policy and the state prosecution of Ojibwe treaty rights escalated pressure to remain at Whitefish. However, even after White's murder, Ojibwe people on the reservation continued to practice traditional and wage labor off-reservation in order to survive. Steve Grover's daughter Susie Levake remembered how her father would journey to Clam Lake, about thirty miles northeast of the reservation, in the winter: "They camped right there for several days and always came back with plenty of venison."[2] Clam Lake was not a traditional area that the Ojibwe community at Whitefish went to but was a destination that was sparsely populated, so the Ojibwe were less likely to have conflict with settlers or game wardens. Even today, miles of national forest surround the area. Likewise, educators continued to have attendance problems when parents took their children off the reservation. In 1911, at the one remaining day school on the reservation, Sister Xavier Grany wrote to La Pointe Agent Major Samuel Campbell echoing the dilemmas faced by her predecessors in the last decades of the nineteenth century: "We wish to inform you that fourteen of our children are in the sugarbush and we feel that they should be in school as they are of no use to their parents."[3]

The accounts of early white settlers also showed Ojibwe presence off-reservation. In Birchwood, Wisconsin (a town about fifteen miles south of the reservation), Allison Stout remembered:

> There was a good sized wild rice bed on Birch Creek just above where it empties into Balsam Lake. Every fall the Indians came down from the Reserve to gather the rice and camped on the north bank of the creek. . . . They stayed there for some time as they came down in time to tie up the green rice stalks in bundles, and waited for it to get ripe. Then they gathered and parched it before returning to Reserve. I venture they camped there about a month as it probably took a week or so to tie the green rice into bundles about the size one could reach around with both hands.[4]

Stout also remembered her father trying to buy rice: "I remember well the cries of outrage when the price went up to 7 cents a pound."[5] Stout remembered that the Ojibwe did not want to sell rice to her father and under pressure would agree to the following day, only to sneak back to the reservation without selling him any. By this time, the prejudice of local whites against Indians had shaped how the Ojibwe related to outsiders. However, according to other Birchwood settlers, Ojibwe people would routinely come down from the reservation selling birch bark, beaded items, and mats.[6]

The murder of Joe White demonstrated that many white settlers were willing to accept violence as a means to keep Ojibwe people on the reservation. However, there were exceptions. As newspaper coverage of the trial of Martin and Hicks suggested, whites at Long Lake were somewhat more tolerant of Ojibwe presence. Six years after the murder of their ogimaa, the Ojibwe community of Bakerville still lived at Long Lake. It was a small community of forty-five people. Only Joe Baker's family, another family headed by a German man, and one other individual had any non-Ojibwe ancestry. Despite the presence of white blood in a small minority of the community, culturally this was an Ojibwe community, more traditional than most families on the reservation. For example, every single person lived in a wigwam at a time when virtually everyone on the reservation lived in a frame house.[7] Bakerville was not a community that sought to assimilate with the whites that surrounded them.

As jobs in the timber industry dried up with the elimination of old-growth forests, the Ojibwe at Bakerville found some work in the developing tourism industry as a way to sustain itself. In 1904, the Rockford Hotel was opened on Long Lake. The hotel was named because its owner, Asaph B. Curtis, was from Rockford, Illinois, as were most of his clients. Ojibwe men drove the buggy from the train stop in Sarona, Wisconsin, about fifteen miles to the west. Ojibwe people sold blueberries and other traditional Ojibwe foods to the guests.[8]

However, the increased enforcement of Wisconsin game laws on Ojibwe people and the end of the timber industry took its toll on the small community. By 1910, the community at Bakerville dwindled to thirteen, consisting only of the families of the brothers Joe and Bill Navaosh and Mary Wiedeman, the Ojibwe wife of a German man, and her four-year-old son. By this time, all three families lived in frame houses. Joe Navaosh's family consisted of his wife and three children. Bill Navaosh's family consisted of his wife, daughter, and three young grandchildren.[9] These families remained at Long Lake, however, and in 1923, Bill Navaosh charged a local tourist one dollar to take a picture of his family in their birchbark canoe.[10]

NOT JUSTIFIABLE IN LAW

While federal officials failed to intervene and protect the Ojibwe treaty rights against Wisconsin's violation of federal law, the Ojibwe had some success taking matters into their own hands. In 1901, Bad River Ojibwe Andrew Blackbird (a direct descendant of ogimaa Makadebinesi, who signed the treaty of 1854) was arrested for netting in a stream on the Bad River Reservation. Blackbird was fined $25 plus court costs and was subsequently jailed for failing to pay the fine. Blackbird sued in federal court, and Judge Romanzo Bunn overturned the citation and ordered Blackbird's release. Bunn ruled, "the prisoner's arrest was the result of overzeal on the part of a fish and game warden, which may be excusable, but is not justifiable in law."

Bunn found that the Ojibwe maintained hunting and fishing rights under the treaty of 1854 throughout the territory ceded (on and off the reservation) that only the federal government could terminate. Bunn ruled:

> Congress might even provide fish and game laws to restrict the Indians in their natural and immemorial rights of fishing and hunting. But it has not seen fit to do so. It would be intolerable if the state, under these circumstances, should have the power to step in, and extend its civil and criminal codes and police power over these people. It would be an invitation to an early conflict of jurisdiction.[11]

While Bunn's ruling helped Blackbird, it did nothing to stop Wisconsin (or Minnesota or Michigan) from enforcing game laws in direct violation of the treaty of 1854. Change did not come until over eighty years later, with the *Voight* decision. In 1972, two Lac Courte Oreilles citizens, brothers Fred and Mike Tribble, moved their ice fishing house on Chief Lake over the reservation boundary, intending to be arrested so as to challenge Wisconsin's prosecution of Ojibwe treaty rights. As a result of the brothers' arrest, the Lac Courte Oreilles Band sued Wisconsin Department of Natural Resources head Lester Voight in federal court. Soon all of the Wisconsin Ojibwe Bands joined the suit. The district court upheld the brothers' arrest in violation of state game laws, ignoring Bunn's ruling in the same district court. However, the circuit court of appeals reversed the lower court ruling and found that Ojibwe treaty rights had never been extinguished and ordered Wisconsin to stop prosecuting the Ojibwe and work with the Ojibwe to create a management plan for the harvesting of resources under treaties. The Supreme Court chose not to hear Wisconsin's appeal of the case.[12]

The practice of Ojibwe Treaty Rights in Wisconsin, in particular the spearing of fish in the spring, angered many whites in northern Wisconsin. In the late 1980s boat landings became increasingly dangerous for the Ojibwe as hundreds of white protesters yelled racist slogans and threw rocks at Ojibwe fishermen. State and local authorities did nothing to stop the protests, often refusing to press charges against violent protesters. The protests drew national media attention, with some media outlets drawing comparisons with racial violence in the Deep South during the 1950s and 1960s. It was only after Judge Barbara Crabb issued an order that interference with Ojibwe treaty rights was a federal crime that the protests slowly died down.[13] At the same time, the state of Minnesota chose to ignore the decision reached in the circuit court of appeals that includes Wisconsin, forcing the Ojibwe bands in Minnesota who were party to the treaties of

1837 and 1854 to bring their own suit in the federal district court of Minnesota. This time the case went all the way to the Supreme Court. In 1999, the US Supreme Court upheld Ojibwe treaty rights, in a very close five to four decision. While there was some opposition to Ojibwe treaty rights in central Minnesota, the fervor did not reach the heights of Wisconsin in the prior decade.[14]

ZIIGWANG (IN THE SPRING)

On a beautiful morning in late March of 2012, I leave the Lac Courte Oreilles Reservation headed for Barron County. This year marks the fifth consecutive spring my family gathers maple sap on Barron County Forest Land just north of Cumberland, Wisconsin. Gathering maple sap on public lands is part of our treaty rights, albeit less practiced and less controversial than spearing fish or deer hunting. I leave the reservation, driving south on State Highway 27 for a few miles before turning west on State Highway 70 for a few more. I then make a left on County Highway B. Two miles up Highway B to my left is Flowage Drive, which leads to Slim Creek Road. Just up this road was where Horace Martin and Josiah Hicks murdered Joe White. I continue on for about twenty miles on County Highway B, winding along the beautiful, towering pines that line Long Lake until I reach Shell Lake. I pass the Washburn County Courthouse, where Martin and Hicks were acquitted of White's murder.

I have passed these places over a hundred times and rarely is their significance lost on me. I finally arrive at the sugar camp. After being cooped up indoors during the long northern Wisconsin winter, it feels great to get outside in the calm winds and clear blue skies, even though the temperatures are only in the upper thirties. It is a true traditional family activity, as my son, my parents, and I collect sap from each tree and lug buckets of sap through the still deep snow. Despite the events that occurred at places I've passed on my way to get here, there are still Ojibwe families in Barron County practicing treaty rights. Removal wasn't fixed in one particular time period. Its significance lies beyond specific legal or policy definition. Removal is foundational to colonialism in its desire create a racially segregated America. Removal is something we live with and must resist today: Ojibwe Akiing (territory) isn't just the reservation; it is the entire ceded territory.

Nena'aangabi, Waabizheshi, and Joe White were American heroes. They accepted Americans in Ojibwe territory but fought hard against those who wished to create a segregated America. The America that Nena'aangabi, Waabizheshi, and Joe White strove for was inclusionary and intercultural, strengthened by the exchange of cultures. While theirs is a unique and interesting story, there were hundreds of other Indian leaders throughout the Western Hemisphere who also resisted colonialism during the nineteenth century. However, tribal sovereignty is not limited to the heroic efforts of these leaders. While we build on what came before, it is up to each generation to practice and define our sovereignty, one bucket of maple sap at a time. It's spring. It's a new day.

Notes

INTRODUCTION

1. All Ojibwe names I have spelled in the Fiero orthography, as it is the most commonly used writing system among contemporary Wisconsin Ojibwe speakers. In all references to Ojibwe names I have included the rendering as it appears in the original document. See John D. Nichols and Earl Nyholm, *A Concise Dictionary of Minnesota Ojibwe* (Minneapolis: University of Minnesota Press, 1995).
2. "Lac Courte Oreilles Band of Lake Superior Chippewa, Tribal Profile," Wisconsin State Tribal Relations Initiative, http://witribes.wi.gov/section.asp?linkid=284&locid=57. Throughout I use the term "tribal citizen" to refer to individuals enrolled in Native nations. While "tribal member" is more common, the use of the word "citizen" better conveys the sovereignty of Native nations. I mean both "tribal citizen" and "tribal member" to be synonymous.
3. Jeffrey Ostler, *The Plains Sioux and U.S. Colonialism from Lewis and Clark to Wounded Knee* (Cambridge: Cambridge University Press, 2004), 2.
4. Patrick Wolfe, "Settler Colonialism and the Elimination of the Native," *Journal of Genocide Research* 8, no. 4 (2006): 392.
5. Patrick Wolfe, "Structure and Event: Settler Colonialism, Time, and the Question of Genocide," in *Empire, Colony, Genocide: Conquest, Occupation, and Subaltern Resistance in World History*, ed. A. Dirk Moses (New York: Berghahn Books, 2008), 103.
6. Ostler, *Plains Sioux and U.S. Colonialism*, 3.
7. Donald Fixico, "Federal and State Policies and American Indians," in *A Companion to American Indian History*, ed. Philip J. Deloria and Neal Salisbury (Malden, MA: Blackwell Publishers, 2002), 379.
8. Indian Removal Act of 1830, 4 Stat. 411 (1830).
9. Sidney L. Harring, *Crow Dog's Case: American Indian Sovereignty, Tribal Law, and United States Law in the Nineteenth Century* (New York: Press Syndicate of the University of Cambridge, 1994), 13.

10. Major Crimes Act of 1885, 23 Stat. 362 (1885) and Ex Parte Crow Dog, 109 U.S. 556 (1883).
11. Robert N. Clinton, "There Is No Federal Supremacy Clause for Indian Tribes," *Arizona State Law Journal* 34, no. 1 (2002): 113–260.
12. United States v. Kagama, 118 U.S. 375 (1886), and Lone Wolf v. Hitchcock, 187 U.S. 553 (1903).
13. Clinton, "There Is No Federal Supremacy Clause for Indian Tribes," 181.
14. For the legacy of plenary power, see Laurence M. Hauptman, "Congress, Plenary Power, and the American Indian, 1870–1992," in *Exiled in the Land of the Free: Democracy, Indian Nations, and the U.S. Constitution* (Sante Fe: Clear Light Publishers, 1992), 317–36.
15. Clinton, "There Is No Federal Supremacy Clause for Indian Tribes," 199. A similar legal rationale for a judicial overturning of plenary power is offered in Nell Jessup Newton, "Federal Power over Indians: Its Sources, Scope, and Limitations," *University of Pennsylvania Law Review* 132, no. 2 (1984): 236.
16. See Newton, "Federal Power over Indians," 195–288.
17. For more on the foundations of the US recognition of the inherent sovereignty of Native Nations, see David Wilkins, *American Indian Politics and the American Political System* (Lanham: Rowman & Littlefield, 2007), 52–54. For more on Native Nations and the Constitution, see Vine Deloria Jr. and David E. Wilkins, *Tribes, Treaties, and Constitutional Tribulations* (Austin: University of Texas Press, 1999).
18. Treaty with the Delaware Tribe, September 17, 1778, 7 Stat. 13. See Wilkins, *American Indian Politics and the American Political System*, 46.
19. An Ordinance for the Government of the Territory of the United States, North-West of the River Ohio, July 13, 1787, and Trade and Intercourse Act, July 22, 1790, 1 Stat. 137.
20. Cherokee Nation v. Georgia, 30 U.S. 1 (1831). In the Cherokee cases, Marshall crafted his decision to avoid a constitutional showdown with the executive branch that would have ended in defeat for the court. Crafting a decision that recognized the inherent sovereignty of the Cherokee would have exposed the violation of Cherokee treaties and the violation of constitutional supremacy of treaties as the "Law of the Land" by the executive branch. For an overview of the circumstances surrounding the Cherokee cases, see Jill Norgren, *The Cherokee Cases: The Confrontation of Law and Politics* (New York: McGraw-Hill, 1996). Early in Supreme Court decisions regarding Native nations, the court made decisions about the nature of individual Native nations that would apply to all the Native nations.
21. On the nature and fluidity of sovereignty, see Stephen D. Krasner, "Sovereignty," *Foreign Policy* 122 (February 2001): 20–29. For more on the

limitations of sovereignty for nations more broadly and its implications for theorizing the sovereignty of Native nations, see David E. Wilkins, *American Indian Sovereignty and the U.S. Supreme Court: The Masking of Justice* (Austin: University of Texas Press, 1997), 375.

22. Michael Witgen, *An Infinity of Nations. How the Native New World Shaped Early North America* (Philadelphia: University of Pennsylvania Press, 2012).
23. Frederick Hoxie, "The Problems of Indian History," *Social Science Journal* 25, no. 4 (1988): 395–96.
24. During the time this study encompasses there were two different Ojibwe ogimaag named Noodin, one from the Snake River Band and the other in the nearby Mille Lacs Band. There were three ogimaag named Bizhiki, the most famous of which was of the La Pointe Band, but also influential ogimaag of the Leech Lake Band and St. Croix Band.

CHAPTER 1. THE RISE OF NENA'AANGABI AND AMERICAN EXPANSION IN THE WESTERN GREAT LAKES, 1825–1837

1. Richard E. Morse, "The Chippewas of Lake Superior," in *Collections of the State Historical Society of Wisconsin*, vol. 3, ed. Lyman Copeland Draper (Madison: Wisconsin Historical Society, 1904; originally published 1857), 341. This book can be accessed online at http://content.wisconsinhistory.org/cdm4/document.php?CISOROOT=/whc&CISOPTR=1793&REC=3.
2. Henry R. Schoolcraft, *Schoolcraft's Expedition to Lake Itasca: The Discovery of the Source of the Mississippi*, ed. Philip P. Mason (1834; repr., East Lansing: Michigan State University Press, 1993), 123–24. Schoolcraft spelled Nena'aangabi's name "Neenaba."
3. One account of Ojibwe migration based on oral tradition from the mid-nineteenth century is found in William W. Warren, *History of the Ojibway People* (1885; repr., St. Paul: Minnesota Historical Society Press, 1984), 76–94.
4. Schoolcraft, *Schoolcraft's Expedition to Lake Itasca*, 118. See also Henry R. Schoolcraft, *Personal Memoirs of a Residence of Thirty Years with the Indian Tribes on the American Frontiers* (Philadelphia: Lippincott, Grambo, 1851), 102–3. Warren discusses Madeline Island as a place where Ojibwe people were once concentrated in one community. See Warren, *History of the Ojibway People*, 95–107. Historian Theresa Schenck disputes Warren's and Schoolcraft's depictions of Madeline Island's importance to Ojibwe people in the nineteenth century based upon its historical role in the concentration of

the Ojibwe population. Citing archival materials from the seventeenth and eighteenth centuries, Schenck argues that there was never a central concentration of Ojibwe people on Madeline Island. Schenck goes so far as to discount the symbolic importance of Madeline Island to nineteenth-century Ojibwe. Schenck also disputes Warren's estimation of the arrival of Ojibwe people on Madeline Island in the late fifteenth century and argues that the Ojibwe arrived there much later. See Theresa M. Schenck, *The Voice of the Crane Echoes Afar: The Sociopolitical Organization of the Lake Superior Ojibwa, 1640–1855* (New York: Garland, 1997), 78. Regardless of whether or not Madeline Island had a large concentration of Ojibwe people prior to the nineteenth century, sources from the nineteenth century indicate that Madeline Island was perceived by the Ojibwe in such a way. Furthermore, that perception remains among Ojibwe people today.

5. Lake Superior Chippewa Annuity, 1857, Chippewa Annuity Rolls, 1841–1907, US Office of Indian Affairs, Minnesota Historical Society (MHS), St. Paul, M390, Roll 1.
6. Warren, *History of the Ojibway People*, 193.
7. John Condecon, "Ottawas," Works Progress Administration (WPA), Chippewa Indian Historical Project, Archives of the Fransciscan Sisters of Perpetual Adoration, La Crosse, Wisconsin. The Bad River WPA project records are an underutlilized treasure of historical information. The originals are located in La Crosse, but they are also available on microfilm at the State Historical Society of Wisconsin's Area Research Center in Ashland, Wisconsin. Condecon was the son of Ontonagon Band ogimaa Waasegiizhig and Ikwezenzish, who was the daughter of Bad River ogimaa Makadebinesi.
8. Reference to Odawa people referred to as *court oreilles* can be found in Johann Georg Kohl, *Kitchi-Gami: Life among the Lake Superior Ojibway*, trans. Lascelles Wraxall (St. Paul: Minnesota Historical Society Press, 1985; originally published 1860), 118. Odawa were called short ears by the French because in the seventeenth and early eighteenth centuries most tribes in the western Great Lakes wore some form of weighted jewelry that elongated the ear lobe. However, the Odawa were the only tribal group in which this was not fashionable. Therefore the Odawa appeared to French traders to have short ears. See Alexander Henry, *Travels and Adventures in the Years 1760–1776* (1809; repr., Chicago: Lakeside Press, 1921), 192.
9. Historian Theresa Schenck argues that villages contained several bands. However, sources from the nineteenth century indicate that the band was the larger structure and the term "village" was used for divisions within the band tied to a specific locality. See Schenck, *Voice of the Crane Echoes Afar*, 78–79. I utilize the terms "village" and "community" interchangeably.

10. Throughout I use "ogimaa," "chief," and "leader" interchangeably. Ogimaa are identified as chiefs in treaties, annuity records, and other historical documents of the nineteenth century. The term "chief" carries with it exoticized notions of Native leadership. As a result, in the historical record many Ojibwe people who were not ogimaa are identified by non-Ojibwe as chiefs.
11. Schoolcraft, *Schoolcraft's Expedition to Lake Itasca*, 94. See also Kohl, *Kitchi-Gami*, 274–75.
12. Warren, *History of the Ojibway People*, 41–53.
13. Ibid., 190–91.
14. Ibid., 191 and 314. Bakweyawaa means where a river bends to resemble a lake. This was explained to me by Lac Courte Oreilles spiritual leader and Tribal Historic Preservation Officer Jerry Smith. Jerry Smith, personal interview, July 26, 2007. A nineteenth-century source that explains this is Joseph N. Nicollet, *The Journals of Joseph N. Nicollet: A Scientist on the Mississippi Headwaters with Notes on Indian Life, 1838–1837*, trans. Andre Frey (St. Paul: Minnesota Historical Society Press, 1970), 149. Bakweyawaa is sometimes rendered "Pahquahwong," and incorrectly translated as "where the river is wide." For example, see Charlie Otto Rasmussen, *Where the River Is Wide: Pahquahwong and the Chippewa Flowage* (Odanah: Great Lakes Indian Fish & Wildlife Commission, 1998).
15. Lake Superior Chippewa Annuity, 1860, MHS M390, Roll 2. Locations for Lac Courte Oreilles Band villages with phonetic spelling of village leaders is in Helen Hornbeck Tanner, ed., *Atlas of Great Lakes Indian History* (Norman: University of Oklahoma Press, 1987), 144.
16. For an overview of how Ojibwe people in northwest Wisconsin lived and spent time in and away from the villages, see Schoolcraft, *Personal Memoirs*. For a description of the Ojibwe labor activities, see Frances Densmore, *Chippewa Customs* (1929; repr., St. Paul: Minnesota Historical Society Press, 1979), 119–23. For an overview of how scholars have depicted Native labor, see Patricia Albers, "Labor and Exchange in American Indian History," in *A Companion to American Indian History*, ed. Philip J. Deloria and Neal Salisbury (Malden, MA: Blackwell Publishers, 2002), 269–86. I use the term "traditional labor" to distinguish between labor activities Ojibwe people participated in historically, such as making sugar, fishing, harvesting wild berries, planting gardens, harvesting wild rice, and hunting, and other forms of labor, such as working in the timber industry. While some may characterize this as "subsistence" labor, this label is inaccurate, as Ojibwe people often sold or exchanged surplus wild rice, maple sugar, and other goods. While "traditional" may seem problematic, it does convey the historical importance of these labor activities as well as the spiritual protocols associated with this

type of labor such as offering tobacco, first harvest ceremonies, and first kill ceremonies. While many scholars may not be comfortable with the term "traditional," it has currency and specific meanings among Native people today.

17. Schoolcraft, *Schoolcraft's Expedition to Lake Itasca*, 93.
18. Schoolcraft, *Personal Memoirs*, 368. Later in Schoolcraft's trip he found the village at Lake Chetac also deserted, noting "at present the whole tendency of the Indian population is to Rice Lake. The war party mustering at that point absorbs all attention." Ibid., 380.
19. Schoolcraft, *Schoolcraft's Expedition to Lake Itasca*, 116, and Ethel Elliot Chappelle, *Around the Four Corners: A Pioneer History of the Washburn, Sawyer, Barron, and Rusk Counties* (Rice Lake, WI: Chronotype Publishing, 1971), 20.
20. William W. Bartlett, *History, Tradition, and Adventure in the Chippewa Valley* (Chippewa Falls: Chippewa Printery, 1929), 65. This book is available online through the Wisconsin Historical Society at http://www.wisconsinhistory.org/turningpoints/search.asp?id=1030.
21. "How Na-non-gabe Was Killed in '55," *Rice Lake Chronotype*, February 18, 1925, 1.
22. Warren, *History of the Ojibway People*, 193. There is no mention of Nena'aangabi by name in Warren's book. However, writing in 1852, Warren identifies Gekek as "the present war-chief of the Chippewa River district." It is likely he is referring to Nena'aangabi, since Gekek was likely dead by this time and Nena'aangabi was at the height of his influence. Warren rendered Gekek "Ka-ka-ke (Hawk)." We do know that Warren was aware of Nena'aangabi. For example, while he was employed as a removal agent in 1851 he wrote to his cousin George Warren and suggested organizing a delegation of the nine most important Ojibwe leaders from Wisconsin to go to Washington in order to convince the Wisconsin Ojibwe to remove to Fond du Lac. In this letter he identifies Nena'aangabi as "Na nuh anung abe." See William Warren to George P. Warren, January 15, 1851, C. F. X. Goldsmith Papers, 1821–1923, State Historical Society of Wisconsin Area Research Center, University of Wisconsin–Eau Claire.
23. For more on Ojibwe migration to this area, see Warren, *History of the Ojibway People*, 314.
24. See Schoolcraft, *Personal Memoirs*, 383.
25. Ibid., 386.
26. Warren, *History of the Ojibway People*, 309. Warren's description of the landscape of Prairie Rice Lake is some of his richest, most evocative writing. While critiques of Warren center on his over-the-top descriptions of Ojibwe warfare, passages such as this are both vital historical information and just plain good writing. Archeological evidence shows a number of pits for

threshing rice on the east side of Prairie Rice Lake. See Charles E. Brown and Robert H. Becker, "The Chetek and Rice Lakes," *Wisconsin Archeologist* 16, no. 3 (1917): 102.

27. Lake Superior Chippewa Annuity, 1850, MHS M390, Roll 1.
28. For more on the importance of wild rice to Ojibwe life, see Thomas Vennum Jr., *Wild Rice and the Ojibway People* (St. Paul: Minnesota Historical Society Press, 1988).
29. Warren, *History of the Ojibway People*, 304. The Red Cedar River was sometimes called the Menominee River in historical sources.
30. Bartlett, *History, Tradition, and Adventure*, 187.
31. Robert E. Ritzenthaler Papers, Milwaukee Public Museum, Spiral Notebook 5, 43.
32. Schoolcraft, *Schoolcraft's Expedition to Lake Itasca*, 117.
33. Schoolcraft, *Personal Memoirs*, 388. Schoolcraft also mentioned numerous hunting camps south of Rice Lake in *Schoolcraft's Expedition to Lake Itasca*, 116.
34. For a brief description of the mounds of Indian Mounds Park in Rice Lake, see "Native Journeys," http://wpt2.org/wisconsinStories/2001season/native/native_journeys.html. More detail is found in Leland Cooper, *Indian Mounds Park, Rice Lake, Wisconsin: Archeological Site* (St. Paul: Science Museum of the St. Paul Institute, 1959).
35. Robert A. Birmingham and Leslie E. Eisenberg, *Indian Mounds of Wisconsin* (Madison: University of Wisconsin Press, 2000). See also Brown and Becker, "The Chetek and Rice Lakes." Both William Warren and Benjamin Armstrong noted that Ojibwe people had no explanation as to the origins of the mounds and that they were not the work of their ancestors. See Warren, *History of the Ojibway People*, 180–82, and Benjamin G. Armstrong, *Early Life among the Indians* (Ashland, WI: A. W. Bowron, 1892), 147–48. Although out of print, Armstrong's book is available online through the Wisconsin Historical Society at http://www.wisconsinhistory.org/turningpoints/search.asp?id=1615.
36. On the Barron County pipestone quarry, see G. A. West, "Pipestone Quarries in Barron County," *Wisconsin Archeologist* 9, no. 2 (1910): 31–34. The land of the site was bought by Cornell University, who later let the land go back to Barron County, who made the land part of the Barron County Forest. However, before letting the land go back to Barron County, Cornell retained the mineral rights. See Bob Heffner, *Rice Lake: Gem of the Red Cedar Valley* (Rice Lake, WI: Chronotype Publishing, 2000), 16. The quarry was mentioned by Henry Schoolcraft during his 1831 trip to Lac Courte Oreilles and Rice Lake. See Schoolcraft, *Personal Memoirs*, 383.
37. In 1925, Lac Courte Oreilles interpreter Ira Isham, who was married to one of Nena'aangabi's granddaughters, claimed in the *Rice Lake Chronotype* that

Nena'aangabi was seventy-six at the time of his death, while former *Rice Lake Chronotype* editor August Ender told historian William Bartlett that Nena'aangabi was "past sixty" when he died. Both accounts agree that the year was 1855. See "How Na-non-gabe Was Killed in '55," *Rice Lake Chronotype*, February 18, 1925, 1, and Bartlett, *History, Tradition, and Adventure*, 64–65. In 1855, Richard Morse estimated Nena'aangabi had "seen about fifty-five winters." However, this was merely an estimate made by an individual who did not have much exposure to Indian people or how they aged. It is likely Nena'aangabi looked much younger to Morse than he actually was. See Morse, "Chippewas of Lake Superior," 341.

38. Census Roll, Lac Courte Oreilles, April 3, 1877, National Archives and Records Administration (NARA), Great Lakes Region, Chicago, Illinois, Record Group (RG) 75, Records of the Bureau of Indian Affairs, La Pointe Agency. The Census role lists Nena'aangabi's son Waabizheshi as "son of Nenaangebi Chief died 1856, son of Gekek, son of Eshpaion."
39. Moozojiid's name literally means "Moose anus," despite the fact it is usually translated more politely in literature from the nineteenth century. For example, Warren translated it as "Moose Tail." See Warren, *History of the Ojibway People*, 318. Schoolcraft noted that Moozojiid was a "red-mouthed and puckered mouth man" and "he was named by the Indians for these two traits." According to Schoolcraft, Moozojiid was a *jaasakiid*. Schoolcraft rendered Moozojiid "Mozojeed." See Schoolcraft, *Personal Memoirs*, 377.
40. Warren, *History of the Ojibway People*, 49. Again, even though Warren identifies "Ka-kaik (the Hawk) of Chippeway River," it is highly likely that he was referring to Nena'aangabi. Warren identified Bagone-giizhig as "Hole-in-the-day (son of the great war chief of that name)" and Bizhiki as "Be-she-ke (Buffalo)." Bizhiki is not to be confused with the highly influential leader from La Pointe or the St. Croix leader of the same name. Much like Waabizheshi, Bizhiki was a very common nineteenth-century Ojibwe name. There is a bust of Bizhiki of Leech Lake in Washington, D.C., which many mistakenly identify as Bizhiki of La Pointe. The bust was made in 1855, the year Bizhiki of La Pointe died. No evidence suggests he was in Washington in 1855. However, Bizhiki of Leech Lake was in Washington and signed the Treaty of Washington, where Mississippi Ojibwe leaders ceded lands to the government. In the treaty, Bizhiki is rendered "Be-sheck-kee, or Buffalo." See Treaty of Washington, February 22, 1855, 10 Stat. 1165.
41. Schoolcraft, *Schoolcraft's Expedition to Lake Itasca*, 126–27.
42. Census of the Chippewas of the Mississippi & Lake Superior within the La Pointe Sub-agency taken September, 1843, NARA, RG 75, Letters Received by

the Office of Indian Affairs, 1824–1881: La Pointe Agency, M234, Roll 388: 0428.

43. Lake Superior Chippewa Annuity, 1850. Starting in 1850, annuity records show more people from the community at Lac Courte Oreilles collecting annuities. However, this is likely due to the provision in the treaty of 1847 that allowed mixed-descent people to collect annuities. In annuity records from 1850 onward a large number of heads of household collecting annuities have French or English surnames, while virtually nobody collecting annuities at Rice Lake had an English or French surname. Many of these mixed-descent people lived south of Lac Courte Oreilles. No evidence suggests that the community at Lac Courte Oreilles actually grew in the mid-nineteenth century.
44. Schoolcraft, *Schoolcraft's Expedition to Lake Itasca*, 124. Schoolcraft spelled Nena'aangabi's name "Neenaba."
45. Ibid., 123–24.
46. For more on Bagone-giizhig's move to farming, see Anton Treuer, *The Assassination of Hole-in-the-Day* (St. Paul: Minnesota Historical Society Press, 2011), 114.
47. Schoolcraft, *Schoolcraft's Expedition to Lake Itasca*, 123.
48. In her attempt to demonstrate how decentralized Ojibwe nineteenth-century leadership was and how American officials at the time and scholars since have given weight to the notion of principal leaders, historian Theresa Schenck overstates the decentralized nature of Ojibwe political life. While Schenck is correct to assert the autonomy of communities and leaders from each other, Schenck goes too far. Schenck fails to discuss the importance of how the legacy of historical connections between Ojibwe communities influenced how communities related to each other and enabled influential leaders to have influence beyond their own community. See Schenck, *Voice of the Crane Echoes Afar*.
49. Warren, *History of the Ojibway People*, 319.
50. Schenck, *Voice of the Crane Echoes Afar*, 80–81. Leadership categories and how they often overlapped are covered in Cary Miller, *Ogimaag: Anishinaabe Leadership, 1760–1845* (Lincoln: University of Nebraska Press, 2010).
51. Kohl, *Kitchi-Gami*, 66.
52. Historian Theresa Schenck discusses the ineffectiveness of traders and government officials appointing Ojibwe chiefs in the nineteenth century, including the failed attempts of American officials to get the Ojibwe to elect their leaders. See Schenck, *Voice of the Crane Echoes Afar*, 73, 80, and 83.
53. Warren rendered Misko-manidoons "Mis-ko-mun-e-dous." Warren, *History of the Ojibway People*, 318. Misko-manidoons's name literally means "Little

Red Spirit" but was always translated as "Red Devil" due to the American habit at the time of translating Native words meaning "spirit" to "devil." In 1996 the Devil's Lake Dakota Reservation in North Dakota legally changed its name to the Spirit Lake Reservation. See "Devil's Lake Tribe Votes for New Name," *Washington Post*, July 21, 1996, A4. Likewise, on the Lac Courte Oreilles Reservation, the Ojibwe name for Devils Lake is Manidoo Zaaga'igan, or Spirit Lake.

54. Schoolcraft, *Personal Memoirs*, 384. For the lineage of Waabizheshi, see ibid., 378. Waabizheshi was a very common nineteenth-century Ojibwe name. There was another Gichi-Waabizheshi in Wisconsin who led the community at Pelican Lake in far northeast Wisconsin. This leader signed the treaty of 1826 as "Gitshee Waubeeshaans: Lac du Flambeau" and 1847 as "Ke che waub ish ash 1st Chief: Pelican Lake." See Treaty of Fond du Lac, August 5, 1826, 7 Stat. 290 and Treaty of Fond du Lac, August 2, 1847, 9 Stat. 904. In 1847 according to annuity records, his community had 261 people. There he is identified as "Ke-che Waub-ish-ash, Big Martin: Pelican Lake." The existing record for the 1847 annuity is found in "Indian Payments," *Boston Herald*, August 27, 1847, 1.
55. Schoolcraft, *Personal Memoirs*, 377.
56. Alfred Brunson to Thomas Hartley Crawford, January 8, 1843, NARA, RG 75, M234, Roll 388: 0390. Waabizheshi is identified by the English translation of his name, Martin.
57. "Indian Payments," *Boston Herald*, August 27, 1847, and Lake Superior Chippewa Annuity, 1850. On the lineage of Gwiiwizenzish, see Census Roll, Lac Courte Oreilles, April 3, 1877.
58. Thomas E. Randall, *History of the Chippewa Valley* (Eau Claire, WI: Free Press Print, 1875), 32. This book is available online through the University of Wisconsin–Madison at http://digital.library.wisc.edu/1711.dl/WI.IHHistChipValley.
59. George Nelson, *My First Years in the Fur Trade* (St. Paul: Minnesota Historical Society Press, 2002), 130. See also 64 and 70–72.
60. John Tanner, *The Falcon: A Narrative of the Captivity and Adventures of John Tanner (U.S. Interpreter at the Sault de Ste. Marie) during Thirty Years Residence among the Indians in the Interior of North America* (1830; repr., Minneapolis: Ross & Haines, 1956), 149.
61. Treuer, *Assassination of Hole-in-the-Day*.
62. Kohl, *Kitchi-Gami*, 341.
63. Treuer, *Assassination of Hole-in-the-Day*.
64. Randall, *History of the Chippewa Valley*, 33.
65. Schoolcraft, *Personal Memoirs*, 293.

66. Witgen, *Infinity of Nations.*
67. Michael Witgen, "The Rituals of Possession: Native Identity and the Invention of Empire in Seventeenth-Century Western North America," *Ethnohistory* 54, no. 4 (2007): 639.
68. Schenck, *Voice of the Crane Echoes Afar.*
69. Bruce M. White, "A Skilled Game of Exchange: Ojibway Fur Trade Protocol," *Minnesota History* 50, no. 6 (1987): 229–40.
70. Kohl, *Kitchi-Gami*, 130.
71. Priscilla K. Buffalohead, "Farmers, Warriors, Traders: A Fresh Look at Ojibway Women," *Minnesota History* 48, no. 6 (1983): 236–44.
72. Armstrong, *Early Life among the Indians*, 101.
73. Nelson, *My First Years in the Fur Trade*, 149, 151, 152.
74. In the council, Eshkibagikoonzh is identified as "Flat Mouth." Proceedings of a Council Held by Governor Henry Dodge with the Chiefs and Principal Men of the Chippewa Nation of Indians, July 20–29, 1837, NARA, RG 75, Documents Relating to the Negotiation of Ratified and Unratified Treaties with Various Tribes of Indians, 1801–1869, T494, Roll 3: 0548.
75. Tim E. Holzkamm, Leo G. Waisberg, and Joan A. Lovisek, " 'Stout Athletic Fellows': The Ojibwa during the 'Big Game Collapse' in Northwest Ontario 1821–71," in *Papers of the 26th Algonquian Conference* (Winnipeg: University of Manitoba Press, 1995), 169–82.
76. Laura Peers, *The Ojibwa of Western Canada, 1780 to 1870* (St. Paul: Minnesota Historical Society Press, 1994), xii.
77. Schoolcraft, *Schoolcraft's Expedition to Lake Itasca*, 90–91.
78. Armstrong, *Early Life among the Indians*, 135.
79. Schoolcraft, *Personal Memoirs*, 292.
80. Ibid., 297. Schoolcraft rendered Gidagaa-bizhiw "Dugah Beshue, or Spotted Lynx."
81. In-depth studies on British-Native relations during the period between the American Revolution and War of 1812 abound. However, these studies tend to focus on often violent encounters in the eastern Great Lakes. See Timothy D. Willig, *Restoring the Chain of Friendship: British Policy and the Indians of the Great Lakes, 1783–1815* (Lincoln: University of Nebraska Press, 2008) and Colin Calloway, *Crown and Calumet: British-Indian Relations, 1783–1815* (Norman: University of Oklahoma Press, 1987).
82. Much of the early American interest in Wisconsin was driven by lead mining in southwest Wisconsin, which was why Prairie du Chien was a center of American power in 1825. For more on the region, see Lucy Eldersveld Murphy, *A Gathering of Rivers: Indians, Métis, and Mining in the Western Great Lakes, 1737–1832* (Lincoln: University of Nebraska Press, 2000). Ironically,

today the region is marginal to the state's economy, as economically bleak as northern Wisconsin only without tourism.

83. Leonard H. Wheeler to David Greene, May 3, 1843, American Board of Commissioners for Foreign Missions Papers, Correspondence 1827–1878, Box 3: Correspondence 1840–April 1844, Minnesota Historical Society, St. Paul.
84. Sometimes headmen evolved into ogimaag as their group became more independent from the original community. One example is the village on Wisconsin Point in modern Superior, Wisconsin, led by Ozaagii. Identified as a Fond du Lac Band headman in the treaty of 1854, he is not identified as a "chief" in any annuity records (annuity records never recorded Ojibwe leaders as ogimaa) until 1865. Before 1865 he was listed as part of the community of Fond du Lac Band ogimaa Naagaanab. See Treaty of La Pointe, September 30, 1854, 10 Stat. 1109; Lake Superior Chippewa Annuity, 1857; and Lake Superior Chippewa Annuity, 1865, MHS M390, Roll 2. Ozaagii is rendered "O-saw-gee" in the treaty of 1854, "Osaw gee" in the 1857 annuity roll, and "Ozawgee" in the 1865 annuity roll. For more on the location of Ozaagii's village and their struggle to remain there after the creation of the Fond du Lac Reservation, see Thomas Peacock, ed., *A Forever Story: The People and Community of the Fond du Lac Reservation* (Cloquet, MN: Fond du Lac Band of Lake Superior Chippewa, 1998), 130–42 and 189–205.
85. Raymond J. DeMallie, "Touching the Pen: Plains Indian Treaty Councils in Ethnohistorical Perspective," in *Ethnicity on the Great Plains*, ed. Frederick C. Luebke (Lincoln: University of Nebraska Press, 1980), 40.
86. Documents Relating to the Negotiation of the Treaty of August 19, 1825, with the Sioux, Chippewa, Sauk and Fox, Menominee, Iowa, and Winnebago Indians and Part of the Ottawa, Chippewa, and Potawatomi of the Illinois Indians, NARA, RG 75, T494, Roll 1: 0710.
87. Ibid. Noodin is identified as "The Wind, Chippewa" in the treaty council minutes. Noodin's fear that the boundaries would "breed new wars" was eerily prophetic since he was killed in battle with the Dakota in 1854. See "The Siouxs and the Chippewas," *Minnesota Pioneer*, June 30, 1854, 2. Noodin was a somewhat prominent ogimaa in Ojibwe politics during the treaty era, signing treaties in 1826, 1837, 1842, and 1847. According to William Warren, Noodin died without a successor. See Warren, *History of the Ojibway People*, 335. In the 1840s, he began to be referred to as Gichi-Noodin, to distinguish himself from another Ojibwe leader from Mille Lacs named Noodin. The close proximity of the Snake River to Mille Lacs compounded by the fact that after 1850 American policy centered on removing the Snake River Band to Mille Lacs creates confusion in distinguishing between the two leaders.

88. Documents Relating to the Negotiation of the Treaty of August 19, 1825. In the treaty council minutes, Bayezhig is identified as "Pi-a-gick, or Single Man, Chippewa of St. Croix River." Snake River leaders were sometimes identified as being from the St. Croix Band, as the communities of the Snake River Band were in close proximity to the St. Croix communities and the Snake River empties into the St. Croix River. Bayezhig was the leader of a community on Pokegama Lake, only twenty miles from the St. Croix River. Bayezhig signed treaties in 1837, 1842, 1847, and 1854. For more on Bayezhig, see Armstrong, *Early Life among the Indians*, 117, 124, 233. Armstrong spelled Bayezhig "Bi-a-jek."
89. Treaty of Prairie du Chien, August 19, 1825, 7 Stat. 272.
90. Schoolcraft, *Personal Memoirs*, 216.
91. Treaty of Prairie du Chien, August 19, 1825, 7 Stat. 272.
92. Schoolcraft, *Personal Memoirs*, 377.
93. Treaty of Prairie du Chien, August 19, 1825, 7 Stat. 272. In the treaty, Gidagaa-bizhiw is rendered "Tu kau bi sho or Crouching Lynx," Misko-manidoons is "The Red Devil," and Babaamikawe is "The Track."
94. Schoolcraft, *Schoolcraft's Expedition to Lake Itasca*, 118.
95. Thomas L. McKenney, *Sketches of a Tour to the Lakes* (1827; repr., Minneapolis: Ross & Haines, 1959).
96. Treaty of Fond du Lac, August 5, 1826, 7 Stat. 290.
97. Schoolcraft, *Personal Memoirs*, 295. Misko-manidoons was rendered "Misco-monetoes, or Red Devil" by Schoolcraft.
98. Treaty of Fond du Lac, August 5, 1826, 7 Stat. 290.
99. McKenney, *Sketches of a Tour to the Lakes*, 312 and 330.
100. The treaty journal is published as an appendix in Ibid., 462. Original found in NARA, RG 75, T494, Roll 1: 0825.
101. Treaty of Fond du Lac, August 5, 1826, 7 Stat. 290.
102. John N. Fonda, "Early Reminiscences of Wisconsin," *Wisconsin Historical Collections* 5 (1868): 247.
103. Chad Delano Ronnander, "Many Paths to the Pine: Mdewakanton Dakotas, Fur Traders, Ojibwes, and the United States in Wisconsin's Chippewa Valley, 1815–1837," (PhD diss., University of Minnesota, 2003). When Lockwood secured approval of the agreement in 1829, Wisconsin was part of the Michigan Territory. Ronnander's dissertation is thoroughly researched; however, he misidentifies Nena'aangabi twice, once in the context of Schoolcraft's 1831 visit to Manoominikaan and the other in Nena'aangabi's arrival at the treaty of 1837. However, without Ojibwe language ability and because Nena'aangabi's name is rendered in different phonetic spellings, he fails to realize that they're the same person. Ibid., 139 and 202.

104. Schoolcraft, *Schoolcraft's Expedition to Lake Itasca*, 124–25.
105. Treaty of Washington, September 29, 1837, 7 Stat. 538, and Treaty of St. Peter's, July 29, 1837, 7 Stat. 536.
106. Samuel C. Stambaugh to Carey A. Harris, September 6, 1836, NARA, RG 75, M234, Roll 387: 0088. Nena'aangabi is rendered "Na nag ag ga bee" and Moozojiid is rendered "Moose Tail Translate moose oojeed." Seven Lac Courte Oreilles Band community members signed the agreement as well including "Ah ke wa zee," which likely refers to Moozojiid's son and eventual successor Akiwenzii.
107. Trade and Intercourse Act, July 22, 1790, 1 Stat. 137.
108. Stambaugh to Harris, September 6, 1836.
109. Schoolcraft, *Schoolcraft's Expedition to Lake Itasca*, 125.

CHAPTER 2. NENA'AANGABI AND THE LANGUAGE OF TREATIES, 1837–1855

1. Richard E. Morse, "The Chippewas of Lake Superior," in *Collections of the State Historical Society of Wisconsin*, vol. 3, ed. Lyman Copeland Draper (Madison: Wisconsin Historical Society, 1904), 344.
2. John D. Nichols, ed. *Statement Made by the Indians: A Bilingual Petition of the Chippewas of Lake Superior, 1864* (London: University of Western Ontario Press, 1988). I have chosen to include the Fiero orthography of the Ojibwe as transcribed by John Nichols. The original document was written by Joseph Gurnoe, a person of mixed Ojibwe descent (and future government farmer on the Lac Courte Oreilles Reservation), who utilized an orthography very similar to Frederic Baraga. For the original document, see "Ojibwe treaty statement and related papers, 1864, 1881–1882"; original manuscript in the Wisconsin Historical Society Archives (SC-O 40); online facsimile at http://www.wisconsinhistory.org/turningpoints/search.asp?id=40. In the petition, Naagaanab is rendered "Na ga nob," Aamoons is rendered "Ah-moonse," and Akiwenzii is rendered "Ake wan zee." Among the La Pointe Band leaders signing the document was "Kish kee tah wog." However, this was a common name for men in the nineteenth century and does not refer to Joe White. Giishkitawag of the La Pointe Band first appears on an annuity record as a "chief" in 1862 as "Kish ke taw wag, Chief" (no. 125). On the same document, Joe White appears as "Kish ke taw wag" (no. 563) in a Lac Courte Oreilles Band community led by his brother Waabizheshi, or as it is spelled in the annuity record "Waw be zha she, Chief" (no. 560). See Lake Superior

Chippewa Annuity, 1862, Chippewa Annuity Rolls, 1841–1907, US Office of Indian Affairs, Minnesota Historical Society (MHS), St. Paul, M390, Roll 2. The petition is explored in Harry Miller, "'These I do not sell': A Statement Made by the Indians," *Wisconsin Magazine of History* 84, no. 4 (2001): 26–33.

3. Excellent analysis of the treaties of 1837 and 1842 appears in Ronald N. Satz, *Chippewa Treaty Rights: The Reserve Rights of Wisconsin's Chippewa Indians in Historical Perspective*, special issue, *Transactions of the Wisconsin Academy of Sciences, Arts and Letters* 79 (1991), and Charles Cleland, "Preliminary Report of the Ethnohistorical Basis of the Hunting, Fishing, and Gathering Rights of the Mille Lacs Chippewa," in *Fish in the Lakes, Wild Rice, and Game in Abundance: Testimony on Behalf of Mille Lacs Ojibwe Hunting and Fishing Rights*, ed. James M. McClurken (East Lansing: Michigan State University Press, 2000), 1–140. While both are excellent, Cleland does a more thorough job of discussing growing tensions between what the treaties designated the "Lake Superior" and "Mississippi" bands.
4. Proceedings of a Council Held by Governor Henry Dodge with the Chiefs and Principal Men of the Chippewa Nation of Indians, July 20--29, 1837, National Archives and Records Administration (NARA), Records Group (RG) 75, Documents Relating to the Negotiation of Ratified and Unratified Treaties with Various Tribes of Indians, 1801–1869, T494, Roll 3: 0548.
5. Cleland, "Preliminary Report," 28.
6. Proceedings of a Council, July 20–29, 1837.
7. Ibid. In the journal of the council, Nena'aangabi is rendered "Ne-non-ga-be or 'The Wounded Man'" and Akiwenzii is rendered "Ke-wat-se, or The Old Man." On Akiwenzii's lineage, see Census Roll, Lac Courte Oreilles, April 3, 1877, NARA, Great Lakes Region, Chicago, Illinois, RG 75, Records of the Bureau of Indian Affairs, La Pointe Agency. According to that census, Moozojiid died in 1839. It is possible the date is incorrect or Moozojiid was in poor health in his later years, as Akiwenzii acted as leader of the community at Lac Courte Oreilles during the treaty of 1837 and after.
8. Treaty of St. Peter's, July 29, 1837, 7 Stat. 536. In the treaty, Bakwe'aamo is rendered "Pa-qua-a-mo, or the Wood Pecker Chief."
9. Proceedings of a Council, July 20–29, 1837. The journal shows no record of these leaders being in attendance. Furthermore, Gichi-Waabizheshi told government officials in 1843, "I was not at St. Peter's (in 1837)." See Alfred Brunson to Thomas Hartley Crawford, January 8, 1843, NARA, RG 75, Letters Received by the Office of Indian Affairs, 1824–1881: La Pointe Agency, M234, Roll 388: 0390.
10. Nichols, *Statement Made by the Indians*, 48.

11. Proceedings of a Council, July 20–29, 1837. Maajigaabaw was rendered "Ma-ghe-ga-bo" in the records of the council.
12. Henry R. Schoolcraft, *Personal Memoirs of a Residence of Thirty Years with the Indian Tribes on the American Frontiers* (Philadelphia: Lippincott, Grambo, 1851), 610–11.
13. Henry R. Schoolcraft, *Schoolcraft's Expedition to Lake Itasca: The Discovery of the Source of the Mississippi*, ed. Philip P. Mason (1834; repr., East Lansing: Michigan State University Press, 1993). Maajigaabaw was rendered "Maji Gabowi" by Schoolcraft, "Major Gaw-bo-way" by James Allen, and "Muchi Gabo" by William Boutwell.
14. Nichols, *Statement Made by the Indians*, 44.
15. Ibid., 45–46.
16. US Senate, Committee on Indian Affairs, *Survey of Conditions of the Indians in the United States: Hearings before a Subcommittee of the Committee on Indian Affairs* (Washington, DC: Government Printing Office, 1930), 1993. Publication of this hearing is available online through the Wisconsin Historical Society at http://www.wisconsinhistory.org/turningpoints/search.asp?id=1623.
17. Bruce M. White, "The Myth of the 'Forgotten' Treaty: Traditions about the St. Peters Treaty of 1837," in *The State We're In: Reflections on Minnesota History*, ed. Annette Atkins and Deborah L. Miller (St. Paul: Minnesota Historical Society Press, 2010), 39–49.
18. Benjamin G. Armstrong, *Early Life among the Indians* (Ashland, WI: A. W. Bowron, 1892), 11.
19. Schoolcraft, *Personal Memoirs*, 583.
20. John D. Nichols, "The Translation of Key Phrases in the Treaties of 1837 and 1855," in McClurken, *Fish in the Lakes, Wild Rice, and Game in Abundance*, 520.
21. White, "Myth of the 'Forgotten' Treaty," 40.
22. Nichols, "Translation of Key Phrases in the Treaties of 1837 and 1855," 519.
23. Lac Courte Oreilles v. Voight, 700 F.2d 341 (1983), and Minnesota v. Mille Lacs, 526 U.S. 172 (1999).
24. Treaty of St. Peter's, July 29, 1837, 7 Stat. 536.
25. Proceedings of a Council, July 20–29, 1837.
26. Frederick Ayer to Martin Van Buren, September 30, 1837, NARA, RG 75, M234, Roll 387: 0101. Ayer rendered Noodin "Nodin (The Wind)," Bizhiki "Besheke (The Buffalo)," and Bwaanens "Bwahnase (Little Sioux)." Bwaanens appears to have been an individual of influence. On his map of the region, Henry Schoolcraft claimed Bwaanens was a chief at Yellow Lake; however, no other surviving record identifies him as a chief. See Schoolcraft, *Personal Memoirs*, 362, 370. Schoolcraft rendered Bwaanens "Bwoinace."

27. Robert Stuart to Thomas Hartley Crawford, September 29, 1842, NARA, RG 75, M234, Roll 389: 0067.
28. Treaty of La Pointe, October 4, 1842, 7 Stat. 591. On the treaty Nena'aangabi is spelled "Ne na nang eb," Akiwenzii is spelled "Ki uen zi," Gichi-Waabizheshi is spelled "Ua be she shi," Gwiiwizenzish is spelled "Que way zhan sis," and Bebookawe is spelled "Be bo kon uen." Neither Bakwe'aamo nor anyone from his community signed the treaty. Nor did anyone from the Lake Chetac community, by this time most likely led by Omadaagami, the son and successor of Gidagaa-bizhiw.
29. Stuart to Crawford, September 29, 1842.
30. Ibid.
31. The best example of how the "Lake Superior" and "Mississippi" designations were a creation of the US government is the Mille Lacs Band, whose lands were ceded in the treaty of 1837 with other "Lake Superior" bands and who maintained significant historical, kinship, and clan ties to the St. Croix Band but were later considered to be part of "Mississippi Chippewa" by the US government.
32. Treaty of La Pointe, October 4, 1842, 7 Stat. 591.
33. Nichols, *Statement Made by the Indians*, 54–55.
34. Ibid.
35. Ibid., 52–54.
36. US Senate, Committee on Indian Affairs, *Survey of Conditions of the Indians in the United States*, 1993.
37. William Bigboy, "The Lost Tribe Comes into Its Own," Works Progress Administration (WPA), Chippewa Indian Historical Project, Archives of the Fransciscan Sisters of Perpetual Adoration, La Crosse, Wisconsin, Envelope 2, 36.
38. Armstrong, *Early Life among the Indians*, 12.
39. Treaty of La Pointe, October 4, 1842, 7 Stat. 591.
40. Ibid.
41. Brunson to Crawford, January 8, 1843.
42. Nichols, *Statement Made by the Indians*, 55–56.
43. Brunson to Crawford, January 8, 1843.
44. In particular, Grand Portage families used the island in the nineteenth century for maple sugaring and other labor activities. Robert Stuart framed the matter as an international dispute between the United States and Great Britain, claiming the Grand Portage group had acknowledged themselves as "British Indians" and were trading with the Canadian Hudson's Bay Company. Furthermore, Stuart pointed out that the British had relinquished claim to the island. See Robert Stuart to Thomas Hartley Crawford, March 29, 1844,

NARA, RG 75, M234, Roll 389: 0054. For more on the Grand Portage Band's use of Isle Royale, see Timothy Cochrane, *Minong—The Good Place: Oijbwe and Isle Royale* (East Lansing: Michigan State University Press, 2009).

45. Compact Between the U.S. & the Chippewa Indians of Mississippi & Lake Superior in regard to Isle Royale, August 20, 1844, NARA, RG 75, M234, Roll 389: 0082. Nena'aangabi's name is spelled "Nay nuh aung abe." Nichols, *Statement Made by the Indians*, 58, 62. On this last point, the Ojibwe text, "Niwanitaas isa ganabaj," translates to just "perhaps I lose," with no mention of the "poor bargain" of the English text. Additionally, it is not "I am the loser," since "Niwanitaas" is a present tense verb, not a noun. A noun meaning "loser" would be read something like "wenitaas."
46. Petition of the Chiefs of the Chippewas for the restoration of the farm and shop to Chippewa Falls, NARA, RG 75, M234, Roll 388: 0419. In this petition, Nena'aangabi is rendered "Wounded Man or Ang-a-be."
47. Armstrong, *Early Life among the Indians*, 44.
48. Raymond J. DeMallie, "Touching the Pen: Plains Indian Treaty Councils in Ethnohistorical Perspective," in *Ethnicity on the Great Plains*, ed. Frederick C. Luebke (Lincoln: University of Nebraska Press, 1980), 50.
49. Russel Lawrence Barsh, "The Nature and Spirit of North American Political Systems," *American Indian Quarterly* 10, no. 3 (1986): 195.
50. Richard White, "The Fictions of Patriarchy: Indians and Whites in the Early Republic," in *Native Americans in the Early Republic*, ed. Frederick E. Hoxie, Ronald Hoffman, and Peter J. Albert (Charlottesville: University Press of Virginia, 1999), 83.
51. Nichols, *Statement Made by the Indians*, 52–54.
52. J. J. Ducatel, "A Fortnight among the Chippewas of Lake Superior," in *The Indian Miscellany*, ed. W. W. Beach (Albany, NY: J. Munsell, 1877), 365. Ducatel spelled Zhingob "Singoup." Zhingob was a prominent Ojibwe leader and signed the 1837 treaty ("Shing-go-be or the Spruce"), the 1842 treaty ("Shin goob"), the 1847 treaty ("Shin goob"), and the 1854 treaty ("Shing goope or the Balsam"). See Treaty of St. Peter's, July 29, 1837, 7 Stat. 536; Treaty of La Pointe, October 4, 1842, 7 Stat. 591; Treaty of Fond du Lac, August 2, 1847, 9 Stat. 904; and Treaty of La Pointe, September 30, 1854, 10 Stat. 1109.
53. David E. Wilkins and K. Tsianina Lomawaima, *Uneven Ground: American Indian Sovereignty and Federal Law* (Norman: University of Oklahoma Press, 2001), 65.
54. Seminole Nation v. United States, 316 U.S. 286 (1942).
55. United States v. Jicarilla Apache Nation, 131 U.S. 2313 (2011).
56. Morse, "Chippewas of Lake Superior," 342.

57. Cleland, "Preliminary Report," 52.
58. Treaty of Fond du Lac, August 2, 1847, 9 Stat. 904.
59. Brunson to Crawford, January 8, 1843.
60. Julia Warren Spears, "My Journey with the Chippewa Indians," Julia A. Spears and Family Papers, Minnesota Historical Society, St. Paul. Spears's claim is backed by the 1850 annuity roll. Of the 207 individuals collecting annuities from the community at Lac Courte Oreilles, 47 had non-Ojibwe names. A similar number of non-Ojibwe names appeared on the annuity collection for the communities led by Ozhaawashko-giizhig and Ginoozhens on the Chippewa River, while only a handful of non-Ojibwe names appears in communities led by Omadaagami at Lake Chetac, Gichi-binesi at Pacwawong Lake, Gichi-Waabizheshi on the Chippewa River, and Nena'aangabi at Rice Lake. See Lake Superior Chippewa Annuity, 1850, MHS M390, Roll 1.
61. Treaty of Fond du Lac, August 2, 1847, 9 Stat. 904. "Indian Payments," *Boston Herald*, August 27, 1847. Akiwenzii is rendered "Kee wan see" in the treaty and "Ah-ke-wan-ze" in the annuity. Gichi-Waabizheshi is rendered "Waub ish ashe" in the treaty and "Waub-ish-esh, Martin" in the annuity. Gichi-binesi is rendered "Pin as see" in the treaty. In the annuity, Gwiiwizenzish is rendered "Que-wee-sans-ish, Bad Boy," Ginoozhens is rendered "Kiu-anoch-ans, Little Pike," and Omadaagami is rendered "Mud-au Gum-me." Of the St. Croix Band leaders, Gabemabi appears in the treaty as "Gab im ub be" and in the annuity as "Gab-am-ub-be, one who changes his seat." Ayaabens appears as "I au bans" in the treaty and "I-au-be-ans, Little Buck" in the annuity. Bizhiki appears as "Ke-che Be-she-ke, Big Buffalo" in the annuity.
62. Letter of Remonstrance of Nine Chippeway Chiefs to Treaty August 21, 1847, NARA, RG 75, M234, Roll 389: 0391.

    Nena'aangabi's name is spelled "Nenangabe," Negwanebi is rendered "Nagonabi," Manoominikeshiinh is rendered "Manominikashe," Zhooniyaa is rendered "Shoniah," and Gegwedaash is rendered "Kakoatash,"
63. William Warren to William Medill, September 1, 1847, NARA, RG 75, M234, Roll 388, and Isaac Verplank to William Medill, November 1, 1847, NARA, RG 75, M234, Roll 389.
64. William Warren to George P. Warren, January 15, 1851, C. F. X. Goldsmith Papers, 1821–1923, State Historical Society of Wisconsin Area Research Center, University of Wisconsin–Eau Claire. Warren spelled Nena'aangabi "Na nuh anung abe" and Gegwedaash "Ka gua dash."
65. Nodin & 5 Other Chippeway Chiefs to the President, NARA, RG 75, M234, Roll 389: 0396. Noodin is spelled "Nodin," Gichi-Noodin is spelled "Gichinodin," Nena'aangabi is spelled "Nenangabe," Negwanebi is spelled "Nagonabi," and Zhooniyaa is spelled "Shoniah." The petition of Noodin

appears to be in same handwriting as the remonstrance, although no writer is credited.

66. Verplank to Medill, November 1, 1847.
67. Enabling Act of Wisconsin, 9 Stat. 56.
68. For the immediate aftermath of the treaties, see Satz, *Chippewa Treaty Rights*, and Cleland, "Preliminary Report."
69. James Taylor Dunn, *The St. Croix: Midwest Border River* (New York: Holt, Rinehart, and Winston, 1965).
70. Armstrong, *Early Life among the Indians*, 115.
71. Thomas E. Randall, *History of the Chippewa Valley* (Eau Claire, WI: Free Press Print, 1875), 34–35, and George Forrester, *Historical and Biographical Album of the Chippewa Valley* (Chicago: A. Warner Publisher, 1892), 78–81.
72. US House of Representatives, Petition of the Head Chiefs of the Chippewa Tribe of Indians on Lake Superior, House Mis. doc. 36 (1849), 30th Congress, 2d session, 1–2.
73. Joint Resolution of the Minnesota Territorial Assembly, November 7, 1849, NARA, RG 75, M234, Roll 428: 0124.
74. Cleland, "Preliminary Report."
75. Ibid.
76. Nichols, *Statement Made by the Indians*, 67–68.
77. Ibid.
78. John Watrous to Alexander Ramsey, December 10, 1850, NARA, RG 75, M234, Roll 767: 0052.
79. *Minnesota Chronicle and Register*, December 17, 1850.
80. *Minnesota Chronicle and Register*, December 23, 1850.
81. *Minnesota Democrat*, July 21, 1851.
82. Selah Treat to Luke Lea, February 15, 1851, NARA, RG 75, M234, Roll 767: 0255.
83. Chief Buffalo to Luke Lea, November 6, 1851, NARA, RG 75, M234, Roll 149, and Chippewa Chiefs to Millard Fillmore, November 1852, NARA, RG 75, M234, Roll 149.
84. James A. Clifton, "Wisconsin Death March: Explaining the Extremes in Old Northwest Indian Removal," *Transactions of the Wisconsin Academy of Sciences, Arts and Letters* 75 (1987): 1–40. The events at Sandy Lake are also covered in Satz, *Chippewa Treaty Rights*. However, the most detailed study of the events at Sandy Lake are in Bruce M. White, "The Regional Context of the Removal Order of 1850," in McClurken, *Fish in the Lakes, Wild Rice, and Game in Abundance*, 141–328.
85. "Indian Payments," *Boston Herald*, August 27, 1847, and Lake Superior Chippewa Annuity, 1857, MHS, M390, Roll 1. All numbers are comparisons

based on the 1847 and 1857 annuities. I chose to use the annuity of 1847 because it includes all Lake Superior Ojibwe communities, including those at Pelican Lake, Lac Vieux Desert, Ontonagon, and L'Anse, all of whom did not attend the annuity payment of 1850 at Sandy Lake.

86. Warren to Warren, January 15, 1851.
87. Theresa M. Schenck, *William W. Warren: The Life, Letters, and Times of an Ojibwe Leader* (Lincoln: University of Nebraska Press, 2007), 125–26. Schenck concludes that Warren supported removal, seeing it as inevitable.
88. William W. Warren to Alexander Ramsey, August 4, 1851, NARA, RG 75, Office of Indian Affairs, Field Office Records, M842, Roll 3. St. Croix communities were pressured to remove to Mille Lacs instead, something they resisted, but not as strongly as other Ojibwe resisted removal to Sandy Lake.
89. Armstrong, *Early Life among the Indians*, 17.
90. Ibid., 18.
91. Ibid., 30.
92. David Aitken to Luke Lea, November 19, 1851, NARA, RG 75, M234, Roll 149.
93. James Scott, "An Old Indian Settler," WPA, Chippewa Indian Historical Project, Envelope 19, 1.
94. Ibid.
95. Henry C. Gilbert to George W. Manypenny, October 17, 1854, NARA, RG 75, T494, Roll 5: 0134.
96. Armstrong, *Early Life among the Indians*, 35.
97. Treaty of La Pointe, September 30, 1854, 10 Stat. 1109. Questions about what communities were included in the Lake Superior bands and Mississippi bands persisted. The Bois Forte Band, who were part of the Lake Superior bands, had not yet been party to any annuities prior to 1854 and were excepted from this separation of interests. Furthermore, as historian Charles Cleland argues, the treaty failed to acknowledge the associations the Mille Lacs, Snake River, and St. Croix Bands had to both the Lake Superior and Mississippi Ojibwe. See Cleland, "Preliminary Report," 84.
98. Armstrong, *Early Life among the Indians*, 42.
99. According to Benjamin Armstrong, it was on his suggestion that this provision was included. See Ibid., 41.
100. Ibid., 77.
101. US House of Representatives, Chippewa Half-Breeds of Lake Superior, House Ex. Doc. 193, 42nd Congress, 2d session.
102. Gilbert to Manypenny, October 17, 1854.
103. Treaty of La Pointe, September 30, 1854, 10 Stat. 1109.
104. Ibid. In the treaty, Nena'aangabi's name is rendered "Nay-naw-ong-gay-be,"

Akiwenzii is rendered "Aw-ke-wain-ze, or the Old Man," Omadaagami is rendered "Maw daw gaw me," Gichi-binesi is rendered "Key-che-pe-nay-se or the Big Bird," Ginoozhens is rendered "Key no zhance or the Little Jack Fish," Gichi-Waabizheshi is rendered "Ke-che-waw-be-shay-she or the Big Marten," and Ozhaawashko-giizhig is rendered "Ozhaw waw sco ge zhick or the Blue Sky."

105. David R. Wrone, "The Economic Impact of the 1837 and 1842 Chippewa Treaties," *American Indian Quarterly* 17, no. 3 (1993): 332.
106. Morse, "Chippewas of Lake Superior," 341.
107. Ibid., 348.
108. Ibid., 361. I have left "Ja-ba-ge-zhick" in the original phonetic spelling as it appears in the text since its meaning is unclear.
109. William W. Bartlett, *History, Tradition, and Adventure in the Chippewa Valley* (Chippewa Falls: Chippewa Printery, 1929), 65.
110. Joseph B. Casagrande Papers, University of Illinois-Urbana Archives.
111. "Court D'Oreilles Reserve," *Barron County Chronotype*, September 25, 1875, 2.
112. "How Na-non-gabe Was Killed in '55," *Rice Lake Chronotype*, February 18, 1925, 1. The account of Nena'aagabi's death by former *Rice Lake Chronotype* editor August Ender in Bartlett's *History, Tradition, and Adventure in the Chippewa Valley*, published in 1929, differs somewhat. Ender said that one hundred Dakota from the vicinity of modern-day Wabasha, Minnesota, overtook Nena'aangabi's party of fifty Ojibwe at the Hay River near modern-day Prairie Farm. See Bartlett, *History, Tradition, and Adventure*, 64–65. Another minor variation in the details of Nena'aangabi's death is that the Lac Courte Oreilles Census of 1877 lists Nena'aangabi's death as occurring in 1856. See Census Roll, Lac Courte Oreilles, April 3, 1877.
113. This account comes from Waabikwe's grandson, Charles "Monte" Diamond, and appeared in Rick St. Germaine, "Odawassagaegun," *Lac Courte Oreilles Journal*, February 1986, 7. Waabikwe's involvement is also found in Benjamin Armstrong's account of Nena'aangabi's death. Armstrong does not identify Waabikwe by name, only as the daughter of Nena'aangabi and the wife of Edward Dingley, a veteran of the Civil War. Edward Dingley is found on the 1887 Lac Courte Oreilles census with a daughter, Eliza. In a letter to Hayward Indian School Agent William Light, Nena'aangabi's youngest daughter Maggie Conger identified all of her siblings and their children. Among Waabikwe's children were Billie Dingley and Eliza Diamond. See Census of the Lac Courte Oreilles Band of Chippewa Indians, 1887, NARA, RG 75, Indian Census Rolls, 1885–1940, La Pointe Agency Census Rolls, 1890–1892, M595, Roll 235, no. 8, and Maggie Conger to William Light, March 11, 1913, NARA, Great Lakes Region, RG 75, Records of the Bureau

of Indian Affairs, La Pointe Agency, Letters Received from the Lac Courte Oreilles Reservation, 1881–1914, Box 4. Conger rendered Waabikwe "Wa bi gwa." Armstrong's account differs slightly. Armstrong claimed Waabikwe killed three Dakota. Also, Armstrong claimed Nena'aangabi's death occurred on his return from the treaty of 1854 at Pacwawong Lake on the Namekagon River, when Nena'aangabi's group was ambushed by Dakotas. However, this is unlikely as all other accounts talk of Nena'aangabi's death as occurring near modern-day Prairie Farm, over one hundred miles to the south and west. Furthermore, the 1854 date is refuted by Richard Morse's account of Nena'aangabi's speech at the 1855 annuity payment, as well as other accounts. Armstrong renders Nena'aangabi "Na-nong-ga-bee." See Armstrong, *Early Life among the Indians*, 199–202. Armstrong's claim that Nena'aangabi died in 1854 at Pacwawong Lake is repeated in Charles E. Brown and Robert H. Becker, "The Chetek and Rice Lakes," *Wisconsin Archeologist* 16, no. 3 (1917): 84. Brown and Becker cite only Armstrong in their discussion of Nena'aangabi's death. There are other inaccuracies in Brown and Becker who, despite their archeological expertise, were not versant in Ojibwe history nor skilled at consulting with archival sources. They claim on page 85 that the Rice Lake Band was in Washington in 1864, but this is the Rice Lake Band of the Mississippi Ojibwe in Minnesota. Later on the same page, they claim that the Lake Chetek they did archeological work at in Barron County was the site of an Ojibwe community led by "Kedug-e-be-shew" (Gidagaa-bizhiw). But this community was located on the Lake Chetac in Sawyer County, and no major Ojibwe community existed on Lake Chetek in Barron County. Lake Chetek (with many variant spellings) is a common name in northern Wisconsin, Michigan, and Minnesota and is an English corruption of an Ojibwe word, *zhede*, meaning "pelican." On page 111, they state that a site on Lower Rice Lake was a community led by "the well known Chippewa chief Chenini" until 1833, when all Native people in the area were removed to the Lac Courte Oreilles Reservation. However, the Lac Courte Oreilles Reservation did not exist until 1873. In addition, "Chenini" (Chi-inini) was not an ogimaa. It is possible that he was a headman of a smaller family group. Brown and Becker's information came from white settlers, who at the time had very limited understandings of Ojibwe political institutions. To many early settlers, every Indian they met was a "chief."

114. Conger to Light, March 11, 1913. Maggie Conger was the married name of Maggie White. The information on the children of Nena'aangabi is also found in Census Roll, Lac Courte Oreilles, April 3, 1877. Aazhaweyaa was known by the shortened version of her full name, Aazhaweyaagiizhigokwe, and was also known by another name, Omoodayens.

115. Minnesota v. Mille Lacs, 526 U.S. 172 (1999), 196.
116. For an analysis of O'Connor's use of the canons in Mille Lacs, see Wilkins and Lomawaima, *Uneven Ground*, 137–39.

CHAPTER 3. WAABIZHESHI'S VISION OF AN INTERCULTURAL COMMUNITY AT RICE LAKE, 1855–1877

1. Richard E. Morse, "The Chippewas of Lake Superior," in *Collections of the State Historical Society of Wisconsin*, vol. 3, ed. Lyman Copeland Draper (Madison: Wisconsin Historical Society, 1904), 341.
2. Throughout I refer to settlers and their descendants as "whites." I employ this term intentionally, as opposed to "Euro-Americans," which is both awkward and somewhat of a misnomer. The views of settlers in northwest Wisconsin in the late nineteenth century of the Ojibwe were shaped not so much by their European heritage but more by an American racial experience that was based on centuries of interactions with Native peoples, African Americans, and others in the Americas. In addition, the term "white" has currency today among both Ojibwe and non-Ojibwe, while "Euro-American" is not a term people utilize, historically or today.
3. Joanne Rappaport, *Intercultural Utopias: Public Intellectuals, Cultural Experimentation, and Ethnic Pluralism in Colombia* (Durham, NC: Duke University Press, 2005), 131.
4. William W. Bartlett, *History, Tradition, and Adventure in the Chippewa Valley* (Chippewa Falls: Chippewa Printery, 1929), 65.
5. Lake Superior Chippewa Annuity, 1857, Chippewa Annuity Rolls, 1841–1907, US Office of Indian Affairs, Minnesota Historical Society (MHS), St. Paul, M390, Roll 1, and Lac Courte Oreilles Annuity, November 14, 1874, MHS, M390, Roll 2.
6. Anton Treuer, *The Assassination of Hole-in-the-Day* (St. Paul: Minnesota Historical Society Press, 2011).
7. John D. Nichols, *Statement Made by the Indians: A Bilingual Petition of the Chippewas of Lake Superior, 1864* (London: University of Western Ontario Press, 1988).
8. "The Indians as Volunteers," *Dunn County Lumberman*, August 27, 1864, 3.
9. William W. Warren, *History of the Ojibway People* (1885; repr., St. Paul: Minnesota Historical Society Press, 1984), 309. Archeological evidence shows a number of pits for threshing rice on the east side of Prairie Rice Lake, known as Prairie Lake after a dam obliterated the rice on the lake. See Charles E. Brown

and Robert H. Becker, "The Chetek and Rice Lakes," *Wisconsin Archeologist* 16, no. 3 (1917): 102.

10. Lake Superior Chippewa Annuity, 1857.
11. A. M. Fitch to Charles E. Mix, May 22, 1858, National Archives and Records Administration (NARA), Record Group (RG) 75, Letters Received by the Office of Indian Affairs, 1824–1881: La Pointe Agency, M234, Roll 391, F:0480.
12. Jacob Thompson to Charles E. Mix, March 22, 1859, NARA, RG 75, M234, Roll 391, F:0713. Michigan Indian Agent A. M. Fitch located areas around Lac Courte Oreilles where he felt the reservation should be located. See A. M. Fitch to Charles E. Mix, March 25, 1859, NARA, RG 75, M234, Roll 391, F:0708.
13. Matthias Martin to Charles E. Mix, June 26, 1859, NARA, RG 75, M234, Roll 391, F:0729.
14. Henry R. Schoolcraft, *Schoolcraft's Expedition to Lake Itasca: The Discovery of the Source of the Mississippi*, ed. Philip P. Mason (1834; repr., East Lansing: Michigan State University Press, 1993), 124.
15. W. S. Cullen to Albert B. Greenwood, July 6, 1859, NARA, RG 75, M234, Roll 391, F:05d55. Waabizheshi is rendered "Waw-be-shay-she or the 'Martin.'" The last annuity Waabizheshi of the Chippewa River village appears in is 1861, where he is listed as "Waw be zha she." See Lake Superior Chippewa Annuity, 1861, MHS, M390, Roll 3, no. 952.
16. Clark W. Thompson to William P. Dole, November 14, 1863, NARA, RG 75, M234, Roll 393, F:0111.
17. "Court D'Oreilles Reserve," *Barron County Chronotype*, September 25, 1875, 2.
18. Commissioner of Indian Affairs, *Annual Report of the Commissioner of Indian Affairs for the Year 1863* (Washington, DC: Government Printing Office, 1864), 300.
19. Luther E. Webb to William P. Dole, January 18, 1865, NARA, RG 75, M234, Roll 393, F:0556.
20. General Land Office to Dennis N. Cooley, July 21, 1866, NARA, RG 75, M234, Roll 393, F:0674.
21. Commissioner of Indian Affairs, *Annual Report of the Commissioner of Indian Affairs for the Year 1868* (Washington, DC: Government Printing Office, 1868), 379.
22. Treaty of La Pointe, September 30, 1854, 10 Stat. 1109.
23. Henry C. Gilbert to George W. Manypenny, October 17, 1854, NARA, RG75, Documents Relating to the Negotiation of Ratified and Unratified Treaties with Various Tribes of Indians, 1801–1869, T494, Roll 5: 0134.
24. Commissioner of Indian Affairs, *Annual Report 1863*, 301.

25. Francis McElroy to William P. Dole, October 18, 1864, NARA, RG 75, M234, Roll 393, F:0466.
26. Commissioner of Indian Affairs, *Annual Report of the Commissioner of Indian Affairs for the Year 1864* (Washington, DC: Government Printing Office, 1865), 41.
27. Akewenzie to William P. Dole, January 25, 1865, NARA, RG 75, M234, Roll 393, F:0456.
28. Ibid. In 1865, Chippewa County consisted of its current location plus much of the areas with then virtually no white settlement that would eventually become Sawyer, Washburn, Rusk, and other counties in present-day Wisconsin.
29. Ibid.
30. Luther E. Webb to Dennis Cooley, April 24, 1866, NARA, RG 75, M234, Roll 393, F:0743. In areas with little effective American control, paper currency was often useless while the value of gold coin was strong in all areas. This was a reoccurring theme throughout the era of annuity payments, which stretched from the Treaty of Fond du Lac in 1826 to the last annuity payment to the Lake Superior Ojibwe in 1875.
31. Nichols, *Statement Made by the Indians*. In his introduction to the document, Nichols does not mention the Bad River removal threat as being the motivation for the trip, but Akiwenzii's letter makes this clear.
32. Commissioner of Indian Affairs, *Annual Report of the Commissioner of Indian Affairs for the Year 1866* (Washington, DC: Government Printing Office, 1866), 59.
33. Commissioner of Indian Affairs, *Annual Report of the Commissioner of Indian Affairs for the Year 1869* (Washington, DC: Government Printing Office, 1870), 426.
34. Commissioner of Indian Affairs, *Annual Report of the Commissioner of Indian Affairs for the Year 1870* (Washington, DC: Government Printing Office, 1870), 309–10.
35. Selden N. Clark to Francis A. Walker, February 1, 1872, NARA, RG 75, M234, Roll 394, F:1009.
36. 17 Stat. 190.
37. Columbus Delano to Francis A. Walker, June 12, 1872, NARA, RG 75, M234, Roll 394, F:1028.
38. Commissioner of Indian Affairs, *Annual Report of the Commissioner of Indian Affairs for the Year 1872* (Washington, DC: Government Printing Office, 1872), 87. Leaders at Fond du Lac claimed their consent was given fraudulently, that federal officials lured some Fond du Lac men to Bad River for jobs logging and not telling them that they were also consenting to removal by doing so. Opposition of Fond du Lac leaders to removal to Bad River

led La Pointe Agent Isaac Mahan to postpone removal in 1874. While the agent remained committed to removal of Fond du Lac and Lac du Flambeau Ojibwe to Bad River, continued opposition of Ojibwe leaders led to nonen forcement of the policy. See Commissioner of Indian Affairs, *Annual Report of the Commissioner of Indian Affairs for the Year 1874* (Washington, DC: Government Printing Office, 1874), 189.

39. Text of the orders is found in Commissioner of Indian Affairs, *Annual Report of the Commissioner of Indian Affairs for the Year 1882* (Washington, DC: Government Printing Office, 1882), 300.
40. Treaty with the Chippewa, February 22, 1855, 10 Stat. 1165.
41. See Frances Densmore, *Chippewa Customs* (1929; repr., St. Paul: Minnesota Historical Society Press), 119–23.
42. Commissioner of Indian Affairs, *Annual Report 1874*, 194.
43. Ibid., 195.
44. Robert F. Fries, *Empire in Pine: The Story of Lumbering in Wisconsin, 1830–1900* (Madison: State Historical Society of Wisconsin, 1951).
45. William Cronen, *Nature's Metropolis: Chicago and the Great West* (New York: W. W. Norton, 1992), 151 and 154.
46. Fries, *Empire in Pine.*
47. Alvah T. Axtell, *The First Fifty Years: Rice Lake, Wisconsin, 1875–1925* (Rice Lake, WI: Chronotype Publications, 1980).
48. Ibid.
49. Robert C. Willging, *On the Hunt: The History of Deer Hunting in Wisconsin* (Madison: Wisconsin Historical Society Press, 2008), 46.
50. Henry R. Schoolcraft, *Personal Memoirs of a Residence of Thirty Years with the Indian Tribes on the American Frontiers* (Philadelphia: Lippincott, Grambo, 1851), 370.
51. Ibid., 375.
52. Schoolcraft, *Schoolcraft's Expedition to Lake Itasca*, 115.
53. Marie D. Livingston, "Blueberrying Forty-Five Years Ago," Works Progress Administration (WPA), Chippewa Indian Historical Project, Archives of the Fransciscan Sisters of Perpetual Adoration, La Crosse, Wisconsin, Envelope 8, 31.
54. Florenia Denomie, "Picking Blueberries in Northern Wisconsin," WPA, Chippewa Indian Historical Project, Envelope 8, 30.
55. Fries, *Empire in Pine.*
56. Nichols, *Statement Made by the Indians*, 44 (Fiero Ojibwe) and 15 (English).
57. "Memoirs of Ward Winton," in *Historical Collections of Washburn County and the Surrounding Indianhead Country*, vol. 1, ed. E. Ward Winton and Kay Brown Winton (Shell Lake, WI: White Birch Printing, 1980), 55.

58. "Indians Again," *Dunn County Lumberman*, August 13, 1864, 3.
59. Newton S. Gordon, *History of Barron County, Wisconsin* (Minneapolis: H. C. Cooper Jr., 1922), 27.
60. "Indians and Logging Camps on Site of Rice Lake in 1877," *Rice Lake Chronotype*, January 18, 1928.
61. The treaty or any mention of it is not included in the Knapp-Stout Company Papers that are held at the University of Wisconsin–Stout in Menomonie.
62. James Bracklin, "A Tragedy of the Wisconsin Pinery," *Wisconsin Magazine of History* 3, no. 1 (1919): 44.
63. Ibid., and Lac Courte Oreilles Chippewa Annuity, November 14, 1874.
64. Bracklin, "Tragedy of the Wisconsin Pinery," 51.
65. Ibid., 50–51. An account of these events also appears in "An Indian Commits Suicide," *Dunn County Lumberman*, September 17, 1864, 3. The newspaper's account of the events is exactly the same with the exception that the newspaper claimed that the murderer tried to fire at Barker and then turned the gun on himself. Bracklin made no mention of this, and it stands to reason that, if the gun failed to discharge on Barker, why would the murderer expect the gun to work when turned on himself? The other murderer took his own life as well, however, without any struggle, near where the crime was committed. See "Another Indian Suicide," *Dunn County Lumberman*, October 1, 1864, 3.
66. Bracklin, "Tragedy of the Wisconsin Pinery," 51.
67. Schoolcraft, *Schoolcraft's Expedition to Lake Itasca*, 123.
68. Commissioner of Indian Affairs, *Annual Report 1870*, 309.
69. Mark Seeley, *Minnesota Weather Almanac* (St. Paul: Minnesota Historical Society Press, 2006). Many thanks to Professor Seeley for sitting down with me and helping me assess the impact of climate variation on Ojibwe labor practices.
70. Isaac Mahan to Ezra A. Hayt, January 11, 1878, NARA, RG 75, M234, Roll 398, F:0177.
71. These are observations based on the author's experience in maple sugar production. This is exactly what happened during the spring of 2012. For more on the role of seasonal climate variables on Ojibwe maple sugar production, see Frances Densmore, *Strength of the Earth: The Classic Guide to Ojibwe Uses of Native Plants* (1928; repr., St. Paul: Minnesota Historical Society Press, 2005), 308–13.
72. These are observations based on the author's experience in wild rice production. For more on the role of seasonal climate variables on Ojibwe wild rice production, see Thomas Vennum Jr., *Wild Rice and the Ojibway People* (St. Paul: Minnesota Historical Society Press, 1988).
73. *Barron County Chronotype*, July 19, 1877, 3.

74. Laura Ingalls Wilder, *The Long Winter* (New York: Harper & Brothers, 1940).
75. Seeley, *Minnesota Weather Almanac.*
76. *Barron County Chronotype*, August 30, 1877, 3.
77. Brown and Becker, "The Chetek and Rice Lakes," 97.
78. "Old Louseberg: A Famed Landmark," *Rice Lake Chronotype*, March 28, 1927.
79. Robert E. Ritzenthaler Papers, Milwaukee Public Museum, Spiral Notebook 6, 8.
80. Dan Morrison, "The Indian as a Skilled Laborer," WPA, Chippewa Indian Historical Project, Envelope 8, 9.
81. Ethel Elliot Chappelle, *Around the Four Corners: A Pioneer History of the Washburn, Sawyer, Barron, and Rusk Counties* (Rice Lake, WI: Chronotype Publishing, 1971), 19.
82. Fries, *Empire in Pine*, 27.
83. Bartlett, *History, Tradition, and Adventure.*
84. There were other ways Ojibwe people got English names, including adopting English names at boarding schools, by church officials, and intermarriage with whites. One interesting discussion of this is in the Bad River WPA history project: Jerome Arbuckle, "How Surnames Were Acquired by the Chippewa," WPA, Chippewa Indian Historical Project, Envelope 2, 8.
85. Isaac Mahan to Ezra A. Hayt, April 23, 1878, NARA, RG 75, M234, Roll 398, F:0258.
86. Patty Loew, *Indian Nations of Wisconsin: Histories of Endurance and Renewal* (Madison: Wisconsin Historical Society Press, 2001), 15–16.
87. Brenda Child, *Holding Our World Together: Ojibwe Women and the Survival of Community* (New York: Viking, 2012).
88. Chappelle, *Around the Four Corners*, 23. Description of labor conditions in Wisconsin's timber industry also appears in Fries, *Empire in Pine.*
89. Victor Barnouw, "Reminiscences of a Chippewa Mide Priest," *Wisconsin Archaeologist* 35, no. 4 (1954): 107. "Tom Badger" was a pseudonym created by anthropologist Victor Barnouw.
90. Ibid., 107.
91. Ibid., 107–8.
92. Ibid., 110.
93. Fries, *Empire in Pine.*
94. William Cronen, *Changes in the Land: Indians, Colonists, and the Ecology of New England* (New York: Hill and Wang, 1983), 170.
95. Fries, *Empire in Pine.*
96. James Willard Hurst, *Law and Economic Growth: The Legal History of the Lumber Industry in Wisconsin, 1836–1915* (Cambridge: The Belknap Press of Harvard University Press, 1964).

97. Fries, *Empire in Pine*, 162.
98. Child, *Holding Our World Together*, 55. Ojibwe people themselves did not employ the term "begging dance" for this performance as the term fundamentally mischaracterizes the reciprocal nature of the performance. Anthropologist Thomas Vennum discussed with Lac Courte Oreilles Ojibwe William Bineshi Baker the "begging dance": "Baker discounted the existence of this genre per se, saying that one simply used a war-dance song, preferably one that 'sounds mournful.'" Thomas Vennum, "The Ojibwa Begging Dance," in *Music and Context: Essays for John M. Ward*, ed. Anne Dhu Shapiro (Cambridge, MA: Harvard University Press, 1985), 60.
99. A description of the dance during the 1826 Treaty of Fond du Lac is in Thomas L. McKenney, *Sketches of a Tour to the Lakes* (Minneapolis: Ross & Haines, 1959), 286–88. Although terming it the begging dance, McKenney emphasized the nature of exchange of the dance as understood by both the Ojibwe and McKenney and other government officials present.
100. J. J. Ducatel, "A Fortnight among the Chippewas of Lake Superior," in *The Indian Miscellany*, ed. W. W. Beach (Albany, NY: J. Munsell, 1877), 366.
101. Morse, "Chippewas of Lake Superior," 351.
102. Ibid.
103. Ibid.
104. *Barron County Chronotype*, October 21, 1876, 3.
105. As Ojibwe relationships to non-Ojibwe were transformed by segregation from non-Ojibwe on reservations, the practice of the dance decreased. Anthropologist Thomas Vennum charted the dance's decline in the twentieth century. Vennum discusses the dance still being performed by Lac Courte Oreilles people in Hayward in the 1920s. The dance held out longer in other areas, still being performed at Red Lake in northern Minnesota in the 1960s. See Vennum, "Ojibwa Begging Dance."
106. Chappelle, *Around the Four Corners*, 21.
107. "Memoirs of Arthur Hovey," in Winton and Winton, *Historical Collections of Washburn County and the Surrounding Indianhead Country*, 1:287. Hovey referred to Niikaanis as a chief, but it is most likely he was a headman, as early settlers had limited understanding of Ojibwe political institutions and tended to call most Ojibwe men "chief." Hovey rendered Niikaanis "Nickonis."
108. Ibid.
109. Ritzenthaler Papers, Spiral Notebook 6, 9.
110. Ibid., Spiral Notebook 7, 3–4.
111. Ned Blackhawk, *Violence over the Land: Indians and Empires in the Early American West* (Cambridge, MA: Harvard University Press, 2006).
112. *Barron County Chronotype*, December 18, 1875, 3.

113. Axtell, *First Fifty Years.*
114. Maggie Conger to William Light, March 11, 1913, NARA, Great Lakes Region, Chicago, Illinois, RG 75, Records of the Bureau of Indian Affairs, Records of the La Pointe Agency, Letters Received from the Lac Courte Oreilles Reservation, 1881–1914, Box 4. Conger recorded her sister's death as happening "about forty years ago" but did not say how she died. Conger rendered Minotaagoz "Me no ta gous."
115. *Barron County Chronotype*, September 20, 1877, 3. Poskin, a small town in central Barron County is named for her. See Gordon, *History of Barron County, Wisconsin*, 1136. In *First Fifty Years* (211), Alvah Axtell also mistakenly identifies Poskin as the daughter of Nena'aangabi.
116. Accounts of Waabizheshi's death appear in the *Barron County Chronotype*, June 27, 1878, 3, and Bartlett, *History, Tradition, and Adventure*. There is a discrepancy in the dates of Waabizheshi's death. Bartlett, based on the account of *Chronotype* editor August Ender, lists it as happening in 1879. I utilize the date from the 1878 newspaper article describing the event as occurring "last fall" as more accurate.
117. Peter C. Mancall, *Deadly Medicine: Indians and Alcohol in Early America* (Ithaca: Cornell University Press, 1995), 85.
118. Ibid., 14.
119. Bartlett, *History, Tradition, and Adventure.*
120. Treuer, *Assassination of Hole-in-the-Day.*
121. Bartlett, *History, Tradition, and Adventure*, and *Barron County Chronotype*, June 27, 1878, 3. There is a discrepancy in the dates of Bidad's death. Bartlett, based on the account of *Chronotype* editor August Ender, lists it as happening in 1882, while the 1878 Chronotype article described it as happening "last week." I utilize the date from the actual 1878 newspaper as more accurate.
122. Schoolcraft, *Schoolcraft's Expedition to Lake Itasca*, 123.

CHAPTER 4. AAZHAWEYAA AND OJIBWE WOMEN IN TRANSITION

1. Thomas Bracklin to Cato Sells, November 10, 1915, National Archives and Records Administration (NARA), Records Group (RG) 75.
2. Writing in 1855, Richard Morse estimated Aazhaweyaa's age at eighteen to twenty. See Richard E. Morse, "The Chippewas of Lake Superior," in *Collections of the State Historical Society of Wisconsin*, vol. 3, ed. Lyman Copeland Draper (Madison: Wisconsin Historical Society, 1904), 350. Writing that

same year, Johann Georg Kohl claimed she was nineteen; see *Kitchi-Gami: Life among the Lake Superior Ojibway*, trans. Lascelles Wraxall (St. Paul: Minnesota Historical Society Press, 1985), 126. In 1893, census records list her age as sixty. This is consistent with subsequent yearly censuses that continued until Aazhaweyaa's death. In the census, Aazhaweyaa is listed by her other name Omoodayens, which is rendered "Mo-dense." See Census of the Lac Courte Oreilles Band of Chippewa Indians, 1893, NARA, RG 75, Indian Census Rolls, 1885–1940, La Pointe Agency Census Rolls, 1893–1894, M595, Roll 236, no. 644.

3. Morse, "Chippewas of Lake Superior."
4. Ibid.
5. An overview of women's participation in warfare in the nineteenth century in the Plains and western Great Lakes, including Aazhaweyaa, is found in Beatrice Medicine, " 'Warrior Women': Sex Role Alternatives for Plains Indian Women," in *The Hidden Half: Studies of Plains Indian Women*, ed. Patricia Albers and Beatrice Medicine (Landham, MD: University Press of America, 1983), 267–80.
6. Morse, "Chippewas of Lake Superior."
7. A good characterization of changes in Ojibwe-Dakota warfare is found in Anton Treuer, *The Assassination of Hole-in-the-Day* (St. Paul: Minnesota Historical Society Press, 2011).
8. Morse, "Chippewas of Lake Superior."
9. Kohl, *Kitchi-Gami.*
10. Morse, "Chippewas of Lake Superior," 350. One rod is equal to 16.5 feet.
11. Kohl, *Kitchi-Gami*, 126.
12. Morse, "Chippewas of Lake Superior," 354.
13. Kohl, *Kitchi-Gami*, 126.
14. Medicine, " 'Warrior Women,' " 269.
15. Angeline Cedaroot, "Chippewa Remedies—Women, Medicine, and War—Indian Prophecies," Works Progress Administration (WPA), Chippewa Indian Historical Project, Archives of the Fransciscan Sisters of Perpetual Adoration, La Crosse, Wisconsin, Envelope 9, 49.
16. Henry R. Schoolcraft, *Schoolcraft's Expedition to Lake Itasca: The Discovery of the Source of the Mississippi*, ed. Philip P. Mason (1834; repr., East Lansing: Michigan State University Press, 1993), 121. The Treaty of Butte des Morts involved settlement of a dispute over the Ojibwe and Menominee boundary set forth in the Treaty of Prairie du Chien in 1825. Treaty of Butte des Morts, August 11, 1827, 7 Stat. 303.
17. John Tanner, *The Falcon: A Narrative of the Captivity and Adventures of John Tanner (U.S. Interpreter at the Sault de Ste. Marie) during Thirty Years Residence*

among the Indians in the Interior of North America (1830; repr., Minneapolis: Ross & Haines, 1956). Nednaakwe is written "Net-no-kwa" in the book. Her name refers to a location on the shores of Lake Huron, where she was born.

18. Kohl, *Kitchi-Gami*, 127.
19. Henry R. Schoolcraft, *Personal Memoirs of a Residence of Thirty Years with the Indian Tribes on the American Frontiers* (Philadelphia: Lippincott, Grambo, 1851), 105.
20. Morse, "Chippewas of Lake Superior," 350.
21. Jim Littlewolf, "Weak of Heart—Strong of Heart," trans. John D. Nichols, *Oshkaabewis Native Journal*, 2 no. 2 (1995): 56–57. This story is in the genre of *dibaajimowin*, which are historical stories that can be told any time of the year. Another major category of Ojibwe stories are *aadizookaan*, which are animate stories, usually dealing with spirits, that can only be told in the winter as to not offend the spirits involved in the story. See John D. Nichols, "Ojibwa Oral Literature," in *Encyclopedia of Literature in Western Canada* (Toronto: University of Toronto Press, 2002), 841–45.
22. Littlewolf, "Weak of Heart—Strong of Heart," 56–57.
23. Benjamin G. Armstrong, *Early Life among the Indians* (Ashland, WI: A. W. Bowron, 1892), 205.
24. Schoolcraft, *Personal Memoirs*, 103.
25. Schoolcraft, *Schoolcraft's Expedition to Lake Itasca*, 218.
26. Tanner, *The Falcon*, 223–24.
27. Schoolcraft, *Schoolcraft's Expedition to Lake Itasca*, 193.
28. Ibid.
29. George Nelson, *My First Years in the Fur Trade* (St. Paul: Minnesota Historical Society Press, 2002), 177.
30. Thomas L. McKenney, *Sketches of a Tour to the Lakes* (Minneapolis: Ross & Haines, 1959), 319.
31. Kohl, *Kitchi-Gami*, 3–4.
32. Armstrong, *Early Life among the Indians*, 191.
33. Ethel Elliot Chappelle, *Around the Four Corners: A Pioneer History of the Washburn, Sawyer, Barron, and Rusk Counties* (Rice Lake, WI: Chronotype Publishing, 1971), 19.
34. David D. Smits, "The 'Squaw Drudge': A Prime Index of Savagism," *Ethnohistory* 29, no. 4 (1982), 281–306.
35. Armstrong, *Early Life among the Indians*, 197. Armstrong noted that Bizhiki participated in the Battle of the Brule River in 1842 and that this was the last battle fought near Lake Superior.
36. Morse, "Chippewas of Lake Superior," 367.
37. Schoolcraft, *Schoolcraft's Expedition to Lake Itasca*, 184.

38. Ibid., 182.
39. Jerome Arbuckle, "The Chippewa and Monogamy," WPA, Chippewa Indian Historical Project, Envelope 6, 82.
40. The various sugar products that resulted from the production of maple sap are detailed in Kohl, *Kitchi-Gami*, 323–24. For a description of the process of Ojibwe maple sugar production, see Frances Densmore, *Strength of the Earth: The Classic Guide to Ojibwe Uses of Native Plants* (1928; repr., St. Paul: Minnesota Historical Society Press, 2005), 308–13. See also Arthur T. Wilcox, "The Chippewa Sugar Camp," *Michigan History* 37, no. 3 (1953): 276–85. A description of an Ojibwe sugar camp in 1823 in the eastern part of the Upper Peninsula of Michigan is in Schoolcraft, *Personal Memoirs*, 162–63. Off-reservation treaty rights to harvest maple sugar are explored in Robert H. Kellar, "America's Native Sweet: Chippewa Treaties and the Right to Harvest Maple Sugar," *American Indian Quarterly* 13, no. 2 (1989): 117–35.
41. Jerry Smith, "Aadizookaan: Iskigamizige giizis—'Sap boiling moon,'" transcribed by Rainbird Winters, *LCO News* 1, no. 5 (2007): 6. Another version of this story is found in Andrew J. Blackbird, *History of the Ottawa and Chippewa Indians of Michigan* (Ypsilanti: Ypsilanti Printing House, 1887), 72–73.
42. J. J. Ducatel, "A Fortnight among the Chippewas of Lake Superior," in *The Indian Miscellany*, ed. W. W. Beach (Albany, NY: J. Munsell, 1877), 370.
43. Alexander Henry, *Travels and Adventures in the Years 1760–1776* (1809; repr., Chicago: Lakeside Press, 1921), 70.
44. Florina Denomie, "An Indian Huntress," WPA, Chippewa Indian Historical Project, Envelope 6, 26–29.
45. Kohl, *Kitchi-Gami*, 319.
46. Ducatel, "Fortnight among the Chippewas," 372.
47. Kohl, *Kitchi-Gami*, 319.
48. Jerome Arbuckle, "Salt," WPA, Chippewa Indian Historical Project, Envelope 2, 74–76.
49. For men's roles in sugar production, see Henry, *Travels and Adventures*, 69–70. Lac du Flambeau Ojibwe Tom Badger noted how in the late nineteenth century his father and brothers participated in sugar making. Later, he participated in sugar making with his wife. See Victor Barnouw, "Reminiscences of a Chippewa Mide Priest," *Wisconsin Archaeologist* 35, no. 4 (1954), 90 and 109.
50. Frances Densmore, "The Native Art of the Chippewa," *American Anthropologist* 43, no. 4 (1941): 678–81.
51. Kohl, *Kitchi-Gami*, 412–14.
52. Densmore, *Strength of the Earth*, 395–96.

53. Densmore, "Native Art of the Chippewa," 679.
54. Ernestine Friedl, "A Note on Birchbark Transparencies," *American Anthropologist* 46, no. 1 (1944): 149–50.
55. An exploration of the decline of birchbark biting among all Algonquian speaking peoples is in Cath Oberholtzer and Nicholas N. Smith, "'I'm the Last One Who Does It': Birch Bark Biting, an Almost Lost Art," in *Papers of the 26th Algonquian Conference* (Winnipeg: University of Manitoba Press, 1995), 306–21.
56. Bernard Coleman, "The Religion of the Ojibwa of Northern Minnesota," *Primitive Man* 10, nos. 3 and 4 (1937): 45–46.
57. Ducatel, "Fortnight among the Chippewas," 370. For description of birchbark torches, see Armstrong, *Early Life among the Indians*, 113.
58. Ibid., 110–11.
59. Schoolcraft, *Personal Memoirs*, 368. Schoolcraft also made similar notice of his impression of the gardens at the Pacwawong Lake community during his 1831 trip in *Schoolcraft's Expedition to Lake Itasca*, 115.
60. For a description of the Ojibwe seasonal labor cycle, see Frances Densmore, *Chippewa Customs* (1929; repr., St. Paul: Minnesota Historical Society Press, 1979), 119–23. See also Maude Kegg, *Portage Lake: Memories of an Ojibwe Childhood*, ed. and transcribed by John D. Nichols (Minneapolis: University of Minnesota Press, 1993).
61. In addition, caches stored other food, such as dried meat. See Ducatel, "Fortnight among the Chippewas," 369. For a description of the use of caches in Ojibwe movement, see Nelson, *My First Years in the Fur Trade*, 141. Caches were particularly important in the fur trade but were utilized by the Ojibwe at wild rice and maple sugar camps for the storage of implements.
62. Schoolcraft, *Personal Memoirs*, 385.
63. See Joseph Casagrande, "John Mink: Ojibwa Informant," *Wisconsin Archaeologist* 26 (1955): 106–28. For an account of dancing on rice, see "Memoirs of Ward Winton," in *Historical Collections of Washburn County and the Surrounding Indianhead Country*, vol. 1, ed. E. Ward Winton and Kay Brown Winton (Shell Lake, WI: White Birch Printing, 1980), 55.
64. For more on the importance of wild rice to Ojibwe subsistence, see Thomas Vennum Jr., *Wild Rice and the Ojibway People* (St. Paul: Minnesota Historical Society Press, 1988). For a description of Ojibwe ricing techniques in the nineteenth century, see Nelson, *My First Years in the Fur Trade*, 56–57. For an account of wild rice harvesting among Ojibwe in Ontario, see Kathi Avery Kinew "Manito Gitigaan: Governance in the Great Spirit's Garden Wild Rice in Treaty #3 from Pre-Treaty to the 1990's," in *Papers of the 26th Algonquian Conference*, 183–94.

65. See "Collections Online," Minnesota Historical Society, http://collections.mnhs.org/cms/display.php?irn=10241408.
66. "Memoirs of Arthur Hovey," in Winton and Winton, *Historical Collections of Washburn County and the Surrounding Indianhead Country*, 1:288.
67. Joseph N. Nicollet, *The Journals of Joseph N. Nicollet: A Scientist on the Mississippi Headwaters with Notes on Indian Life, 1838–1837*, trans. Andre Frey (St. Paul: Minnesota Historical Society Press, 1970), 188.
68. Ibid., 188.
69. Ducatel, "Fortnight among the Chippewas," 371.
70. McKenney, *Sketches of a Tour to the Lakes*, 294.
71. Ducatel, "Fortnight among the Chippewas," 371.
72. Tanner, *The Falcon*, 101.
73. Armstrong, *Early Life among the Indians*, 103.
74. Schoolcraft, *Personal Memoirs*, 376.
75. Ibid., 377. Schoolcraft spelled Moozojiid "Mozojeed" and Bakwe'aamo "Pukquamoo." This chief is also known as Odabasaa spelled "Odabossa" by Schoolcraft.
76. Lake Superior Chippewa Annuity, 1857, Chippewa Annuity Rolls, 1841–1907, US Office of Indian Affairs, Minnesota Historical Society (MHS), St. Paul, M390, Roll 1. Aazhaweyaa is rendered "Aw-zhaw-way-aw" in this annuity.
77. This practice was continued into the twentieth century. In Tom Badger's account of his life, one his brothers dies in prison, leading his other brother to marry the widow. See Barnouw, "Reminiscences of a Chippewa Mide Priest," 99.
78. Kohl, *Kitchi-Gami*, 111.
79. Schoolcraft, *Personal Memoirs*, 124. Schoolcraft rendered Metaakozige "Me-ta-koos-se-ga, i.e. Smoking-Weed, or Pure Tobacco." There was a leader from the Lac du Flambeau Band named Metaakozige who signed the treaty of 1826 and treaty of 1842, but it is unknown if this is the same individual. In the treaty of 1826, Metaakozige is rendered "May-tau-koos-ee-gay." Treaty of Fond du Lac, August 5, 1826, 7 Stat. 290. In the treaty of 1842 Metaakozige is rendered "May tock cus e quay." Treaty of La Pointe, October 4, 1842, 7 Stat. 591.
80. Schoolcraft, *Personal Memoirs*, 377.
81. One of his Tanner's mother's relatives had two wives and his son did also. See Tanner, *The Falcon*, 18 and 82.
82. Arbuckle, "Chippewa and Monogamy," 82.
83. Nelson, *My First Years in the Fur Trade*, 61 and 177. Nelson's vivid descriptions of husbands abusing their wives (and other incidents of violence usually

related to alcohol; see 51, 99, and 128) are disturbing. While Nelson was only in his teens when the events happened, it should be remembered that he wrote the memoir much later in life, after decades of being a fur trader. This gave him years of interacting with Native people to temper the extreme biases he may have had in his teens. Other accounts such as Tanner's do not feature abusive husbands so prevalently. However, Tanner's account does note the destructive effects of alcohol in ways similar to Nelson's memoir. After telling of a trader who beat his Ojibwe wife, J. J. Ducatel noted, "The Indians themselves never beat their wives." See Ducatel, "Fortnight among the Chippewas," 373.

84. Armstrong, *Early Life among the Indians*, 124. Armstrong renders Bayezhig "Bi-a-jek."
85. See Sylvia Van Kirk, *Many Tender Ties: Women in Fur-Trade Society, 1670–1870* (Norman: University of Oklahoma Press, 1983) and Susan Sleeper-Smith, *Indian Women and French Men: Rethinking Cultural Encounter in the Western Great Lakes* (Amherst: University of Massachusetts Press, 2001).
86. William W. Bartlett, *History, Tradition, and Adventure in the Chippewa Valley* (Chippewa Falls: Chippewa Printery, 1929), 66.
87. Robert E. Ritzenthaler Papers, Milwaukee Public Museum, Spiral Notebook 8, 7–8.
88. Bartlett, *History, Tradition, and Adventure*, 66.
89. Ibid. Ogimaabinesikwe is rendered "Ogimabinensikwe" in the 1877 census of Lac Courte Oreilles. See Census Roll, Lac Courte Oreilles, April 3, 1877, NARA, Great Lakes Region, Chicago, Illinois, RG 75, Records of the Bureau of Indian Affairs, La Pointe Agency. The author's son is a direct descendant of Ogimaabinesikwe.
90. Lake Superior Chippewa Annuity, 1859, MHS M390, Roll 1, no. 751. Aazhaweyaa is rendered "Aw-shaw-wa-yah," in the annuity record. It is likely that Ogimaabinesikwe was an infant at the 1859 annuity payment, as census records list her birth as occurring in 1859. Census of the Lac Courte Oreilles Band of Chippewa Indians, 1923, NARA, RG 75, Hayward Superintendency, 1916–1923, M595, Roll 179, F:0700, no. 982. Ogimaabinesikwe is identified as "Ogemibinikikwe or Quaderer, Julia" in the census. However, it is possible that Ogimaabinesikwe was slightly older, as the earliest surviving annuity record that lists Aazhaweyaa as a head of a family is 1857, and her family includes one child. Lake Superior Chippewa Annuity, 1857. In this annuity, Aazhaweyaa is rendered "Aw-zhaw-way-aw."
91. Bartlett, *History, Tradition, and Adventure*.
92. George Forrester, *Historical and Biographical Album of the Chippewa Valley* (Chicago: A. Warner Publisher, 1892), 451–52.

93. Nellie Bracklin's exact year of birth is unknown since she does not appear on any Lac Courte Oreilles census records. According to annuity records, the first year that there were two girls in Aazhaweyaa's family was 1862. In the annuity, Aazhaweyaa is rendered "Aw shaw wa yaw." See Lake Superior Chippewa Annuity, 1862, MHS M390, Roll 2. In a 1905 letter regarding the heirs of Aazhaweyaa's allotment, Lac Courte Oreilles Reservation farmer David E. Jacobs noted, "Nellie is married to a white man and lives in Denver." See David E. Jacobs to Samuel W. Campbell, March 12, 1905, NARA, Great Lakes Region, RG 75, Letters Received from the Lac Courte Oreilles Reservation, 1881–1914.
94. Thomas Bracklin is listed in the Lac Courte Oreilles census of 1887 as being twenty-three. Census of the Lac Courte Oreilles Band of Chippewa Indians, 1887, NARA, RG 75, Indian Census Rolls, M595, Roll 235, no. 961. The first annuity list where a boy appears in Aazhaweyaa's family is in 1865. Lake Superior Chippewa Annuity, 1865, MHS M390, Roll 2. In the annuity, Aazhaweyaa is identified by her other name Omoodayens, which is rendered "Omodaiance."
95. Sylvia Bracklin, personal interview, August 13, 2013.
96. Forrester, *Historical and Biographical Album*, 451–52, and Newton S. Gordon, *History of Barron County, Wisconsin* (Minneapolis: H. C. Cooper Jr., 1922), 85.
97. Sylvia Bracklin, personal interview, August 13, 2013.
98. Personal Record of Thomas Bracklin, February 18, 1915, NARA, Great Lakes Region, RG 75, Records of the Bureau of Indian Affairs, Red Cliff Agency, Administrative Correspondence of the Superintendent, 1908–1922, Box 2.
99. Lake Superior Chippewa Annuity, 1868, MHS M390, Roll 2. Aazhaweyaa is listed under her other name Omoodayens which is rendered "Omodaiance."
100. Lake Superior Chippewa Annuity, 1873, and Lake Superior Chippewa Annuity, 1874, MHS M390, Roll 1. In both records Aazhaweyaa is rendered "Ashaweia."
101. "Mayor Bracklin Dead," *Rice Lake Chronotype*, August 3, 1900, 5.
102. *Barron County Shield*, March 30, 1877, 1.
103. James Bracklin, "A Tragedy of the Wisconsin Pinery," *Wisconsin Magazine of History* 3, no. 1 (1919): 45.
104. *Barron County Shield*, March 30, 1877, 1.
105. Census of the Lac Courte Oreilles Band of Chippewa Indians, 1887. Aazhaweyaa is identified by her other name, Omoodayens, which is rendered "Mo-dense" (no. 958). Mary Barker is listed as "Mani" (no. 959), which is how Mary is said in Ojibwe since there is no "r" sound in the Ojibwe language.

106. *Barron County Chronotype*, April 15, 1876. Samuel and Susan Barker's only child, a boy, died in infancy a few months after his father's death. *Barron County Chronotype*, June 26, 1876.
107. Armstrong, *Early Life among the Indians*, 133.
108. See Gordon, *History of Barron County, Wisconsin*, 1136, and Rick St. Germaine, "Old Post: A History," *Lac Courte Oreilles Journal*, October 1985, 8. Thomas Tainter's year of birth is found in Census of the Lac Courte Oreilles Band of Chippewa Indians, 1916, NARA, RG 75, Hayward Superintendency, M595, Roll 179, F:0088.
109. Forrester, *Historical and Biographical Album*, 397.
110. Gordon, *History of Barron County, Wisconsin*, 942.
111. Ibid., 29.
112. "Indian Hearing Marked by Humor and Tragedy," *Milwaukee Journal*, July 14, 1929.
113. US Senate, Committee on Indian Affairs, *Survey of Conditions of the Indians in the United States: Hearings before a Subcommittee of the Committee on Indian Affairs* (Washington, DC: Government Printing Office, 1930), 2035. Bracklin's claim that the medal was given to his great-grandfather suggests that it was given to Nena'aangabi's father, Gekek, who signed the Treaty of Prairie du Chien in 1825. The medal does not survive today. Thomas Bracklin's house was broken into shortly after his death in 1950, and the house was set on fire to cover up the break-in. It is likely the medal was destroyed in the fire. Sylvia Bracklin, personal interview, August 13, 2013.

CHAPTER 5. GIISHKITAWAG CONFRONTS REMOVAL, 1879–1894

1. "Proceedings of the Barron County Board of Supervisors," *Barron County Chronotype*, January 24, 1878, 2. The petition was sent to the secretary of the interior. N. H. Rockman to Carl Schurz, January 18, 1878, National Archives and Records Administration (NARA), Record Group (RG) 75, Letters Received by the Office of Indian Affairs, 1824–1881: La Pointe Agency, M234 Roll 398, F:0562.
2. Jerome Arbuckle, "Fishing on the Bad River Reservation in the Early Days," Works Progress Administration, Chippewa Indian Historical Project, Archives of the Fransciscan Sisters of Perpetual Adoration, La Crosse, Wisconsin, Envelope 7, 4.
3. Isaac Mahan to Ezra A. Hayt, April 8, 1878, NARA, RG 75, M234, Roll 398, F:0243.

4. See Commissioner of Indian Affairs, *Annual Report of the Commissioner of Indian Affairs for the Year 1882* (Washington, DC: Government Printing Office, 1882), 177.
5. *Barron County Chronotype*, August 1, 1878, 3.
6. Isaac Mahan to Ezra A. Hayt, June 20, 1878, NARA, RG 75, M234, Roll 398, F:0322.
7. Treaty of La Pointe, September 30, 1854, 10 Stat. 1109. In 1892, Congress passed a comprehensive liquor law that made sale of alcohol to Indians by anyone (Indians and non-Indians) a federal offense on- or off-reservation. Under the statute, only the person selling alcohol was prosecuted: it was not illegal for Indians to possess alcohol. The wording of the law included any Indian who "exercised guardianship." July 23, 1892, 27 Stat. 260. The law was complicated by allotment. When patents for allotments were issued, making owners of allotments citizens, the federal courts were flooded with appeals of convictions (mostly whites) of the 1892 Indian liquor law, arguing that the Indians buying liquor were citizens and not under "guardianship." In 1915, the Seventh Circuit Court of Appeals ruled in *Katzenmeyer v. United States* that Indians were still subject to federal liquor laws even if they were citizens. The court based its decision on *United States v. Noble*, where the Supreme Court ruled that Indians were still under federal guardianship even when citizenship was bestowed. See Katzenmeyer v. United States, 225 F. 523 (1915), and United States v. Noble, 237 U.S. 74 (1915).
8. Felix S. Cohen, *Handbook of Federal Indian Law* (Washington, DC: Government Printing Office, 1945), 353.
9. Isaac Mahan to Ezra A. Hayt, June 20, 1878, NARA, RG 75, M234, Roll 398, F:0322.
10. "Proceedings of the Barron County Board of Supervisors," *Barron County Chronotype*, December 12, 1878, 2. The petition was sent to the commissioner of Indian affairs. N. H. Rockman to Ezra A. Hayt, December 18, 1878, NARA, RG 75, M234, Roll 398, F:0573.
11. *Barron County Chronotype*, June 27, 1879, 3.
12. Isaac Mahan to Ezra A. Hayt, October 29, 1879, NARA, RG 75, M234, Roll 399, F:0299.
13. In 1864, Gurnoe transcribed the bilingual petition of Akiwenzii and other Ojibwe leaders that was presented to President Lincoln. Gurnoe's desire to become the farmer at Lac Courte Oreilles and his motivation for doing so are covered in Joseph Gurnoe to E. J. Brooks, June 23, 1879, NARA, RG 75, M234, Roll 399, F:0045, and Joseph Gurnoe to E. J. Brooks, July 7, 1879, NARA, RG 75, M234, Roll 399. La Pointe Agent Isaac Mahan was quite frustrated with Gurnoe, calling him "crass," and tired of his demands for

increased pay. However, Mahan was beholden to Gurnoe's language ability, writing Commissioner of Indian Affairs Ezra Hayt, "I do not see how I can now get along without him *but I am determined to try*." See Isaac Mahan to Ezra A. Hayt, July 17, 1879, NARA, RG 75, M234, Roll 399, F:0254. Indeed, the documents left behind by Gurnoe in Ojibwe such as census records and the 1864 petition to President Lincoln are clearly legible and utilize the Baraga writing system in a way that is very accessible to modern readers. Over a hundred years later, we too rely on Gurnoe much in the way Mahan did. Background information on Gurnoe, such as his age and prior position as interpreter, is found in List of Employees at La Pointe Agency Wisconsin to be Prepared to be Retained in 1880, May 12, 1879, NARA, RG 75, M234, Roll 399, F:0215.

14. Joseph Gurnoe to William Durfee, June 21, 1881, NARA, Great Lakes Region, Chicago, Illinois, RG 75, Records of the Bureau of Indian Affairs, La Pointe Agency, Letters Received from the Lac Courte Oreilles Reservation, 1881–1914, Box 1.
15. Joseph Gurnoe to William Durfee, March 22, 1882, NARA, Great Lakes Region, RG 75, Letters Received from the Lac Courte Oreilles Reservation, 1881–1914, Box 1.
16. While there is no study of the relationship between persons of mixed descent and traditional Ojibwe at Lac Courte Oreilles, an excellent study of this conflict elsewhere is Melissa L. Meyer, *The White Earth Tragedy: Ethnicity and Dispossession at a Minnesota Anishinaabe Reservation, 1889–1920* (Lincoln: University of Nebraska Press, 1994). Two mixed-descent communities in the nineteenth century in northwest Wisconsin were Flambeau Farm (today called Ladysmith) and Eagleton, ten miles north of modern Chippewa Falls. Many individuals in these communities moved to the Lac Courte Oreilles Reservation when white settlers came. A description of this is in Sirilla LaRush, "Lola—Later, Sister M. Sirilla, OSF," in *Cadotte Family Stories*, ed. Thomas Henry Tobola (Cadott, WI: Cadott Printing, 1974), 124–45. Sirilla LaRush was the first Lac Courte Oreilles Catholic nun and was the author's grandfather's second cousin. It is important to remember that these characterizations are particular to this time period and have nothing to do with descendants of these individuals or persons of mixed Ojibwe descent more generally. The way we think about Ojibwe identity today is vastly different than it was during this period. Furthermore, even in the nineteenth century, being Ojibwe was more about cultural practice than biological heritage. As Meyer notes at White Earth in the nineteenth century, not all those labeled "full bloods" were solely of Ojibwe heritage. People of mixed descent who lived in Ojibwe communities, engaged in traditional seasonal labor, and

practiced traditional beliefs were considered Ojibwe, regardless of the exact details of their ancestry.

17. George Forrester, *Historical and Biographical Album of the Chippewa Valley* (Chicago: A. Warner Publisher, 1892), 312–13.
18. Ethel Elliot Chappelle, *Around the Four Corners: A Pioneer History of the Washburn, Sawyer, Barron, and Rusk Counties* (Rice Lake, WI: Chronotype Publishing, 1971), 20.
19. Ibid., and "Memoirs of Lena Larson," in *Historical Collections of Washburn County and the Surrounding Indianhead Country*, vol. 1, ed. E. Ward Winton and Kay Brown Winton (Shell Lake, WI: White Birch Printing, 1980), 286.
20. Treaty of La Pointe, September 30, 1854, 10 Stat. 1109, Article 3.
21. *Barron County Chronotype*, July 1, 1876, 3.
22. Commissioner of Indian Affairs, *Annual Report of the Commissioner of Indian Affairs for the Year 1878* (Washington, DC: Government Printing Office, 1878), 146, and Commissioner of Indian Affairs, *Annual Report of the Commissioner of Indian Affairs for the Year 1880* (Washington, DC: Government Printing Office, 1880), 172. Allotment selections were made even earlier at Bad River, with 160 selected by September 1875. See Commissioner of Indian Affairs, *Annual Report of the Commissioner of Indian Affairs for the Year 1875* (Washington, DC: Government Printing Office, 1875), 371.
23. B. Cornell to Carl Schurz, January 6, 1879, NARA, RG 75, M234, Roll 399, F:0026.
24. Joseph Gurnoe to William Durfee, June 27, 1881, NARA, Great Lakes Region, RG 75, Letters Received from the Lac Courte Oreilles Reservation, 1881–1914, Box 1. Once again, Gurnoe did not identify Giishkitawag by name, instead calling him the "(Chief?) of the Red Cedar band."
25. Ibid.
26. Joseph Gurnoe to William Durfee, July 18, 1881, NARA, Great Lakes Region, RG 75, Letters Received from the Lac Courte Oreilles Reservation, 1881–1914, Box 1. Gurnoe wrote Bakweyawaa "Bakweiawa."
27. Commissioner of Indian Affairs, *Annual Report 1882*, 175.
28. Commissioner of Indian Affairs, *Annual Report of the Commissioner of Indian Affairs for the Year 1883* (Washington, DC: Government Printing Office, 1883), 159, and Commissioner of Indian Affairs, *Annual Report of the Commissioner of Indian Affairs for the Year 1884* (Washington, DC: Government Printing Office, 1884), 180.
29. Giishkitawag's allotment was the E ½ SE ¼ Section 25 Township 39 Range 9. See US Senate, Committee on Indian Affairs, *Chippewa Allotments of Land and Timber Contracts*, Senate Report 2710, 50th Congress, 2d session (Washington, DC: Government Printing Office, 1889), 1278. Giishkitawag is

rendered "Gish-ki-ta-wag." Today the land is tribal land. The Senate report includes a complete inventory of allotments for Lac Courte Oreilles, Bad River, Red Cliff, Fond du Lac, and Lac du Flambeau through 1889.

30. Aazhaweyaa's allotment was the SW ¼ SW ¼ Section 30 and NW ¼ NW ¼ Section 31 Township 39 Range 8. See ibid., 1277. Aazhaweyaa received her patent under her other name, Omoodayens, rendered "O-mo-da-i-nis." Today the land is tribal land.
31. Under the 1854 treaty, patents were issued at Bad River at the same time as Lac Courte Oreilles with 131 patents issued by August 1882. See Commissioner of Indian Affairs, *Annual Report 1882*, 173. On the much smaller Red Cliff Reservation, the entire reservation was allotted in 1876 and all had patents by August 1883. See Commissioner of Indian Affairs, *Annual Report of the Commissioner of Indian Affairs for the Year 1876* (Washington, DC: Government Printing Office, 1876), 159, and Commissioner of Indian Affairs, *Annual Report 1883*, 149.
32. Commissioner of Indian Affairs, *Annual Report of the Commissioner of Indian Affairs for the Year 1887* (Washington, DC: Government Printing Office, 1887), 229.
33. Anthony Godfrey, *A Forest History of Ten Wisconsin Indian Reservations under the Great Lakes Agency: Precontact to the Present* (Salt Lake City: U.S. West Research, 1996).
34. United States v. Cook, 86 U.S. 591 (1873).
35. David E. Wilkins and K. Tsiamina Lomawaima, *Uneven Ground: American Indian Sovereignty and Federal Law* (Norman: University of Oklahoma Press, 2001), 58–60.
36. Dead and Down Timber Act, February 16, 1889, 25 Stat. 673.
37. Leo G. Waisberg and Tim E. Holzkamm, "'A Tendency to Discourage Them from Cultivating': Ojibwa Agriculture and Indian Affairs Administration in Northwestern Ontario," *Ethnohistory* 40, no. 2 (1993): 193.
38. Commissioner of Indian Affairs, *Annual Report 1875*, 373 and Godfrey, *Forest History of Ten Wisconsin Indian Reservations.*
39. For Rust's biography, see Forrester, *Historical and Biographical Album*, 424–26.
40. Joseph B. Casagrande Papers, University of Illinois-Urbana Archives.
41. For more on Menominee management of their forest resources, see Brian C. Hosmer, *American Indians in the Marketplace: Persistence and Innovation among the Menominees and Metlakatlans, 1870–1920* (Lawrence: University of Kansas Press, 1999) and David R. M. Beck, *The Struggle for Self-Determination: History of the Menominee Indians since 1854* (Lincoln: University of Nebraska Press, 2005).

42. Godfrey, *Forest History of Ten Wisconsin Indian Reservations.* United States v. Cook, 86 U.S. 591 (1873).
43. Godfrey, *Forest History of Ten Wisconsin Indian Reservations.*
44. Eldon Marple, *The Visitor Who Came to Stay: Legacy of the Hayward Area* (Hayward, WI: Country Print Shop, 1971), 49.
45. Thaddeus Thayer v. United States, 20 Ct. Cl. 137 (1885). Biidaanakwad is rendered "Bi-da-na-kwad." I have left the name "Chiz-ai-aw" in the original phonetic spelling, as the meaning of this name is unclear. It may be Chi-sayenh. Biidaanakwad's allotment was Lots 4 and 5 Section 31 Township 40 Range 6. Chiz-ai-aw's allotment was SE ¼ SE ½ and Lot 3 Section 31 Township 40 Range 6. See US Senate, Committee on Indian Affairs, *Chippewa Allotments of Land and Timber Contracts*, 1271.
46. Thaddeus Thayer v. United States, 142.
47. Petition to James Gregory, October 28, 1886, NARA, Great Lakes Region, RG 75, Letters Received from the Lac Courte Oreilles Reservation, 1881–1914, Box 2.
48. William Rusler to James Gregory, January 3, 1887, NARA, Great Lakes Region, RG 75, Letters Received from the Lac Courte Oreilles Reservation, 1881–1914, Box 2.
49. Godfrey, *Forest History of Ten Wisconsin Indian Reservations.*
50. US Senate, Committee on Indian Affairs, *Chippewa Allotments of Land and Timber Contracts*, vii.
51. Godfrey, *Forest History of Ten Wisconsin Indian Reservations.*
52. Ibid.
53. Lac Courte Oreilles Annuity, November 14, 1874, Chippewa Annuity Rolls, 1841–1907, US Office of Indian Affairs, Minnesota Historical Society (MHS), St. Paul, M390, Roll 2.
54. Victor Barnouw, "Reminiscences of a Chippewa Mide Priest," *Wisconsin Archaeologist* 35, no. 4 (1954): 95.
55. US Senate, Committee on Indian Affairs, *Chippewa Allotments of Land and Timber Contracts*, 817–18. Giishkitawag is rendered "Gesk kit a wag."
56. Lac du Flambeau had a very similar experience with allotment as Lac Courte Oreilles. The main difference was that during the late nineteenth century, the white settlers moved into the territory near the Lac du Flambeau Ojibwe a decade or more later than at Lac Courte Oreilles. Godfrey, *Forest History of Ten Wisconsin Indian Reservations*, 40.
57. Barnouw, "Reminiscences of a Chippewa Mide Priest," 95.
58. "Married Here 50 Years Ago," *Rice Lake Chronotype*, March 3, 1924, 8. Mary Dingley was the daughter of Edward Dingley and Giishkitawag's sister Waabikwe. See Maggie Conger to William Light, March 11, 1913, NARA,

Great Lakes Region, RG 75, Letters Received from the Lac Courte Oreilles Reservation, 1881–1914, Box 4.

59. "Memoirs of Arthur Hovey," in Winton and Winton, *Historical Collections of Washburn County and the Surrounding Indianhead Country*, 1:287, and "Charles White Obituary," *Sawyer County Record and Hayward Republican*, October 7, 1954, 8.
60. "Memoirs of Arthur Hovey," 287–88.
61. "Memoirs of Lena Larson, 1886," 286.
62. Barnouw, "Reminiscences of a Chippewa Mide Priest," 108.
63. Leo G. Waisberg, Joan A. Lovisek, and Tim E. Holzkamm, "Ojibwe Reservations as 'An Incubus upon the Territory': The Indian Removal Policy of Ontario 1874–1982," in *Papers of the 27th Algonquian Conference* (Winnipeg: University of Manitoba Press, 1996), 337–52.
64. James W. Oberly, "Land, Population, Prices, and the Regulation of Natural Resources: The Lake Superior Ojibwa, 1790–1920," in *The Other Side of the Frontier: Economic Explorations into Native American History*, ed. Linda Barrington (Boulder: Westview Press, 1999), 190–205.

CHAPTER 6. THE MURDER OF JOE WHITE AND THE CULMINATION OF REMOVAL

1. Robert Traver, *Anatomy of a Murder* (New York: St. Martin's Press, 1958), 376. *Anatomy* is often cited as the birth of the modern legal thriller, which means it in turn influenced the dozens of procedural crime dramas now flooding the schedules of network television. *Anatomy* was set in Upper Michigan although Upper Michigan's Ojibwe people were not part of the story. However, Voelker was very interested in the Ojibwe communities of the Upper Peninsula. His follow-up work, *Laughing Whitefish* (East Lansing: Michigan State University Press, 2011), was a fictionalized version of a real-life case where an Ojibwe woman sought compensation due her father from a mining company because her father was promised an interest in an ore deposit to which he led company officials. Also, in 1989 he established the Voelker Foundation, which provided scholarships for Native students in law school.
2. Court documents do not identify the name of Joe White's daughter. Census records from the time of the murder identify two daughters in Joe White's family. These same records identify Charles White as being nine at the time of Joe White's murder, but later census records as well as his obituary indicate he was eighteen when his father was murdered. Census of the Lac Courte Oreilles

Band of Chippewa Indians, 1892, National Archives and Records Administration (NARA), Record Group (RG) 75, Indian Census Rolls, 1885–1940, La Pointe Agency Census Rolls, 1890–1892, M595, Roll 235, no. 1075. The *Shell Lake Watchman* and the *Spooner Register* identified Charles White as Joe White's stepson. However, even if this was the case, all historical evidence suggests that Joe White raised Charles White as his own son, something attested to by the fact that they shared the same last name.

3. Details of the murder are in State Against S.M. Hicks, ST 113, State Against Horace Martin, ST 114, State Historical Society of Wisconsin, Ashland Area Research Center, Washburn Series 27: Wisconsin Circuit Court Washburn County, Case Files, 1886–1982; "About Finished!," *Shell Lake Watchman*, March 21, 1895; and "The Slayers of Joe White," *Spooner Register*, December 29, 1894.
4. State Against S.M. Hicks, ST 113.
5. "Is Very Much Mixed," *Spooner Register*, December 22, 1894.
6. J. F. Riordan to W. A. Mercer, December 14, 1894, NARA, Great Lakes Region, Chicago, Illinois, RG 75, Records of the Bureau of Indian Affairs, La Pointe Agency, General Letters Received, 1871–1914.
7. Sidney L. Harring, *Crow Dog's Case: American Indian Sovereignty, Tribal Law, and United States Law in the Nineteenth Century* (New York: Press Syndicate of the University of Cambridge, 1994), 206.
8. Ibid., 174.
9. Tenth Census of the United States, 1880, Town of Shetec, Wisconsin, Enumeration District: 196, NARA, Bureau of the Census, T621, Roll 1417, 2B.
10. Tenth Census of the United States, 1880, Town of Clear Lake, Wisconsin, Enumeration District: 209, NARA, Bureau of the Census, T621, Roll 1440, 3B.
11. "The Slayers of Joe White," *Spooner Register*, December 29, 1894.
12. State Against S.M. Hicks, ST 113.
13. Ibid.
14. Clare V. McKanna Jr., *The Trial of "Indian Joe"* (Lincoln: University of Nebraska Press, 2003).
15. State Against Horace Martin, ST 114.
16. Twelfth Census of the United States, 1900, Town of Long Lake, Wisconsin, Enumeration District: 166, NARA, Bureau of the Census, T623, Roll 1821, 9A. The census taker lists Joe Baker of being of half "white" blood; however, many persons of mixed descent at this time were considered "white." Therefore, it is possible that Baker's father was himself of mixed descent.
17. State Against Horace Martin, ST 114.
18. State Against S.M. Hicks, ST 113.

19. Ibid.
20. Ibid.
21. Ibid.
22. Ibid.
23. It is likely his name was Waabizheshi (like Joe White's brother), as this was a very common Ojibwe name in the nineteenth century. There are a few individuals in the Lac Courte Oreilles census records of the time with the name Waabizheshi, and there is no individual in census records named "Wabasha" or "Ooshkoshur." See Census of the Lac Courte Oreilles Band of Chippewa Indians, 1890 and 1891, NARA, RG 75, M595, Roll 235.
24. State Against S.M. Hicks, ST 113.
25. Ibid.
26. Ibid. This reference to Joe White as the "second highest chief" reflects how Akiwenzii had sustained his influence over the decades. Much of this was due to the establishment of the reservation and the fact that by 1894 most people in the Lac Courte Oreilles Band lived on the reservation. Because they sought to manage day-to-day life on reservations, federal officials weakened the position of traditional leaders overall during this time. However, in other ways they bolstered the power of leaders like Akiwenzii by referring to them with decisions such as who was entitled to allotments. This was a new avenue for asserting leadership that leaders like Joe White, who refused to have anything to do with the reservation, did not have access to. Akiwenzii was succeeded by his son-in-law George Sheff, who by virtue of being the "head chief" of the reservation in issues such as who was entitled to allotments maintained Akiwenzii's influence.
27. Ibid. Information on Joe Navaosh's age is from Thirteenth Census of the United States, 1910, Town of Loomis, Wisconsin, Enumeration District: 223, NARA, Bureau of the Census, T625, Roll 2020, 15A. Navaosh's last name is spelled in trial documents "Navaosh" while in the census is spelled "Neveach."
28. State Against S.M. Hicks, ST 113.
29. State Against Horace Martin, ST 114. The connection of these men to Hicks is unclear.
30. "Game Warden Shoots," *Shell Lake Watchman*, December 20, 1894.
31. *Hayward Republican*, December 20, 1894, 5.
32. "Joe White Again," *Shell Lake Watchman*, January 31, 1895.
33. "Ghost of Joe White," *Shell Lake Watchman*, January 24, 1895, 1.
34. "The District Attorneys," *Spooner Register*, January 5, 1895.
35. "Chairman Todd of Long Lake," *Spooner Register*, December 22, 1894.
36. "The Slayers of Joe White," *Spooner Register*, December 29, 1894.

37. "Is Very Much Mixed," *Spooner Register*, December 22, 1894.
38. In coverage of the trial, the *Watchman* referred to Joe White as "the ill-fated chief." See "About Finished!," *Shell Lake Watchman*, March 21, 1895.
39. "The Slayers of Joe White," *Spooner Register*, December 29, 1894.
40. "District Court Proceedings," *Spooner Register*, March 23, 1895.
41. "The Court Calendar," *Shell Lake Watchman*, March 14, 1895, 1.
42. *Commemorative Biographical Record of the Upper Lakes Region* (Chicago: J. H. Beers, 1905), 124–25.
43. Newton S. Gordon, *History of Barron County, Wisconsin* (Minneapolis: H. C. Cooper Jr., 1922), 85.
44. Ibid., 86. See also George Forrester, *Historical and Biographical Album of the Chippewa Valley* (Chicago: A. Warner Publisher, 1892), 882, and Alvah T. Axtell, *The First Fifty Years: Rice Lake, Wisconsin, 1875–1925* (Rice Lake, WI: Chronotype Publications, 1980), 41.
45. Gordon, *History of Barron County, Wisconsin*, 258, and Axtell, *First Fifty Years*, 203.
46. Forrester, *Historical and Biographical Album*, 874.
47. "Everything Goes Republican Throughout the Country," *Shell Lake Watchman*, November 8, 1894, 1. The *Watchman* was a Republican paper. Accordingly, in the article about the Republican landslide of 1894, the paper proclaimed "The world is ours!"
48. "District Court Proceedings," *Spooner Register*, March 23, 1895. The defense affidavits are contained in State Against Horace Martin, ST 114.
49. Goss's affidavits are contained in State Against S.M. Hicks, ST 113.
50. "District Court Proceedings," *Spooner Register*, March 23, 1895.
51. Ibid.
52. For the early history of Shell Lake, see A. L. Stouffer, *The Story of Shell Lake* (Shell Lake: Washburn County Historical Society, 1961).
53. *Commemorative Biographical Record of the Upper Lakes Region*, 88–90; "Memoirs of Maude Ferguson Pratt," in *Historical Collections of Washburn County and the Surrounding Indianhead Country*, vol. 2, ed. E. Ward Winton and Kay Brown Winton (Shell Lake, WI: White Birch Printing, 1980), 467–87; and "Memoirs of William S. Ferguson II," in Winton and Winton, *Historical Collections of Washburn County and the Surrounding Indianhead Country*, 2:490–91. Niizhoodenh is identified as "Ne-Io-da, meaning 'a twin' (also spelled Ne-Sho-Dar and Ne-Sho-Te)" and Gekek is identified as "Ke-kek" in the "Memoirs of Maude Ferguson Pratt."
54. "District Court Proceedings," *Spooner Register*, March 23, 1895.
55. "Oliver Purdy Dead," *Shell Lake Watchman*, December 12, 1901, 1.
56. Illustrating how intense Scandinavian immigration to the area was in the late

nineteenth century is the fact that there were two Ole Erricksons in the town of Shell Lake. One was fifty-five and the other was thirty-one. Twelfth Census of the United States, 1900, Township of Shell Lake, Wisconsin, Enumeration District: 166, NARA, Bureau of the Census, T623, Roll 1821, 6A, 7A, and 2B.

57. Thirteenth Census of the United States, 1910, Village of Shell Lake, Wisconsin, Enumeration District: 224, NARA, Bureau of the Census, T625, Roll 2020, 5A. See also "Obituary: Artemus B. Crandall," *Shell Lake Watchman*, July 17, 1915, 5.
58. The only record of these jurors in Washburn County is the Wisconsin State Census, 1895, Wisconsin Historical Society, Madison, Wisconsin. Little is known about the background of these jurors, since state census records did not provide such information. The twelfth juror, reported in the *Watchman* as "R. Mooney," does not show up on any federal or state census records for Washburn County. The only possible record of this person is an individual on the Shell Lake baseball team in 1896 named Dick Mooney. See Winton and Winton, *Historical Collections of Washburn County and the Surrounding Indianhead Country*, 1:254.
59. "About Finished!," *Shell Lake Watchman*, March 21, 1895. Trial testimony is not included in the circuit court files. The only testimony included in the circuit court files is from the arraignment on December 27, 1894. Therefore, the only source of the trial testimony is from the *Shell Lake Watchman* and *Spooner Register*, neither of which provided an exact transcription of the trial. According to historian Clare V. McKanna this was not unusual for the time: "Preliminary hearings sometimes provide the only factual testimony by witnesses. Trial transcripts are seldom available unless the case was appealed." Clare V. McKanna, *Homicide, Race, and Justice in the American West, 1880–1920* (Tucson: University of Arizona Press, 1997), 11.
60. "About Finished!," *Shell Lake Watchman*, March 21, 1895, and "District Court Proceedings," *Spooner Register*, March 23, 1895.
61. "About Finished!," *Shell Lake Watchman*, March 21, 1895, and "District Court Proceedings," *Spooner Register*, March 23, 1895.
62. "About Finished!," *Shell Lake Watchman*, March 21, 1895, and "District Court Proceedings," *Spooner Register*, March 23, 1895.
63. "About Finished!," *Shell Lake Watchman*, March 21, 1895, and "District Court Proceedings," *Spooner Register*, March 23, 1895.
64. "About Finished!," *Shell Lake Watchman*, March 21, 1895, and "District Court Proceedings," *Spooner Register*, March 23, 1895.
65. "About Finished!," *Shell Lake Watchman*, March 21, 1895, and "District Court Proceedings," *Spooner Register*, March 23, 1895.

66. Biographical information on Franklin Angel is in Forrester, *Historical and Biographical Album*, 627.
67. "About Finished!," *Shell Lake Watchman*, March 21, 1895, and "District Court Proceedings," *Spooner Register*, March 23, 1895.
68. "About Finished!," *Shell Lake Watchman*, March 21, 1895.
69. "About Finished!," *Shell Lake Watchman*, March 21, 1895, and "District Court Proceedings," *Spooner Register*, March 23, 1895.
70. "About Finished!," *Shell Lake Watchman*, March 21, 1895, and "District Court Proceedings," *Spooner Register*, March 23, 1895. Biographical information on John Harrington is in Forrester, *Historical and Biographical Album*, 632–33.
71. "About Finished!," *Shell Lake Watchman*, March 21, 1895, and "District Court Proceedings," *Spooner Register*, March 23, 1895.
72. "About Finished!," *Shell Lake Watchman*, March 21, 1895; "District Court Proceedings," *Spooner Register*, March 23, 1895; and "Session Finished," *Shell Lake Watchman*, March 28, 1895.
73. See Richard White, *The Middle Ground: Indians, Empires, and Republics in the Great Lakes Region, 1650–1815* (Cambridge: Cambridge University Press, 1991) and Michael Witgen, *An Infinity of Nations: How the Native New World Shaped Early North America* (Philadelphia: University of Pennsylvania Press, 2012).
74. "District Court Proceedings," *Spooner Register*, March 23, 1895.
75. "Session Finished," *Shell Lake Watchman*, March 28, 1895.
76. "Be Sure You Are Right," *Shell Lake Watchman*, March 28, 1895.
77. "Martin & Hicks Trial," *Hayward Republican*, March 28, 1895.
78. "Justifiable Homicide," *Rice Lake Chronotype*, March 22, 1895, 1.
79. Ned Blackhawk, *Violence over the Land: Indians and Empires in the Early American West* (Cambridge, MA: Harvard University Press, 2006), 9.

CHAPTER 7. MAGGIE QUADERER, STEVE GROVER, AND THE CREATION OF COMMUNITY AT WHITEFISH, 1894–1920

1. Eliza Diamond was the daughter of Edward Dingley and Waabikwe, Nena'aangabi's daughter.
2. David E. Jacobs to Samuel W. Campbell, February 8, 1910, National Archives and Records Administration (NARA), Great Lakes Region, Chicago, Illinois, Record Group (RG) 75, Records of the Bureau of Indian Affairs, La Pointe Agency, Letters Received from the Lac Courte Oreilles Reservation, 1881–1914.

3. John Dady to William Light, February 11, 1915, NARA, Great Lakes Region, RG 75, Records of the Red Cliff Agency, Administrative Correspondence of the Superintendent, 1908–1922, Box 2.
4. John Dady to Cato Sells, February 22, 1915, NARA, Great Lakes Region, RG 75, Administrative Correspondence of the Superintendent, 1908–1922, Box 2.
5. E. B. Meritt to Thomas Bracklin, January 6, 1916, NARA, Great Lakes Region, RG 75, Administrative Correspondence of the Superintendent, 1908–1922, Box 2.
6. E. B. Meritt to John Dady, January 6, 1916, NARA, Great Lakes Region, RG 75, Administrative Correspondence of the Superintendent, 1908–1922, Box 2.
7. Thomas Bracklin, April 20, 1934, personal collection of Sylvia Bracklin.
8. Ethel Elliot Chappelle, *Around the Four Corners: A Pioneer History of the Washburn, Sawyer, Barron, and Rusk Counties* (Rice Lake, WI: Chronotype Publishing, 1971), 28.
9. Ibid., 29–32.
10. Rick St. Germaine, "Reserve: A Village Grows," *Lac Courte Oreilles Journal*, March 1986, 6–11.
11. At Long Lake, old-growth pine was depleted by 1900, and railways facilitated the harvest of hardwoods. See Chappelle, *Around the Four Corners*, 79.
12. Ibid.
13. Rick St. Germaine, "Signor: A Look into the Past," *Lac Courte Oreilles Journal*, December 1985, 8–11.
14. David E. Jacobs to Samuel W. Campbell, March 12, 1905, NARA, Great Lakes Region, RG 75, Letters Received from the Lac Courte Oreilles Reservation, 1881–1914.
15. For more on Campbell and his critics at Bad River, see Patty Loew, "Natives, Newspapers and 'Fighting Bob': Wisconsin Chippewa in the 'Unprogressive Era,'" *Journalism History* 23, no. 4 (1997/98): 149–59.
16. "Conditions of Indian Affairs in Wisconsin: Hearings before the Committee on Indian Affairs, United States Senate [61st Congress, 2d session], on Senate Resolution no. 263" (Washington, DC: The Committee, 1910). Publication of this hearing is available online through the Wisconsin Historical Society at http://www.wisconsinhistory.org/turningpoints/search.asp?id=1101.
17. See Patty Loew, "Newspapers and the Lake Superior Chippewa in the 'Unprogressive Era,'" (PhD diss., University of Wisconsin–Madison, 1998).
18. Anthony Godfrey, *A Forest History of Ten Wisconsin Indian Reservations under the Great Lakes Agency: Precontact to the Present* (Salt Lake City: U.S. West Research, 1996).

19. R. L. McCormick, *Evolution of Indian Education: Mission, Public School, U.S. Auspices in Sawyer County, Wisconsin* (Hayward, WI: Hayward School Board, 1901).
20. Denomie reported sixteen students in 1897, fifteen in 1898, sixteen in 1899, and fourteen in 1900. See William Denomie to Samuel Campbell, July 1, 1897, June 2, 1898, June 6, 1899, and March 1, 1900, NARA, Great Lakes Region, RG 75, Letters Received from the Lac Courte Oreilles Reservation, 1881–1914, Boxes 3 and 4.
21. William Denomie to Samuel Campbell, November 30, 1899, NARA, Great Lakes Region, RG 75, Letters Received from the Lac Courte Oreilles Reservation, 1881–1914, Box 4.
22. Brenda Child, *Boarding School Seasons: American Indian Families, 1900–1940* (Lincoln: University of Nebraska Press, 1998).
23. Paulette Molin Fairbanks, "'Training the Hand, the Head, and the Heart': Indian Education at Hampton Institute," *Minnesota History* 51, no. 3 (1988): 82–98.
24. Petition, April 22, 1901, NARA, Great Lakes Region, RG 75, Letters Received from the Lac Courte Oreilles Reservation, 1881–1914, Box 4.
25. Rose Martin, personal interview, March 31, 2003. Martin was the author's great-aunt.
26. Child, *Boarding School Seasons.*
27. Fairbanks, "'Training the Hand, the Head, and the Heart.'"
28. Alice Littlefield, "Indian Education and the World of Work in Michigan, 1893–1933," in *Native Americans and Wage Labor: Ethnohistorical Perspectives*, ed. Alice Littlefield and Martha C. Knacks (Norman: University of Oklahoma Press, 1996).
29. An account of Ojibwe baseball is in Patty Loew, "Tinkers to Evers to Chief: Baseball from Indian Country," *Wisconsin Magazine of History* 87, no. 3 (2004): 2–13. Charles Bender is the subject of a full-length biography: Tom Swift, *Chief Bender's Burden: The Silent Struggle of a Baseball Star* (Lincoln: University of Nebraska Press, 2010). Gus Welch quarterbacked the Carlisle team that included Jim Thorpe and famously defeated the US Military Academy led by future president Dwight Eisenhower at West Point in 1912. After that game, Welch went on to play five seasons in the National Football League for the Canton Bulldogs, then went on to coach college football for over two decades. See Sally Jenkins, *The Real All-Americans* (New York: Anchor Books, 2007).
30. Vine Deloria Jr., ed., "Testimony Taken at Hayward, Wisconsin, April 23 & 24, 1934," in *The Indian Reorganization Act: Congresses and Bills* (Norman: University of Oklahoma Press, 2002), 379.

31. Benjamin G. Armstrong, *Early Life among the Indians* (Ashland, WI: A. W. Bowron, 1892), 246.
32. Joseph B. Casagrande Papers, University of Illinois–Urbana Archives.
33. Brenda Child, "Wilma's Jingle Dress: Ojibwe Women and Healing in the Early Twentieth Century," in *Reflections on American Indian History: Honoring the Past, Building a Future*, ed. Albert L. Hurtado (Norman: University of Oklahoma Press, 2008), 115.
34. Many Ojibwe succumbed to tuberculosis at this time including Lac du Flambeau Ojibwe Tom Badger's son. The grief that this produced for Badger is discussed in Victor Barnouw, "Reminiscences of a Chippewa Mide Priest," *Wisconsin Archaeologist* 35, no. 4 (1954): 112.
35. Albert E. Jenks, *The Wild Rice Gatherers of the Upper Lakes: A Study in American Primitive Economics,* Nineteenth Annual Report of the Bureau of American Ethnology to the Secretary of the Smithsonian Institution 1897–98, pt. 2 (Washington, DC: Government Printing Office, 1900).
36. S. A. Barrett, "The Dream Dance of the Chippewa and Menominee Indians of Northern Wisconsin," *Bulletin of the Public Museum of the City of Milwaukee* 1, no. 4 (1911).
37. Nancy Oestreich Lurie, *A Special Style: The Milwaukee Public Museum, 1882–1982* (Milwaukee: Milwaukee Public Museum, 1983).
38. Nancy Oestreich Lurie, "Robert Eugene Ritzenhauler, 1911–1980," *American Anthropologist* 83, no. 3 (1981): 607–11.
39. Joseph Casagrande, "John Mink, Ojibwa Informant," *Wisconsin Archaeologist* 36, no. 4 (1955): 106–28, and Ernestine Friedl, "Persistence in Chippewa Culture and Personality," *American Anthropologist* 58, no. 5 (1956): 814–25.
40. Victor Barnouw, *Wisconsin Chippewa Myths & Tales and Their Relation to Chippewa Life* (Madison: University of Wisconsin Press, 1977).
41. Robert E. Ritzenthaler and Pat Ritzenthaler, *The Woodland Indians of the Western Great Lakes* (1970; repr., Prospect Heights, IL: Waveland Press, 1988).
42. In particular, see Thomas Vennum Jr., *The Ojibwa Dance Drum: Its History and Construction* (Washington, DC: Smithsonian Institution Press, 1982); Vennum, *Wild Rice and the Ojibway People* (St. Paul: Minnesota Historical Society Press, 1988); and Vennum, *Just Too Much of an Indian: Bill Baker, Stalwart in a Fading Culture* (LaPointe, WI: Just Too Much of an Indian Press, 2008).
43. See James Clifford, *The Predicament of Culture: Twentieth-Century Ethnography, Literature, and Art* (Cambridge, MA: Harvard University Press, 1988) and James Clifford and George E. Marcus, eds., *Writing Culture: The Poetics and Politics of Ethnography* (Berkeley: University of California Press, 1986).
44. For example, anthropologist Ruth Landes's many works are often critiqued

for casting her southwestern Ontario Ojibwe subjects as timeless, even going so far as to blame Ojibwe culture for the poverty and social dysfunction in Ojibwe communities she encountered during her fieldwork in the early twentieth century. However, by failing to consider the historical changes in the communities she encountered and assuming that Ojibwe culture was static and incapable of changing, Landes failed to realize that the poverty she encountered was a direct result of Canadian Indian policy in the late nineteenth century, which dispossessed the communities she studied from successful agricultural economies on lands near Lake of the Woods. When Landes encountered these communities several decades later, they were still reeling from the effects of being relocated on reserves not suitable for farming. See Joan A. Lovisek, Leo G. Waisberg, and Tim E. Holzkamm, "'Cultural Leprosy': The 'Aboriginal Ethnology' of Ruth Landes," in *Papers of the 27th Algonquian Conference* (Winnipeg: University of Manitoba Press, 1996), 164–79.

45. Barrett, "Dream Dance of the Chippewa and Menominee," 255.
46. Vennum, *Ojibwa Dance Drum*, 56.
47. Ibid., 44–45.
48. Armstrong, *Early Life among the Indians*, 158.
49. Vennum, *Ojibwa Dance Drum*, 70–71. Another account of Tailfeather Woman's vision is by Bad River Ojibwe Drum Keeper James Scott. See Chief James Scott, "The Origin of the Ceremonial Powwow Drum," Works Progress Administration, Chippewa Indian Historical Project, Archives of the Franciscan Sisters of Perpetual Adoration, La Crosse, Wisconsin, Envelope 2, 21–26.
50. Truman Michelson, "On the Origin of the So-Called Dream Dance of the Central Algonkians," *American Anthropologist* 25, no. 2 (1923): 277–78.
51. Armstrong, *Early Life among the Indians*, 156–60.
52. Alanson Skinner, "A Further Note on the Origin of the So-Called Dream Dance of the Central Algonkian and Southern Siouan Indians," *American Anthropologist* 25, no. 3 (1923): 427–28.
53. Truman Michelson, "Further Remarks on the Origin of the So-Called Dream Dance of the Central Algonkians," *American Anthropologist* 26, no. 2 (1924): 293–94.
54. Alanson Skinner, "Final Observations on the Central Algonkian Dream Dance," *American Anthropologist* 27, no. 2 (1925): 340–43.
55. M. R. Harrington, "Alanson Skinner," *American Anthropologist* 28, no. 1 (1926): 275–80.
56. Truman Michelson, "Final Notes on the Central Algonkian Dream Dance," *American Anthropologist* 28, no. 3 (1926): 573–76.

57. Vennum, *Ojibwa Dance Drum*, 71. An account of Big Drum ceremonies among Sauk in Oklahoma is Michael Reinschmidt, "Historical and Contemporary Aspects of the Algonquian Drum Dance," in *Papers of the 26th Algonquian Conference* (Winnipeg: University of Manitoba Press, 1995), 431–56.
58. On the music of Mide ceremonies as interpreted by scholars, see Thomas Vennum Jr., "Ojibwa Origin-Migration Songs of the Mitewiwin," *Journal of American Folklore* 91, no. 361 (1978): 753–91.
59. Anthony F. C. Wallace, *The Death and Rebirth of the Seneca* (New York: Vintage, 1969).
60. Anthony F. C. Wallace, "Revitalization Movements," *American Anthropologist* 58, no. 2 (1956): 265.
61. Isaac Mahan to William Leads, June 22, 1878, NARA, RG 75, M234, Roll 398, F:0315. It is unknown who the third ogimaa at Bakweyawaa was. In the 1877 Lac Courte Oreilles census, long-time ogimaa Ozhaawasho-giizhig is listed along with Ogabebinens, who succeeded his father Ginoozhens. In the census, Ozhaawasho-giizhig is rendered "Ojawashogijig." Census Roll, Lac Courte Oreilles, April 3, 1877, NARA, Great Lakes Region, RG 75.
62. Isaac Mahan to William Leads, June 22, 1878, NARA, RG 75, M234, Roll 398, F:0315.
63. Susie Daughtery to M. A. Leahy, October 17, 1890, NARA, Great Lakes Region, RG 75, Letters Received from the Lac Courte Oreilles Reservation, 1881–1914, Box 2.
64. While distinct from the Ghost Dance, scholars have argued that Big Drum did inherit much of its ceremonial structure from the more secular Grass Dance, which spread through the Northern Plains in the mid-nineteenth century. See Vennum, *Ojibwa Dance Drum*, 51–61.
65. James Mooney, *The Ghost Dance Religion and the Sioux Outbreak of 1890*, Fourteenth Annual Report of the Bureau of American Ethnology to the Secretary of the Smithsonian Institution 1892–93, pt. 2 (Washington, DC: Government Printing Office, 1896).
66. Big Drum is even referred to as the Ghost Dance in Armstrong's account. See Armstrong, *Early Life among the Indians*, 160.
67. For example, missionaries working in Ojibwe communities in Minnesota were concerned Big Drum came to Ojibwe communities from neighboring Dakota communities. See Joseph A. Gilfillan, "The Ojibways in Minnesota," in *Collections of the Minnesota Historical Society*, vol. 9 (St. Paul: Minnesota Historical Society, 1902), 117.
68. Jeffrey Ostler, *The Plains Sioux and U.S. Colonialism from Lewis and Clark to Wounded Knee* (Cambridge: Cambridge University Press, 2004).

69. Vennum, *Ojibwa Dance Drum*, 125.
70. Barrett, "Dream Dance of the Chippewa and Menominee," 313.
71. Vennum, *Ojibwa Dance Drum*, 269.
72. Ibid., 260.
73. Ibid., 101.
74. Ibid., 97–98.
75. Frances Densmore, *Chippewa Music II*, Bureau of American Ethnology 53 (Washington, DC: Smithsonian Institution Press, 1913), 142.
76. Vennum, *Ojibwa Dance Drum*, 264. Big Drum ceremonies at Lac du Flambeau are mentioned in the narrative Lac du Flambeau Ojibwe Tom Badger gave in Barnouw, "Reminiscences of a Chippewa Mide Priest," 96, 108.
77. For Steve Grover's lineage, see Maggie Conger to William Light, March 11, 1913, NARA, Great Lakes Region, RG 75, Letters Received from the Lac Courte Oreilles Reservation, 1881–1914, Box 4.
78. Maggie Quaderer is listed as a student at the Whitefish School from 1897 to the school's closing in 1900. See William Denomie to Samuel Campbell, January 1, 1898, June 2, 1898, June 6, 1899, March 1, 1900, and June 1, 1900, NARA, Great Lakes Region, RG 75, Letters Received from the Lac Courte Oreilles Reservation, 1881–1914, Box 4. In these records Quaderer is anglicized "Quarters."
79. Barrett, "Dream Dance of the Chippewa and Menominee," 327–32.
80. Census of the Lac Courte Oreilles Band of Chippewa Indians, 1901, NARA, RG 75, Indian Census Rolls, 1885–1940, M595, Roll 238, F:0541, no. 904. Maggie Quaderer died in 1926, leaving no children. Census of the Lac Courte Oreilles Band of Chippewa Indians, 1926, NARA, RG 75, Indian Census Rolls, M595, Roll 180, F:0211, no. 770.
81. Barrett, "Dream Dance of the Chippewa and Menominee," 301. Interestingly, Barrett never mentioned that Steve Grover and Maggie Quaderer were related.
82. Census of the Lac Courte Oreilles Band of Chippewa Indians, 1923, NARA, RG 75, Indian Census Rolls, M595, Roll 179, F:0660, no. 537.
83. Conger to Light, March 11, 1913, NARA, RG 75, and William W. Bartlett, *History, Tradition, and Adventure in the Chippewa Valley* (Chippewa Falls: Chippewa Printery, 1929), 66. Conger rendered Minotaagoz "Me no ta gous" and Bartlett spelled it "Minotagas."
84. Rick St. Germaine, "Whitefish: A Village of Legacy," *Lac Courte Oreilles Journal*, January 1986, 7.
85. Barrett, "Dream Dance of the Chippewa and Menominee," 286–87.
86. Ibid., 325.
87. Ibid., 333–34.

88. Ibid., 334–35.
89. Ibid., 342.
90. Ibid., 344–45, 349.
91. Ibid., 306.
92. Ibid., 310, 342.
93. Ibid., 319–20.
94. Ibid., 346.
95. Ibid., 347.
96. Ibid., 349.
97. Ibid., 319.
98. Ibid., 310.
99. Vennum, *Ojibwa Dance Drum*, 82–87.
100. Barrett, "Dream Dance of the Chippewa and Menominee," 350.
101. Vennum, *Ojibwa Dance Drum*, 82–87.
102. Barrett, "Dream Dance of the Chippewa and Menominee," 327.
103. Vennum, *Ojibwa Dance Drum*, 308.
104. Casagrande Papers.
105. Ibid.
106. For more on Smith's notions of the place of recovery in the process leading to indigenous self-determination, see Linda Tuhiwai Smith, *Decolonizing Methodologies: Research and Indigenous Peoples* (Dunedin: University of Otago Press, 1999), 116.
107. Anton Treuer, *Ojibwe in Minnesota* (St. Paul: Minnesota Historical Society Press, 2010), 78.

CONCLUSION

1. Frank Zufall, "Blood on the Trail: The Killing of Joe White, Ojibwa Chief," *Spooner Advocate*, March 17, 2007. Joe White has very few direct descendants living on the reservation, while there are hundreds of people living on the reservation from the Bracklin, Grover, Quaderer, and Isham families who are descendants of White's sisters.
2. Quoted in Rick St. Germaine, "Whitefish: A Village of Legacy," *Lac Courte Oreilles Journal*, January 1986, 6.
3. Xavier Grany to Samuel Campbell, March 23, 1911, National Archives and Records Administration (NARA), Great Lakes Region, Chicago, Illinois, Record Group (RG) 75, Records of the Bureau of Indian Affairs, La Pointe Agency, Letters Received from the Lac Courte Oreilles Reservation, 1881–1914, Box 8.

4. Ethel Elliot Chappelle, *Around the Four Corners: A Pioneer History of the Washburn, Sawyer, Barron, and Rusk Counties* (Rice Lake, WI: Chronotype Publishing, 1971), 98.
5. Ibid., 99.
6. Ibid.
7. Twelfth Census of the United States, 1900, Town of Long Lake, Wisconsin, Enumeration District: 166, NARA, Bureau of the Census, T623, Roll 1821, 9A, 9B, and 10A.
8. Chappelle, *Around the Four Corners*, 86. The Rockford House still stands as a tavern on County Highway B on Long Lake.
9. Thirteenth Census of the United States, 1910, Town of Long Lake, Wisconsin, Enumeration District: 223, NARA, Bureau of the Census, T625, Roll 2020, 16A, and Thirteenth Census of the United States, 1910, Town of Loomis, Wisconsin, Enumeration District: 223, NARA, Bureau of the Census, T625, Roll 2020, 15A. In the 1910 Census Navaosh is spelled "Neveash."
10. Chappelle, *Around the Four Corners*, 86. Chappelle spelled Navaosh "Naviach."
11. In re: Blackbird, Western District of Wisconsin, 109 F. 139 (1901).
12. Lac Courte Oreilles v. Voight, 700 F.2d 341 (1983).
13. Ronald N. Satz, *Chippewa Treaty Rights: The Reserve Rights of Wisconsin's Chippewa Indians in Historical Perspective*, special issue, *Transactions of the Wisconsin Academy of Sciences, Arts and Letters* 79 (1991) and Larry Nesper, *The Walleye War: The Struggle for Ojibwe Spearfishing and Treaty Rights* (Lincoln: University of Nebraska Press, 2002).
14. Minnesota v. Mille Lacs, 526 U.S. 172 (1999).

Select Bibliography

COLLECTIONS

Casagrande, Joseph B., Papers, University of Illinois–Urbana Archives

Chippewa Annuity Rolls, 1841–1907, US Office of Indian Affairs, Minnesota Historical Society, St. Paul

Documents Relating to the Negotiations of Ratified and Unratified Treaties with Various Indian Tribes, 1801–1869, Record Group 75, National Archives and Record Administration Microfilm T494

Goldsmith, C. F. X., Papers, 1821–1923, State Historical Society of Wisconsin Area Research Center, Eau Claire

Hayward School, 1894–1934, Record Group 75, National Archives and Record Administration Great Lakes Region, Chicago

Hayward Superintendency, 1916–1923, Records Group 75, National Archives and Record Administration Microfilm M595

Indian Census Rolls, 1885–1940, La Pointe Agency Census Rolls, Records Group 75, National Archives and Record Administration Microfilm M595

La Pointe Agency, 1869–1931, Record Group 75, National Archives and Record Administration Great Lakes Region, Chicago

Letters Received by the Office of Indian Affairs, 1824–1881: La Pointe Agency, Record Group 75, National Archives and Record Administration Microfilm M234

Ritzenthaler, Robert E., Papers, Milwaukee Public Museum Archives

Spears, Julia A., and Family Papers, Minnesota Historical Society, St. Paul

Tenth Census of the United States, 1880, Bureau of the Census, National Archives and Record Administration Microfilm T621

Thirteenth Census of the United States, 1910, Bureau of the Census, National Archives and Record Administration Microfilm T625

Twelfth Census of the United States, 1900, Bureau of the Census, National Archives and Record Administration Microfilm T623

Works Progress Administration, Chippewa Indian Historical Project, Archives of the Franciscan Sisters of Perpetual Adoration, La Crosse, Wisconsin

GOVERNMENT DOCUMENTS

Commissioner of Indian Affairs. *Annual Report of the Commissioner of Indian Affairs for the Year 1863*. Washington, DC: Government Printing Office, 1864.

———. *Annual Report of the Commissioner of Indian Affairs for the Year 1864.* Washington, DC: Government Printing Office, 1865.

———. *Annual Report of the Commissioner of Indian Affairs for the Year 1866.* Washington, DC: Government Printing Office, 1866.

———. *Annual Report of the Commissioner of Indian Affairs for the Year 1868.* Washington, DC: Government Printing Office, 1868.

———. *Annual Report of the Commissioner of Indian Affairs for the Year 1869.* Washington, DC: Government Printing Office, 1870.

———. *Annual Report of the Commissioner of Indian Affairs for the Year 1870.* Washington, DC: Government Printing Office, 1870.

———. *Annual Report of the Commissioner of Indian Affairs for the Year 1872.* Washington, DC: Government Printing Office, 1872.

———. *Annual Report of the Commissioner of Indian Affairs for the Year 1874.* Washington, DC: Government Printing Office, 1874.

———. *Annual Report of the Commissioner of Indian Affairs for the Year 1875.* Washington, DC: Government Printing Office, 1875.

———. *Annual Report of the Commissioner of Indian Affairs for the Year 1876.* Washington, DC: Government Printing Office, 1876.

———. *Annual Report of the Commissioner of Indian Affairs for the Year 1878.* Washington, DC: Government Printing Office, 1878.

———. *Annual Report of the Commissioner of Indian Affairs for the Year 1880.* Washington, DC: Government Printing Office, 1880.

———. *Annual Report of the Commissioner of Indian Affairs for the Year 1882.* Washington, DC: Government Printing Office, 1882.

———. *Annual Report of the Commissioner of Indian Affairs for the Year 1883.* Washington, DC: Government Printing Office, 1883.

———. *Annual Report of the Commissioner of Indian Affairs for the Year 1884.* Washington, DC: Government Printing Office, 1884.

———. *Annual Report of the Commissioner of Indian Affairs for the Year 1887.* Washington, DC: Government Printing Office, 1887.

"Conditions of Indian Affairs in Wisconsin: Hearings before the Committee on Indian Affairs, United States Senate [61st Congress, 2d session], on Senate Resolution no. 263." Washington, DC: The Committee, 1910.

US Senate, Committee on Indian Affairs. *Chippewa Allotments of Land and Timber Contracts*, Senate Report 2710, 50th Congress, 2d session. Washington, DC: Government Printing Office, 1889.

———. *Survey of Conditions of the Indians in the United States: Hearings before a Subcommittee of the Committee on Indian Affairs.* Washington, DC: Government Printing Office, 1930.

LEGAL CASES

Cherokee Nation v. Georgia, 30 U.S. 1 (1831)
In re: Blackbird, Western District of Wisconsin, 109 F. 139 (1901)
Lac Courte Oreilles v. Voight, 700 F. 2d 341 (1983)
Lone Wolf v. Hitchcock, 187 U.S. 553 (1903)
Minnesota v. Mille Lacs, 526 U.S. 172 (1999)
Thaddeus Thayer v. United States, 20 Ct. Cl. 137 (1885)
United States v. Cook, 86 U.S. 591 (1873)
United States v. Kagama, 118 U.S. 375 (1886)

TREATIES

Treaty of Prairie du Chien, August 19, 1825, 7 Stat. 272.
Treaty of Fond du Lac, August 5, 1826, 7 Stat. 290.
Treaty of St. Peter's, July 29, 1837, 7 Stat. 536.
Treaty of La Pointe, October 4, 1842, 7 Stat. 591.
Treaty of Fond du Lac, August 2, 1847, 9 Stat. 904.
Treaty of La Pointe, September 30, 1854, 10 Stat. 1109.

NEWSPAPERS

Barron County Shield
Dunn County Lumberman
Lac Courte Oreilles Journal
Rice Lake Chronotype
Sawyer County Record
Shell Lake Watchman
Spooner Register

OJIBWE LANGUAGE TEXTS

Baraga, Frederic. *A Dictionary of the Ojibway Language*. St. Paul: Minnesota Historical Society Press, 1992.

Jones, William. *Ojibwa Texts*. Edited by Truman Michelson. New York: G. E. Steechert, 1917.

Kegg, Maude. *Portage Lake: Memories of an Ojibwe Childhood*. Edited and transcribed by John D. Nichols. Minneapolis: University of Minnesota Press, 1993.

Littlewolf, Jim. "Weak of Heart—Strong of Heart." Translated by John D. Nichols. *Oshkaabewis Native Journal* 2, no. 2 (1995): 52–59.

Nichols, John D., ed. *Statement Made by the Indians: A Bilingual Petition of the Chippewas of Lake Superior, 1864*. London: University of Western Ontario Press, 1988.

Nichols, John D., and Earl Nyholm. *A Concise Dictionary of Minnesota Ojibwe*. Minneapolis: University of Minnesota Press, 1995.

Treuer, Anton. *Living Our Language: Ojibwe Tales and Oral Histories*. St. Paul: Minnesota Historical Society Press, 2001.

PUBLISHED WORKS: PRIMARY SOURCES

Armstrong, Benjamin G. *Early Life among the Indians*. Ashland, WI: A. W. Bowron, 1892.

Barnouw, Victor. "Reminiscences of a Chippewa Mide Priest." *Wisconsin Archeologist* 35, no. 4 (1954): 83–112.

Barrett, S. A. "The Dream Dance of the Chippewa and Menominee Indians of Northern Wisconsin." *Bulletin of the Public Museum of the City of Milwaukee* 1, no. 4 (1911).

Casagrande, Joseph. "John Mink, Ojibwa Informant," *Wisconsin Archeologist* 36, no. 4 (1955): 106–28.

Densmore, Frances. *Chippewa Customs*. 1929. Reprint, St. Paul: Minnesota Historical Society Press, 1979

———. *Strength of the Earth: The Classic Guide to Ojibwe Uses of Native Plants*. 1928. Reprint, St. Paul: Minnesota Historical Society Press, 2005.

Ducatel, J. J. "A Fortnight among the Chippewas of Lake Superior." In *The Indian Miscellany*, ed. W. W. Beach. Albany, NY: J. Munsell, 1877. 361–78.

Henry, Alexander. *Travels and Adventures in the Years 1760–1776*. 1809. Reprint, Chicago: Lakeside Press, 1921.

Kohl, Johann Georg. *Kitchi-Gami: Life among the Lake Superior Ojibway*, trans. Lascelles Wraxall. St. Paul: Minnesota Historical Society Press, 1985.

McKenney, Thomas L. *Sketches of a Tour to the Lakes*. Minneapolis: Ross & Haines, 1959.

Morse, Richard E. "The Chippewas of Lake Superior." In *Collections of the State Historical Society of Wisconsin*, vol. 3, ed. Lyman Copeland Draper, 338–69. Madison: Wisconsin Historical Society, 1904.

Nelson, George. *My First Years in the Fur Trade*. St. Paul: Minnesota Historical Society Press, 2002.

Nicollet, Joseph N. *The Journals of Joseph N. Nicollet: A Scientist on the Mississippi Headwaters with Notes on Indian Life, 1838–1837*. Translated by Andre Frey. St. Paul: Minnesota Historical Society Press, 1970.

Schoolcraft, Henry R. *Personal Memoirs of a Residence of Thirty Years with the Indian Tribes on the American Frontiers*. Philadelphia: Lippincott, Grambo, 1851.

———. *Schoolcraft's Expedition to Lake Itasca: The Discovery of the Source of the Mississippi*. Edited by Philip P. Mason. 1834. Reprint, East Lansing: Michigan State University Press, 1993.

Tanner, John. *The Falcon: A Narrative of the Captivity and Adventures of John Tanner (U.S. Interpreter at the Sault de Ste. Marie) during Thirty Years Residence among the Indians in the Interior of North America*. 1830. Reprint, Minneapolis: Ross & Haines, 1956.

Warren, William W. *History of the Ojibway People*. 1885. Reprint, St. Paul: Minnesota Historical Society Press, 1984.

PUBLISHED WORKS: LOCAL HISTORIES

Axtell, Alvah T. *The First Fifty Years: Rice Lake, Wisconsin, 1875–1925*. Rice Lake, WI: Chronotype Publications, 1980.

Bartlett, William W. *History, Tradition, and Adventure in the Chippewa Valley*. Chippewa Falls: Chippewa Printery, 1929.

Chappelle, Ethel Elliot. *Around the Four Corners: A Pioneer History of the Washburn, Sawyer, Barron, and Rusk Counties*. Rice Lake, WI: Chronotype Publishing, 1971.

Forrester, George. *Historical and Biographical Album of the Chippewa Valley*. Chicago: A. Warner Publisher, 1892.

Gordon, Newton S. *History of Barron County, Wisconsin*. Minneapolis: H. C. Cooper, Jr., 1922.

Marple, Eldon. *The Visitor Who Came to Stay: Legacy of the Hayward Area*. Hayward, WI: Country Print Shop, 1971.

McCormick, R. L. *Evolution of Indian Education: Mission, Public School, U.S. Auspices in Sawyer County, Wisconsin*. Hayward, WI: Hayward School Board, 1901.

Randall, Thomas E. *History of the Chippewa Valley*. Eau Claire, WI: Free Press Print, 1875.

Tobola, Thomas Henry, ed. *Cadotte Family Stories*. Cadott, WI: Cadott Printing, 1974.

Winton, E. Ward, and Kay Brown Winton, eds. *Historical Collections of Washburn County and the Surrounding Indianhead Country*. Shell Lake, WI: White Birch Printing, 1980.

PUBLISHED WORKS: SECONDARY LITERATURE

Albers, Patricia. "Labor and Exchange in American Indian History." In *A Companion to American Indian History*, ed. Philip J. Deloria and Neal Salisbury, 269–86. Malden, MA: Blackwell Publishers, 2002.

Alfred, Taiaiake. *Peace, Power, and Righteousness: An Indigenous Manifesto*. Oxford: Oxford University Press, 1999.

Bieder, Robert E. *Native American Communities in Wisconsin, 1600–1960: A Study of Tradition and Change*. Madison: University of Wisconsin Press, 1995.

Borrows, John. *Recovering Canada: The Resurgence of Indigenous Law*. Toronto: University of Toronto Press, 2002.

Child, Brenda. *Boarding School Seasons: American Indian Families, 1900–1940*. Lincoln: University of Nebraska Press, 1998.

———. *Holding Our World Together: Ojibwe Women and the Survival of Community*. New York: Viking, 2012.

Clifford, James. *The Predicament of Culture: Twentieth-Century Ethnography, Literature, and Art*. Cambridge, MA: Harvard University Press, 1988.

Clifford, James, and George E. Marcus, eds. *Writing Culture: The Poetics and Politics of Ethnography*. Berkeley: University of California Press, 1986.

Clinton, Robert N. "There Is No Federal Supremacy Clause for Indian Tribes." *Arizona State Law Journal* 34, no. 1 (2002): 113–260.

Connor, Walker. *Ethnonationalism: The Quest for Understanding*. Princeton: Princeton University Press, 1994.

Cronen, William. *Changes in the Land: Indians, Colonists, and the Ecology of New England*. New York: Hill and Wang, 1983.

———. *Nature's Metropolis: Chicago and the Great West*. New York: W. W. Norton, 1992.

Danziger, Edmund Jefferson. *The Chippewas of Lake Superior*. Norman: University of Oklahoma Press, 1979.

DeMallie, Raymond J. "Touching the Pen: Plains Indian Treaty Councils in Ethnohistorical Perspective." In *Ethnicity on the Great Plains*, ed. Frederick C. Luebke, 38–51. Lincoln: University of Nebraska Press, 1980.

Fries, Robert F. *Empire in Pine: The Story of Lumbering in Wisconsin, 1830–1900.* Madison: State Historical Society of Wisconsin, 1951.

Godfrey, Anthony. *A Forest History of Ten Wisconsin Indian Reservations under the Great Lakes Agency: Precontact to the Present.* Salt Lake City: U.S. West Research, 1996.

Harring, Sidney L. *Crow Dog's Case: American Indian Sovereignty, Tribal Law, and United States Law in the Nineteenth Century.* New York: Press Syndicate of the University of Cambridge, 1994.

Holzkamm, Tim E., Leo G. Waisberg, and Joan A. Lovisek. "'Stout Athletic Fellows': The Ojibwa During the 'Big Game Collapse' in Northwest Ontario 1821–71." In *Papers of the 26th Algonquian Conference*, 169–82. Winnipeg: University of Manitoba Press, 1995.

Hoxie, Frederick E. *A Final Promise: The Campaign to Assimilate the Indians, 1880–1920.* Lincoln: University of Nebraska Press, 1984.

Hurst, James Willard. *Law and Economic Growth: The Legal History of the Lumber Industry in Wisconsin, 1836–1915.* Cambridge, MA: The Belknap Press of Harvard University Press, 1964.

Krasner, Stephen D. "Sovereignty." *Foreign Policy* 122 (February 2001): 20–29.

Kugel, Rebecca. *To Be the Main Leaders of Our People: A History of Minnesota Ojibwe Politics, 1825–1898.* East Lansing: Michigan State University Press, 1998.

Loew, Patty. *Indian Nations of Wisconsin: Histories of Endurance and Renewal.* Madison: Wisconsin Historical Society Press, 2001.

Lovisek, Joan A., Leo G. Waisberg, and Tim E. Holzkamm. "'Deprived of Part of Their Living': Colonialism and Nineteenth-Century Flooding of Ojibwa Lands." In *Papers of the 26th Algonquian Conference*, 226–39. Winnipeg: University of Manitoba Press, 1995.

Lurie, Nancy Oestreich. *A Special Style: The Milwaukee Public Museum, 1882–1982.* Milwaukee: Milwaukee Public Museum, 1983.

Mancall, Peter C. *Deadly Medicine: Indians and Alcohol in Early America.* Ithaca: Cornell University Press, 1995.

McClurken, James M., ed. *Fish in the Lakes, Wild Rice, and Game in Abundance: Testimony on Behalf of Mille Lacs Ojibwe Hunting and Fishing Rights.* East Lansing: Michigan State University Press, 2000.

McKanna, Clare V. *Homicide, Race, and Justice in the American West, 1880–1920.* Tucson: University of Arizona Press, 1997.

———. *The Trial of "Indian Joe."* Lincoln: University of Nebraska Press, 2003.

Meyer, Melissa L. *The White Earth Tragedy: Ethnicity and Dispossession at a Minnesota*

Anishinaabe Reservation, 1889–1920. Lincoln: University of Nebraska Press, 1994.

Miller, Cary. *Ogimaag: Anishinaabe Leadership, 1760–1845*. Lincoln: University of Nebraska Press, 2010.

Nesper, Larry. *The Walleye War: The Struggle for Ojibwe Spearfishing and Treaty Rights*. Lincoln: University of Nebraska Press, 2002.

Oberly, James W. "Land, Population, Prices, and the Regulation of Natural Resources: The Lake Superior Ojibwa, 1790–1920." In *The Other Side of the Frontier: Economic Explorations into Native American History*, ed. Linda Barrington, 190–205. Boulder: Westview Press, 1999.

Ostler, Jeffrey. *The Plains Sioux and U.S. Colonialism from Lewis and Clark to Wounded Knee*. Cambridge: Cambridge University Press, 2004.

Peers, Laura. *The Ojibwa of Western Canada, 1780 to 1870*. St. Paul: Minnesota Historical Society Press, 1994.

Rappaport, Joanne. *Intercultural Utopias: Public Intellectuals, Cultural Experimentation, and Ethnic Pluralism in Colombia*. Durham, NC: Duke University Press, 2005.

Satz, Ronald N. *Chippewa Treaty Rights: The Reserve Rights of Wisconsin's Chippewa Indians in Historical Perspective*. Special issue, *Transactions of the Wisconsin Academy of Sciences, Arts and Letters* 79 (1991).

Schenck, Theresa M. *The Voice of the Crane Echoes Afar: The Sociopolitical Organization of the Lake Superior Ojibwa, 1640–1855*. New York: Garland, 1997.

———. *William W. Warren: The Life, Letters, and Times of an Ojibwe Leader*. Lincoln: University of Nebraska Press, 2007.

———. "William W. Warren's History of the Ojibway People: Tradition, History, and Context." In *Reading beyond Words: Contexts for Native History*, ed. Jennifer S. H. Brown and Elizabeth Vibert, 193–210. Peterborough, Ont.: Broadview Press, 2003.

Seeley, Mark. *Minnesota Weather Almanac*. St. Paul: Minnesota Historical Society Press, 2006.

Silvern, Steven E. "Reclaiming the Reservation: The Geopolitics of Wisconsin Anishinaabe Resource Rights." *American Indian Culture and Research Journal* 24, no. 3 (2000): 131–53.

Sleeper-Smith, Susan. *Indian Women and French Men: Rethinking Cultural Encounter in the Western Great Lakes*. Amherst: University of Massachusetts Press, 2001.

Smith, Linda Tuhiwai. *Decolonizing Methodologies: Research and Indigenous Peoples*. Dunedin: University of Otago Press, 1999.

Smits, David D. "The 'Squaw Drudge': A Prime Index of Savagism." *Ethnohistory* 29, no. 4 (1982): 281–306.

Tanner, Helen Hornbeck, ed. *Atlas of Great Lakes Indian History*. Norman: University of Oklahoma Press, 1987.

Treuer, Anton. *The Assassination of Hole-in-the-Day*. St. Paul: Minnesota Historical Society Press, 2011.

Van Kirk, Sylvia. *Many Tender Ties: Women in Fur-Trade Society, 1670–1870*. Norman: University of Oklahoma Press, 1983.

Vennum, Thomas, Jr. *The Ojibwa Dance Drum: Its History and Construction*. Washington, DC: Smithsonian Institution Press, 1982.

———. *Wild Rice and the Ojibway People*. St. Paul: Minnesota Historical Society Press, 1988.

Vizenor, Gerald. *The People Named the Chippewa: Narrative Histories*. Minneapolis: University of Minnesota Press, 1984.

Waisberg, Leo G., and Tim E. Holzkamm. " 'A Tendency to Discourage Them from Cultivating': Ojibwa Agriculture and Indian Affairs Administration in Northwestern Ontario." *Ethnohistory* 40, no. 2 (1993): 175–211.

Waisberg, Leo G., Joan A. Lovisek, and Tim E. Holzkamm. "Ojibwe Reservations as 'An Incubus upon the Territory': The Indian Removal Policy of Ontario 1874–1982." In *Papers of the 27th Algonquian Conference*, 337–52. Winnipeg: University of Manitoba Press, 1996.

Wallace, Anthony F. C. *The Death and Rebirth of the Seneca*. New York: Vintage, 1969.

White, Bruce M. "A Skilled Game of Exchange: Ojibway Fur Trade Protocol." *Minnesota History* 50, no. 6 (1987): 229–40.

White, Bruce M. "The Myth of the 'Forgotten' Treaty: Traditions about the St. Peters Treaty of 1837." In *The State We're In: Reflections on Minnesota History*, ed. Annette Atkins and Deborah L. Miller, 39–49. St. Paul: Minnesota Historical Society Press, 2010.

White, Richard. "The Fictions of Patriarchy: Indians and Whites in the Early Republic." In *Native Americans in the Early Republic*, ed. Frederick E. Hoxie, Ronald Hoffman, and Peter J. Albert, 62–84. Charlottesville: University Press of Virginia, 1999.

———. *The Middle Ground: Indians, Empires, and Republics in the Great Lakes Region, 1650–1815*. Cambridge: Cambridge University Press, 1991.

Wilkins, David E. *American Indian Sovereignty and the U.S. Supreme Court: The Masking of Justice*. Austin: University of Texas Press, 1997.

Wilkins, David E., and K. Tsianina Lomawaima. *Uneven Ground: American Indian Sovereignty and Federal Law*. Norman: University of Oklahoma Press, 2001.

Willging, Robert C. *On the Hunt: The History of Deer Hunting in Wisconsin*. Madison: Wisconsin Historical Society Press, 2008.

Witgen, Michael. *An Infinity of Nations: How the Native New World Shaped Early North America*. Philadelphia: University of Pennsylvania Press, 2012.

Wolfe, Patrick. "Settler Colonialism and the Elimination of the Native." *Journal of Genocide Research* 8, no. 4 (2006): 387–409.

———. "Structure and Event: Settler Colonialism, Time, and the Question of Genocide." In *Empire, Colony, Genocide: Conquest, Occupation, and Subaltern Resistance in World History*, ed. A. Dirk Moses. New York: Berghahn Books, 2008. 102–32.

Wrone, David R. "The Economic Impact of the 1837 and 1842 Chippewa Treaties." *American Indian Quarterly* 17, no. 3 (1993): 329–40.

Index